ENGLISH—PANJABI

DICTIONARY

COMPILED BY

Rev. Grahame T. Bailey

EDITED & INTRODUCED BY

Shreeram Vidyarthi

AND

SOME MUSINGS

by Dr. Mulk Raj Anand

LINGUASIA

Published by
LINGUASIA
(*An Imprint of* ASIA PUBLISHING HOUSE LIMITED)
Borden Villa, Borden Lane,
SITTINGBOURNE, Kent ME10 1BY

Original Edition March 1919
This Edition August 1996

ISBN 1 870836 14 6

PHOTOTYPESET & PRINTED IN INDIA BY
REKHA PRINTERS PVT. LTD., NEW DELHI-110 020, INDIA

ROMANIZING INDIC LANGUAGES
A Prefatory Misgiving

The history of these ROMANIZED dictionaries of different Indic languages such as this unfurls with the spread of the Union Jack over India. With the spread of the Raj, armies of civil servants and hordes of priests came in to consolidate what had been carved out in the name of the British Crown.

This imperial march necessitated some level of communication with the 'natives'—however rudimentary such communication was to be. (After all, what the rulers lacked in the quality of their 'communication', they could make up through the imposition of their authority.)

So some of these half-baked, but crafty and clever 'linguists' set to work—like fuel gatherers—on the vocabulary of the natives, indexed and listed them, spelt them in their familiar Roman script, without too much regard or care for the phonetics and/or accuracy of pronunciations.

I have had a chance to glance through a whole range of these ROMANISED grammars, language manuals and dictionaries, purporting to deal with the character and complexities of various Indic languages. I find them deficient in their grammatical profiling of words, missing on subtelties and nuances of native speech and rather limited in their grasp and range.

But these very 'deficient' compilations were nontheless sufficient for the administrator to grasp the gist of natives' petitions, to dispense a bit of 'justice' and to help the local padre explain the parables of the *Holy Bible*.

This dictionary, the one in your hand, was compiled by the Reverend Grahame Bailey, of the Scottish Mission, Wazirabad, in 1919. It is one of the better and more comprehensive works in this range. The other two compilations—one compiled by Munshi Jawahir Singh and the other prepared by Lala Salig Ram Bajaj had enjoyed limited use: Munshi Jawahir Singh's work was only good for the army sergeant-majors on the parade ground; and Lala Salig Ram's book, which purported to be a trilingual work—English–Punjabi and Hindi, did not distinguish Punjabi words from the Hindi. The latter work also had no positive use for the '*Goraa Saahib Log*' because they could not read the native scripts.

All my working life, in the course of written dissertations and during 'live' discussions with students and scholars alike, I have set myself against these 'Romanised' specimens of linguistic anthropology. I find them totally inadequate for any serious teaching or learning of Indic languages in the West. Why? Let me explain why...

If they are loaded with scores of diacritical markings and various weird shaped, reversed and upside-down letters of the Roman alphabet, in order to indicate phonetic values for each printed stroke, then they become totally inaccessible for the layman—the two week tourist, the rushed-off-his-feet businessman, or the casual, friendly neighbour just trying to be nice to his next door 'Aizian'. If these works are written in straightforward English script, then the pronunciation of the Indic words gets heavily distorted. English speech is used to a very limited sound box and cannot reproduce the many variants on basic consonants. (Trying to praise a woman for being a '*Moti*–a pearl—for her contribution to a situation, an Englishman is more likely to end up calling her a '*Moatee*', 'the fat one'.

In any case, I find it extraordinary that the *Goraa Saahib Log* still insist on the languages of the world being transcribed for them in 'English script'. To me, this attitude not only smacks of cultural arrogance, but also indicates a deplorable intellectual lethargy.

Here, while being critical of the limited vocabulary being enlisted in this volume, one must not forget that by the early 20th century, primary education had spread far and wide; the administrative machinary was running smoothly throughout the land—on the back of Arabo-Persian administrative terminology, established by the Muslim rulers of India long before the arrival of the British on the subcontinent.

This brought about a sort of familiarity, with words of common parlance, taken from Hindi, English, Arabic, Persian etc. even amongst the illiterate and semi-literate rural people. This on the one hand enriched their daily speech and enhanced their skills of social communication; on the other hand, it also bred a kind of cultural, or at least linguistic, chauvinism whereby a whole range of Sanskrit, Persian and Arabic words were presumed and claimed to be Punjabi words, although they had no roots in the peasant speech of this 'land of five rivers'.

[The most concrete example of this cultural chauvinism can be seen in the common belief in modern day Punjab that 'all the contents' of the Holy Granth Saahib are 'written in Punjabi'. While even a lay reader of linguistics can discern therein the 'baani' of various saintly contributors, in Persian, in Sadhukkadi, in Siraiki, in Braj-Bhaashaa, and so on. Out of sincere respect for the religious feelings of those devoted to the Granth Saahib, people generally avoid discussion on this matter, but the linguistic facts are there for all to see and study.]

Therefore, in spite of my reservations about the deficient vocabulary and the phonetic innacuracies inherent in the 'English' script—when employed in the transliteration of Indic words—this volume is being reissued in a new edition purely to serve those who shun the idea of learning a new script and yet seek to communicate with their Punjabi friends and neighbours in the West.

It was originally designed for Europeans in India. Today it has assumed another function—that of helping the second and third generation Punjabi immigrant who might learn rudiments of Punjabi speech at home, but fails to acquire any serious, scriptive knowledge of his/her native language. The Roman script is the only one they can read. This way, at least they will not lose their mother-tongue entirely.

In order to explain the methodology of word-profiling used in this volume by Reverend Bailey, we have retained the original introduction written by the author himself, all those years ago, in March 1919.

We recommend this volume to you, not so much for its profundities, but for its practical, functional usefulness.

–Shreeram Vidyarthi
August 1996
Sittingbourne, Kent

MUSINGS OF AN ANGLICISED PUNJĀBI
by Mulk Raj Anand

I was just a child of ten when, one day, I boasted to my silversmith uncle, Chāchā Piaru, that I had obtained ten-out-of-ten marks for reciting a Urdu poem from my textbook. The poem in question was a popular, and rather tender rhyme—

Suvéré Jo Kal Aankh Méri Khuli.

Chacha Piāru had never been to school, though he could recite long passages from the Sikh book of prayers, called Japji Sāhib, in Punjābi. He had never been to school and knew neither Urdu, nor 'Angrézi' (English). But he was proud of being Punjābi and of his command of his mother tongue.

He reacted to my boast with an uncanny and direct retort—"Son, I may not know Angrézi. And Urdu is not as heart-warming as Punjābi. To speak in one (English), you have to keep your mouth half shut; and to speak in the other (that being Urdu), you have to speak with a bit of *Nakharaa* (contrived mannerism). Punjābi is an honest man's language: We open our mouths wide and speak warmly from our hearts!"

I suddenly found myself on the defensive—".. But Chāchā Ji, The *Angrézi sarkaar* despises Punjābi. Our Urdu Master tells us that"

"Urdu comes from Iran, Son. Punjābi is our own tongue. The saints sang in it long before the Pathān sant Bābā Farid came on the scene. And even he chose to learn Punjābi before singing his praises of the Lord." —said Chāchā Piaru.

That day, in the course of a longish conversation, chāchā Piaru impressed me with his command of a vast vocabulary of my native tongue', a tongue which I was not too proud of. But from that day on I became very alert to the Punjābi words being spoken around me, by my friends and family members. I even started paying attention to the regular readings of the Holy Granth in our *Gurudwārā.*

On festival days, I would go to listen to Bhāi Faiz, the musician at the *darbār sāhib,* reciting Guru Nānak's *Bārahmāsa* (the song of twelve months).

But I really fell in love with my native tongue when I heard first ever recitation of the epic love poem HEER RAANJHAA of Syed Waaris Shah. That even inspired me to write some half-baked love poems addressed to my baby-love Yasmin, the sister-in-law of my classmate, Noor Mohammad.

Later on, when I went to London to study philosophy, I felt very homesick and often attempted to put down my thoughts in Punjābi free verse, just to console myself as well as to preserve the privacy of my thoughts of loneliness.

Intensely aware of the shortcomings, of my knowledge of Punjābi language, I looked up Dr T. Cummings' PUNJABI MANUAL AND GRAMMAR in the library of the School of Oriental & African Studies (SOAS). I also discovered for the first time the existence of the English Punjabi Dictionary in Roman script, compiled by T. Grahame Bailey which was published in Wazirābād, Punjab.

Later on, I even met Dr Bailey, who was teaching in SOAS. He was cordial and happy to talk to me in Punjabi, bang in the heart of London. We would sometimes adjourn to tea in Student's Christian Movement in the Club House, near Russell Square, and chat through many hours.

I soon realised that whatever had inspired other British scholars to study Punjabi, and one such motive must have been to win the hearts and minds of simple-minded, hard-working Punjabis, by delivering their sermons in Punjabi to the native converts to Christianity, the assiduity and dedication of this padre to master 'my mother tongue' deserved my salute.

There have been many other salutary examples of high quality lexicography, of Indian languages, undertaken and completed by many an English scholar in the course of the British Raj: Dr William Carey's Bengali dictionary, Molesworth's work on Marathi language, Reverened Winslow's Tamil English and English Tamil dictionaries, H.H. Wilson's studies in Sanskrit Philology and Monier Williams' classic English-Sanskrit and Sanskrit-English dictionaries....... Only difference is, those were compiled using the scripts of the native languages in question....

It fell to Reverend Bailey and to Reverend Hares to change the mode and compile the first native language dictionaries in Roman script so that a civil servant of the Raj, and/or a missionary of the Church, moving from camp to camp and mission to mission, though might be obliged to encounter various languages, in the course of discharging his duties, but will not have to subject himself to the task of learning all the native scripts.

This move, though phonetically a retrograde step, and accounts for a considerable loss of pronunciation quality of the native tongues when subjected to European utterances, was definitely a bold one and a brave one: In one swift move, this innovation had liberated the working energy of these ambassadors of the Raj from the shackles of 'local knowledge' for the smooth running of their show; now they could function anywhere as long as they could read English... fortunately that is all they could read.

Alas, the bold venture was not to benefit the Raj-wallahs for long. A couple of decades later, the Raj was wound up and this experiment never extended beyond the realms of Punjabi and Hindi/Hindustani.--

Like many bold and brave projects, undertaken by the operators of the Raj, like the railways and the telegraph, and the newspapers, with a view to improving the efficient running of the Crown machinery, today, even this experiment is proving handy for the benefit of the 'natives' like me—Anglicised, urbanised, cultural refugees, alienated from our mother tongues and visiting our mother cultures only through the tinted (or you might want to call it, 'tainted') glasses of English.

Amongst these anglicised, urbanised, alienated children of mother India, I also count the second and third generation emigrants to Europe and America who can only read the Roman (English) script and can only gain access to their mother tongues through this kind of a work.

It is true that, owing to the age of the work in question, the word-lists will be somewhat outdated and somewhat out-of-touch with the reality of today. But once a start is made in the use of these tools of learning, a need for updating and revision of such works will also be felt and the task likely to be undertaken...

And that surely won't be a retrograde a step.

—Mulk Raj Anand

The readers will note two different spellings for the word Punjabi/Panjabi being used in the early part of this volume. This confusion has been going on for long many years. When we spell it with 'a' and the word is pronounced by anglophiles as *'Pen-jaabi'*; if we spell it with a 'u' we end up with a pronunciation sounding as *'Poon-jaabi'*. Since neither is phonetically correct, we decided in this case to stick to the original spellings used by T.Grahame Bailey in the part compiled by him and resort to new spellings, incorporating 'u', which is the common practice today.

We hope the readers will understand the difficulty and won't allow it to interfere with their use of the dictionary.

INTRODUCTION

This book has been issued primarily to meet the need of those Europeans who use Panjabi in their intercourse with the people of the country, and secondarily to enable Panjabis, schoolboys and others, to ascertain the meanings of the commoner English words which they daily come across. No English-Panjabi dictionary at present exists. It did not, however, seem desirable to compile an exhaustive dictionary : that would have been both bulky and expensive. What appeared to be required was a volume, which, while containing a large selection of words likely to be useful, would be small enough to be easily handled, and cheap enough to be within the reach of all. The price has been increased by the war, but it has been kept as low as possible, and no attempt has been made to do more than cover expenses.

The number of English words translated is about 5800, a number sufficiently large for most purposes. The idea of this work was suggested by Col. D.C. Phillott's excellent "English-Hindustani Vocabulary."

Panjabi may be divided into two main dialects, the northern or western, and southern or eastern. The former is spoken west and north of Amritsar and is used throughout in this Vocabulary. It is commonly called northern Panjabi to distinguish it from the southern dialect.

Special Features:—(i) As most of those who use this book will possess the "Panjabi Manual and Grammar"* written some years ago by Dr. T.F. Cummings and myself, I have made frequent references to it. In this way it has been possible to refer the student to fuller explanations of words and phrases.

(ii) Nouns: The gender of every noun is given. It is indicated in most cases by m. or f., but when the infinitive or the sign of the genitive (***dā***) is given along with a noun the letters m. and f. are omitted. The endings of the infin. ***-ā, -i, -e, -iā̃*** or the variations of the genitive sign ***dā, dī, de, dīā̃*** show the gender. When both m. and f. are used the word may be either masc. or fem., the commoner gender being given first. The addition of "pl." means that the word is nearly always plural.

*This title is currently out of print. Re-issue under consideration.

In Appendix-I several pages have been added containing notes on the grammatical portion of the "Panjabi Manual" including a complete conjugation of the verb with pronominal suffixes.

(iii) Verbs: Both trans. and intr. forms are frequently given the latter often correspond to the English passive. Occasionally the causal is added. Irregular past participles are generally mentioned. With one or two exceptions intensive compound verbs (such as ***mukā chaḍḍṇā***, ***wēkh laiṇā***) have not been used in the Vocabulary. There are not more than one or two verbs of which it can be asserted that the compound form is always necessary. Another reason is that in most cases several different compound forms are possible; and finally Europeans when they learn a compound form generally employ it to excess. See Compound Verbs, p. 150. See also (iv).

(iv) Construction: A special effort has been made to show the construction of verbs, what prepositions they use, and how the object is expressed. This is a matter of importance as foreigners are often in difficulties about these points. It should be noted that when there is no indication of how to express the object, it is usually the direct accusative with ***nū̃***, or it may be without ***nū̃***, in which case it is the same as the nominative.

(v) Idioms: Special pains have been taken to include as many idioms as possible. They will be found throughout the Vocabulary.

(vi) Cross references: By means of these much space has been saved. The student should always look up the references even though the connection may not be obvious. A great deal of additional information will in this way be obtained.

(vii) It often happens that words used by Hindus are not used by Muhammadans and vice versâ. Hindu and Muhammadan words have been distinguished. Christians employ the one or the other according to the majority of the people by whom they are surrounded. There are also specifically Christian words, which will be found in their proper places. See also the letters K. and U. in the list of abbreviations.

(viii) Word jingle: This is so usual a feature of Panjabi speech that it has been thought advisable to include the commonest examples: such are ***kūṇā saihṇā***, speak: ***gohā gaṭṭā***, cowdung.

(ix) At the end of Appendix I are notes on the agreement of adjectives, the uses of ***calṇā*** and ***paiṇā***, the formation of the past part. and causal verbs, on verbal roots in ***g*** and ***kh***, and a few hints on common mistakes.

(x) In Appendix II are additions to the Vocabulary.

(xi) Special lists: Names of birds are given under "bird" in the Vocabulary; names of stars under "stars" in Appendix II; weights and measures under "Weights and Measures" in Appendix II.

SPELLING.—The chief difficulties in spelling are due to the existence of different pronunciations and, in the case of words common to Urdu and Panjabi, to doubt as to how far removed from literary Urdu the normal pronunciation of a word is. Some educated speakers, not realising that Panjabi is a language distinct from Urdu, endeavour to assimilate words to their Urdu forms, and thus spoil the pronunciation. The best rule is to follow the pronuciation of those who have a little, but not too much, education. Lest anyone should think that some of the forms in this book are vulgar it may be mentioned that the proofs have been shown to three educated Indian gentlemen whose names are given at the end of this introduction. Two are Hindus and one a Muhammadan. The Muhammadan is a graduate of the Panjab University and a teacher of Panjabi. Of the Hindus one has, for many years, been a school-teacher and has wide experience of teaching Panjabi; the other has taught in school for some years and this year is going up for his B.A. It is not likely that these gentlemen would pass vulgar forms. They did not try to Urduise the spelling, on the contrary in some cases they suggested that my spelling too closely resembled Urdu and advised a change.

An unaccented vowel in Panjabi always tends to become the short neutral vowel heard in the first syllable of the English words "along", "announce", "America", hence ***milkiyat***, ***shikāyat***, etc. generally become ***malkīat***, ***shakait*** and so on. Frequently this neutral vowel is omitted as in ***zindgī***, ***bandgī*** where we might anticipate ***zindagī, bandagī***.

Further difficulties arise in connection with the length of vowels, the doubling of consonants at the end of accented syllables (e.g. ***ghaṭṇā*** or ***ghaṭṭṇā***, ***Panjābī*** or ***Panjābbī***), the omission or insertion of ***y*** (***dhyān*** or ***dhiān***) and in a number of other cases. It should also be borne in mind that words with the low tone may often be written in at least two ways without affecting the pronunciation. Thus it is immaterial whether we write ***dhigāṇe*** or ***tighāṇe***, uselessly : ***kandhāṛe*** or ***ghandāṛe***, on one's shoulders : ***culhānī*** or ***jhulānī***, village kitchen : ***panjihāḷ*** or ***bhanjāḷ***, partner : again ***hanerā***, ***nherā***, and ***anherā*** are pronounced practically alike. The high tone is not constant and depends partly upon the accent. Thus the word for sahib is pronounced ***sāho*** when the accent falls upon it, but when in a compound word it follows the syllable with the accent, it is simply ***sāb***, as ***lāṭ sāb***, ***miss sāb***, ***mem sāb***. In such cases it is not certain which is the better way to write the word. Occasionally a word is here spelt in two different ways. It will be found that both may be defended. See also next heading.

PRONUNCIATION.—Differences of pronunciation are due to (i) individual idiosyncracy : (ii) difference of degree of education: (iii) difference of district. In a few words ***ḷ*** or ***l*** and ***ṇ*** or ***n*** are both correct. The commonest are—

melā, ***meḷā***, fair.
dil, ***diḷ***, heart.
din, ***diṇ***, day.
waḷgan, ***walgan***, courtyard.
naṇān, ***nanāṇ***, husband's sister.
aglā, ***agḷā***, former.
paulī, ***pauḷī***, four-anna bit.
hanekeā jāṇā, ***haṇekeā jāṇā***, get out of order.
kalpā, ***kaḷpā***, goatherd's crook.

City dwellers are often unable to distinguish between ***ḷ*** and ***l***.

EXPLANATION OF CONTRACTIONS.—A list of abbreviations is given after the table of contents. Further points are now mentioned: (i) When a word has occurred as a heading, it is referred to within the limits of that one entry by its first letter: e.g. "acquit, ***chaḍḍṇā***, ***barī k.***: be a. etc.;" here "be a." means "be acquitted."

(ii) There is a difference between "or" and a comma: thus ***zore laiṇā*** or ***ugrāhṇā*** would mean that one may say ***zore laiṇā*** or ***zore ugrāhṇā*** but "***zore laiṇā, ugrāhṇā***" means either ***ugrāhṇā*** or ***zore laiṇā***, but not ***zore ugrāhṇā***. The very few cases where to save space this rule has been departed from will not cause confusion.

(iii) A hyphen has sometimes been employed with ***k*** and ***h***. This is to show that the whole is regarded as one verb : e.g.

natthī-k means that ***natthī karnā*** is all one verb, and one might have ***natthī kītā*** or ***natthī kīte*** or ***natthī kītīā̃*** according to the gender of the word with which the past part. agrees. But when we have ***pakkī karnī*** or ***jhī̃ karnī*** the past part. must remain fem. and we should have ***ohnū̃ pakkī kītī*** or ***jhī̃ kītī*** (not ***kītā***).

Students must be prepared to find in use words, genders and constructions differing from those in this work. Only in a few words will difference be observable as regards gender. It is due sometimes to local variations but not infrequently to mistakes on the part of men who have learnt Urdu and use Urdu genders. Certain words common in one district are rare in another, or if used, assume a different form. Only after much inquiry can one venture to say that any particular word is wrong. One must remember that village speech is the real standard in Panjabi.

In conclusion I desire to express my grateful thanks to three Indian gentlemen whose assistance throughout has been of much value to me. They are Lālā Sundar Dās, teacher in the Church of Scotland High School, Gujrāt; Qāzī Muhammad Zafr Ali, B.A., holder of the Govt. Oriental Language Teachership, Certificate in Panjabi; and Lālā Dēw Datt, teacher in the Church of Scotland High School, Wazīrābād. I have been fortunate in enlisting the interest of gentlemen so competent and so willing to help.

T Grahame Bailey.

Wazirabad:
March 22, 1919

CONTENTS

1. Romanizing Indic Languages:
A Preferatory Misgiving
by Shreeram Vidyarthi iii

2. Musings of an Anglicized Punjabi
by Mulk Raj Anand vii

3. Introduction
by Rev. Grahame T. Bailey xi

4. Key of Abbreviations xix

5. Key to Pronunciation xxi

6. Vocabulary A-Z 1–153

7. Appendix 1: *Additions to Vocabulary* 155

8. Appendix 2: *List of Main Birds* 159

9. Appendix 3: *Weights & Measures* 161

KEY TO ABBREVIATIONS

A, App. refers to Appendix II, Additions to Vocabulary.
acc., accus., accusative.
adj., adjective.
adv., adverb.
aux. v., auxiliary verb.
bet., between.
caus., causal.
d., ***dēṇā***.
educ., used in schools.
f., fem., feminine : f. pl., feminine plural : f. m., feminine or masculine.
fr., from.
G., refers to the last or Grammar section of the "Panjabi Manual and Grammar."*
gen., in general, generally.
H., word used by Hindus.**
h., ***hōṇā*** : ***-h.***, e.g., ***jārī-h.,*** *see* Introduction, Explanation of Contractions, p. vi.
inf., infin., infinitive.
infl., inflec., inflected.
interj., interjection.
int., intransitive.
k., ***karnā*** : ***-k.***, e.g., ***natthī-k.***, *see* Introduction, Explanation of Contractions, p. vi.
K., khansama's language.
leg., legal language.
loc., locative case.
M. (alone) word used by Muhammadans.**
M. followed by number refers to the earlier parts of the "Panjabi Manual and Grammar."*
m., masculine: m. pl., masculine plural: m. f., masculine or feminine.
metaph., metaphorical.
neg. negative.
obj., object.
obl., oblique.
occ., occasionally.
pa. p., past participle.
pl., plur., plural.
prep., preposition.
pres., present.
pron., pronoun.
pronom. suff., pronominal suffix. rel., relig., religious.
Rom. Cath., Roman Catholic.
sthg., something.
tr., transitive.
U., word or expression borrowed or altered from Urdu, Urduised Panjabi.
v., verb.
verb subst., verb substantive, the same as auxiliary verb.
W., *see* Weights and Measures in Appendix.

* This title is currently out-of-print.

** Linguistically this difference is rather illogical and baseless. (Ed.)

KEY TO PRONUNCIATION

CONSONANTS.

b, g, j, m, n, s, z are nearly as in English.

d, t are made with the tongue covering the inner side of all the upper teeth, both front and side teeth. ('d' as 'th' in there 't' as in french coup de ta).

c, j are approximately as in English, but the tongue is further forward, and ***c*** is unaspirated. (C as 'ch' in Church/J as in Judge)

The cerebral letters ***ḍ, ṭ, ḷ, ṇ, ṛ*** the tongue strikes or touches the hard palate rather far back.

kh̲ is approximately the ***gh*** in Irish "lough" or the ***ch*** in Scotish "loch": ***g*** is the same sound voiced.

l is nearly as in English "willing."

ñ is like ***ñ*** in Spanish "señor" or ***gn*** in Italian and French words, practically the same as ***ni*** in English "lenient" (nasalized).

ṅ is like ***ng*** in "singing."

r is made with a single tap of the tongue, like the so-called trilled ***r*** in Scotland. In genuine Panjabi words it is never found doubled.

w has hitherto been described by all writers (including myself) as a bilabial letter made by the lips without the use of the teeth. It is not bilabial; it is made by the contact of the upper teeth with some part of the lower lip, either where it is visible or lower down, but the contact is so faint that the acoustic effect is quite different from that of English ***v***. ***f*** is the same letter unvoiced.

y is like English ***y***, but when doubled tends towards an attenuated ***zh***, written phonetically ***J***.

h :—(i) ***h*** is like English ***h*** when it occurs in ***ch, kh, ph, th, ṭh;*** in the word ***āho***, yes; and occasionally in ***āhā̃***, no; ***oe hoe***, alas or oh; ***āe hāe***, alas or oh; ***īho***, this very one; ***ūho***, that very one; and possibly two or three more words.

(ii) ***h*** coming after, even though not immediately after, the vowel of an accented syllable is not pronounced, but gives the high-falling tone to the syllable.

(iii) ***h*** coming before, even though not immediately before, the vowel of an accented syllable, is not pronounced, except when it stands alone, but gives to the syllable the low-rising tone. When the ***h*** is alone, i.e. without another consonant, it is faintly pronounced as a sonant ***h***, and the syllable has the low-rising tone.

Tones.—Panjabi is a tone language like Chinese, but the tones do not play so important a part in speaking. There are four tones:—

(i) level tone found in about 75% of the words. It might also be described as absence of tone.

(ii) high-falling. The syllable is begun about six or seven semitones above the lowest note that the speaker can reach, and falls about two semitones. If no pause follows, the fall is in the following syllable.

(iii) low-rising. The syllable is begun about a tone above the lowest note that the speaker can reach, and rises one or two semitones. If no pause follows, the rise is in the following syllable.

(iv) A combination of low-rising and high-falling, the former, always coming first. See "Punjabi Manual," pp. xvii-xix.

The following points connected with consonants are worth remembering:—

(1) The surd letters ***c, k, p, t, ṭ*** must be kept unaspirated (unlike the corresponding English letters which always have slight aspiration). ***ch, kh, ph, th, ṭh,*** are strongly aspirated.

(2) Some letters when occurring undoubled after a vowel are frequently, but not always, changed to certain others. Thus ***g*** becomes *g*; ***tagṛā*** strong, not ***tagṛā*** : ***kh*** becomes ***k̲h̲***, as ***āk̲h̲dā*** saying for ***ākhdā*** ; ***nj*** becomes ***ñ***, as ***aiñ***, thus, rather than ***ainj*** : ***s*** becomes English ***h***, as ***maĩ tenū̃ dahnā̃ dah paihe ditte hāhū***, I tell you he gave ten pice. This is extremely common rapid conversation, but Panjabis have not, as a rule, observed it themselves and most of them will not admit that they pronounce in this way. A little careful listening will convince the student that they do.*

* This is applicable to the Doābi dialect—spoken in the Doābā region of present day Punjāb. (Ed.)

(3) Foreigners have a strong tendency to allow the letters ***r, ṛ, ḍ, ṭ, ṇ, ḷ*** to alter the sound of vowels immediately preceding or following. This must be avoided. They have no effect upon vowels (in Punjabi).

VOWELS.

ă, ***a*** are like ***u*** in "mutton" when stressed, and like ***a*** in "along" when unstressed.

ā, ī, ū are like Italian ***a, i, u,*** and approximately like English ***a*** in "clam," ***ee*** in "seen" and ***u*** in "rule."

ē is between French ***é*** and ***è*** not unlike the Scottish vowel in "lane."

e, ĕ are the same but shorter.

ō is approximately like ***o*** in Schottish "mote", not like the English diphthongal sound, ***o*** is the same but shorter.

i is like English ***i*** in "linen."

u is like ***u*** in pull. Scottish and North Irish speakers should note that it is quite different from ***ū*** which is like ***u*** in "rule" or ***oo*** in "pool."

ai is almost identical with ***a*** in English "man," i.e. it is longer than the same vowel in 'mat." It is far removed from the vowel in "height," "like," "side," etc.

au is not far from ***aw*** in "shawl." More exactly it begins with the vowel of "shawl" and goes on with the "***o***" in "O'Neill," the two being combined into a diphthing. It is utterly unlike the English diphthing in "how" "mound," "shout," etc. The ***au*** in ***maulwī*** is practically the same as that in English "maul."

Nasal vowels are as in French except that nasalisation does not change the vowels.

— (Minor updating by Shreeram Vidyarthi)

ERRATA

jamhā (karnā), add, collect, is preferably ***jamhā***, not ***jamā***.

li<u>kh</u>ṇā, write, is ***li<u>kh</u>ṇā***, not ***likhṇā*** or ***likkhṇā***.

To express the idea of drawing or painting (pictures, maps, etc.) the Panjabi tendency is to use ***baṇāṇā***, make, and to reserve ***khiccṇā*** for photographs, a distinction being made between what is done by hand and what is mechanical.

The short *a* usually written in the following words is better omitted: ***bar<u>kh</u>lāf***, contrary : ***kīmtī***, costly : ***baṇāwḷī***, counterfiet, etc.: ***nazāktā̃, nazāktī,*** *see* delicacy, delicate: ***dadēhs*** and ***patēhs***, see father : ***saltnat***, kingdom.

English—Panjabi Dictionary

A

a, an, omit or use ***ikk***, one : ***koī***, some.
abandon, ***chaḍḍṇā*** : (an idea) ***dilõ kaḍḍhṇā***, or ***bhulāṇā***.
abate, *see* lessen.
ability, ***liākat***, f. : ***jinnī pujj e***, up to one's : ***jinnā sare***, as far as one can financially.
able, ***laik***, ***tagṛā*** : able for, ***de jogā***, or ***jogā*** w. inflec. infin., G. 95
able, to be, ***sakṇā***, ***koḷõ*** w. tr. passive or int. or inflec. inf., G. 66, 96, 97, 112.
ablution, perform (relig.) ***wuzū karnā*** (M.), ***ashnān karnā*** (H.) : *see* wash.
abnormal, *see* strange, wonderful.
abolish, ***maukūf k.*** : ***band k.*** : ***band karāṇā***.
abominable, ***burā***, ***ghinaoṇā***, ***makrūh***.
abound, ***bauht hōṇā*** : *see* much.
(1) about, ***eddhar oddhar*** (here and there) : *see* round, approximately, concerning.
(2) about to do, verb w. ***wālā***, ***ḍigganwāḷā***, a. to fall : G. 44, 45, 98, 99 : sometimes w. ***caleā***, G. 67 : a. to go, come, ***ṭureā***, ***āyā cāhndā e***, G. 112 : *see* ready.
above, prep., ***de utte***, ***de te***, ***te*** : *see* upon : adv., ***utte*** : *see* up : from a., ***uttõ*** : by way of a., ***uttõ dī***.
above-mentioned, use ***jihdā utte zikar hoeā*** or ***āyā e***.
abroad, ***pardēs***, m., foreign country : ***wilait***, f., Europe, America.
abrogate, *see* abolish, cancel, repeal.
abscond, ***nass jāṇā***, ***bhajj jāṇā***.
absence, ***gair-hāzrī***, f. : in my a., ***mere picche***, ***merī gair hāzrī wicc*** : *see* back.
absent, adj., ***gair-hāzar***.
absolute, ***jihnū̃ sārā ikhtyār e***.
absolutely, ***ukkā***, ***atte***, ***aslõ***, ***mūḷõ***, ***bilkul*** A.
abstain (from forbidden food), ***thõ parhēz*** (m.f.) ***k.*** : (from defiled food), ***thõ choh karnī*** : (give up doing sthg.), ***muṛnā***, ***chaḍḍṇā***.
abundant, *see* much.
abuse, n, v., ***gāḷ*** (plur. ***gāhḷā̃***) ***kaḍḍhṇī*** (gen. indecent); be abused, ***gāḷ laiṇī***, ***khāṇī***; ***gāḷ paiṇī*** (***nū̃***), M. 125. 9 : (very bad) ***phakkaṛ tōlnā*** : (very mild) ***phiṭak dēṇī***; be a., ***phiṭak laiṇī***, ***khāṇī*** : use badly, *see* injure, spoil.
abusive, ***gandī zabān-wālā***, ***baṛiā̃ gāhḷā̃ kaḍḍhaṇwāḷā***, ***trakkī hoī zabān-wāḷā***.

acacia (various kinds), ***kikkar***, m. : ***kikkrī***, f. : ***phulāh***, f. : ***sharīh̃*** (siris), m.
accent (in language), ***laihjā***, m. : (stress), ***zōr***, m. (d).
accept, *manzūr k., kabūlnā, kabūl k.* : *see* agree, assent.
acceptable, use like.
acceptance, *manzūrī*, f.
accident, *hādsā*, m., ***durghaṭnā***, (f.) (U.) : use injury.
accidental, *takdīrī, itfākī, itfāk dā*.
accidentally, *sbabb nāḷ, aĩwẽ, ẽwẽ, takdīr nāḷ, itfāk nāl.*
accommodation, *gunjaish*, f. : place, ***thā̃***, m. f. : ***jaghā***. f.
accompany, *de nāḷ jāṇā* or ***calṇā.***
accomplice, *bhētī*, m., ***nāḷ raḷeā hoeā.***
accomplish, *mukāṇā* (int. ***mukkṇā***) : ***kar laiṇā, kar chaḍḍṇā*** : *see* finish, complete.
accomplished, *see* learned, able.
accomplishment, *hunar*, m. : ***ilm***, m. (knowledge).
according to, *de mūjab.*
accordingly, *so, bas pher.*
account (money, etc.), ***lēkhā***, m. : ***hisāb***, m. : settle a., ***hisāb k.*** or ***mukāṇā*** : to his account, ***ohde peṭe pāṇā*** : *see* responsibility : (narration), ***bĕān*** (m.) ***k.*** : on no a., ***kadī nehī̃, kise tarhā̃ nehī̃*** : on a. of, *see.* because of.
account-book (village) ***behī***, f. : ***wehī***, f. : (gen.) ***hisāb dī kitāb***, f., or ***pōthī***, f.
accountable, *see* responsible.
accountant, village, ***paṭwārī*** : his business, ***paṭwār***, f. : head a., ***gardaur, kānūgo*** : his business, ***gardaurī***, f.
accumulate, *kaṭṭhā k., jamā k.*
accurate, *thīk, durust.*
accuse, accusation, ***ilzām lānā*** (***utte***) : ***cuglī khāṇī*** or ***k.*** (***dī***) : ***bhaṇḍī karnī*** (***dī***) : ***nindyā karnī*** (***dī***) : ***bhaṇḍṇā*** (***nū̃***) : ***shikait karnī*** (***dī***, lit. complaint) : *see* slander.
accused, *mulzam.*
accuser, *ilzām lāṇwāḷā* : (in court) ***nālish karnwāḷā.***
accustom, v. tr., ***haḷāṇā, gijhāṇā.***
accustomed, become, ***gijihṇā*** (pa. p. ***giddhā, gijjheā***), ***hiḷṇā***, both w inflec. inf. as ***iṭṭā̃ ḍhōṇ hiḷeā hoeā e***, or ***gijjhā e***, he is a. to transporting bricks : state of being a., ***gējh***, f., ***hiḷtar***, f. : *see* habit.
ache, *see* pain, hurt.
acid, sour, ***khaṭṭā, tezāb***
acidity, *khaṭeāī*, f.
acknowledge (saint, prophet, ruler, error, sin) ***mannṇā.***
acquaintance (person), ***jāṇū̃, wākaf***, m.f. : *see* information, knowledge.
acquire, *see* obtain.
acquit, *chaḍḍṇā, barī k.* : be a., ***chaḍḍeā jāṇā, barī h., k̲halāsī hōṇī*** (***dī***).
acquittal, *k̲halāsī*, f.
acre, *ghumā*, m. : ***ēkar***, m. : *see* ***killā*** App. weights and meas.

acrobat, *see* tumbler.
across, ***-õ pār, de pār, de parle pāse*** : *see* crosswise.
act, v., drama, *see* imitate.
act, n. (law), ***kanūn***, m. : of God, ***Khudā dā kamm***.
action, ***fēhl***, m. : ***kamm***, m. : ***amal***, m. : ***karam***, m. : *see* deed.
active, ***kamm karnwāḷā***, ***tagrā***, ***cust***.
actual, ***aslī***.
actually, ***asl wicc***; ***saccī muccī*** (truly).
acute (severe) ***sakht*** : (clever) ***siāṇā***, ***aklwāḷā***, ***chalāk/chattar***.
Adam's apple, ***ghaṇḍī***, f.
add, ***jōṛnā***, ***jamā k***.
address (residence), ***patā***, m. : on letter, ***patā***, m. : ***sarnāmā***, m. : short, relig. a., ***nasīhat***, f. (***k.***) : *see* sermon, lecture, speech.
address, v, ***kise nāḷ gall karni***
adhere (of stamp, etc.) ***laggṇā***; to opinion, ***apṇi gall nā chaḍḍṇī*** : to someone, ***cambaṛnā*** (***nū̃***).
adherent, *see* follower.
adhesive, ***lēsḷā***.
adieu, *see* farewell.
adjacent, ***nāḷ dā***.
adjoin, *see* adjacent.
adjourn, ***chaḍḍṇā*** (for two days, ***dūh diṇā̃ wāste***, etc.) : *see* postpone : (legal), ***pher tarīk pai geī e***, another date fixed.
adjure, *see* conjure.
administer, ***bandobast karnā*** (***dā***), ***intizām karnā*** (***dā***) : *see* arrange, settle, oath.
admire, ***wēkhke khush hōṇā***, ***acchā*** or ***sohṇā laggṇā*** (***nū̃***) : *see* praise.
admit (acknowledge), ***mannṇā*** : (person) ***wāṛnā***, ***andar auṇ d.*** : not be admitted, ***ḍhoī nā hōṇī or milṇī*** (women's talk).
admittance, ***ḍhoī***, f. (***milṇī***).
admonish, ***samjhāṇā***, ***nasīhat dēṇī*** (***nū̃***) : *see* reprimand.
adopt (boy) ***putrēla baṇāṇā*** : (girl) ***dhī karke rakkhṇī***.
adopted son, ***putrēlā*** : daughter, ***dhī karke rakkhī hoī*** or ***pāḷī hoī***.
adore, no good word, use worship.
adorn, ***sajāṇā*** (int. ***sajjṇā***) : ***sajāwat karnī*** (***dī***).
adorned, ***sajjeā hoeā***.
adult (man) ***gabbhrū***, ***juān*** : (woman) ***muṭeār***, ***juān*** : *see* young.
adulterate, ***ohde wicc pāṇī***, ***trāmma***, etc., ***raḷāṇā*** or ***pāṇā***, a.w. water, copper, etc. A.
adulterated, ***raḷā miḷā***, ***malāwaṭ wālā***.
adulterer, fornicator, ***zanāhī***, ***harāmkār***.
adultery, fornication, ***zanāh karnā*** (***nāḷ***), ***burāī karnī*** (***nāḷ***), ***haramkārī karnī*** (***nāḷ***).
advance, ***trakkī karnī***, ***agā̃ waddhṇā*** : (money) ***pēshgī dēṇī*** (int. ***milṇī***) : *see* earnest.
advantage, ***fāidā***, m. (***uṭhāṇā***) : ***nafā***, m. (***uṭhāṇā***) : *see* profit. good : a. and disadvantage, ***nafā nuksān***, m.

advantageous, ***mufid, fāide. wāḷā*** : *see* useful.
adversary, *see* enemy : man of other side, ***dujjī dhir dā, dujje pāse*** or ***dhaṛe dā.***
adversity, *see* misfortune, poverty.
advertise-, -ment, ***ishtihār dēṇā*** (***dā***).
advice, advise, ***matt,*** f. : ***salāh,*** f. : ***nasīhat,*** f. : ***hidait,*** f. : (all w. ***dēṇī*** and ***nū̃***) : *see* consult.
advisable, ***cāhidā*** w. inf., G. 67, 96 : *see* necessary, duty, require, have to.
adze, ***tēsā,*** m.
aeroplane, ***jahāz,*** m. : ***hawāī jahāz,*** m.
aesophagus, ***shāh rag,*** f. ***saṅgh,*** m.
affair, ***gall,*** f. : ***bāt,*** f. : ***kamm,*** m. : ***muāmlā,*** m.
affection, *see* love, friendship.
affix, ***lāṇā*** (int ***laggṇā***).
affliction, *see* grief, pain, misfortune.
afford, ***dē sakṇā, sarnā*** (***nū̃***), M. 248. 6.
affray, ***fasād,*** m. : ***daṅgā fasād,*** m.
aforesaid, *see* above-mentioned.
afraid, *see* fear.
afresh, ***nawī̃ suanni, nawẽ sireõ*** : *see* beginning.
after, ***de picche, de magar*** : from a., ***de picchõ, de magarõ*** : after all, ***aksar*** : *see* behind, finally.
afterwards, ***magarõ, picche, picche nū̃, picchõ.***
afternoon, ***pishlā paihr,*** m : divisions w. approximate times (which vary with the season) are : —***kaccī pēshi,*** 1-0 P.M.; ***pēshī,*** 2-0; ***nikkī ḍigar,*** 3-0; ***dīgar*** 4 or 5; ***lauḍhewelā,*** 5 or 6 : in the a., ***pishle paihr, ḍigarī, pēshī, lauḍhewēḷe,*** etc. : *see* morning, evening, A.M.
again, ***mur, phēr, watt*** ; a second time, ***dujjᵒ phēre, dujjī wārī*** : *see* repeatedly.
against, ***de k͟halāf, de bark͟hlāf.***
age, ***umar,*** f. : present a., ***hāl dā zamānā*** : past a., ***parāṇā z.*** : old age, *see* old : of same a., *see* equal : *see* hair.
aged, ***buḍḍhā, buḍhrā*** : *see* old.
agent (advocate, lawyer) ***wakīl, muk͟hteār, muk͟htār*** : (land -a., etc.) ***gumāshtā*** : a. in gen., verb w. ending ***-wāḷā,*** G. 44, 45, 98, 99, or -ū, G. 45.
agitation, be in state of, ***taṛapṇā, dil taṛapṇā*** (or ***taṛafṇā***).
agitate, *see* excite, incite, shake.
agitator, ***lokā̃ nū bhaṛkāṇwāḷā*** or ***cukkaṇwālā.***
ago, five years ago; ***panjā̃ warheā̃ dī gall e paī, panj warhe hoe ne paī*** : *see* since.
agree, ***mannṇā, manzūr k., rāzī h.*** : a. w., ***itfāk k.*** (***nāḷ***), *see* assent : a. to take, pay money, ***karnā,*** M. 119. 38 : G. 118.
agreeable, ***dil nū̃ caṅgā laggṇā***; ***suādlā*** (tasty).
agreement, ***itfāk,*** m. : ***mēḷ,*** m. : written a., ***karārnāmā*** : written reconciliation, ***rāzīnāmā,*** m. : *see* settle, covenant.

agriculture, ***wāhi***, f. : ***khēti***, f. : ***khētī bāṛī***, f. : *see* plough.
agriculturist, ***zamindār*** : ***wāhi karnwāḷā*** : (legal) ***kāshtkār.***
ague, ***kāmbū***, m. : ***kāmbū tāp***, m. (both ***caṛhnā, nū̃***).
ahead, *see* front.
aim, ***irādā***, m. : ***matlab***, m. : ***manshā***, f. : a. at target, etc., ***nishānā***, m. (***mārnā***) : *see* intention, object, interest.
air, ***wā***, f. : ***hawā***, f. : in the open a., ***waule*** : airs, give oneself, ***nakhre karne*** : ***nazākatā karniā̃*** : ***shēkhi mārni*** : ***ākaṛnā*** : *see* conceit, show, tune.
air (clothes, etc.) ***sukāṇā***, ***sukṇe pāṇā.***
airing, go for, ***wā bhakhṇi.***
alarm, *see* fear, start, startle.
alarming, ***ḍaraoṇā***, ***ḍarnwāḷā***, ***ḍarāṇwāḷā.***
alas! ***hāe hāe***, ***āe hāe***, ***hoe hoe***, ***oe hoe.***
alert, ***hushyār***, ***cukannā***, ***khabardār.***
alight, ***laihṇā*** (pa. p. ***latthā***), ***uirnā.***
alike, ***ikse kism de***, ***ikkojehe***, ***āpe icc raḷde ne.***
alienate (person) ***apṇe wallõ dil khaṭṭā k.*** (***kise, dā***).
alive, ***jiūndā***, ***jiūndā jāgdā.***
all, ***sabbh***, ***sāre***, ***sārā***, ***sāre de sāre*** : not at all, ***ukkā nā***, ***atte nā*** : nothing at all, ***kujjh wī nehī̃.***
allay, *see* lessen, quench.
alliance, ***aihd***, m. : ***dōsti***, f.
alligator, ***sansār***, m. : ***magarmacch***, m. (U).
allow, ***dēṇā*** w. inflec. inf., G. 66 : ***ijāzat dēṇi*** (***dī***).
allowance (food) ***rāshan***, m. : ***rasad***, m. : food a. in travelling, ***bhattā***, m. : travelling a. (money). ***safar kharc***, m. : famine a., ***mahṅgāi***, f. (pron. ***maṅghāi***) : *see* famine.
allude, ***ishārā karṇā*** (***ohde wall***, to him) : hit at someone, ***nōk lāṇi*** (***nū̃***), *see* hit.
almanac, ***jantri***, f.
almond, ***badām***, m.; w. thin shell, ***kāgzī badām***, m. : colour, ***badāmī.***
almost, ***karīb*** : *see* approximately : a. falling, ***digg caleā e***, G. 67.
alms, give alms, ***khair***, m. (***pāṇā***, M.), ***khairāt***, f. or ***kharait***, f. (***d.***, M.), ***luṭāṇā***, G. 109 : ***dāt***, f. (***dēṇi***, M.), ***dān***, m. (***d.***, H.) : ***dānpun***, or ***pundān*** m. (***d.*** or ***k.*** H.)
aloe, ***keoṛā***, m. : soft kind, ***kuār gandal***, f.
alone, ***kallā***, ***chaṛā***, ***kall mukallā chaṛā muṛā***, ***charā chāṇḍ***, ***dam dā dam*** : *see* unmarried.
along (road, bank, etc.), locative case repeated; a. bank, ***dande dande*** or ***kandhe kandhe*** : a. road, ***sarke sarke*** : a. side, ***nāḷ***, ***nāḷo nāḷ***
aloud, ***uccī*** : *see* loudly : ideas hardly distinguished.
alphabet, ***allaf bē̃***, f. ***harf***, m. ***bārā̃khari.***
also, ***wī***, ***bī*** : *see* moreover.

alter, *see* change.
altercation, *see* quarrel.
alternate, on a. days, ***dujje dujje dihāṛe, ikk ikk din chaḍḍke.***
alternately, ***wārī wārī, wāro waṭṭī.***
alternative, ***koī hōr tajwīz*** (f.) or ***gall*** (f.)
although, ***bhāwẽ, bhāwẽ jīkar, hālā̃*** : conjunct. part. of verb, as ***sārī gall wekhke wī nehī muṛeā,*** he did not desist a. he had seen the whole thing.
altitude, *see* height.
altogether, ***kull, sārā, sāre dā sārā*** : *see* absolutely.
alum, ***phaṭkarī.*** f.
always, ***hamēshā, hamēsh, sadā, nitt*** : *see* continuously.
amass, *see* collect.
A.M., P.M., use ***rāt de, shām de; din de do-waje,*** 2 P.M.; M. 61.
amazed, ***harān, hakkā bakkā*** : *see* astonished.
amazement, ***harānī,*** f. : *see* astonishment.
ambassador, ***wakīl : ēlcī*** (U.).
ambiguous, ***shakkī, dū̃h maihṇeā̃ wālī gall, gōḷ mōḷ*** : *see* obscure.
ambition, no word : use ***waḍḍe waḍḍe khyāl karne,*** have high thoughts : ***waddhaṇ dī barī kōshish karnī,*** try to increase.
amble (of horse), ***rawhāl calṇā.***
amend, *see* improve.
amiable, ***khushmizāj, khushta-bīat.***
amicable, *see* friendly.
amidst, ***de wicc, de wishkār, de darmiān*** : *see* between.
amiss, take, ***burā mannṇā*** (***gall nū̃***).
amnesty, ***muāfī,*** f. : general a., ***ām muāfī.***
among, *see* amidst.
amount, n., ***rakam,*** f. : a. to, ***banṇā,*** h.
amputate, ***waḍḍhṇā.***
amulet, ***tawīt,*** m. : ***tāwīz,*** m. (U.).
amuse, ***dil parcāṇā*** (int. ***parcṇā***): ***dil bhulāṇā*** (int. ***bhullṇā***) : ***khush k.*** (int. ***h.***) : ***mauj karnī*** : ***bullhe luṭṭne*** : ***lillā̃ luṭṭṇiā̃*** : ***noshe luṭṭne*** : *see* delight, charm.
amusement, ***tamāshā,*** m. (often suggests dancing girls) : ***mauj mēlā,*** m.
amusing, ***hasāṇwāḷī gall*** : *see* amuse.
anarchy, ***mulkh wicc gaṛbaṛī*** (***paiṇī***), ***hanēr*** (***macṇā***).
ancestors, ***pyōdādde, waḍḍe, waḍēre,*** m. pl.
anchor, ***langar,*** m. : weigh a., ***cukkṇā*** : let down, ***saṭṭṇā.***
ancient, ***kadīm, muṇḍh kadīm dā, purāne zamāne dā.***
and, ***te, nāḷe*** : both this and that, ***nāḷe eh te nāḷe oh, eh wī te oh u'ī.***
anecdote, *see* story.
angel, ***farishtā,*** m.
angle, corner, ***nukkar,*** f. : ***guṭṭh,*** f.
anger, ***gussā*** (***k.*** and ***h.***) : ***tā,*** m. (heat, ***auṇā***) : ***lāl h., lālo lāl h.*** : God's wrath, ***kahr,*** m. : swallow

down one's a., ***gussā pī laiṇā*** : *see* angry, flare, rage.

angry, ***gussā auṇā*** or ***caṛhnā*** (***nū̃***) M. 117. 3 : G. 117 : ***gusse h., saṛnā, balṇā, lūsṇā*** : *see* annoy, displease, frown. A.

animal, ***hawān***, m. : ***jānwar*** or ***janaur***, m. (gen. means bird).

animosity, *see* enmity, envy.

aniseed, ***saũf***, f.

ankle, ***giṭṭā***, m.

anklet, ***kaṛī***, f. : ***toṛā***, m. A

anna, ***ānnā***, m. : two a., ***duānnī***, f. : four a., ***paulī, pauḷī***, f., ***cuānnī***, f. : eight a., ***dhēllī***, f., ***aṭhiāṇṇī***, f. : half a., ***adhiānnī***, f. ***ṭaga***, m.

annihilate, ***fanā k.*** : *see* exterminate.

announce, ***khabar dēṇī*** : ***itlāh dēṇī*** : *see* proclaim, inform.

annoy, ***satāṇā***, or ***satā mārnā, dikk k., ḍicc k., taṅg k., akāṇā, chēṛnā*** : int. ***satṇā, dikk h., ḍicc h., akkṇā***, also ***wiṭarnā, kiṛnā, ciṛhṇā*** : *see* tease, displeased, angry, bore.

annual, *see* year, yearly.

anoint, ***lēp karnā (tē)*** : ***copaṛnā***, put on oil, ***ghi***, butter, etc. : *see* ointment, apply, rub.

anonymous, ***gumnām***.

another, ***ikk hōr, dujjā***.

answer, ***juāb***, m. (***d.***) : flat refusal, ***sukkā juāb*** : know the a, ***juāb auṇā***, (***nū̃***), M. 117. 2, G. 117. *see* refusal.

ant, ***kīṛī*** f. : whiteants, ***syõk***, f. or ***simak***, f. (used collectively in sing.).

antagonist, *see* enemy, adversary.

antagonism, ***mukhālfat***, f. (***k***) : ***wair***, m. (***k.***) : ***dushmaṇī*** (***k.***), 2nd and 3rd mean enmity : *see*, enmity, envy.

antelope, ***harn***, fem. ***harnī***.

antecedents, ***paihlā hāl*** or ***cāl caln***.

antimony, ***surmā***, m., ***kajjal***, m.

anvil, ***airan***, f., ***aihran***, f.

anxiety, ***waswās***, m. : ***fikr.*** m. : ***andēshā***, m. : ***sōc.*** f. (thought)

any, anyone, ***koī***.

anyhow, ***ẽwẽ, aĩwẽ, kiwẽ, kise taṛhā̃***.

anything, ***kujjh***.

anywhere, ***kitale, kite***.

apart, adv., ***nawēkḷā, pasittā, alagg, ikk pase, alaihḍā*** : *see* separate.

aperient, *see* purgative.

apologise, ***muāfī maṅgṇī***. A.

apostle, ***rasūl***, m.

apostleship, ***rasālat***, f.

apparatus, ***samān***, m.

apparent, ***zāhr*** ; *see* appear, seem, visible.

apparently, ***wēkkhaṇ wicc*** : of person's professions, ***uttõ-wālī, uttõdī***.

appeal (legal), ***apīl***, f. (***k.***) : as interj., ***duhāī*** : ***duhāī Rabb dī***, I a. to God : *see* ask, beseech.

appear, *see* seem, visible.

appearance, ***sūrat***, f. : ***shakl***, f. : ***raṅg rūp***, m. : *see* form.

appease, ***manāṇā, rāzī k.*** A.

appetite, no word, use ***bhukkh***, f., hunger : ***shauk***, m., desire, liking.

apple, ***syō***, m. : crab-a., ***cōṭā***, m. : custard a., ***sharīfā***.
applicant, ***umēdwār***, ***jihdī darkhāst e***, etc. : *see* beggar.
apply (ointment, varnish, etc.), ***lāṇā*** (int. ***laggṇā***) : *see* anoint, ointment : apply to, use ask, speak to, write to.
appoint (servant) ***rakkhṇā*** : sometimes ***lāṇā***, M. 196. 18 : (*see* servant) : (day) ***din mitthṇā*** : (date) ***tarīk*** or ***tārīkh pāṇī*** (int. ***paiṇī***) or ***rakkhṇī***.
appointment, ***naukrī***, f.
apprentice, ***shagird***, m.
approach, ***nēṛe auṇā*** : ***ḍhukkṇā*** (esp. of marriage procession, or ox to yoke).
approximately, ***nēṛe trēṛe***, ***nēre***, ***aṭā saṭā***, ***aṭkal paccū***, ***duāle*** : ***koī***, ***ko*** and ***ku***, as ***koī trai***, ***trai ku***, about three, G. 87.
apricot, ***khurmānnī***, f.
April, ***aprail***, m. : ***ēpril***, m. : ***wasākh***, m. (about Apr. 13 to Mar. 12).
apt to, *see* prone.
arbiter, ***tarfain***, m. : *see* mediator.
arch, n., ***ḍāṭ***, f.
arena, ***akhāṛā***, m. : ***piṛ***, m.
argue, ***baihsṇā***, ***baihs karnī***, ***dalīlā̃ chāṇṭṇiā̃***, ***dalīlī laggṇā***, M. 131. 8.
argument, ***dalīl***, f. : quibble, ***hujjat***, f., *see* quibble.
argumentative, ***hujtī***, ***baihsaṇwāṭā***, etc. : *see* argue.
arid, ***sukkā***, ***jitthe pāṇī nehī̃***, ***barānī***.
arise, ***uṭṭhṇā*** : *see* stand, happen, rise.
arithmetic, ***hisāb***, m. : (educ.) ***riāzī***, f., (mathematics).
arm (whole), ***bā̃h***, f. : fore-a., ***wīṇī***, f. : upper, ***ḍauḷā***, m. : *see* biceps; a. of river, ***shākh***, f. : in arms (of child) ***kucchar*** (m.) ***wicc***. : *see* arms, tie. A.
armpit, ***kacch***, f.
arms, ***hathyār***, m.
army, ***fauj***, f. : ***lashkar***, m.
around, *see* round.
arouse, *see* wake, incite, excite.
arrange, arrangement, ***ṭhīk ṭhāk k.*** : ***sajāṇā*** (adorn), ***sāmbhṇā*** or ***sambhālnā*** (look after) : a. about, ***āhr karnā***, ***āhr pāhr karnā*** (***dā***) : ***intizām karnā*** (***dā***) : ***bandobast karnā*** (***dā***) : ***tajwīz kaṛnī*** (***dī***) : make some arrangement or other, ***koī bhantrik karnā*** : *see* settle : a. to pay, take money, *see* agree.
arrears, ***bakāyā***, m.
arrest, ***pharnā***.
arrival, ***auṇā*** (come) : news of a., ***awāī***, f.
arrive, ***apparnā***, ***auṇā***, ***paūhoṇā***, ***ḍhukkṇā*** (esp. of marriage procession).
arrow, ***tīr***, m.
artery, ***nāṛ***, f. : (also vein, sinew).
artful, ***calāk***, ***hīlebāz***, and words for deceitful.
artifice, *see* trick, deceit.
artificer, ***kārigar***, m.
artificial, ***baṇāwṭī*** (also of made-up story or excuse).
artillery, ***tōpkhāṇā***, m.
as, adj., ***jehā***, ***jaisā*** : adv. ***jīkaṇ***, ***jīkar***, ***jīkarā̃***, ***jiwẽ***, ***jis tarhā̃***, ***jiñ***

(rare) : as if, ***jiwẽ***, ***goyā***, ***jāttā***, ***jāṇo***.
ascend, ***caṛhnā***, ***utā̃ jāṇā*** (tr. ***cāṛhnā***, ***caṛhāṇā***).
ascent, ***caṛhāī***, f.
ascertain, *see* discover, investigation.
ashamed, ***sharmindā***, ***lāzam*** (both gen. of actual shame, not shyness) : *see* shame, shy.
ashes (from fire) ***sāh***, f., ***suāh***, f. : (still hot) ***bhubbaḷ*** f. : (from decomposition), *see* dust.
aside, *see* apart, aside.
ask (question), ***pucchṇā***, ***pucchṇā gicchṇā*** : ***suāl karnā*** (also make petition) : ask for, ***maṅgnā***, (*see* beg); ask after health, *see* inquire : *see* beg, beseech.
aslant, *see* slanting.
asleep, ***suttā hoeā***; while people are a., ***suttī̃ bandī̃***, G. 78 : half a., ***jāggo miṭī*** : a. (of limb) ***suttā hoeā***, ***sunn*** : *see*, numb, sleepy.
aspire, *see* ambition, desire.
ass, ***khōtā***, fem. ***khōtī*** ; ***waihtar*** m. (any beast of burden) : *see* horse, mule.
assafoetida, ***hiṅg***, ***f.***
assault (leg.), ***mār piṭṭ***, f. : *see* attack.
assemble, ***kaiṭhā k.*** (int. ***h.***) : ***jamā k.*** (int. ***h.***).
assembly, ***majlis***, f. : ***jalsā***, m. (of large a.) ***: manḍlī***, f. (company) : *see* company, meeting.
assent, ***hā̃ karnī***, ***huṅgārā bharnā***, ***mannnā***.
assert, ***zor nāḷ ākhṇā***, ***takīd nāḷ ākhṇā***.
assess (of land), ***muāmlā lāṇā*** : *see* settlement, tax.
assessment, ***muāmlā***, m.
assist, *see* help.
assistant, ***madadgār***, m. : Asst. Commissioner, ***Ạshṭanṭ Sāhb***.
associate, n., *see* companion : v., ***joṛidār***, ***sāthi milṇā juḷṇā*** (***nāḷ***), ***wartṇā*** (***nāḷ***), ***wāh painā*** (***nāḷ***).
assure, ***tsallī duāṇī***, ***yakīn duānā*** : *see* insure.
astonish, ***harān k.*** : ***hakkā bakkā k.*** : astonished, be, ***harān h.***, ***hakkā bakkā h.*** : ***tajjab k.***, ***h.*** and ***acarj h.*** (mildly) : *see* wonderful.
astonishment (mild), ***tajjab***, m. : (great) ***harānī***, f. : interj. of a., ***balle balle***, ***bāī bāī***.
astray, go, ***(rāhō) khunjhṇā*** or ***ghussṇā***, ***kurāhe*** or ***kurāh paiṇā*** : *see* way, seduce.
astrologer, ***ramḷī***, m.; ***naiūmī***, m. : ***jōtshī***, m.
asylum (lunatic), ***pāgalkhānā***, m.
at, ***wicc*** : at well, shop, tank, railway station, etc., ***te*** : for at often use loc.. G. 9, 10, 77 : at of time loc, G. 10, 34, 78.
asylum (political), (***siāsi***) ***panāh***, f. ***sharaṇ***, f.
atheist, ***daihriā***.
athlete, *see* wrestler, tumbler.
atone, atonement, ***kafārā***, m. (***d.***, ***h.***)
attach, ***lāṇā*** (int. ***laggnā***) : *see* file (papers), tie, apply.
attachment, *see* love.
attack, ***hamlā***, m. (***k.***, ***utte***) : of dog, ***paiṇā*** (***nū̃***), G. 120, M. 125, 8.

attain, *see* obtain, reach.
attempt, *see* try.
attend (to someone), ***dhiān karnā*** (***de wall***) : a. upon, serve, ***ṭaihl karnī*** (***dī***), ***khidmat karnī*** (***dī***) : *see* serve : a. sick person (of doctor), ***ilāj karnā*** (***dā***).
attendance (being present), ***hāzrī***, f. (***lāṇī***, to enter attendance in book, int. ***laggṇī***) : *see* call.
attendant, *see* servant.
attention, ***dhiān***, m. (also meditation).
attentive, use ***dhiān nāḷ***, ***dil nāḷ***, ***dilō̃ wajhō̃ hōke***.
attribute, *see* quality.
auction, n., ***lalāmī***, f. : v., ***lalām-k.*** (***nū̃***)
audience (people present), ***hāzrīn***, m. pl. (U) :.jehre ***hāzir*** or ***baiṭhe ne*** : ***jamāt***, f. : *see* congregation, spectator.
audit, ***paṛtāḷ***, ***k.*** (***dī***, rarely ***nū̃***).
auger, ***warmā***, m.
August, ***agast***, m. : ***bhādrō̃***, m. (about 13th Aug. to 12th Sep.).
aunt, father's sister, ***phupphī***, ***bhūā*** : mother's sister, ***māssī*** : father's elder brother's wife, ***tāī*** : father's younger brother's wife, ***cāccī*** : mother's brother's wife, ***māmmī*** : wife's or husband's aunt, *see* father.
auspicious, ***nēk*** (M.), ***mubārak*** (M.) : ***shubh*** (H.), ***mahūrat caṅgā*** (H.) : *see* fortunate.
author, (***kitābā̃***) ***likkhaṇwālā***.
authorise, ***ikhtiār dēṇā***, ***mukhtār rakkhṇā*** or ***baṇāṇā*** (*see* advocate) : ***hukam dēṇā*** (order) : ***ijāzat dēṇī*** (permit).
authority, ***ikhtiār***, m. : ***ijāzat***, f. (permission) : ***hukam***, m. (order) : ***hakk***, m. (right) : ***kadr***, m. f. (value, i.e. who was he to do so and so?) : ***tākat***, f. (power).
avarice, avaricious, *see* covetous, covetousness.
avenge, *see* revenge.
average, n., ***ausat***, ***aust***, f. : adj., ***wishkārle***, ***mēḷ dā***; strike an a., ***aust kaḍḍhnī*** : *see* approximately, mediocre.
avert, ***ṭaḷṇā***, ***rōkṇā***, ***rafā dafā k.*** (int. ***ṭaḷṇā***, ***rukkṇā***, ***rafā dafā h.***).
avidity, *see* desire, wish, long.
avoid (food, actions), ***parhēz*** (f.m.) ***k.*** (***-ō̃, te***) : avoid meeting someone, ***matthe nā laggṇā*** (***de***), ***neṛe nā jāṇā*** (***de***) : *see* escape.
avow, ***saūh khānī***, f. also *see* admit, confess.
await, *see* wait.
awake, adj., ***jāgdā*** : v., *see* wake.
aware, ***patā h.*** or ***laggṇā***, ***khabar hōṇī***, ***mālūm h.*** (all ***nū̃***).
away (from home on visit) ***wāhṇḍā*** : begone! ***jā parū̃***, ***parā̃ hō***, ***dūr hō***, ***radd hō***, ***dafā hō*** : ***jā***, ***ṭur jā*** : (*see* rise) : (to dog) ***dūr dūr***, ***dūre*** : (to cat) ***chir chir***, ***chire***.
awe (person's influence), ***rohb***, m. : *see* fear.
awkward, ***bhaddā***, ***kōjhā***, ***kuḍhabbā***.

awning (over shop), ***chappar***, m. (strictly thatch) : kind of large tent), ***shāmiānā***, m.
axe (large) ***kuhāṛā***, m. : (small) ***kuhāṛī***, f.
axle, *dhurā*, m.
azure, *asmānī* (***raṅg***, m.).

B

baby, *baccā*, m. (***kucchaṛ wicc***, in arms).
bachelor, *kuārā* : ***chaṛā*** (alone).
back, ***piṭṭh***, f. : upper b., ***kaṇḍ***, f. : lower, ***lakk***, m. (*see* waist) : b. of shoulders, ***maur***, m. : *see* spine : b. of book, paper, ***pusht***, f. : behind one's back, ***picchõ kaṇḍī***, ***piṭṭh picche*** : *see* absence : (carry) on one's b, ***kandhāṛe***, shoulders : at the b. of, *see* behind, after. A.
back, adv. (as send b., go b.), ***partāke***, ***partke*** : *see* return.
back out of, ***phirnā***, ***thiṛnā***, ***pasrnā***.
backbite, *see* tale, slander, accuse.
bad, *burā*, ***k͟harāb***, ***mandā***, ***bhaiṛā***, ***raddī*** : rotten, ***trakkā hoeā*** ; slightly, ***musseā hoeā*** : go bad, ***trakkṇā***, *see* rot ; slightly, ***mūssṇā*** : (of milk) *see* sour : *see* worthless, useless : a bad business, ***maṭṭhī gall***, ***burī gall***, ***mandī gall*** : (of land) ***niras***, ***raddī***, ***karlāṭhī*** : *see* coin, evil, soil, sin.
badness, *burāī*, ***bureāī***, f. : ***k͟harābī***, f. : *see* sin.
badge, *nishān*, m. : (for ***caprasī***) ***capṛās***, f.
baffle, *see* bewilder.
bag (large) ***thailā*** : (small) ***thailī***, f. : for schoolbooks, ***bastā***, m. : ***jhōḷī***, chudder or front of shirt used as b. : *see* purse, sack : b. and baggage, ***gaṇdh gaṭṭhrī***, ***grām gaṭṭhrī***, f. : ***bistrā bōriā***, m. : ***bhāṇḍā ṭiṇḍar***, m. **:** ***bā̃ bistar***, m. : (all w. ***bannhṇā***, tie up).
baggage, *samān*, m. : ***asbāb***, m. : *see* bag and baggage.
bail, *zamānat*. f. (security) : release on b., ***zamānat te chaḍḍṇā*** ; person going b., ***zāman***, m
bake, *pakāṇā*, ***bēk k.*** (K).
baker, *roṭiā̃wāḷā*, or as U ***roṭīwāḷā*** : village b., ***māchī***, fem. ***māchaṇ*** : ***nānwāī***, no fem.
balance, *see* scales : (financial) ***bakāyā***, m.
bald, (head b. and face bare) ***rōḍḍā*** : b. through disease (favus), ***ganjā*** : *see* hairless.
ball (for play), ***khehnū̃***, m. : ***gēnd***, m. : ***bāl***, m. : ***khiddo***, m. (made of cloth) : bullet, ***gōḷī***, f. : cannon-b., ***gōḷā***, m.
bamboo, *wanjh*, m. **:** ***bā̃s***, m.
banana, *kēlā*, m. : more often ***phaḷī*** or ***kēle dī phaḷī***, f.
band (music) ***wājewāḷā***, m. pl. : *see* company.
bandsman, *wājewāḷā*, m.
bandage, *paṭṭī* f. : (v., ***paṭṭī bannhṇī***) : over ointment, etc., ***phāh***, m. (***lāṇā***).
bangle, *cūṛī*. f., ***kaṛā***, m. *see* bracelet.

banish, ***mulkhõ*** or ***watnõ bāhr kaḍḍhṇā.***
banjo, *see* guitar.
bank (of river, lake, etc.) ***kaṇḍhā,*** m. : ***dandā***, m. : (for money), ***bańk***, m. : (actual building) ***bańk-ghar***, m.
banker (Indian) ***shāh***, ***shāhūkār*** : (European) ***bańkwāḷā.***
banknote, ***nōṭ***, m.
bankrupt, become, ***duāḷā nikḷnā*** : he has become b., ***ohdā duāḷā nikḷeā e*** : he claims to be b., ***oh duāḷā kaḍḍh baiṭhā e.***
banner, *see* flag.
banquet, ***khāṇā***, m. : invite to, ***dāwat karnī*** : *see* invite.
banyan tree, ***bōṛh.*** f.
baptise, ***baptismā*** (m.) ***d.*** (***nū̃***) : be b., ***baptismā h.*** (***dā***) or ***laiṇā.***
bar (for door), ***hohṛkā***, m. : ***hohṛā***, m. : ***arl***, m. : *see* rod.
barbarian, ***waihshī***, ***jāṅglī*** : original inhabitants of canal districts called ***jāṅglī.***
barber, ***nāī***, fem. ***naiṇ.***
bare, ***naṅgā*** : barefooted, ***naṅgī̃ pairī̃*** (G. 10, 78), ***pairā̃ tõ wāhṇā*** : bareheaded, ***naṅge sir*** : lay bare, ***naṅgā k.*** : lay bare thoughts, ***thullṇā*** : matter, ***phōlṇā.***
barely, *see* scarcely.
bargain, ***saudā***, m. : good b., ***caṅgā saudā*** : a b. ***i.e.*** cheap, ***sastā.***
bark, v., ***bhauṅkṇā.***
bark, n., *see* tree.
barley, ***jaū̃***, m. : barle and wheat, ***gojī***, f.
barracks, ***bārak***, f.
barrel (of gun) ***nāḷī***, f. : (cask) ***pīpā***, m.
barren (land), ***kallar***, ***banjar*** : (of tree) ***apphal*** : (woman) no good word, say ***baccī baccā*** or ***dhī puttar koī nehī̃***, etc. : ***autrī nakhattrī*** means either barren or children dead : often as abuse.
barrow, ***reṛhī***, f. : *see* cart.
barter, exchange, ***waṭāṇā.***
base, adj., (low family or ideals) ***kamīnā*** : (evil) *see* bad, wicked.
base, n. (plinth) ***kursī***, f. : *see* foundation.
bashful, *see* shy, shyness.
basin, ***cilamcī***, f.
bask (in sun) ***siyā sēkṇā*** : ***siye*** or ***dhuppe baihṇā*** : ***dhupp sēkṇī.***
basket, ***ṭōkrā***, m. : ***ṭōkrī***, f. : ***caṅer***, f. : for winnowing, ***chajj***, m. : for fruit, vegetables, sweets, ***chābṛī***, f. : of fruit, vegetables, presented to superior, ***ḍāhḷī***, f. : in scales, ***chābbā***, m.
bastard, ***harām dā.***
bastion, ***burj***, m.
bat (animal) ***cāmcṛikk-*** or ***-ī***, f. : ***cāmciṭṭh***, f.
bat, for playing, ***ballā***, m. : ***baiṭ***, m. : village bat and ball, ***khehnū̃ ṭallā.***
bath, n. (the article) ***ṭapp***, m. : *see* cistern : Turkish b., ***hamām***, m. : *see* boiler, bathe : bathroom, ***guslkhānā***, m.
bathe, ***nhauṇā*** (pa. p. ***nhātā***), ***gusl karnā*** : b. someone else,

nalwhāṇā, nuhānā, gusl dēṇā (***nū̃***) : *see* wash ablution.
battalion, ***baṭālyan***, f.
bawl, *see* scream, shout.
battle, ***laṛāī***, f.: *see* war.
bay (of horse) ***kumaid, kumait.***
bayonet, n. and v., ***saṅgīn mārnī*** (***nū̃***).
bazar, ***bazār***, m.
be, to, verb subst., am, was, etc., only pres, and past : G. 50, 55, 56 : become, ***hōṇā*** : let it be, ***raihṇ dē*** : *see* mind.
bead, ***maṇkā***, m.
beadle, ***capṛāsī***, m.
beak, ***cunjh***, f. : ***cinjh***, f. : *see* peck.
beam, large, ***shatīr***, m. : small, ***shatīrī***, f. : ***bāllā***, m. : small cross bit in ceiling, ***kaṛī***, f. : *see* log.
bean, ***sēm***, f., French, ***frās bīn***, f.
bear, n., ***ricch***, m : fem. ***ricchṇī*** : sometimes ***bhālū***, m.
bear, *see* endure : b. children, ***jammṇā*** : b. young (cattle) ***sūṇā*** (int.) : in gen. ***baccā dēṇā*** : *see* born.
beard, ***dāṛhī***, f.
bearded, ***dāṛhīwāḷā***, m.
beardless (because too young), ***alū̃*** : (older person) ***khōddā*** : gen., ***andāṛhīā*** : *see* bald, hairless.
bearer (servant), ***baihrā***, m.
beast, ***hawān***, m. (not much used, if possible name animal) : ***jānwar, janaur***, m. (nearly always means bird).
beat, ***mārnā, kuṭṭnā, phaṇḍṇā***, b. w. shoe, stick, blows of fist, etc., ***mārnā*** w. word for shoe, stick, etc., and ***nū̃*** of person struck : *see* blow, strike : rush at to strike, ***ṭuṭṭke paiṇā*** (***nū̃***)***,*** G. 120, M. 125. 14***, mārn paiṇā*** (***nū̃***), G. 120, M. 125. 13 : drum, ***wajāṇā*** : carpets, ***phaṇḍṇā, phaṇḍākā mārnā*** : whisk eggs, ***phēṇṭṇā.***
be beaten, ***mār khāṇī***, or passive of ***mārnā*** or ***phaṇḍṇā***; ***khāṇā*** w. word for shoe, stick, etc., or these words w. ***paiṇā*** and ***nū̃*** of person beaten.
beautiful, ***sohṇā : khūbsūrat*** (U.).
beauty, ***suṇh-ippaṇ, -appaṇ***, m.
because, ***kyū̃ jo, ēs wāste paī, ēs karke paī, es laī paī, kyū̃ paī*** : ***jo*** as enclitic, M. 221. 12.
because of, on account of, ***de sadkā*** : G. 37, 38 : ***de sbabb, de sbabbō̃*** : ***dā mārā, de māreā̃*** (last two of intellectual condition), G. 37, 38.
beckon, ***hatth nāḷ saddṇā, sainat karnī*** (***nū̃***) : *see* wink.
become, ***hōṇā, ho jāṇā*** : *see* suit, suitable.
becoming, *see* beautiful, suitable.
bed, ***manjī***, f. : (large) ***palaṅgh***, m. : side-piece, ***hī***, f. : end-piece, ***sērū***, m. : head, ***sarhāndī***, f. : foot, ***puāndī***, f. : make b., ***wachauṇā*** or ***bistrā wachāṇā*** : sometimes ***bistrā k.*** : bedding, ***sōt***, f., ***wachauṇā***, m., ***bistrā***, m : bed-room, ***sauṇā kamrā***, m.

bed *see* flower-bed.
bee, ***mākhyõ dī makkhī***, f.
beef, any word for meat w. ***waḍḍā***, big. or ***gōkā***, cow's, or ***gā̃ dā***, cow's, prefixed : also ***bīf***, m. (K.).
beer, ***bīr sharāb***, m. (K.).
beetle for levelling road, ***durmaṭ***, m. : ***damūsā***, m.
beetroot, ***cakundar***, m.
before, adv. of time (both previously and in future), ***agge***, ***agge, nū̃*** : (previously only), ***paihlā̃***, ***paihle***, ***paihlū̃***, ***paihle nū̃***, ***agētre***, ***agdū̃*** : adv. of place, ***agge***, ***sāhmṇe*** : forward, ***agā̃*** : from before, from in front of, ***aggō, sāhmṇeõ*** : by way of in front, ***aggõ dī***, ***sāhmṇeõ dī***.

prep., ***de agge***, ***de sāhmṇe*** : one in front of the other, ***agge picche***, ***aggaṛ picchaṛ*** : *see* front, face :

conj., inflec. inf. w. ***tõ*** or ***thõ*** or ***thī̃*** or ***-õ*** followed by ***agdū̃*** or ***paihlū̃*** : G. 95.
befriend, *see* help.
beg, ***mangṇā***, ***suāl karnā*** : *see* ask, beseech.
beggar, ***manganṇwāḷā***, ***suālī***, ***mangtā***, ***fakīr***, fem. ***fakīrnī***.
beggary, *see* poverty.
begin, ***laggṇā*** (pa. p. ***lagā***, when unemphatic, and ***laggā*** when stressed) w. inflect. inf. : ***shurū k.*** (w. inf. agreeing w. object) : to begin w., ***paund saṭṭe***.
beginner, ***aje hune sikkaṇ lagā***.
beginning, ***shurū***, m. : from the b., ***muḍḍõ***, ***muhḍḍõ*** : from b. to end, ***alfõ laike yē tōṛī*** : ***muḍḍõ laike akhir tōṛī***.
begone, *see* away.
behalf, on my, etc., ***mēre wallõ*** from me : ***mērī khātar***, for my sake : ***mēre lai***, ***mēre wāste***, for me : *see* for.
behaviour, *see* character.
behead, ***sir waḍḍhṇā*** (***dā***).
behind, adv., ***picche***, ***pichēre***, ***pishēre*** : *see* afterwards : towards behind, ***pishā̃*** : from b., ***picchõ***, ***pichēreõ***, ***pishēreõ*** prep., ***de picche***, ***de magar*** : sheltered b. or hidden b., ***de ohle*** : pass b., ***picchõ dī*** or ***magarõ dī langhṇā*** : *see* after, before.
belie, ***jhūṭhā k.*** or ***baṇāṇā***.
believe (a fact) ***mannṇā***, ***yakīn k.*** or ***h.*** or ***auṇā*** (M. 153. 30, 31) : b. in (God, Christ, etc.) ***imān leauṇā*** (***utte***), M. 154. 33-6, 155 : *see* faith, trust, confide, reliance.
bell, large, ***ghaiṇṭā***, m., ***ṭall***, m. : gong, ***ghaṛeāḷ***, m. : iron bar, ***ghaiṇṭī***, f. : bicycle, dinner bell, ***ṭallī***, f. : tongue of b., ***dur***, m. : ring b., strike gong, ***wajāṇā*** : (***ṭallī***) ***chaṇkāṇī***, ***wajāṇī***, int. ***chaṇakṇī***, ***wajjṇī*** : tiny bells on hands, feet, neck of horses, etc., ***ghunghrū***, m. (***chaṇakṇā***).
belly, *see* stomach.
beloved, ***pyārā*** : *see* lover.
below, adv., ***hēth***, ***hēṭhā̃***, ***thalle***, ***hēṭhle pāse*** : downwards, same words : from b., ***hēṭhõ***, ***thalleõ*** : prep. ***de hēṭh***, etc. same words : pass b., ***hēṭhõ dī***, ***hēṭh dū̃***, ***thalleõ dī***, all ***w. langhṇā***.

belt, ***pēṭī***, f. : ***bilṭ***, m. (***k***) : *see* badge.
bench, ***banc***, f. : *see* seat, chair.
bend, ***lafāṇā*** : be bent, ***lifṇā*** : b. head, ***sir jhukāṇā*** : *see* crooked, stoop.
beneath, *see* below.
benediction, ***barkat dā kalmā*** (pronounce, ***suṇāṇā***) : *see* blessing.
benefactor, ***murabbī***, ***mehrbān*** (kind).
beneficial, *see* advantageous.
benefit, v. tr., ***fāidā***, m. (***karnā***) : int. ***fāidā h.*** (***dā***) : arrogantly claim to have benefited someone, ***ahsān*** (pron. ***as-hān***) or ***ṭhāhrā cāṛhnā*** (***utte***) : admit being benefited, ***ahsān*** or ***ṭhāhrā mannṇā*** (***dā***) : *see* obligation.
benefit, n., ***fāidā***, m. : ***ahsān*** m. (kindness) : *see* profit.
benumbed, *see* numb.
bequeath, ***wasīat karke d.*** : ***wasiatnāme wicc d.***
beseech, ***tarle karne***, ***tarlā karnā***, ***miṇtā̃ karniā̃***, ***miṇt tarlā k.***, ***miṇt mājrā karnā*** (all w. gen.); ***hatth bannhke arz karnī*** (***de agge***) : *see* ask.
beside, *see* near.
besides, ***ehnū̃ chaḍḍke***, ***ehde suā*** : *see* without.
besiege, ***ghērnā***, ***muhāsrā karnā*** (***dā***).
bet, ***shart***, f. : v., ***lāṇī*** : int. ***laggṇī***.
best, ***sāreā̃ tõ*** or ***sāreā̃ wiccõ caṅgā*** : best man, ***sarbāhlā***, m.
betel-leaf, ***pān***, m. :—nut, ***sipārī***, f.
between, ***wicckār***, ***de darmiān*** : *see* through : go-between, *see* mediator.
bewilder, v.tr., ***ghabrāṇā*** : be b. ***ghābbarnā***.
bewitch, *see* charm.
beyond, adv., ***pare***, ***parle pāse***, ***pār*** : towards b., ***parā̃*** : prep., ***de pare***, ***de parle pāse***, ***de pār***.
Bible, ***baibal***, f. : ***Khudā dī*** (***dā***) ***kalām***, or ***dī kitāb***, f. : *see* Testament.
bhang, ***bhaṅg***, f. : ***cars***, f. (a preparation of b.) : man who uses b., ***bhaṅgī***.
bias, *see* partiality.
biceps, triceps, ***ḍauḷe dā paṭṭhā***, m.
bicycle, ***bāiskal***, ***sāikal***, m. : among children, ***aṅgrēzī ghōṛā***, m.
bid (at auction), ***bōlī dēṇī***.
big (age, size) ***waḍḍā***, G. 34 : *see* great; so b., ***ēḍḍā***, ***ōḍḍā*** : how b., ***kēḍḍā*** : as b., ***jēḍḍā*** : as b as I, ***mēre jēḍḍā*** : G. 91, 92.
bigoted, ***tassabī***.
bigotry, ***tassab***, m.
bill (of exchange), ***huṇḍī***, f. : *see* cheque, beak.
bind, *see* tie : b. books, ***jild bannhṇī*** (int. ***bajjhṇī***).
binoculars, ***dūrbīn***, f.
bird, ***jānwar***, m. : ***janaur***, m. : ***painchī***, f. : ***pakhērū***, m. : small, ***ciṛī***, masc. ***ciṛā*** (esp. sparrow) : *see* fledgling.
birth, ***jamm***, m. ***padaish***, f. : when was she (he) born, ***oh***

kadõ dī (***dā***) ***jamm e***? : *see* bear, born.
birthday, *jaṇam din*, m.
biscuit, *biskut*, m. : very thin, ***tunkī***, f. : Indian, ***khatāī***, f.
bit, *see* piece, mouthful : horse's, ***kaṛeāḷā*** m : *see* bridle.
bite, *waḍḍhṇā, waḍḍh khāṇā* : ***dandiā̃ waḍḍhṇiā̃*** : of horse, ***cak mārnā*** (all ***nū̃***) of rats, mice, ***ṭukkṇā, kutarnā*** : *see* gnaw, attack (dog).
bitter, *kauṛā* : of person, ***kauṛā, saṛeā baḷeā*** : *see* annoy : of mind, ***khaṭṭā*** : *see* embitter.
bitterly, *saṛke* : weep b., ***ucci ucci***, loudly. or ***bauht***, very much. &c., ***rõṇā***.
black, *kāḷā* : *see* jet-black.
blackness, *kāḷakh*, f. (especially from soot, smoke).
blackguard, *badmāsh, sharārtī*, immoral, ***luccā***.
blacking, for boots, ***syāhī***, f. *see* polish.
blacksmith, *luhār*, fem. ***luhārī***.
blade, of knife, etc., ***phaḷ***, m.
bladder, *bhakānnā*, m.
blame, *ilzām lāṇā*, (***utte***) : ***pēṭe gall pāṇī*** (***de***) : *see* reprimand, accuse, sit upon.
blameless, *bēkasūr, bēgunāh* : *see* sinless, innocent.
blank (paper), ***kōrā*** : *see* unused.
blanket, *kambaḷ*, m. : ***jhull***, f. : ***loī***, f. (fine) : ***bhūrā, dōṛa*** m. (esp. for horses, cattle) : *see* quilt, sheet, shawl.
blasheme, blasphemy, ***kufar***, m. : (***bakṇā, bōlṇā***).
blasphemer, *kāfar*, M. : ***kufr bakaṇwāḷā*** : *see* atheist, unbeliever.
blaze up, *bhakhṇā, bhakh paiṇā* : *see* burn, heat.
bleat, of sheep, goats, ***maīkṇā***.
blemish, *nuks*, m. : ***dāg***, m. (spot, stain) : ***aib***, m.
bless, blessing, God to man ***barkat dēṇī*** : ***asīs dēṇī*** (H.) : man God, *see* praise : man man, ***duā dēṇī*** : *see* benediction, curse.
blessed, *mubārak, dhann*.
blind, *annhā* : (title by courtesy), ***hāfaj*** (for ***hāfiz***, : *see* Quran) : of one eye, ***kāṇā*** : *see* see.
blindly, *annhe wā* or ***wāh***.
blindness, at night, ***artānnā***, m. ***andhrātā***, m.
blister, *chāllā, phōṛā* m. (***paiṇā***) : *see* water.
blood, *ratt*, f. : ***khūn***, m. : ***lahū***, m.
bloody, *ratt nāḷ bhareā hoeā*.
blossom, n., ***kalī***, f. : ***phull***, m. v. : *see* flower.
blot, *dāg*, m. : moral, ***dhabbā*** m. : *see* disgrace, delete.
blotting paper, *syāhīcaṭ*, m., ***blāṭin***, f.
blow, n., ***dhapphā***, m. slap ***saṭṭ*** (***laggṇī, wajjṇī*** : tr., ***lāṇī, mārnī***) : *see* wound : b.w. fist, ***hūrā***, m., ***ghasunn***, m., ***gubbh***, f. : slap, ***capēṛ***, f. : w. stick, ***hujj***, f. (*see* prod), or ***sōṭī*** f. : w. shoe, ***chittar***, m., ***juttī***, f. : verb for all, ***wajjṇā, khāṇā, paiṇā*** ; tr. ***mārnā*** : *see* beat : come to blows,

hatthī paiṇā : struggled w. me, tried to strike me, ***mērī hatthī peā*** : G. 120, m. 125. 7.

blow, v., ***phūk mārnī*** : trum. pet, bugle, &c., ***wajāṇā*** : of wind, ***wagṇā*** : b away (of wind), ***uḍāṇā.***

blue, light, ***asmānī (rang)*** : darker, ***lillā, nillā*** : very dark, ***kāḷā.***

blunt, ***khunḍhā.***

boar, same as pig : wild, ***bēlle dā.***

board, large, ***phaṭṭā***, m. : ***ta<u>kh</u>tā***, m. : small, ***phaṭṭī***, f., ***ta<u>kh</u>tī***, f.

boast, ***phaṛā mārniā*** : ***baṛiā gallā karniā : shē<u>kh</u>ī mārni, gapp mārnī.***

boat, ***kishtī***, f., ***bēṛī***, f. : ***bēṛā***, m. (esp. raft).

boatman, ***mallāh***, m. : ***mānjhī*** (Hindu caste).

body, ***piṇḍā***, m. : ***jussā***, m. : ***wujūd***, m. : ***jism***, m. : ***badan***, m. : ***sarīr, sharīr***, m. : one's form, outline, ***but***, m. : *see* corpse, carcase.

boil, n., ***phōṛā***, m. : small. ***phimhṇī***, f. : ***gaṛ***, m. : in armpit, ***kachrāḷī***, f.

boil, v. tr, ***kāṛhnā, khulāṇā, ubāḷṇā*** (make bubble) : (int. ***kaṛhnā. khaulṇā, ubbaḷṇā***) : cook, ***rinnhṇā*** (pa. p. ***riddhā***) (also stew : int. ***rijjhṇā***).

boiled, ***kaṛheā hoeā, riddhā hoeā.***

boiler, for heating water, ***hamām***, m.

boiling, ***khauldā.***

bold, *see* brave, forward.

boldness, including forwardness, ***jurat***, f. : ***dalērī***, f.

bolt, n., ***ciṭ<u>kh</u>anī***, f. : screw-b., ***kāblā***, m. : v., ***ciṭ<u>kh</u>anī mārnī*** or ***lāṇī*** (int. ***wajjṇī, laggṇī***).

bomb, ***bamb***, m.

bond, ***karār***, m. : ***li<u>kh</u>at paṛht***, f. : *see* agreement, covenant.

bondage, *see* slavery, imprison.

bone, ***haḍḍī***, f.

book, ***kitāb***, f. : ***pōthī***, f. (esp. relig. H.) : note-b., copy-b., ***kāpī***, f. : b.-language, ***kitābī bōlī*** : *see* account.

bookcase, (***kitābā wāḷī***) ***almārī***, f.

bookseller, ***kitābā wēccaṇwāḷā, kutub-farōsh*** (U).

book, v., ticket, ***ṭikaṭ laiṇā*** : seat, ***thā ra<u>kh</u>āṇā*** : b.-ing office, ***ṭiktā dā daftar*** : b.-ing clerk, ***ṭiktā wāḷā bābu*** : b. luggage, ***asbāb tulāṇā*** (have weighed), ***buk karāṇā***

boot, *see* shoe.

booty, ***luṭṭ dā māl***, m.

border, *see* boundary, edge, skirt.

bore, ***mōrī kaḍḍhṇī*** or ***karnī*** : ***chēk kaḍḍhṇā*** : (worry) ***akāṇā***, (int. ***akkṇā***); ***sir khapāṇā*** : *see* annoy.

borer, *see* auger.

born, be, ***jammṇā, paidā h.*** : b. (blind), ***jaṇāhndrū*** (***annhā***).

borrow, ***udhār laiṇā*** (money) ***karrz cukkṇā*** (money) : ***mang leauṇā*** (gen.).

borrowed, ***udhār, udhārā*** (money) ***: mangwā*** (gen.).

both, ***dowẽ*** : *see* also.

bottle, ***bōtal***, f. : small, ***shīshī***, f.

bottom, of vessel, box, almirah, ***thallā***, m. : *see* foot.

boundary, ***hadd***, ***phirnī*** f. : narrow, bet. fields, ***bannā***, m., ***bannī***, f., ***waṭṭ***, f.; *see* path : b. pillar, ***buttī***, f.; bet, three villages, ***tarhaḍḍā***.

boundless, ***bēant***, ***bēbahā***.

bow, for arrows, ***kamān***, f. : b. and arrow, ***tīr kamān***, f. : for pellets, ***gulēl***, f. *see* sling, pellet.

bow, v., ***matthā ṭēknā*** (esp. relig.), *see* salute, stoop.

bowels, ***āndrā̃***, f. pl.

bowl, n., ***pyālā***, m. : ***bōl***, m. (K.).

bowl, v., (cricket) ***bāl dēṇā***.

box, ***sandūk***, m. : ***sandūkṛī***, f. : ***bakas***, m. : ***pēṭī***, f. (esp. wooden) : rough wooden, ***khōkhā***, m. : steel, ***ṭarank***, m. : very small, ***ḍabbī***, f. : for measuring ***kankar***, lime, etc., large, ***sandūkṛī***, f. : small, ***ḍaggā***, m.

boy, ***muṇḍā***, ***kākkā***, ***jātak*** : *see* child, son.

boyishness, ***muṇḍpuṇā***, m. : ***muṇḍeā̃***- or ***añāṇeā̃-wāḷī tabīat***, f.

bracelet, ***cūṛī***, f. : ***cūṛā***, m. : ***wanī***, f. : ***gajrā***, m. : ***kaṅnaṇ***, m. : ***gokhṛū***, m. : ***pariban***. m. : ***pauṇcī***, f., ***juṭ***, m. A.

braces, ***gālas***, f.

brackish, ***kaurā***, ***khārā***.

brain, ***bhējā***, m. : ***magz***, m. : ***damāg***, m. : (3rd gen. of conceit) : *see* sense, intelligence, conceit, pride.

brake-van, ***birk***, m. : ***brēk***, m.

bran, ***cōkar***, m. (wheat and gram) ***: chāṇ***, m. : *see* straw.

branch, large, ***ḍāhṇ***, m. : ***ḍāhḷ***, m. : smaller, ***ṭāhṇī***, f. : ***ḍāhḷī***, f. : small switch, broken off, ***chamak***, f. : shoot, ***gullā***, m. : thorn b., ***mōṛhā***, m. : ***mōṛhī***, f. : ***ḍhīṅghrī***, f.

brand, ***dāg***, (***lāṇā***) : morally ***dhabbā***, (***lāṇā***) : int. ***laggṇā***.

brandy, ***brā̃ḍī***, f.

brass, ***pittal***, m. : b. worker, ***ṭhaṭhyār***.

brave, ***bahādar***, ***dalēr*** : *see* courage.

bravo ! ***sadke***, ***balle balle***, ***shābāse***, ***shāhbā***, ***bāī bāī***.

bray, of ass, ***hiṅgṇā***.

bread, ***rōṭī***, f. : made of maize, millet, ***ḍhōḍḍā***, m. : *see* loaf, food.

breadth, ***pēṭ***, m. : ***cuṛāī***, f.

break, ***bhannṇā*** (int. ***bhajjṇā***) : ***ṭōṛnā***, ***trōṛnā*** (int. ***ṭuṭṭṇā***) : b. into bits, ***ṭōṭe ṭōṭe k.*** : b. against, *see* knock : b. open (box, etc.), ***jandrā trōṛnā*** : b. down (become ill) of well, cart, man, animal (not woman), ***hanēkeā jāṇā***, M. 118. 32 : into house, ***sannh mārnī*** : b. fast, at right time, ***rōzā kholhṇā*** : at wrong time, *see* fast : b. in for ploughing, ***hāḷī kaḍḍhṇā*** (***nū̃***) : for burdens, ***lādū kaḍḍhṇā*** (***nū̃***) (int. of both ***nikḷṇā***) : b. off habit, ***ādat chaḍḍṇī*** (for someone else, ***chuḍāṇī***).

breakfast, ***hāzrī***, f. : early b., ***chōṭī hāzrī***.

breast, ***hikk***, f. : ***chātī***, f. (U.) :

breath, breathe, ***sāh***, m. (***laiṇā***, also stop talking) **:** ***dam laiṇā*** : *see* rest : out of b. become, ***haff jāṇā***, ***sāh caṛhnā*** (***nū̃***).

bribe, ***waḍḍhī***, f. : take b., ***laiṇī***, ***khāṇī*** : give b., ***dēṇī*** : ***rishwat***, f. : taker, of b's ***waḍḍhikhōr***, ***rishwatkhōr*** (U.).

brick, ***iṭṭ***, f. : well-baked, ***pakkī*** : half-baked, ***pillī*** too-much baked, ***khangar*** : sun-dried, ***kaccī*** : broken bit, ***rōṛā***, m.; small, ***rōṛī***, f. : b-powder, ***surkhī***, f. : b-maker, ***pathēra***, m. : b-making, ***pathēr***, f. : b-layer, ***rāj***, m. : *see* layer.

bride, use ***kuṛī***, girl. A.

bridegroom, ***lāṛā***, m. : *see* best man.

bridge, ***puḷ***, m. : make b., ***puḷ bannhṇā*** : (int. ***bajjhṇā***).

bridle, ***lagām***, f. (***cāṛhnī***).

brief, ***mukhtsar***, ***thoṛeā̃ lafzā̃ wicc***.

bright, ***baṛī lō***, ***baṛā cānaṇ*** or ***cānṇā***, ***baṛī rōshnī*** : *see* shine : colour, ***gūṛhā***, ***shōkh***, ***tez***.

brim, ***kaṇḍhā***, m. : of hat, ***kannī***, f. : *see* edge.

bring, ***leauṇā***, ***laiauṇā*** : pa. p. ***le-***, ***lai-āndā*** or ***-āyā*** : take w. one, ***kharṇā*** : b. near of cattle to yoke, ***ḍhōṇā*** (int. ***ḍhukkṇā***) : cause to be brought, ***aṇwāṇā***.

brinjal, *see* egg-plant.

brink, *see* edge.

brittle, ***ṭuṭṭaṇwāḷā*** : *see* crisp.

broad, ***cauṛā***, ***caiṛā*** : broadways, across, ***cauṛe dā***.

broad-cloth, ***banāt***, f.

broker, ***dalāl***.

bronze, ***kaĩh***, f.

brook, ***nāḷā***, m. (wet or dry) : ***nadī***, f.

broom, ***jhāṛū***, m. : ***bauhkar***, f. : ***bahārī***, f. : ***kharkṇā***, m. : ***mānjā***, m. : *see* sweep.

broth, ***shurūā***, m.

brother, ***bhrā***, ***bhāī*** : full b., ***sakkā bhrā*** : step b., ***matrēā bhrā*** : wife's b., ***sāḷā*** : ***sāḷā's*** wife, ***sāḷihār***, ***sāḷihāj*** : sister's husband, ***bhaṇūjā*** : husband's elder b., ***jēṭh*** (***jēṭh's*** wife, ***jaṭhāṇī***) : husband's younger b., ***deōr*** (***deōr's*** wife, ***darāṇī***) : ***jēṭh's*** son, ***jaṭhullar*** : husbands of two sisters are ***sāṇḍhū*** to each other : *see* sister.

brotherhood, ***birādrī***, f.

brown, ***bhūsḷā***, ***bhūrā*** : ***badāmī***, almond colour : ***khākī***, dustcolour **:** ***naswārī rang***, snuff colour.

brush, n., v., ***burs***, ***bursh*** (***karnā***, ***nū̃***) : *see* sweep, broom.

bubble, ***buḷbuḷā***, m.

bubo, ***phōṛā***, m. : ***giḷṭī***, f. : ***phimhṇī***, f.

bucket, ***bāḷṭī***, f. (pail) : leather b., ***bōkkā***, m. : iron, ***ḍōḷ***, m.

buckle, ***bagsūā***, m.

bud (flower) ***kalī***, f. : tiny shoot, ***kõpal***, f. : *see* sprout, branch.

buffalo, ***sanḍhā***, m. : ***majjh***, ***maīh***, f. : gen. ***mehrū***, m. : b. calf, ***jhōṭṭā*** : smaller, ***kaṭṭā*** : adj., ***mājhā***.
bug, ***khaṭmaḷ***, m., ***caṛ***, f.
bugle, ***bigal***, m. (***wajāṇā***, ***wajjṇā***).
build, ***baṇāṇā*** : raise walls, ***usārnā***, (int. ***usrnā***).
building, ***makān***, m. : large, ***hawēlī***, f. : ***amārat***, f. (U.).
bull, ***ḍhaggā***, ***baḷd*** : for breeding, ***sāhn*** : *see* calf, ox.
bullet, ***gōḷī***, f.
bullock, *see* bull, calf.
bundle, ***ganḍhṛī***, f. : of corn, etc., ***pūḷī***, f., ***thabbā***, m., ***bharī***, f., ***panḍ***, f.
bunch, of flowers, grapes, keys, ***gucchā***, m.
burden, *see* load, weight.
burdened, ***bhār hēṭh dabbeā hoeā***.
burn (as fuel), ***bāḷṇā***, int. ***baḷṇā*** : b. up, ***sāṛnā***, int. ***saṛnā*** : ***phūkṇā*** : *see* firewood.
burning, n., ***sāṛā***, m. (fire, also feeling mental or physical).
burrow, *see* hole.
burst, ***pāṭṇā*** (tr. ***pāṛnā***) : by crushing, squeezing, ***phissṇā*** (tr. ***phehṇā***).
bury, ***dabbṇā*** : ***dafn k.*** (U.).
bush ***jhāṛī***, f.
busy, be, ***rujjhṇā*** (pa. p. ***ruddhā***, ***rujjhā***) : being b., n., ***rujjh***, f : b., adj., ***ruddhā hoeā***, ***laggā hoeā***.
butcher, ***kasāī***, fem. ***kasaiṇ***.
but, conj. ***par*** : *see* only, except.
butt, v., ***mārnā***, ***siṅg mārnā***.
butter, ***makkhaṇ***, m. : *see* ghee.
butter-dish, ***makkhaṇdān***, m.
butterfly, ***titlī***, f. ***bāhmaṇ baccā***, m. A.
buttermilk, ***lassī***, f. A.
button, ***bīṛā***, m. : ***baṭaṇ***, m. (***mēḷṇā***, ***mārnā***, rarely ***band k.***). unbutton, ***bīṛā kholhṇā*** : put on b., ***bīṛā lāṇā*** : *see* stud : b.-hole, ***kāj***, m.
buy, ***mull laiṇā*** : ***kharidnā*** (U.) : *see* purchases.
buyer, ***gāhk***, ***laiṇwāḷā***.
buzz, of bees, mosquitoes, etc., ***ghankūr***, f., ***shukāṭ***, f.
by (agent), use agent case, G. 8, 74 : ***koḷõ***, G. 66, 90, 112 : by himself, *see* alone : of himself, *see* spontaneously : one by one, ***ikk ikk karke*** : ten by ten, ***das das karke***.
by and by, *see* afterwards.
byre, ***kuṛh***, f.

C

cabbage, ***gobhī***, f. : ***band gobhī*** : ***pattā gobhī***.
cactus, flat, ***chittar thōhr***, m. : round, ***thōhr ḍanḍā*** m.
cage, ***pinjrā***, m.
cake, ***kēk***, m. (K.) : of soap, ***gācī***, f.
calamity, ***baḷā***, f. : ***āfat***, f. : ***biptā***, f. : ***musībat***, f.: ***ākhar*** (***auṇī***).
calculate, ***lēkhā lāṇā*** : ***hisāb karnā*** : ***kiās karn-ī***, ***-ā*** : *see* guess, approximately, counf, estimate.
calf, ***wacchā***, m. : bigger, ***waihṛā***

: *see* buffalo : calf of leg, ***pinnī***, f. : ***pinnī dī machḷī***, f.
caligraphy, *khatt*, m. : ***khush-khattī***, f. : -ist, ***khush nawīs***.
call, *saddṇā*, *kuānā*, *bulāṇā* : ***wāz***, or ***awāz mārnī*** (***nū̃***) : *see* name, remember : c. out, *see* shout, scream, proclaim : pay a call, ***miḷṇ jāṇā*** : ***mulākāt wāste jāṇā*** : c. attendance, ***hāzrī laiṇī*** or ***lāṇī***.
calm, adj., of water ***khlōtā hoeā*** : of person, neg of excited, or use calmly : *see* still, quiet.
calm, v. tr., ***phēr rāzī k.***, ***ṭhaṇḍā, k.***, ***gussā ṭhaṇḍā*** or ***maṭṭhā karnā*** : *see* peace, quiet, appease.
calmly, *hausle nāl*, *saihe nāḷ*, *saihj nāḷ*, *amn nāḷ*.
calumniate, *see* slander.
camel, *ūṭh*, fem. ***uṭhṇī***, ***ḍācī***, ***sāhnṇī*** : young c., ***bōttā***, m.
camp, *kamp*, *tambū* m. : *see* tent.
camping ground, *paṛā*, m.
camphor, *kāfūr*, m.
can, *see* tin.
canal, *naihr*, f. : branch c., ***sūā***, m. : channel made by farmers, ***mohgā***, m., ***khāl***, m. : to make such, ***khāḷṇā*** c. bank, ***paṭrī***, f.
cancel, order ***hukm band ka*r*nā*** : name, ***nā̃ kaṭṭṇā***.
candidate, *umēdwār*, m. : in exam., ***imtihān deṇwāḷā***.
candle, *mōmbattī*, f.
candle-stick, *battīdān*, m.
candour, *safāī*, *sāfdilī*, *sāf sāf ākhṇā*.
cane, *baint*. m. (***mārnā***, ***nū̃***) : *see* sugar-cane : be caned, ***baint khāṇā***, ***paiṇā***.
canister, *see* tin.
cannibal, *ādamkhōr* (U.) : ***bandeā̃ dā gōsht khāṇwāḷā***.
cannon, *tōp*, f. (***calāṇī***, int. ***calṇī***).
canopy, *see* awning.
canter, (horse) ***poiā calṇā***.
cantonment, *chāoṇī*, f.
cap, *ṭōpī*, f.
capable, *laik* : *see* able.
capacious, *mōkḷā*.
capacity, *gunjaish*, f. ***samās***, f. : *see* ability.
capital, *pū̃jī*, *mūṛī*, f., ***sarmāyā***, m., ***rās***, m., ***rupayye***, m. pl. : chief town, ***dār ul khalāfa***, m. (U.).
captive, in war, ***asīr***, ***bandī*** : prisoner, ***kaidī*** : take c., ***phaṛnā***, ***kaid k***.
captivity, *kaid*, f. : ***asīrī***, f. (U.).
caravan, *kāflā*, m., ***kārawān***, m., ***ṭōllā*** m., ***ṭōllī***, f.
carcase, *murdār*, m. (collective term) : ***lōth***, f. : *see* corpse.
card, v., cotton, etc., ***piññā***, ***jhambhṇā***. A.
card, n., post c., ***kāṭ***, m. : ***khatt***, m.
cards, *tāsh*, m. (***khēḍṇā***)
cardamum, *lācī*, f.
care, *see* anxiety, look after, protect, like : take c., interj., ***backe***, ***khabardār***, ***sambhaḷke***. I don't care, ***menū̃ koī parwāh nehī***.
caretaker, *rakhwālā*, *rakhwāl*, *caukīdār*.
careless, *lāparwāh*, *bēparwāh* *see* thoughtless.

carelessness, ***lā-*** or ***bē-parwāhī,*** ***gaflat,*** f.

caress, ***pyār dēṇā***; *see* fondle, kiss.

carpenter, ***tarkhāṇ*** : fem. ***tarkhāṇī.***

carpet, ***darī,*** f. : rug, ***galīcā,*** m.

carriage, driving, ***bagghī,*** f. : ***ṭamṭam,*** f. : (tonga) ***ṭāṅgā,*** m. : phaeton, ***fiṭn,*** f. : (railway) ***gaḍḍī,*** f. (also train) : *see* class : ladies only, women only, ***zanānī gaḍḍī*** : servants, ***sarwaṇṭī,*** f. : act or price of carrying, *see* cartage.

carrion, ***murdār,*** m. (including animal dead, not killed).

carrot, ***gājar,*** f.

carry, ***cukkke*** or ***uṭhāke khaṛnā*** or ***laijāṇā*** : c. bricks, earth, ***dhōṇā*** : be carried, ***hūṇṭe*** or ***hūhṇṭe laiṇe*** (M. 122. 34 : tr. ***dēṇe***), *see* ride, swing, back : c. on work, ***kamm ṭōrnā*** or ***calāṇā*** (int. ***ṭurnā, calṇā***).

cart, for two bullocks, ***gaḍḍā,*** m. : for one bullock, handcart, wheel-barrow, ***reṛhī,*** f.

cartage, act or price, ***ḍhuāī,*** f.

cartridge, ***kārtūs,*** m.

carve, ***ghaṛnā, trāshnā.***

case, *see* cover : lawcase, ***mukadmā,*** m. : bring c. ag., ***kise te arzī pāṇī*** or ***dāhwā karnā*** or ***nālish karnī*** : in this c., ***es hālat*** or ***sūrat wicc*** : in no c., ***cāre banne*** w. neg., or ***kise sūrat wicc*** and neg. : *see* lose.

cash, ***nakad,*** m. : v., ***tōṛnā.*** A.

cask, ***pīpā,*** m.

cast, *see* throw, lots.

caste, ***zāt,*** f. : ***gōt,*** f. (division of c.) : low, ***niwī*** : high, ***uccī*** : put out of c., ***chēkṇā, hukkā pāṇī band k.*** (***dā***).

castor-oil plant, ***harnōḷā,*** m.

cat, ***billā,*** fem. ***billī.***

cataract (in eye) ***mōtiā,*** m. A.

catarrh, ***sardī,*** f.: ***zukām,*** m.

catastrophe, *see* calamity, accident.

catch, ***phaṛnā, phagaṛnā*** : ball, etc., ***jhōpṇā, jhaṛapṇā*** : *see* seize : allow oneself to be caught, ***phaṛā dēṇā, phaṛāī dēṇī*** : G. 74, 75. A.

catch, n., in door, window, ***huḍhkā,*** m., ***billī,*** f.

catechumen, ***mutlāshī,*** m.

caterpillar, ***suṇḍī,*** f. : ***bhaṅgū kuttā,*** m., ***bhaggū kuttā.***

cattle (horned), ***māl,*** m. : ***ḍaṅgar,*** m. : ***caukhar,*** m.

cauliflower, ***phull gobhī,*** f.

cause, n., ***wajhā,*** f. (reason) : ***sbabb,*** m. : *see* reason, purpose : causeless, *see* reason, useless.

cause, v., use causal vv. w. direct acc. or ***koḷō*** of agent : G. 41-3, 109, 110 : *see* force.

caution, ***hōsh,*** f., ***hushyārī,*** f. ***khabardārī,*** f.

cautiously, words for caution w. ***nāḷ*** : ***samjhke.***

cavalry, ***risālā,*** m.

cave, ***guphā, khundhar,*** f. : ***gār,*** f. (U.).

ceaselessly, *see* continuously.

cedar, ***diār,*** m. : ***biāṛ,*** m.

ceiling, ***chatt,*** m. : thin planks, ***pakkhar,*** m.

celebrated, *see* famous : be c., of fair, festival, ***laggṇā***, ***manneā jāṇā.***
cement, *see* mortar, glue.
cemetery, *see* graveyard.
centre, ***markaz***, m. (U.) : adj., ***wiclā***, ***wishkārlā*** : *see* middle.
ceremony, ***rīt***, f. : ***rasm***, f.
certain, ***pakkā***, ***yakīnī*** : a. c. man, ***fulāṇā.***
certainly, ***bêshakk***, ***nishaṅg***, ***zarūr***, ***lājarūr*** ; ***hōr kī***? ***te hōr***? ***hā̃ te.***
certainty, ***yakīn***, m.
certificate, ***sāṭifkaṭ***, m.; ***sanad***, f.
certify, ***zimewār*** or ***zimmewār h.***, ***guāhī dēṇī***, ***tsallī dēṇī.***
chafe, *see* rub, annoy, grief : be chafed (of skin, etc.) ***ucchṇā***, ***ambṇā.***
chaff, of rice, barley, etc., ***phakk***, f. : *see* bran : chopped straw from wheat, ***tūṛī***, f., ***ciṭṭā bhoh*** : from gram, etc., ***bhoh***, m., ***missā bhoh.*** A.
chain, ***saṅgal***, m. : smaller, ***saṅgḷī***, f. : very small, ***zanjīrī***, f. : e.g. watch-c. A.
chair, ***kursī***, ***khursī***, f. : low, all wood, ***caukī***, f. : of reeds, ***mūṛhā***, m. : easy c., ***arām kursī***, f. : *see* stool, seat.
chalk, ***cāk***, m., ***khaṛiā miṭṭī***, f.
chamber, *see* room : c. pot, ***pāṭ***, m.
champ (horse) ***cabakṇā.***
chance, ***sbabb***, m. : by c., ***sbabb nāl***, ***ẽwẽ***, ***aĩwẽ***, ***kār e kazā.***
change, ***tabdīlī***, f. : *see* difference : for rupee, etc., ***bhangbaṛ***, m., ***bhān***, m., but *see* rupee : whole unchanged rupee, ***baddhā rupayyā.***
change, v., ***badalnā*** : c. person, animal, regiment for other, ***badlī karnī*** (int. ***hōṇī***) : *see* exchange : c. several things, ***adal badal k.*** : c. notes. rupees, ***tōṛnā*** : get them changed ***tuṛāṇā*** (int. ***ṭuṭṭṇā***) : give back, ***partāṇā*** : c. opinions, ***phir jāṇā***, ***dalīl badalnī.***
changeable, ***kacce khyāl dā***, ***dudilā*** : *see* vacillate.
channel, ***nāḷā***, m. : small, ***nālī***, f. : *see* stream, drain, brook.
chap, (hands, feet) ***biāī pāṭṇī***
chapter, ***bāb***, ***m.***
character, no good word, use (***dī***). adj. describing person, or word for disposition, temperament : of good moral c., ***nēkcalan*** : of bad, ***badcalan*** : *see* good : life and actions. ***cāl calan***, m.
characteristic, ***sift***, f.
charcoal, ***koḷā***, m. : ***koḷe***, m. pl. : ***lakkaṛ de koḷe***, m. pl. : *see* coal : small broken bits. ***kērī.*** f.
charge, give into c., ***de hawāle k.*** : ***de pēṭe pāṇā*** : give over c., ***cāraj d.*** : take over c., ***cāraj laiṇā*** : c. price, ***lāṇā*** (int. ***laggṇā***) : M. 122. 27 : *see* cost.
charity, *see* alms.
charm, please, ***baṛā <u>kh</u>ush k.*** : bewitch, ***jādū k.*** or ***pāṇā*** (***utte***), ***mantar paṛhnā*** (***utte***) : *see* amuse, delight.
charmer, *see* magician, snake.

chase, *see* pursue, hunt.
chaste, ***pāk***.
chatter, foolishly, ***yabbhā̃ mārniā̃***, ***yabbhṇā***, ***bakṇā***, ***cilkṇā*** : of birds, ***cī̃ cī̃ karni*** : of teeth, ***dandoṛikke wajjṇe*** (***de***) : *see* talkative.
cheap, ***sastā***, ***suwallā***.
cheat, ***rupayye*** or ***paise mārne***, M. 123, 46 : *see* deceit, deceive.
check, *see* hinder, stop, compare, examine.
cheek, ***gallh***, f.
cheer, *see* amuse, comfort.
cheers, applause, ***cirs dēṇe*** : *see* clap.
cheerful, ***khush***.
cheese, ***panīr***, m.
cheque, ***cikk***, m. : *see* bill.
cherish, *see* support.
chess, ***shatranj***, m. (***khēḍṇā***).
chest, (body), ***hikk***, f. : ***chāti***, f. (U.) : of drawers, ***almārī***, f. : *see* drawer, box.
chew, grain, etc., ***cabbṇā*** : suck, ***cūpṇā***.
chick, *see* chikk.
chicken, ***cūccā***, m. : for table, *see* fowl.
chief, chieftain, ***sardār***, fem ***sardārnī***.
chikk, hanging screen, ***cikk***, f. : ***cikh*** ; f.
child, ***baccā***, m. ***jwāk***, ***bāl***, m. : ***añāṇā***, m. : ***bacṛā***, m. : European, ***bāwā***, fem. ***bāwī*** : plur., ***dhī puttar***, m. : ***dhiā̃ puttar***, m. pl. : ***muṇḍe kuṛiā̃***, m. pl. : *see* descendants.
childish ***mū̃dpuṇā̃***, ***añāṇeā̃wāṇg***.
childishness, *see* boyishness.
childless, ***dhī puttar nehī̃*** : ***autrā*** or ***autrā nikhattrā*** is mild abuse or self pity.
chimney, of lamp, ***cimṇī***, f. : for fire, ***dhū̃kash***, m. : for sugarcane furnace, ***lūhmbā***, m. : *see* funnel.
chimneypiece, ***paṛchatti***, f.
chin, ***ṭhōḍḍī***, f.
china (ware), ***cīnī***, f. (***de bhāṇḍe*** or ***bartaṇ***).
chip, of wood, ***sakk***, m. ***sakṛā***, m.
chocolate, ***caklēṭ***, f. : *see* cocoa.
choice, use ***marzī***, f. (will) : *see* select.
choke (food going wrong way), ***athrū auṇā*** (***nū̃***) : from disease, ***galghōṭū hōṇā*** : v. tr., *see* smother, strangle, hang : by pressure, ***saṅgh ghuṭṭṇā***.
cholera, ***haizā***, m. (gen. merely severe vomiting).
choose, *see* select.
chop, n., (meat) ***cā̃p***. f. (K.).
chop, v. tr., wood, ***lakkar dalṇī*** : cut long piece into thick bits, ***mōche pāṇe*** : into long thin bits, ***phāṅgā̃ karniā̃***.
chopper, farmer's, ***tōkkā***, m. : kitchen, ***cāpaṛ*** m. (K.).
Christ, ***Masīh***.
Christian, ***Isāī***, ***As-hāī***, fem. ***Isaiṇ***, ***As-haiṇ***.
Christmas Day, ***waḍḍā din***.
chudder, *see* veil.
church; building, ***girjā***, m. : congregation, ***jamāt***, f. : many congregations, ***kalīsyā***, f.
chutney, ***caṭṇī***, f.

cinnamon, ***dāḷcīnī***, f.
circle, ***ghērā***, ***m. dāirā***, m. (educ.)
circuit, ***cakkar***, m. : *see* tour, round.
circuitous, use ***waḷā paiṇā*** : *see* round.
circular, ***gōl*** : *see* roundness.
circumcise, ***suntī bahāṇā*** (***nū̃***) : be c., ***suntī baihṇā***.
circulate, (money), ***calṇā*** (tr. ***calāṇā***) : *see* pass : (story) ***dhummṇā*** (tr. ***dhumāṇā***).
circumstance, ***gall***, f. : ***wākiā***, m. : ***hāl***, m. : ***hāl hakīkat***, f. : in no c. : *see* case.
cistern, ***hauz***, m. : ***hauzī***, f. : (also place for bath in bathroom).
citizen, ***shaihrīā***, ***shaihrī***, ***shaihrdār*** (all city-dweller) : *see* subject.
citron, ***khaṭṭā***, m.
city, ***shaihr***, m.
civil, not military, ***mulkhī*** : not criminal, ***duānī*** : *see* polite.
civilised ***muhazzab*** (U.).
claim, ***dāhwā***, m. (*k.*)
claimant, ***mudaī***, m. (leg.).
clandestine, *see* secret.
clap hands, ***māhngā mārnā*** (approval, applause) : ***tāṛī mārnī*** (derision).
class, in school, ***jamāt***, f. : of people, railway, ***darjā***, m. : first c., ***paihlā darjā***, ***fast klās*** (*see* excellent); second c., ***dujjā darjā***, ***sikanḍ klās***, ***sĕkanḍ klās***, m. : intermediate, ***ḍeoḍhā darjā***, ***iṇṭar***, m. : third c., ***trijjā*** or ***tīsrā darjā***, ***ṭhaḍḍ klās***, m.
claw, ***naũh***, m. : whole foot, ***panjā***, m.
clay, ***miṭṭī***, f. : *see* mud.
clean, ***sāf***, ***suthrā*** : ceremonially, *see* holy : *see* scrub, wash, pure.
cleanliness, ***safāī***, f. : *see* purity.
clear (water, sentence, meaning ***sāf*** : (water) ***nitreā hoeā*** : v., water, meaning, etc., ***natārnā*** (int. ***nitrnā***) : *see* evident, acquit : c. up (weather), *see* weather; (difficulty, *see* solve : c. away table), *see* table.
clerk, ***munshī***, ***bābū***, ***klārak***.
clever, *see* able, intelligent : ***hushyār***, ***kārīgar***, ***ustād***, ***siāṇā*** : (bad sense) ***calāk***, ***hikmatī***, ***catur***.
cleverness, ***hushyārī***, f. : ***hikmat***, f. : ***kārīgarī***, f. : ***ustādī***, f. : bad sense, ***calākī***, f., ***catrāī***, f. : *see* intelligence, ability.
climate, ***hawā***, f. : ***āb hawā***, f. ***mausam***, m.
climb, ***caṛhnā*** (***utte***) : climbing plant, ***wēl***, f. : ***wall***, f
cling to, ***cambaṛnā*** (***nū̃***).
clip (w. scissors) ***katrnā*** *see* prune.
clique, ***dharā***, m. : *see* party.
cloak, ***cogā***, m. : *see* coat : v., ***paṛdā pānā*** (***utte***) : *see* screen.
clock, ***ghaṛī***, f. : *see* o'clock.
clockmaker; ***ghaṛīsāz***, m.
clod, ***dhehm***, f., ***dhīhm***, f.
clogged, dirty, ***jaḍḍā***.
close, v. tr., door, window : ***phērnā***, ***ḍhoṇā***, ***bhīṛnā*** : *see* shut : w. closed doors, ***wajjī̃ būhī̃***, G. 78 : *see* shut.
close, adj., *see* near.
cloth, ***kapṛā***, m. : *see* sheet,

skirt, shawl, etc. : c.-merchant, ***bajāj*** : trade of selling c., ***bajājī***, f.

clothe, oneself, ***kapṛe pāṇe*** : another, ***kapṛe pāṇe*** (***nū̃***) : make him put on clothes, ***kapṛe puāṇe*** : in gen. clothe, ***kapṛe dēṇe***.

clothes, ***kapṛe***, m. pl.

cloud, ***baddaḷ***, m. : clouds all over, ***jhaṛ***, m., ***baddaḷ ghuḷeā hoeā e*** : c-less, *see* weather.

clove, ***lauṅg***, f.

clown, *see* jester.

club (building) ***kalafghar***, m. : wooden, *see* stick.

clue, ***patā***, m. : *see* discover.

clumsy, *see* awkward.

cluster, *see* bunch.

coach-house, ***bagghī-k͟hāṇā*** m.

coagulate, ***jammṇā*** (tr. ***jamāṇā***).

coal, ***patthar dā kōḷā*** : *see* charcoal : live coal, ***bhak͟heā hoeā koḷā***, m. : small broken bits, ***kērī***, f.

coarse, not fine, ***mōṭā***.

coast, ***samundar dā kaṇḍhā*** or ***dandā***, m.

coat, ***kōṭ***, m. : servant's double breasted, ***aṅgā***, m. : *see* over-coat, waterproof.

coax, ***k͟hush karke manāṇā*** : ***parcāṇā***.

cob of maize, ***challī***, f. : without grain, ***tukkā***, m.

cobbler, ***mōcī***, fem. ***mōcaṇ***.

cobweb, ***jāḷā***, m. : single thread, ***tār***, f., ***cinā̱kh***, m.

cock (bird) ***kukkaṛ***, m. : of gun, ***ghōṛā***, m.

cocoa, ***kōkō***, f. : *see* chocolate.

cocoanut, whole, ***nanyēr***, m. : half of kernel, ***ṭhūṭhī***, f. : ***khōppā***, m. : kernel in gen., ***garī***, f. (cf. ***girī***, f., kernel of other fruit, pith).

coffee, ***kāfī***, f. : -pot, ***kāfīdān***, m.

coffin, ***sandūk***, m. : *see* shroud.

coin, no word, use rupee, pice. etc., good, ***kharā*** : bad, ***khōṭā***.

coincide, ***raḷnā***, ***miḷnā***.

cold, n., ***pāḷā***, m. : ***sardī***, f. : ***sīt***, f. : ***ṭhaṇḍ***, f. : feel cold, ***pāḷā***, etc., w. ***laggṇā***, G. 108 : hands, feet feel c., ***hatth***, ***pair ṭharne*** : air get c., ***pāḷā uttō̃ paiṇā*** : catch c., ***sardī laggṇī***, ***zukām hōṇā*** or ***laggṇā***.

colic (***ḍhiḍḍh wicc***) ***waṭṭ***, m.

collar, ***kālar***, m.

collect, ***kaṭṭhā k.***, ***jamā k.*** : money, ***ugrāhṇā*** (int. ***uggharnā***).

college, ***kālij***, m.

coll-ide, -ision, ***ṭakkar khāṇī***, ***mērī ṭakkar wajjī*** (***nāḷ***); tr. ***mērī ṭakkar mārī*** (***nāḷ***) : *see* knock.

colloquial, ***ām bōl cāl dī***.

colonel, ***karnail***.

colonise, *see* people (2).

colony (canal), simply ***naihr***, f. : in the c., ***naihr te***.

colour, ***raṅg***, m. : dark, *see* dark in A. : *see* light, fast, bright : faint, ***maddham***.

coloured, ***raṅgdār***, ***raṅgwāḷā*** : many-c., ***raṅg baraṅgī***.

colt, ***wachērā***, m.

comb, ***kaṅghī***, f. : of cock, ***kalgī***, f., ***pagg***, f.

come, ***auṇā*** (pa. p. ***āeā***) : c. in,

see enter : c. out, ***nikḷ auṇā*** ; of sun fr. clouds, ***dhupp nikḷṇī*** ; of stain, *see* delete.

comet, ***bōdī āḷā tārā***, m.

comfort, ***tsall-ī*** or ***-ā dēṇī nū̃*** : be c.-ed., ***tsallī hōṇī*** (***nū̃***) : *see* ease, condole, soothe.

Comforter (Holy Spirit), ***Tsallī Dēṇwāḷā.***

command, ***hukm*** m. (d.) : unwarrantably, ***hukm cāṛhnā.***

commander-in-chief, ***jaṅgī lāṭ***., ***jarnail.***

commemoration, ***yādgārī***, f.

commence-, -ment, *see* beginning.

commend, *see* recommend, praise.

commentary, ***tafsīr***, f.

commerce, *see* trade, intercourse.

commercial, ***tajārtī*** : c. usage, ***sudāgrī*** or ***bazār dā dastūr.***

commission (discount, percentage) ***dastūrī***, f. : (written authority), ***sanad***, f.; *see* order : seller on c., ***āhṛtī***, ***āhṛtaḷī*** : his c. is ***āhṛtaḷ***, f. : (a committee) ***kamēṭī***, f.

committee (of all kinds, relig. and secular) ***kamēṭī***, f. : c-meeting, ***kamēṭī***, f.

common, ***ām***, ***mamūlī*** : *see* much : shared by others, ***sānjhā*** : c. village land, ***shāmlāṭ***, f. : c. people, ***ām lōk***, ***kamīne lōk*** (low), *see* everyone, people.

commonly, ***ām taur tē***, ***aksar.***

commotion, *see* disturbance.

communication, *see* intercourse, information.

communion, *see* intercourse : Holy C., ***Ashā Rabānī***, f. : celebrate H.C., ***karnī***, take, ***laiṇī.***

companion, ***sāthī***, ***jōṛīdār***, ***mēre nāḷ dā*** : bet. men, ***yār*** : bet. women, ***sahēlī***, f. : *see* partner, equal.

company, of people, ***kaṭṭh***, m. : ***ṭōllā***, m., ***ṭōllī***, f. ***: jatthā***, m. : ***taraṇḍī***, f. : ***taraṇḍā***, m. : *see* assembly, congregation : business c., ***kaumpaṇī***, f. : good or bad c., ***baihṇī***, f. : M. 127. 3 : G. 121.

compare, ***raḷāṇā***, ***miḷāṇā***, ***mukāblā karnā*** : c. weights, size, etc., ***hāṛnā*** : comparison of size, cost, etc., *see* time, G. 23 : compared w., ***ohde mukāble wicc.***

compass, ***kutabnumā***, m.

compassion, *see* pity.

compassionate, ***raihm-dil***, ***tars karnwāḷā*** : God, ***rahīm.***

compatriot, *see* fellow-countryman.

compel, *see* force, cause.

compensation, ***harjānnā***, m. : ***iwzānnā***, m. : in c. for, ***ohde***, ***badle*** : *see* loss, damage in A.

compet-e, -ition, *see* emulate.

competent, ***laik***, ***samajhdār***, ***k͟habardār*** : *see* able, clever.

complain-, -t, ***shaikait***, f. (***k.***, ***dī***) : ***faryād***, f. (***k.***, ***dī***) : leg. ***nālish***, f. (***k.***, ***utte***).

complainant, *see* plaintiff.

complete, ***pūrā***, ***mukammal*** : *see* finish.

complex : *see* intricate.
complexion, ***rang***, m.
complication, *see* intricate, entangle.
compliment, *see* praise : present my compliments, ***mēre wallō̃ salām ākhṇā*** or ***hatth bannhṇā***.
comply, *see* agree, assent.
composed of, ***dā baṇeā hoeā***.
compromise, leg., ***rāzīnāmā***, m.
compulsion, *see* force.
compulsory, subject in exam., ***lāzmī***.
comput-ation, -e, *see* calculate, count
comrade, *see* companion, friend.
conceal, *see* hide.
conceit, ***baṛī mizāj***, f. : ***baṛā damāg***, m. : *see* pride, sense.
concentrate, *see* attend.
concerning, ***dī bābat***, ***de bāre wicc***.
concession, ***riait***, f. : adj. ***riaitī***.
conciliate, ***razī k.***, ***manāṇā***.
concise, *see* brief.
conclude, draw conclusion, ***natījā kaḍḍhṇā*** *see* settle, finish.
concussion, ***ṭakkar***, f. : *see* collide.
condemn, ***mujrim k.***, ***baṇāṇā*** : be c., ***mujrim h.***, ***jurm sābit hōṇā*** : *see* guilt.
condemnation, ***sazā dā hukm***, m.
condition, ***hāl***, m. : ***hālat***, f. : ***hāl hakīkat***, f. : ***hawāl*** m. (often story) : make c., ***eh shart e*** : on c. that, ***es shart te paī***.
conditional, ***shartī***, ***bā-shart***.
condole, (go to), ***mukāṇī jāṇā*** : *see* comfort, mourn-, -ers, -ing, sympathise.
conduct, *see* character, lead.
confectioner, ***halwāī***, fem. ***halwaiṇ*** : ***miṭhāī-wāḷā***.
confederate, *see* partner.
conference (meeting) ***kamēṭī***, f. : (consultation) ***salāh mashwarā***, m.
confess, ***mannṇā*** : c. under torture, ***bakṇā*** (tr. ***bakāṇā***) : force to c., without torture, ***dhakke naḷ*** or ***zōre manāṇā***.
confidant, ***bhētī***, m., fem. ***bhētaṇ***.
confide, ***wasāh karnā*** (***dā***) : ***wasāh hōṇā*** (***menū̃ ohdā***) : *see* trust.
confidence, ***wasāh***, m. : lack of c., ***bēwasāhī***, f.
confidently (speak), ***dāhwe nāḷ***.
confirm, ***pakkā k.*** : *see* ratify.
confiscate, ***ghar kurk*** (***k., h.***), house confiscated : ***ghar dī kurkī*** (***k., h.***), furniture, etc., c-ed.
conflicting, ***āpe wicc nehī̃ raḷde***.
confront, ***mū̃h te ākhṇā*** : *see* face.
confuse, things, ***rauḷā mārnā*** : ***gaṛbaṛī pāṇī*** : persons, ***ghabrāṇā***, ***ghobrā chaḍḍṇā*** (int. ***ghābbarnā***, ***ṭhiṭham-barnā***) : *see* perplex.
confusion, ***gaṛbaṛī*** f. : mistake, ***ṭapḷā***, m. : *see* disorder.
confute, ***jhūṭhā sābit k.***
congeal, int. ***jammṇā*** : tr. ***jamāṇā***.

congratulate, ***mubārakbādī dēṇī*** : *see* bravo.

congregation, ***jamāt,*** f. (either audience or settled c.).

conjecture, *see* guess, calculate, estimate, approximately.

conjectural, ***kiāsī.***

conjure, adjure, ***saũh duāṇī*** (***nū̃***).

conjurer, ***madārī,*** fem. ***madāran.***

connection, ***tallak,*** m. : ***wāstā,*** m. (both ***menū̃ ohde nāḷ***) : *see* relative relationship.

conquer, ***jittṇā, fatā-karnā*** (***fatā*** used alone is fem.) : *see* possess, defeat.

conscience, ***dil,*** m.

conscious, ***hōsh wicc*** : *see* aware, remember.

consciousness, ***hōsh,*** f. (also sense).

consecrate, ***K͟hudā de hawāle k., mak͟hsūs k.*** (U.) ***bilkull K͟hudā dā samjhṇā*** : give in charity, ***K͟hudā de nā̃ dēṇā.***

consecutive, ***suāhrā,*** or use ***nā chaḍḍṇā.***

consent, v., *see* agree, assent.

consent, n., ***razāmandī,*** f. : ***manzūrī,*** f. : ***marzī,*** f. : ***razā*** f. : w.c. of all, ***sāreā̃ dī razā*** or ***marzī nāḷ.***

consequence, ***natījā,*** m. : of no c., ***koī gall nehī̃,*** *see* matter : *see* useless, worthless.

consider, ***sōcṇā, gaur karnā.***

consideration, ***sōc,*** f. : ***gaur,*** m. : ***dhiān,*** m. : out of c. for ***ohdā lihāz karke*** : *see* concession, esteem, partiality, deference.

considering, conj., *see* since.

consist, *see* composed.

console, *see* comfort, condole.

conspicuous, ***jehṛā sāf disse,*** etc. : *see* visible.

conspire, ***de k͟halāḷ gall pakāṇī*** (int. ***pakkṇī***).

constant, *see* faithful, resolute, continuous, repeatedly.

consternation, ***harānī,*** f. : *see* astonish-, -ishment.

constipation, ***kabzī,*** f. : the pain and straining, ***marōṛā,*** m.

consult, ***salāh karnī*** (***nāḷ***) : ***mashwarā karnā*** (***nāḷ***) : ***rā pucchṇī*** (***dī***).

consum-e, -ption, ***k͟harc karnā*** (int. ***h.***) : *see* waste, phthisis.

contagious, disease, ***lagganwāḷī bimārī,*** f.

contain, be contained, ***auṇā*** (come) : *see* room.

contaminate, *see* defile, unclean.

contemplate, *see* think, consider.

contemplation (relig.) ***dhiān,*** m.

contempt, ***hikārat,*** f. : *see* despise, scorn.

contemptible, ***kamīnā, burā.***

contend, *see* argue, fight.

content, ***rāzī, k͟hush.***

contentious, *see* argumentative, quarrelsome.

contents, ***jehṛā wicc e*** : (of letter, book) ***mazmūn,*** m.

continual-, -ly, *see* always, repeatedly, daily.

continue, ***raihṇā*** : c. throwing, ***saṭṭdā rehā, saṭṭī geā*** : G. 68.

continuously, ***lagātār, barābar*** : *see* continual.

contract, ***ṭhēkā***, m. (***d., laiṇā***) : *see* settle.
contract, v., *see* shrink.
contractor, ***ṭhēkedār-***, fem. ***-nī***.
contradict, ***jhūṭheā̃ k.*** : ***gall mōṛnī***.
contrary, ***de khalāf, de barkhalāf, de ulṭ*** : *see* opposite : on the c., ***sagõ sagõ***.
contrast, ***fark***, m. : *see* compare.
contribution, ***madad, madat***, f. : ***rupayye***, m. pl. : ***candā***, m.
contriv-e, -ance, *see* arrange : c.w. difficulty : ***taradad***, or ***taraddad***, m. (***k.***), ***taragas***, m. (***k.***).
control, ***kābū***, m. : ***ikhtiār***, m. : ***wass***, m. : ***hatth***, m (all w. ***wicc rakkhṇā*** or ***h.***) : self-c., ***hauslā*** : *see* patience.
controversy; *see* argu-e, -mentative, quarrel-, -some.
convalescent, ***kujjh wall, wall hōṇ lagā e***.
convene, ***karāṇā, jamā k.*** (both w. word for meeting as object).
convenien-ce, -t, -tly, *see* ease, inconvenience : use ***je taklīf nā hōwe, lokā̃ wāste eh weḷā ṭhīk e***, etc., *see* inconvenience.
conversational, ***bōl cāl dā***.
convers-e, -ation, ***gall katth***, f. : ***gallā̃ katthā̃***, f. pl. (***k.***) : ***carcā*** f m. (***k.***) : ***bāt cīt***, f. (***k.***) : ***gallā̃***, f. pl. (***k.***).
conversion (rel.) ***dil dā badalnā, nawẽ sireõ jammṇā, dil dī tabdīlī***.
convert, v. (make) ***baṇāṇā*** : to Christianity, etc., ***Isāī k.*** (often used of baptism) : be converted, *see* conversion.
convert, n., ***Isāī, Musalmān, Āryā***, etc., ***ho geā***.
convey, *see* carry.
conveyance, *see* carriage, cart.
convict, ***kusūr***, m. : ***galtī***, f. (etc. all w. ***sābit k.***) : *see* condemn, convince.
convict, n., ***kaid-ī***, fem. ***-an***.
convince, ***kail k., manāṇā, yakīn karāṇā***.
cook, n., ***khānsāmā̃, bāorcī, lāṅgrī***.
cook, v., ***pakāṇā*** (int. ***pakkṇā***) : roast, ***bhunnṇā*** (int. ***bhujjṇā***) : bread, ***pakāṇā***). ***lāṇā***, M. 121, 10 (int. ***laggṇā***.) A. : c. in pot, ***rinnhṇā*** (pa. p. ***riddhā***, int. ***rijjhṇā***) : put on pot, put on to c., ***cāṛhnā*** (int. ***caṛhnā***) : M. 118, 23, 26. : ready cooked, ***pakkā pakāeā***.
cool, *see* cold : nice and cool (wind, water, etc.) ***ṭhaṇḍā ṭhaṇḍā***.
coolie, ***kulī, mazdūr***.
co-operate, ***nāḷ raḷke kamm k.***
copper, ***tāmbā, trāmmā***, m.
coppersmith, ***ṭhaṭhiār***.
copse, few trees, ***jhaṅghī***, f.
copy, n., ***nakl***, f. : sample, ***namūnā***, m. : (book), ***kāpī***, f. v., ***nakl k.*** : boy at school ***nakl mārnī*** : *see* imitate.
copyist, ***kātib, naklnawīs***.
cord, of leather, ***waddhrī***, f. : *see* string, rope.
cordial-, -ity, use love, friendship.

coriander, ***dhaniā***, m.
cork, ***daṭṭ***, m. (any stopper, plug) : ***kāg***, f. : of maize-cob, ***tukkā***, m.
corkscrew, ***pēckass***, m.
corn, on toe, etc., ***caṇḍī***, f. : on sole, ***bhaurī***, f.
corn, *see* grain, maize, oats, wheat.
corner, of room, box (outside or in), ***nukkar***, f. : ***guṭṭh***, f. : four -ed, ***caunukrā***, ***cauguṭṭhā*** : c-dish, ***ḍōṅghā***, m.
coronation, ***tājpōshī***, f. : of ***raja***, ***gaddī te bahāṇā*** (int. ***baihṇā***).
corpse, ***lōth*** f. : ***murdā*** (dead person) : *see* carcase.
corpulent, ***mōṭā*** jocular, ***dhiḍḍhū***, ***ḍhiḍḍhal***.
correct, ***ṭhīk*** (***k.***) : ***durust*** (***k.***) : c. character, ***sudhārnā*** : *see* rebuke, reprimand, improve.
correspond, ***ralṇā***, ***milṇā*** : (write letters) ***ikk dujje nū̃ ciṭṭhiā̃ likh̲ṇiā̃ : kh̲att kitābat karnī*** (U.).
corrupt, v. tr., ***wigāṛnā***, ***kh̲arāb k.*** (int. ***wigaṛnā***, ***kh̲arāb h.***) : adj., ***wigṛeā hoeā*** : *see* bad, bribe.
cost, n., ***mull***, m. : ***kīmat***, f. : costs (leg.) ***kh̲arcā***, m., ***kh̲arc***, m. : v., how much c.? ***kinnā mull e***, ***kinnā laggā***, ***kinne tõ āeā*** : *see* spend, expense.
costly, ***bare mull dā***, ***kīmatī*** : ***maihṅgā*** (dear).
cottage, ***nikkī kōṭhī***, f : *see* hut.
cotton, growing, ***kapāh***, f., ***phuṭṭī***, f : wool, ***rū̃***, m. : c.-seeding machine, ***welṇī***, f. : c.-seed, ***waṇẽwā***, m.
couch, *see* sofa.
cough, n., ***khaṅgh***, f. : v., ***khanghṇā***, ***khaṅgh auṇī*** (***nū̃***) : severe c. and sneezing, ***dhraññā***, ***dhrā̃sṇā***.
council, ***kamēṭī***, f. : ***kaunsal***, f.
count, ***giṇṇā***, ***gintrī karnī*** : *see* calculate.
countenance, *see* face.
counteract, *see* hinder.
counterfeit, ***baṇāwaṭī***, ***naklī*** : forged, ***jāhlī*** : (coin) ***khōṭā***.
countermand, *see* cancel.
countless, *see* innumerable.
country, ***mulkh̲***, ***muḷkh̲***, m. : ***dēs***, m. : native c., ***waṭan***, m. : in c. (not town) ***piṇḍā̃ wicc*** : adj., not foreign, ***dēsī***.
countryman (fellow), ***mērā watnī***, ***mēre dēs*** or ***mulkh̲ dā***.
couple, ***jōṛā***, m. : ***jōṛī***, f.
courage, ***bahādrī***, f. : ***dalērī***, f., *see* boldness : patient c., ***himmat***, f., ***hauslā***, m.
courageous, *see* brave : patiently c., ***himmatwāḷā***, ***hausle wāḷā***.
course, *see* method, arrangement, way, path : of c., ***hōr kī***, ***bêshakk***, ***nishaṅg***, ***hā̃ te***, G. 94 : of c. (concessive), ***hā̃***.
court, of law, ***kacaihrī***, f. : official, royal, raja's darbar, ***darbār*** m. : person w. right to sit in darbar, ***darbārī*** : court dress, ***darbārī kapṛe***.
courteous, no real word, use ***sharīf***, or kind, good : *see* polite.

courtesy, *see* favour, kindness.
courtier, *see* court.
courtyard, ***waḷgan***, m. : ***walgaṇ***, m. : ***wehṛā*** m.
cousin, use brother : on father's side, ***cācce bābbeõ bhrā*** : mother's, ***māmmeõ bhrā***, etc.
covenant, ***kaul karār***, m. : ***aihd***, m. : ***shṭāmp***, m. : ***rajisṭrī***, f. : *see* agreement, bond.
cover, v. ***kajjṇā***, ***ḍhakkṇā*** : *see* hide, screen.
cover, n. (also lid) ***ḍhakkaṇ***, m. : ***ḍhakkṇā*** m. : for earthen pots, ***capṇī***, f., ***chūṇī***, f., ***chūṇā***, m. : of dried earth, ***cāppaṛ***, m. : for umbrella, hat, pillow, ***uchār***, m.
coverlet, *see* quilt.
covet-, -ousness, ***lālac***, m. (***k.***) : ***tamā***, m. (***k.***) : *see* desire, greed.
covetous, ***lālcī***.
cow, ***gā̃*** : adj., ***gōkā*** : -dung, ***gohā***, m.
coward, ***ḍarākaḷ***, ***ḍarū***, ***ḍarnwāḷā***.
cowherd, ***chēṛū***, ***wāggī***.
cowhouse, ***kuṛh***, f.
coxcomb, *see* fop.
crack, n., ***trēṛ***, f. : v., ***trēṛ paiṇī*** (***nū̃***) : of glass, ***tiṛakṇā*** : china, ***līk paiṇī*** : wood, ***kaṛkṇā*** : (split, ***pāṭṇā***, tr. ***pāṛnā***).
cradle, ***paṅghūṛā***, m.
craft, *see* cleverness, deceit, profession
cram, ***tunnṇā***.
cramp, get, ***bakhōṛ paiṇā*** : ***nāṛ caṛhnī***.
cramped (no room), ***saurā***, ***taṅg***, ***bhīṛā***.
crash, ***ḍiggaṇ***, etc. ***dā khṛāk***.
crawl : creeping things, use ***ḍhiḍḍh parne ṭurnā*** : child, ***riṛhnā*** : go very slowly, ***jū̃ dī ṭōr calṇā*** : *see* creep.
crazy, *see* mad.
creak, ***cī̃ cī̃ karnī***, ***cikṇā*** : *see* squeak.
cream, ***maḷāī***, f.
crease, ***bhann***, f. (***paiṇī***) : *see* fold.
create, ***paidā k***.
creation, ***k͟halkat*** f. : ***mak͟hlūk***.
Creator, ***Paidā karnwāḷā***, ***K͟hālik*** : *see* God.
credible, ***mannaṇwāḷī gall***.
credit, *see* belief, trust : on c., ***udhār***, *see* borrow, debt.
creditor, ***laiṇdār***, or use ***laiṇā***.
credits, ***laihṇā***, m.
credulous, ***shtābī mannaṇwāḷā***, ***siddhā*** (simple).
creed, ***akidā***, m. : ***imān***, m. : brief M. sentences, ***kalmā***, m.
creep, *see* crawl : -ing plant, ***wēl***, f., ***wall***, f. : -ing things : *see* insect, ant.
crest, on bird, ***kalgī***, f. : *see* comb.
cricket, insect, ***biṇḍā***, m. : game, ***kirkaṭ***, m.
crime, ***jurm***, m. : *see* sin.
criminal, *see* guilty, prisoner : adj. (leg.), ***faujdārī***, *see* civil.
crimson, ***kirmzī***, ***kirmcī*** : *see* red.
cripple, ***lūhlā***. : lame, ***laṅgā*** : *see* hand.
crisp, ***kṛākēdār***.
crisis, ***nāzak wakat***, m.

critical, *see* critical, crisis, delicate.
criticise, ***nuks kaḍḍhnā, nuktācinī karnī, ghutkḷā̃ chēṛniā̃*** or ***kaḍḍhṇiā̃.***
crocodile, *see* alligator.
crook, shepherd's, ***ḍhāṅgā***, m. : ***kalpā***, m.
crooked, ***ḍiṅgā, ḍiṅg phaṛiṅgā*** : bent at end, ***muṛeā hoeā*** : c. matter, ***puṭṭhī*** or ***kuāsī*** or ***kasūṭī gall*** : *see* intricate.
crookedness, ***ḍiṅg***, m. : ***ḍiṅg phaṛiṅg***, m.
crop, n., ***fasl***, m. : spring c. (***rabī'***), ***hāṛhī***, f. : autumn c. (***kharīf***), ***sauṇī***, f. : *see* produce.
crop-eared, ***buccā.***
cross, ***salīb***, f. : ***sūḷī***, f. (lit stake) : c. temper, ***kauṛī tabīat***, f.
cross-examination, ***jarhā***, f. (***k.***)
cross-legged, ***caukṛī mārke baihṇā*** : *see* squat.
crossroads (four), ***curastā***, m., ***curāhā***, m.; ***caũk***, m. (in town).
crosswise, ***cauṛē dā*** : M. 128. 8 : G. 122 : *see* direction.
crow, v., ***bāṅg dēṇī*** (of cock).
crow-bar, ***bārī***, f.
crowd, ***kaṭṭh***, m. : ***baṛā mulkh***, m. : ***baṛā ādam, baṛī khalkat*** : ***jhurmaṭ*** (***pāṇā***) : *see* company.
crown, ***tāj***, m.
crucify, ***sūḷī*** or ***salīb utte cāṛhnā.***
crude, of word, ***dagg.***
cruel, ***bêraihm, zālim, sakht, betars.***
cruel-ly, -ty, ***bĕraihmī nāl*** f. : ***betarsī***, f. : ***sakhtī***, f. : all w. ***k.***, and ***nāḷ*** : *see* oppression.
crumble, (e.g. food, bricks, earthen pots), become powder, ***bhurnā*** : tr. ***bhōrnā.***
crumb, ***bhōrā***, m. : ***krām***, collective term (K.).
crunch, *see* gnaw.
crush, ***citthṇā, ghōṭṇā, dabāṇā, mandhāṛnā*** : *see* squeeze, trample, pound, beetle.
crust, ***krās*** (K.).
cry, *see* call, weep, shout, scream.
crystal, ***bilaur***, m.
cubit, ***hatth***, m.
cucumber, ***tar***, f., ***khīrā***, m.
cud, chew, ***ugāḷī karnī.***
cudgel, *see* stick.
cuff, ***kaff***, f. : *see* blow (1).
culprit, *see* guilty.
cultivate, ***wāhī karnī, khētī karnī*** : ***wāhṇā*** (int. ***waggṇā***) : *see* plough.
cultivation, ***wāhī***, f. : ***khētī***, f. : leg, ***kāshtkārī***, f.
cultivator, ***wāhk***, leg. ***kāshtkār*** : *see* farmer.
cunning, *see* clever, deceitful.
cup, ***pyālā***, m. : *see* drinking vessel.
cupboard, ***almārī***, f.
cupola, ***gumbaz.*** m.
curb, *see* bit, bridle, restrain.
curdle, ***jammṇā*** (tr. ***jamāṇā***) : *see* rennet.
curds ***dahī̃***, m. : *see* rennet.
cure, ***wall k.*** : ***caṅgeā̃ k.*** : *see*
curious, *see* strange.
curly, ***challeā̃wāle wāḷ*** : *see* hair. treat.

curry, food, ***kārī*** : c. and rice, ***kārī caul***, m. pl.
curry, curry-comb (horse), ***kharkṇā phērnā***.
curse, ***bad duā dēṇī*** (***nū̃***) : of God, ***lānat karnī*** (***nū̃***).
cursed, ***lāntī***.
cursory reading, etc., ***sarsarī nazr mārnī*** (***te***).
curtain, ***paṛdā***, m. : *see* screen, mosquito, cikk.
curved, ***gōḷ*** (round), *see* crooked.
custodian, *see* guardian, watchman.
custom, gen., ***dastūr***, m., ***riwāj***, m. : esp. rel., ***rīt***, f. ***rasm***, f. : *see* habit, rule.
customer, ***gāhk***, m. : ***laiṇwāḷā***, m.
customs, ***maihsūl***, m. : ***caṇgī***, f. (octroi); *see* tax.
cut, gen., ***waḍḍhṇā*** : clip w. scissors, ***katrnā*** : hair, ***katrnā*** (get cut, ***katrāṇā***) : pay, ***kaṭṭṇā*** : grass, ***mārnā*** (int. ***marnā***), ***khōtarnā*** : teeth, ***dandiā̃ nikḷṇiā̃*** (tr. ***kaḍḍhṇiā̃***) : c. up fodder, ***kutrnā*** : c. up wood, *see* chop : *see* prune. A.
cutting (of flowers, trees for sowing), ***kalam***, f. : of pay, *see* deduction.
cymbal, ***channā***, m.

D

dagger, ***k͟hanjar***, m. : ***churā***, m.
dacoit, ***ḍākū***, m.
dacoity, ***ḍākā***, m. (***mārnā***).
daily, ***rōz***, ***rōz dihāṛī***.
dam, n., ***bann***, m.
damage, ***nuksān***, m. : *see* loss, injure, hurt : leg., *see* A : v., ***nuksān k.*** (***dā***), be damaged, ***nuksāneā jāṇā***, ***nuksān h.*** (***dā***).
damp, n., ***sill***, f. ***sējjaḷ***, f. : *see* moisture, wet : adj., ***gillā*** : become d., ***sill*** or ***sējjal caṛhnī*** (***nū̃***) : ***sill ghattṇā***.
dance, gen., ***naccṇā*** : special d., ***bhaṅgṛā*** (***mārnā***) or ***dhamāḷ*** (***pāṇī***).
dandy, *see* fop. : sedan chair, ***ḍāṇḍī***, f.
danger, ***k͟hatrā,*** m.
dangerous, ***k͟hatrewāḷā***.
dare, ***dalērī***, ***karnī***, ***jurat karnī***.
dark, n. and adj., ***hanērā*** : get d., ***hanērā paiṇā*** : at d., ***hanēre paie*** : very d., ***ghupghēr***, m. : d. of colour, ***kāḷī bhai mārda e*** *see* somewhat *see* A.
darling, *see* dear : rather spolit, ***lāḍlā***.
dash, *see* run, throw.
date, fruit; dried, ***chuhārā***, m. : green, ***khajūr***, f. : tree, ***khajūr***, f.
date, time. ***: tārīk͟h***, f. : ***tarīk***, f. : *see* appoint : useful dates for computing middle-aged and old persons' age : ***maiṇe wāḷā sāl***, Apr. 1877 to Apr. 1878 : mutiny, ***gadar***, m. (1857) : ***Sikkhā̃ dā rāj***, rule of the Sikkhs, later forties : *see* era, year.
daub, *see* plaster, smear.
daughter, ***dhī*** : leg. document, ***bint*** (always called ***bannat***) :

European's, ***bāwī***, ***miss bāwā*** : d. in-law, ***nū̃h***.
dawn, day, ***diṇ*** or ***diū̃h caṛhnā***.
day, ***dihāṛā***, m. (gen.) : ***wār***, m. (day of week) : ***diṇ***, ***din***, m. (daylight, also 24 hours) : ***rōz***, m. (rare except meaning daily) : ***aṭṭh paihr***, eight watches, one day : d.'s work or wages, ***dihāṛī***, f. : in course of day or less, ***sādihāṛī*** : by day, ***diṇe*** : day and night, ***rātī diṇe***, ***dẽh rātī̃*** : long days of hot weather : ***mōkle dihāṛe***, ***lamme dihāṛe***, ***mōklī bahār***, f. : next d., ***agle bhaḷak***, ***dujje bhaḷak*** : few days ago, ***agle dihāṛe*** or ***diṇ*** (the other day) : *see* time, year : that d., ***ōddiṇ*** : what d., ***kiddiṇ*** ? which d., ***jiddiṇ*** : (or ***ōddihāṛe***, etc.) : d. for, fever, ***wārī***, f. (turn).
dead, ***moeā hoeā***, ***murdā*** : *see* die.
deadly; disease, ***marnwāḷī***, ***mautwāḷī*** : snake, ***zaihrī*** : *see* fatal.
deaf, ***ḍōrā***, ***bōḷā*** : ***uccā suṇnā***, M. 129. 24 : ears stopped, ***jhappe auṇe*** (***nū̃***), M. 117. 8.
deal, *see* associate.
dealings, ***laihṇā dēṇā***, m., ***lāho deī***, f., ***laihṇ dēṇ***, m. : ***kamm***, m.
dear; loved, ***pyārā***, ***azīz*** (U.) : money, ***maihṅgā***, ***pyārā***, ***tēz***.
dearness, money, ***maihṅgāī***, f. (pron. ***maṅghāī***) : *see* rise.
death, ***maut***, f. : *see* die.
debar, *see* forbid hinder.
debauchee, ***sharābī***, ***nashebāz***, ***nashaī***, ***luccā***.
debris, ***malbā***, m. (also wood. bricks of house).
debt, ***karz***. m. : get into d., ***karz cukkṇā***, ***de sir karz caṛhnā*** : M. 118. 20 : *see* owe.
debtor, ***karzāī***.
decadence, ***rauṇak ghaṭṇī***, ***zōr***, etc., ***ghaṭnā***.
decamp, ***cupp capītā nass jāṇā***.
decapitate, *see* behead.
decay, ***trakkṇā*** : *see* bad : get soft, ***gaḷṇā*** : get spoiled, ***wigaṛnā*** : *see* decadence.
deceased, *see* dead, late.
deceit, deceive, ***dhōkhā***, m. (***d.***, ***nū̃***) : ***farēb***, m. (***k.***, ***nāḷ***) : ***dhroh***, m. (***k.***, ***nāḷ***) : ***ṭhaggī***, f. (***k.***, ***nāḷ***) : ***ṭhaggṇā***, ***luṭṭnā*** (both lit. rob) : *see* trick : be d., ***dhōkhā khāṇā***, ***farēb khāṇā*** : *see* put off.
deceitful, ***dhōkhebāz***, ***farēbī***, ***dhrohī***, ***ṭhagg*** : *see* double (-tongued).
decaitfulness, ***dhōkhebāzī***, f.
December, ***dasambar***, m. : ***poh***, m., about Dec. 13 to Jan. 12.
decide, ***faislā karnā*** : *see* settle, arrange, umpire.
decline, day, ***diṇ ḍhaḷṇā*** : *see* sink : in years, ***umr ḍhaḷṇī*** ; 5 *see* old : see refuse (1), decadence, lessen.
decorate, *see* adorn.
decrease, *see* lessen, decadence.
decree, ***ḍigrī***, f. : *see* lose, command, regulation, law.
deduce, ***natījā kaḍḍhṇā***.
deduct, ***mujrā*** m. (***mujre laiṇā***, ***d.***) : d. pay, *see* cut : *see* subtract.

deduction, of pay, ***kāṭ***, f. (***k.***).
deed, *see* action : ***amal***, m. : ***kartūt***, f. (gen. bad).
deep, ***ḍūṅghā*** (water, thoughts, matters), ***gaihrā*** (thoughts, matters, U) : *see* cunning.
deer, ***harn***, fem. ***harnī***.
defame, *see* accuse, slander.
defeat, v. int. ***hārnā*** (tr. ***harāṇā***) : n., ***hār***, f. : *see* conquer, vanquish.
defect, ***nuks***, m., ***aib***, m., ***kasr***, f. : *see* fault.
defective, ***nākas***.
defence, ***bacā***, m.
defenceless, ***māṛā*** (weak) : ***hathyār nehī̃***.
defend, ***bacāṇā*** (save) : ***hifāzat karnī*** (protect).
deference, ***lihāz***, m. : ***ādar***, f. : ***izzat***, f. : *see* consideration, favour, partiality.
deficient, ***ghaṭṭ***, ***kassā***, ***kam*** : *see* paucity.
defile (dirty) ***mailā k.*** : ceremonially, ***palīt k.*** : ***bhēṭ chaḍḍṇā*** (int. ***bhiṭ jāṇā***) : ***choh chaḍḍṇā*** (only by touch, int. ***choh ghattṇā***) : *see* unclean, abstain.
deformed, *see* cripple, hunchback.
defraud, ***hakk dabāṇā*** or ***mārnā***, M. 123. 46.
defy, ***laṛn nū̃ teār h.*** : *see* disobedient.
degrade, in rank, ***trõṛnā***, ***tōṛnā*** (int. ***ṭuṭṭṇā***).
degree, rank, ***darjā***, m. : by degrees, ***hōndeā̃ hōndeā̃***, ***hōndeā̃ hawāndeā̃***, ***hauḷī hauḷī***.
delay, ***cir lāṇā*** (int. ***laggṇā***) : ***dēr lāṇī*** (int. ***laggṇī***) : ***ḍhill karnī***, ***ḍhill maṭṭh karnī***.
delete, ***ḍhāṇā***, ***miṭāṇā***, ***lāhṇā*** (int. ***ḍhaiṇā***, ***miṭṇā***, ***laihṇā***) : strike off name, ***kaṭṭṇā***, ***khārij***.
delegate, ***wakīl*** ; ***ūmidwār***, ***pratnīdhī ēlcī***, (U.).
deliberately, ***jāṇke***, ***sōc k.*** ***samjhke***, ***jāṇ bujhke***, ***aiwẽ nehī̃*** : *see* purposely.
delicacy, esp. affected, ***nazākatā̃***, f. pl. (***k.***) : ***nakhre***, m. pl. (***k.***) : ***nakhrebāzī***, f. (***k.***) : real, use ***bimār raihṇā***, ***tagrā nā raihṇā***, ***nāzak***.
delicate, matter, person, ***nāzak*** *see* delicacy, weak : affectedly, ***nazākatī***, ***nakhrebāz***.
delicious, ***suādlā***, ***mazedār***.
delight (int. sense,) ***suād auṇā*** (***nū̃***), ***khush h.***, ***rāzī h.*** : tr., ***khush-k.***, ***rāzī-k.*** : *see* charm, rejoice.
delightful, *see* good, beautiful, delicious, etc.
delinquent, ***kusūrrwār***, *see* guilty.
delirious (raving) ***bĕhōshī wicc bakṇā***.
deliver, ***chuḍāṇā*** : d. address, ***d., k.***, etc., or ***suṇāṇā*** : of mid-wife, ***jamāṇā***.
deluge *see* flood.
delusion, ***waihm***, m. : *see* deceit
demand, *see* ask, claim : commercial d., ***mā̃g***, f.; ***wikrī***, f. (sale).
demolish, ***ḍhāṇā***, ***ḍēgṇā*** : *see* destroy.
demoralised, become, ***wigaṛnā***.

demur, ***cū̃ carā karnī, kusakṇā*** : *see* refuse (1).
den, animals, ***khundhar,*** f.
dense, trees, population, ***sañhṇā*** : *see* stupid.
dent, in metal, soft brick, ***cibb,*** m., (***paiṇā,*** tr. ***pāṇā*** : *see* straighten) : in wood, ***ṭoā,*** m. (***paiṇā,*** tr. ***kaḍḍhṇā***).
deny, ***mukkarnā, inkāri karnī, namukkar jāṇā, nā̃h karnī.***
depart, ***ṭur jāṇā, Allāh Belī h.; alī panj h.*** : *see* start, farewell.
department, ***maihkmā,*** m. : of education, ***sarishtā e tālīm,*** m.
depend, *see* confide, trust : my visit d. upon my getting leave, use "If" clause, or ***shart,*** f., condition : *see* condition
deplore, ***menū̃ ohdā baṛā afsōs*** e.
deport, *see* exile, banish.
deposit, n., ***amānat,*** f. : v., d. in bank, ***jamā k., rakkhṇā.***
depressed, *see* sad, sorry.
deprive, ***khohṇā*** : *see* defraud.
depute, ***mukhtār banāṇā*** : ***wakil karke, ghallṇā.***
depth, ***ḍuṅghiāī,*** f.
deputy, ***naib.***
deride, *see* ridicule.
derogatory, ***eh- de wicc sāḍḍī bêiztī e.***
descend, ***laihṇā,*** G. 64 : ***utrnā, ḍhaḷnā.***
descendant (s), ***aulād,*** f., ***uḷād,*** f. : ***āl aulād,*** f., ***aṇs,*** f., ***aū̃s,*** f., ***nasl,*** f. : of Muhammad, ***sayyad,*** fem. ***sayyadzādī*** : *see* tree.
descent, ***lahāī,*** f. : ***utrāī,*** f.
describe, ***bĕām karnā*** (***dā***).
desert, n., ***rēgistān,*** m.; ***ujār,*** m. : ***barētā,*** m., ***barētī,*** f., bit of dry sand in water : *see* waste : -ed, ***ujjareā hoeā.***
desert, v., ***nass jāṇā, chaḍḍṇā.***
deserve, ***oh dā hakk e.***
design, ***matlab,*** m., ***wiclā matlab*** ; *see* intention : drawing, ***nakshā,*** m. (***baṇāṇā***).
desire, n., ***cāh,*** f. : ***hirs,*** f. : ***shauk,*** m. : ***khāhsh,*** f. : ***rījh,*** f. : *see* taste : v., above nouns w. ***hōṇā*** : ***jī,*** m., ***rūh,*** m., ***dil,*** m., all w. ***karnā*** (M. 119. 35, 37) : ***cāhṇā*** G. 67 : ***auhkṇā*** (w. hestitation) : ***pucchaṇ pucchaṇ*** (etc.) ***k.,*** d. but hesitate to ask, G. 112 : cause to d., afflict, ***tarsāṇā*** : I wish for, want, ***mênū̃ cāhīdā e,*** or ***lōṛīdā e,*** G. 67 : *see* long.
desist, ***muṛnā, chaḍḍṇā.***
despair, ***nāumēdī,*** f. (h.) : ***udāsī,*** f., (***h.***).
desolate (place) ***ujār, wīrān*** : *see* desert (l).
despatch, *see* send.
despise, ***kujjh nā samjhṇā, kutte de barābar samjhṇā*** : *see* contempt, scorn.
despot-, -ic, *see* cruel.
destiny, *see* fate.
destitute, *see* fate.
destitute, *see* poor.
destroy, ***barbād k., kharāb k., nās karnā*** (***dā***), ***cauṛ k., cauṛ capaṭṭ k.*** : ***traṭṭī cauṛ karnī*** (***dī***) : lay waste, ***ujāṛnā*** (int. ***ujjaṛnā***) : money, ***phūkṇā, uḍāṇā*** : *see*

demolish, devastate, waste, downfall, perish, ruin.

detail, n., ***tafsīl***, f. : in d., ***sāriā̃ gallā̃***, ***tafsīlwār*** (U.), ***mufassal*** (U.) : v., *see* relate.

detain, someone, ***bahāī rakkhṇā***, ***khalhāṛī rakkhṇā***, ***jāṇ nā d.***

detect, ***tāṛ laiṇā***, ***wēkh laiṇā***, ***jāc, laiṇā***, ***samjhṇā*** : *see* trace, discover.

detective, ***khufyā pulswāḷā***.

detenu, ***nazrband***, m. : *see* surveillance.

deteriorate, ***wigaṛnā***, ***kharāb hōjāṇā***.

determin-ation, -e, ***pakkā irādā karnā*** : *see* inten-d, -tion, purpose.

dethrone, ***takhtõ haṭāṇā***, ***gaddīõ lāhṇā***.

devastate, ***wirān k.***, ***ujāṛnā*** (int ***ujjaṛnā***) : *see* destroy, waste, desert (l).

devi-ce, -se, mechanism, ***kalā̃***, f., ***kalā***, f., : *see* arrange, plan, trick.

devil, ***shatān***, m.

devote, time, ***lāṇā***, ***kharc k.*** : *see* consecrate.

devoted, *see* love.

devour, ***khā laiṇā***, ***ragaṛ laiṇā***,

devout, *see* religious.

dew, ***trēḷ***, f. (***paiṇī***).

dhak, tree, ***chichrā***, m.

dialect, ***bōlī*** f.

dialogue, *see* conversation.

diamond, ***hīrā***, m.

diarrhoea, ***baṛe dast***, m. pl. (***laggṇe***, ***nū̃*** : ***auṇe*** motions) : *see* dysentery.

dice, ***dāṇā***, m. : ***pāshā***, m. : ***nard*** f.

dictat-e, ion, (in school) ***imlā likhāṇī*** : gen., ***kise nū̃ koī gall likhāṇī***.

dictionary, ***lugāt***, f. : ***ḍikshnarī***, f. (educ.).

die, v., ***marnā***, ***guzar jānā***, ***pūrā h.*** : trees, plants, ***sukkṇā***, ***marnā*** : *see* death.

die, n., ***mohr.***, f. (***lāṇī***) : *see* dice.

diet, ***khurāk***, f. : ***gazā***, f.

differ, ***nā ralṇā***, ***nā milṇā*** : words for difference w. ***hōṇā***.

difference, ***fark***, m. : ***wērwā***, m. : great d., ***zamīn asmān dā fark*** : slight d., ***rawāl jehā fark***.

different, ***wakkhrā***, ***hōr*** : *see* differ, separate.

difficult, ***aukkhā***, ***mushkil***, ***sakht***.

difficulty, ***aukh***, m. : ***aukhat***, f. : ***mushkil***, f. : ***aukkar***, f. : *see* inconvenience, trouble; straits : w. d., adv., words for difficulty, trouble, etc., w. ***nāḷ*** : also ***masā̃ masā̃ masā̃***, ***kiwẽ***, ***aukkheā̃ hōke***, ***marke***, *see* scarcely.

dig, ***puṭṭṇā*** : *see* hoe, weed : d. hole, ***ṭoā kaḍḍhṇā***.

digested, be, ***pacṇā***, ***hazm h.***, (tr. ***k.***).

digestion, ***hāzmā***, m.

dignity, (honour) ***izzat***, f. : (rank) ***darjā***, m.

diligent, ***mehntī***, ***kamm karnwāḷā***.

dim, ***maṭṭhā***, ***maddham*** : sight, ***maṭṭhī***, ***mārī***.

dine, ***khāṇā khāṇā*** : -ingroom, ***khāṇā kamrā***, m.

dinner, ***khāṇā***, m.
direct, adj., *see* straight : v., ***rāh pāṇā*** or ***dassṇā*** (***nū̃***).
direction, in what d. : ***kehṛī guṭṭhe***, ***kehṛe pāse***, ***kehṛī sehde*** : *see* north, south : lengthwise, ***lamme dā***, M. 128. 8 : crosswise, ***cauṛe dā*** : in this way, ***ēs dā***.
dirt, ***gand***, m. : ***mail***, f. : in well, ***jīndar***, f. : *see* rubbish.
dirty, ***gandā***, ***mailā*** ; *see* bad : of water, *see* muddy : of machine, *see* clogged : v., ***gandā k.***, ***mailā k.***
disabled, well, cart, animal, man, but not woman, ***hanēkeā jāṇā*** : for woman use ill, injured, etc.
dissadvantage, ***nuksān***, m. ***ghāṭā***, m. : *see* defect.
disaffected, ***badniyyat***, ***badkhāh*** (U.) : *see* disloyal.
disagree, ***khiāl nā ralṇā*** : ***rā nā ralṇī*** : food, ***menū̃ muāfik nehī̃, mēre, laī cangā nehī̃.***
disagreeable, affair, ***maṭṭhī*** or ***burī*** or ***mandī*** or ***kauṛī gall.***
disagreement, *see* discord, quarrel.
disappear, ***disṇõ raih jāṇā***, ***gaib hōjāṇā*** : *see* run, visible.
disappoint, no exact, word, ***nāumēd k.***, ***umēd jāndi rehī***, ***umēd pūrī nehī̃ hoī.***
disapprove, ***cangā nā laggṇā*** (***nū̃***).
disaster, ***hanēr***, m. : *see* calamity.
discharge, gun, arrow, etc., *see* fire : debt, *see* pay : servant, ***juāb d.*** (***nū̃***) : *see* dismiss.
disciple, ***cēllā*** (H.) : ***murīd*** (M.) : ***shagird*** : *see* pupil scholar.
discipline, ***intizām***, m. (arrangement).
discomfort, ***bēarāmī***, f. : ***taklīf***, f. : *see* inconvenience.
discontented, ***rāzī nehī̃*** : *see* displeased.
discord (tune), *see* tune : unfriendliness, (*see* tune), ***nāitfākī***, f. : ***phuṭṭ***, f. : ***wigāṛ***, m. : *see* enmity, quarrel.
discordant, *see* tune.
discourage, ***dil tōṛnā*** (int. ***ṭuṭṭṇā***), ***bedil k.*** (int. ***h.***) : be d., ***hauslā chaḍḍṇā***, ***dil chaḍḍṇā.***
discover, ***malūm k.*** : ***daryāft k.*** (inquire) : by asking, ***patā karnā*** : by looking for one-self, ***patā lāṇā*** (int. ***laggṇā***).
discuss, ***gall karṇī***, ***salāh karnī***, ***salāh mashwarā karnā*** : *see* argue.
disease, ***rōg***, m. : ***bamārī***, f. : ***marz***, f. : contagious or infectious, ***lagganwālā.***
disembark, *see* land.
disgrace, ***beiztī*** f., ***bepatī***, f., (both ***k., h., dī***) : ***namōshī***, f. (***h., dī*** or ***auṇī nū̃***, M. 117. 3) : *see* dishonour.
disgraceful, ***sharm dī gall*** : *see* bad, mean.
disguised, ***bhēs badalke.***
disgust, ***krīc***, f. : ***kraiht***, f. : ***nafrat***, f. : all w. ***auṇā*** and ***wallõ***, ***tõ***, M. 117.3 : or ***k.*** and ***nāḷ.***
dish, ***bhāṇḍā***, m., ***bartaṇ***, m., ***ḍis***, m. (K.) : ***kunāḷ***, m., ***kunāḷī***, f. : *see* plate.

dishcloth, ***jhāṛan***, m.
disheartened, *see* discourage.
dishonest, ***beīmān***, ***badniyyat*** (in intention)
dishonour, ***pat lāhṇī*** (int. ***laihṇī***, ***dī***, M. 121. 19 : 122. 32) : ***beiztī k.***, ***dī*** : ***izzat lāhṇī*** (int. ***laihṇī***, ***dī***) : *see* disgrace.
disinclined, *see* sick of.
disinfect, ***pōcā pherna*** (plaster) : ***fanail chiṇkṇī*** or ***traũkṇī*** (phenyle) : *see* fumigate.
dislike, ***burā laggṇā*** (***nū̃***, M. 121. 11) : ***caṅgā*** or ***acchā nā laggṇā*** (***nū̃***) : *see* disgust, annoy, displeased.
dislocated, be, of joint, ***ṭalṇā***, ***laihṇā***, ***utrnā*** : adj., ***ṭaḷeā hoeā***.
disloyal, ***khaikhāh nehī̃*** : *see* disaffected.
dismay, v., tr. ***ghabrāṇā***, ***gnabrā dēṇā*** : int. ***ghābbarnā***.
dismiss, ***kaḍḍhṇā***, ***ṭōr d.***, ***juāb d.***, (***nū̃***) : permit to go, ***rukhsat-karnā*** (***nū̃***) . A.
disobedient, ***ākkhe nā laggṇā*** : ***gall na mannṇī*** : ***hukm nā mannṇā***.
disobliging, no word, say ***puṭṭhā ādmī*** ; ***kise dā faidā nehī̃ cāhndā*** : ***badniyyat***.
disorder, ***gaṛbaṛī***, f. : ***bēintizāmī***, f. : ***bētartībī***, f. : *see* confus-e, -ion, tidy, untidy.
dispensary, ***haspatāḷ***, m. : *see* hospital.
disperse, ***khalārnā***, ***ēddhar ĕddhar k.***, ***urā̃ parā̃ k.***
display, *see* show.
displease, ***narāz k.*** : -d., ***ranj***, ***narāz***, ***wiṭreā hoeā***, ***mū̃h waṭṭṇā*** (***mēre wallõ***) : *see* angry, annoy.
disposition, ***tabīat***, f. : ***mizāj***, f. : *see* pride.
disprove, ***jhūṭhā*** or ***galt sābit*** [***k.***
disqualify, ***nā̃ kaṭṭṇā*** (***dā***). A.
dissension, *see* discord, quarrel, disturbance.
dissuade, ***mōṛnā***, ***manā k.***, ***samjhāṇā***.
distance, ***paiṇḍā*** m. : ***wāṭ***, f. : ***witth***, f. (very small space) : ***dū̃h paiḷīā̃ ḍī wāṭ***, two fields d. : ***kukkaṛ uḍārī*** f., ceckfly, short d. : *see* near.
distant, ***durāḍḍā*** : ***dūr*** (fem., as ***kinnī dūr*** how far ?) : *see* far.
distinct, *see* different, separate.
distinguish, ***nakhēṛā karnā***, ***fark kaḍḍhṇā***, ***pachāṇṇā*** (pa. p. ***pachā-ttā***, ***-ṇeā***) : ***tamīz karnī*** (U.).
distinguished, *see* famous.
distressed, be, (heat worry) ***hussaṛnā*** : *see* worry, trouble.
district, gen., ***alākā***, m. : small, ***tappā***, m., ***halkā***, m.: Govt. d., ***zilā***, m. : ***taihsīl***, or ***tasīl*** f. : ***pargaṇa***, m. : ***zail***, f.
disturbance, ***rauḷā***, m. : ***raṭṭā***, m. : ***rēṛkā*** m. : ***rapphar***, m. : ***bakhēṛā***, m. (all w. ***pāṇā***, int. ***paiṇā***, h.) : ***halcal***, f. (***paiṇī***, h.) : ***rohḷī***, f. (***macāṇī***, int. ***macṇī***) : serious d., ***fasād***, m. (***k.***, ***h.***) : ***daṅgā fasād***, m. ***k.***, ***h.***) : *see* quarrel, noise, excitement, riot.
ditch, ***ṭoā***, m. (***kaḍḍhṇā***) : *see* pit.

dive, ***cubbhi mārnī*** : go under accidentally, ***gōtā khāṇā.***
diver, ***ṭōbhā***, m.
divert, ***dil parcāṇā***, (int. ***parcṇā***) : ***dil bhulāṇā***, int. ***bhullṇā*** : *see* delight, please, game.
divide, ***wandṇā, taksīm-k.***
division, ***taksīm***, f. : of school class, ***farik***, m. : *see* part.
divorce, paper of, ***likhat***, f. (M.) : ***tiāg pattrī***, f. (H.), ***tiāg pattar***, m. (H.) : v. tr., ***likhat dēṇī (nū̃) : tiāg dēnā (nū̃) : tiāgṇā, talāk dēṇī (nū̃).***
divulge, ***bhēt dassṇā, zāhr k.***
dizz-y, -iness, ***nhērnī auṇī (nū̃), bhuāṭṇī auṇī (nū̃), sir sakrāṇā, sir cakkar khāṇā, akkhiā̃ agge nhērā auṇā.***
do, ***karnā*** (pa. p. ***kīlā***) : *see* accomplish, finish, work : d. without, ***ohde bājhō̃ guzārā karnā*** or ***kamm calāṇā.***
docile, animal, ***asīl.***
doctor, ***ḍāgdār***, m. : ***ḍākṭar***, m. : ***hakīm***, m. : d.'s work, practice, ***ḍākṭarī***, f.
doctrine, ***tālīm***, f. (teaching) : ***akīdā***, m. (creed) : ***maslā***, m. (one point of d.).
dog, ***kuttā***, m. : *see* puppy.
doll, ***guḍḍī*** f.
dome, ***gumbaz***, m.
donation, ***candā***, m.
donkey, *see* ass.
dooly, ***dōlī***, f.
door, ***būhā***, m.. ***darwāzā***, m. : rough wooden, ***bhitt*** m. and ***khiṛk***, m. : one side of double door, ***bhitt***, m. : w. open doors, ***latthī̃ būhī̃*** G. 78 : w. shut d., ***wajjī̃ būhī̃***, indoors, ***ghare, andar*** : d.-frame, ***cugāṭh***, m. : side of d., ***muhāṭh***, f. : wood above, ***sardal***, m. : below, ***brū̃***, f. : lean against doorpost, ***muhāṭhī̃ laggṇā*** (M. 120. 5) : through door, ***būhe rāh*** : *see* socket, pivot.
dot, ***nukhtā, nuktā***, m.
double (size, price, distance, etc.) ***dūṇā*** : (two layers, etc.) ***dohrā*** : on both sides, ***duallī***, thus ***dūṇī sazā***, double punishment ; ***duallī sazā***, punishment to both parties : *see* fold, time : v. tr., ***dūṇā k., dohrā k.*** : d.-entendre, ***domaihṇī gall***, f. : double-tongued, ***duragā, dubājrā*** : *see* deceit-, -ful.
doubt, ***shakk***, m. (***k., h.***).
doubtful, ***shakkī.***
doubtless, ***beshakk, nishaṅg.***
dough, ***tauṇ***, f., ***guddhā hoeā āṭā*** : for pudding, cake scones, ***māwā***, m.
dove-cot, ***kābuk***, f. : in ground, ***ghumail***, f, : roost, ***chatrī***, f.
down-, -wards, *see* below.
downfall, ***nās***, m. : ***barbādī***, f. : *see* destroy.
dowry, ***dāj***, f. : *see* marr-y, -iage.
dozen, ***darjaṇ***, m.
drag, ***dhrūhṇā, ghasīṭnā*** : d. in, *see* rake up.
drain, ***waihṇī***, f. : ***nāḷī***, f.
drama, ***nāṭak*** m.
draught, rough, of deed, etc., ***masaudā***, m. (***baṇāṇā***).

draw, ***khiccṇā*** : *see* drag : d. water, ***bharnā***, rarely ***kaḍḍhṇā*** : of tea, ***rang auṇā*** (***nū̃***, M. 50. 4) : *see* drawing.

drawer, ***drāz***, f.

drawers, ***drāz***, f. sing. : very small, ***jānghiā***, m. sing.

drawing, ***taswīr***, f. (***khiccṇī***) : plan, map, ***nakshā***, m. (***baṇāṇā***).

drawingroom, ***gōl kamrā***, m.

dread, *see* fear.

dream, ***khāb*** f. m. : ***sufnā***, m. (both ***auṇā***, M. 117.6, and ***wēkhṇā***).

dress, n.v. : *see* clothes, clothe : lady's d., ***ḍrēs***, m. : d. wound, ***paṭṭī bannhṇī***, ***phāh lāṇā*** (int. ***laggṇā***) : *see* ointment.

dressingroom, ***sangār-kamrā***, m.

drill n., ***kawaid***, f. (***k.***)

drill (hole) ***chēk kaḍḍhṇā***.

drink, ***pīṇā*** (pa. p. ***pītā***) : caus, ***piāṇā***, ***piāḷṇā***.

drink, intoxicating, ***sharāb***, m. : ***nashā***, m. (both w. ***pīṇā***) : *see* drunk-, -ard.

drinking-vessel, ***channā***. m. : ***kaul***, m. : ***kaṭōrā***, m. : ***garwā*** m. : ***garwī***, f. : ***gilās***, m. : *see* cup.

drip, (of vessel, house, water), ***cōṇā*** : (of vessel, water), ***wagṇā*** : *see* ooze, trickle.

drive, horse, etc., ***ṭōrnā***, ***calāṇā*** : d. fast, ***bhajāṇā*** : d. on or away, ***hikkṇā*** : *see* hammer.

drizzle, ***phak***, f. : ***phūhr***, f. (both ***paiṇī***).

drop, n., ***būnd***, f. : ***chitt***, f. (fr. splashed or falling water), both ***paiṇī***.

drop, v., ***ḍiggṇā***, ***paiṇā*** : let fall, ***ḍiggaṇ d.*** : *see* drip.

drought, ***rōṛā***, m. : ***auṛ***, f. : ***sōkā***, m. (all w. ***laggṇā***).

drown, ***duobke marnā***, ***ruṛhke marnā*** (in flowing water); tr. ***ḍōbṇā***.

drowsy, *see* sleepy.

drum, ***ḍhōl***, m. : smaller, ***ḍholkī***, f. : double, ***tablā***, m. : all w. ***wajāṇā*** (int. ***wajjṇā***).

drunk, ***matwālā***, ***nashe wicc***.

drunkard, ***nashebāz***, ***nashaī*** (both also of drugs), ***sharābī***.

drunkenness, ***nashebāzī***, f.

dry, ***sukkā*** : d. bread, ***rukkhī rōṭī***, f., bread alone : ***sukkī rōṭī***, actually dry : *see* insipid.

due, n., ***hakk***, m. : adj., d. to me, ***menū̃ aundā e*** (money). train due, ***gaḍḍī āī cāhndī e***, (G. 112), ***hun āī khlōtī e***.

dumb, ***gūngā***.

dumbbell, village, ***bugdar***, m. : ***mungḷī***, f. Indian club.

dung, horse, ass, ***lidd***, f. : cattle, ***gohā***, m., ***gohā gaṭṭā***, m. : sheep, camel, rats, mice, ***mengnā̃***, f. pl. : dogs, human, ***gū̃h***, m. : birds, ***wiṭṭh***, f. (all w. ***k.***).

dunghill, ***rūṛī***, f.

dupe, *see* prey.

durable, *see* lasting.

dusk, ***muhānjlā***, ***mū̃h anhērā*** m.

dust, n., ***dhūṛ***, f. : ***dhuddaḷ***, f. : ***ghaṭṭā***, m. : of decayed body, ***khāk***, f. : ***miṭṭī***, f. : v., ***jhāṛnā***, ***jhāṛ pōc karnī*** (***dī***) : *see* sweep.

duster, ***jhāṛan***, m.

duty, ***farz***, m. (***pūrā k.***) : of work, ***naukrī*** (***laggṇī***, M. 121. 7) **:** ***ḍyūṭī***, f. (***h.***).

dwarf, ***giṭh miṭhīā***, ***ṭhiṅgṇā***, ***ṭhigṇā***, ***gīṇḍhā***, ***bauṇā*** (all for very small man).

dwell, ***wassṇā***, ***raihṇā*** (pa. p. ***rehā***) : *see* resident.

dye, n., ***raṅg***, m. : for hair, beard, ***was nā***, m. and ***kalf***, f., indigo : ***mehndī***, f., red dve, (all with ***liṇā***) : v., ***raṅgṇā***.

dyer, ***lalār-ī***, fem. ***-an***.

dysentery, ***pēcish***, f. : griping pain, ***marōṛā***, m. : *see* diarrhoea.

E

each, *see* every : two e., three e., etc., ***dō dō*** : ***trai trai***, etc., G. 24 : at certain rate for e., ***sēṭī***, ***picche***, ***fī*** (U.) : *e.g.* ***jaṇe sēṭī***, per man : *see* per.

eager, *see* desire.

ear, ***kann***, m. : w. cropped ears, ***buccā*** : poison ears, *see* incite.

early, ***sawēḷe***, ***sājhre***, ***sawakhte*** *see* morning.

earn, ***khaṭṭṇā***, ***kamāṇā*** : *see* deserve, obtain.

earnings, ***khaṭṭī***, f. : ***kamāī***, f. : *see* advantage, profit.

earnest, ***sargarm***, ***jōshwāḷā*** : in e., truly, ***saccī muccī***.

earnest money, ***sāī***, f.

earth, *see* world, soil : filling up w. e., ***bhartī***, (***pāṇī***) : e. coloured, ***ghasmailṛā***, ***khākī***.

earthquake, ***bhucāl***, m.

ease (rest), ***arām***, m. : (easiness), ***sukhall***, m., ***asānī*** f., at e., ***maze wicc***, ***maze nāḷ*** : *see* rest, convenience.

easily, ***saukh nāḷ***, ***asānī nāḷ***, ***cuṭkī wicc*** ; ***hāī̃ maī̃***, used only in neg. sentences.

east, ***caṛhdā***, m. : ***caṛhdā pāsā***, m. : e.-wards, ***caṛhde wall***.

easy, ***sukhallā***, ***saukkhā***, ***saihl***, ***asān*** : *see* chair.

eat, ***khāṇā***, pa. p. ***khādhā*** : e. greedily, ***ragaṛnā*** : e. orange, lime, lemon, mango, sugarcane, ***cūpṇā*** : parched grain, ***cabbṇā***.

eavesdropping, ***cōrī suṇṇā*** : *see* overhear.

eccentric, ***laihrī***.

echo, ***dūhrī***, ***awāz***, f. (***auṇī***).

eclipse, ***cugarn***, m. : solar, ***sūraj*** or ***diṇ dā*** : lunar, ***cann dā*** : among educated people, ***graihṇ***, e. (gen.) ; ***cugarn***, lunare.

economy, ***sarfā***, m. (k.) : ***ghaṭṭ kharc***, m. (***k.***)

edge, of instrument, ***dhār***, f. : or river, lake, etc., ***kaṇḍhā***, m., ***dandā***, m. : of garment, ***kannī***, f. : raised e. round roof, ***banērā***, m.

educat-e, -ion, *see* teach : educated, ***paṛheā likheā***, ***widwāṇ***.

efface, *see* delete : mental, ***dūr k.***, ***haṭāṇā***.

effect, ***asar***, m. (gen.).

efficacious, ***asarwāḷā*** : *see* advantageous.

efficacy, *see* effect, advantage.

efficient, *see* able.

effort, ***kōshish***, f. or ***kōsht***, f.

(*k.*) : ***dill***, m. (***lāṇā***, int., ***laggṇā***) : great e., ***jataṇ***, m. (***k.***) ; ***zōr***, m. (***lāṇā***) : w. an e., ***dill nāl***, ***zōr***, ***nāḷ*** : *see* difficulty.
egg, ***āṇḍā***, m. : (lay, ***d.***,) : white of, ***safēdi***, f. : yellow, ***zardī*** f. : hatch e., ***bacce kaḍḍhṇe*** : e.-shell, ***chill***, f.
egg-plant, ***batāū̃***, m., ***wainnaṇ***, m.
eight, ***aṭṭh*** : eighth, ***aṭṭhwā̃*** : G. 19-24 : eighth part, see time, wts. and meas.
eighteen, ***aṭhārā̃*** : -th, ***aṭhāhrwā̃*** : eighteen-finger shoe, ***aṭhāhri jutti***, f., G 19-24, 123.
eighty, ***assī*** : -one, ***ikāsī*** : -two, ***beāsī*** : three, ***tirāsī*** : -four, ***curāsī*** : -five, ***panj-*** or ***pacāsī*** : -six, ***cheāsī*** : -seven, ***satāsī*** : -eight, ***aṭhāsī*** : -nine, ***unānwe*** : G. 19-24, 123 : ordinals : 80, ***assīwā̃*** : 81 to 88 end in ***-āhsīwā̃*** with high tone or occ. ***āsīwā̃*** : -nine, ***unāhnwewā̃*** : G. 22, 123.
either .. or, ***cāhe..cāhe***, ***yā̃..yā̃ bhāwē̃....bhāwē̃***.
eject, *see* expel.
ekka, ***yakkā***, m.
elapse, time, ***laṅghṇā***.
elastic, ***lifṇwāḷā***.
elbow, ***ark***, f. ***kūṇī***.
electric, -ity ***bijlī***, f. : e. light, ***bijlī dī battī***.
elder, ***waḍḍā***, ***thō̃ waḍḍā*** : *see* old : church-e., ***ělḍar***, m.
electroplate, ***giṭ***, m.
elephant, ***hāthī***, fem. ***hāthnī***.
eleven, ***yārā̃*** : -th, ***yāhrwā̃*** : G. 19-24, 123.
eliminate, ***kaḍḍhṇā***.
elope, of woman, ***uddhaḷṇā***, ***nikḷ jāṇā*** : of man, ***udhāḷṇī*** w. woman as obj.
elopement, ***udhāḷā***, m.
else (e.g., who e., what e.) ***hōr*** : *see* otherwise, course.
elude, ***dhōkhe nāḷ nikḷṇā*** or ***bacṇā***.
emaciated, ***baṛā māṛā*** or ***patlā***.
embankment, ***bann***. m
embark, ***jahāz utte suār-h***. or ***caṛhṇā***.
embers, *see* coal, ashes.
embezzle, ***rupayyā khāṇā*** (***beimānī nāḷ***).
embitter, ***ohdā dil mere wallō̃ khaṭṭā k***.
embrace, ***gaḷ nāḷ*** or ***hikk nāḷ lāṇa*** (int. ***laggṇā***, M. 1.2.31) : ***jappḥā***, ***japphī mārn-ā***, ***-ī***, ***nāḷ*** : ***kaḷāwē̃ wicc laiṇā***.
embroil, ***phasāṇā*** (int. ***phasṇā***) w. word for quarrel.
emerge, ***nikḷṇā***.
emergency, *see* crisis.
emigrate, ***dujje mulkh wicc jāke wassṇā*** or ***raihṇā***.
emperor, empress, *see* king, queen.
emphasis, particle of, ***ī***, ***hī*** : also expressed by ***chaḍḍṇā*** (***charnā***, ***sarnā***), ***dēṇā***, ***laiṇā***, ***suṭṭṇā***, ***jāṇā*** compounded w. verbs, G. 65, 110, 111 : never by repetition of words, G. 71 : *see* very.
emphasise, ***zōr dēṇā*** (***utte***).
empower, *see* authorise.
empty, ***sakkhṇā*** (***k.***), ***khālī*** (***k.***) :

e. handed, ***sakkhṇe hatth*** : *see* unoccupied.
emulate, ***rīs***, f. or ***barābrī***, f. (***k.***).
enable, ***es gall jogā k.*** or ***baṇāṇa*** : ***tākat dēṇī*** (***nū̃***).
enamel, gen. ***lohā***, m. (iron).
encamp, ***ḍērā*** or ***tambū lāṇā*** (int. ***laggṇā***) : *see* tent, camp.
enclose, a place, ***duāḷe wāṛ dēṇī*** or ***jaṅgḷā banāṇā*** : *see* shut up, hedge, railing.
enchant, *see* charm.
encourage, ***dil wadhāṇā*** : *see* comfort.
end, ***a<u>kh</u>īr***, m. : ***ant***, m. : ***natījā***, m. (result) : to the e., ***tōṛ tīkar*** : in the e., *see* finally : *see* head, foot, object, edge, boundary.
endanger, ***<u>kh</u>atre wicc leauṇā***.
endeavour, *see* try.
endless, ***beant***, ***bēbahā***, ***behadd***, ***jehṛā nā mukke***.
endow, paraphrase, or ***wazīfā dēṇā*** (scholarship) : rupayye ***dēṇē***, etc.
endure, ***jhallṇā***, ***jhāgṇā***, ***saihṇā***, ***jarnā*** : ***bhugtṇā*** (go through w.) : *see* remain lasting, strong.
enemy, ***wair-ī***, fem. ***-an*** : ***dushmaṇ***, ***dōkh-ī***, fem. ***-aṇ*** : deadly c., ***jānī dushmaṇ*** : *see* enmity, envy.
energetic, ***cust***, ***mehntī***, ***himmatwāḷā***.
enervate, *see* weaken.
enforce, ***zōre karāṇā*** : *see* force.
engage, servant, ***naukar rakkhṇā*** : e. a seat, ***thā̃ ra<u>kh</u>āṇā*** : (but keep seat, ***rakkhṇā***) : be e. to be married, *see* fiancé : be e. in work, ***ḍaihṇā*** (pa. p. ***ḍehā***) : G. 67, 68.
engagement, (marriage), ***kuṛmāī***, f. : ***maṅgṇī***, f.
engine, ***iñaṇ***, m. : small mechanical contrivance, ***kalā̃***, f., ***kalā***, f.
engrave, ***ghaṛnā*** : signet, ***ukkarnā*** (caus. ***ukrāṇā***), ***ukkhaṇṇā*** (caus. ***ukhṇāṇā***).
enjoy-, -ment, ***suād***, m. : ***mazā***, m. (both ***auṇā***, ***nū̃***) : *see* amuse, delight.
enlist, tr., ***bhartī-k.*** (int. ***h.***) : ***nā̃wā̃ li<u>kh</u>āṇā***. have one's name entered.
enmity, ***wair***, m. : ***dushmaṇī***, f. : mutual ill-feeling, ***aṇ baṇ***, f. : *see* envy.
enough, ***bas. kāfī*** (U.) : words for much : ***jinnā lōṛīdā e*** or ***cāhīdā e*** ; ***jinnī lōṛ e***.
enrage, ***baṛā gussā duāṇā*** (***nū̃***) : *see* excite, incite : be e., ***baṛā gusse h.*** : *see* angry, displeased, rage.
enquire, etc., *see* inquire, etc.
entangle, ***phhāṇā***, ***phasāṇā*** (int. ***phasṇā***).
enter, ***waṛnā*** (tr. ***wāṛnā***) : ***andar jāṇā*** : e. name, ***nā̃ li<u>kh</u>ṇā*** (caus. ***li<u>kh</u>āṇā***) : e. pupil in school, ***dā<u>kh</u>il h.*** (of pupil); ***dā<u>kh</u>il k.*** (of teacher); ***dā<u>kh</u>il karāṇā*** (of guardian).
enteric, ***mohrkā tapp***, m.
entertainment, ***tamāshā***, m. : w. name, as ***bhaṇḍā̃ dā***, clowns' : ***madāriā̃ dā***, conjurers' :

otherwise dancing-girls suggested : *see* amuse, delight.
enthusiasm, ***jōsh***, m. : ***sargarmī***, f.
enthusiastic, ***baṛī cāh rakhdā e. baṛā shukīn.***
entice, ***hirs***, f., or ***tamā***, m., or ***lālac***, m., ***kujjh duāke manāṇā.***
entire, not broken or incomplete, ***sābat*** : *see* all, bag and baggage.
entitled, *see* right.
entrance fee, *see* fee.
entrails, ***āndrā̃***, f. pl.
entreat, *see* beseech, ask.
entrust, ***kōḷ chaḍḍṇā, de pēṭe pāṇā, hawāle karnā***
envelope, ***lafāfā***, m.
envy, ***khār***, f. (***h. nāḷ***); ***kiṛ***, f. (***k. nāḷ***); ***mērā sāṛā*** (***ohnū̃ paiṇā***); ***dukh***, m. or ***dukh-waidā***, m. (***h nāḷ***); ***cōbh***, f. (***h. nāḷ***); or ***mērā dukh k.*** or ***mēre nāḷ dukh rakkhṇā***, or ***ohnū̃ mērā dukh e*** : this last also means sympathise : M. 130 33-6 : *see* enmity.
epilepsy, ***mirgī***, f.
equal, ***barābar***, ***barabbar***, ***barōbbar*** : in age, ***hāṇī***, m., fem ***hānnaṇ*** : ***mēre jehā*** (like), ***jēḍḍā*** (size), ***jinnā*** (amount, number), G. 91.
equality, ***barābrī***, f.
equip, ***sārā samān d.***, etc.
equipage, *see* retinue.
era, ***sammat***, m., esp. that of Wikramaditya, in which 1975 = Apr. 13, 1918 to Apr. 12, 1919 : year A.D., ***san Iswī*** : *see* date.
eradicate, *see* expel, annihilate, destroy, exterminate.
erase, *see* delete.
erect, ***khaḷhārnā*** : *see* build.
err, error, *see* mistake.
escape, ***bacṇā***, ***bac nikḷṇā***, ***chuṭṭṇā***, ***maḷ jāṇā***; ***phaṛā nā dēṇā***, ***phaṛāī nā dēṇī*** : *see* run.
escort, *see* retinue.
especial, ***khāss*** : -ly, of set purpose, ***ucēcā.***
espionage, ***jāsūsī***, f. : ***mukhbarī***, f. : *see* spy.
essence, ***asl*** f.
essentially ***asl wicc*** : *see* real, necessary.
establish, ***kaim k.*** : *see* build, found.
estate, landed, ***malkīyat***, f. : ***jagīr***, f. (given as reward) : ***jāēdāt***, f. (property).
esteem, ***izzat***, f. (***k.***) : ***ādar***, f. (***k.***) : ***acchā*** or ***nēk samjhṇā*** : *see* consideration, partiality.
estimate, n., ***takhmīnā***, m. (of cost, ***baṇāṇā*** or ***lāṇā***) : ***jāc***, f. (***k.***, less formal, v., ***jācṇā***) : *see* calculate, guess, approximately.
estrangement, *see* discord, quarrel, enmity.
eternal, ***hamēshār dā***, ***azlī*** (without beginning), ***sadā dā***, ***abdī*** (without end) : *see* life.
eternally, ***azlō̃ abad tīkar*** : ***hamēshā toṛī***, etc.
etiquette, *see* custom, rule.
Eurasian, ***dōglā*** : (jocular), ***bērrā***, m.
evacuate, *see* empty, leave.
evade, *see* escape, put off.

evaporate, ***sukk jāṇā.***
evasion, *see* evade.
even, not odd, ***jist*** : *see* level, smooth.
even, adv. ***sagō***, ***wī***, ***bī*** : *see* emphasis.
evening, ***shām***, f. (sunset : in e., ***shāmī̃***) : ***tarkāḷā̃***, f. pl., about half hour after sunset : ***khaupīyyā***, m., time of e. meal, about 8 : ***sōtā***, m., sleeping time, about 9 or 10 **:** ***ḍūnghī shām***, when full darkness comes : *see* afternoon.
event, ***wākiā***, m : ***gall***, f., ***ghaṭnā***, f.
ever, ***kade*** : for e., *see* always, eternal.
every, as in e. eighty day, ***aṭṭhī̃ diṇī̃***, ***aṭṭhwē̃*** (or ***aṭṭhwē̃ de aṭṭhwē̃***) ***dihāṛe***.
everyone, ***har koī***, ***sabbh koī***, ***hamā shamā***, ***jaṇā khaṇā*** : *see* all, people, common.
everything, ***sabbh kujjh.***
everywhere, ***sabbhnī̃ pāsī̃***, ***sabbh dare***, ***sabbhnī̃ thāī̃*** : *see* side.
evidence, ***guāhī***, f. (***d.***, ***dī***) : ***sabūt***, m. (proof, d., ***dā***).
evident, ***zāhr***, ***sāf zāhr***, ***ujāgar*** : self-e., ***apū̃ malūm hondā e.***
evil, adj., *see* bad : n. ***bureāī***, f. : ***burāī***, f. : ***k͟harābī***, f. : ***badī***, f. : *see* sin.
evil eye, be injured by; ***nazreā*** or ***nazrāṛeā jāṇā***, ***nazr*** or ***nazrāṛ ghattṇā*** : ***tērī ohnū̃ nazr laggī.***
exact, ***ṭhīk***, ***bilkul ṭhīk.***
exact, v., ***zōre laiṇā*** or ***ugrāhṇā.***
exactly, ***hū bahū***, ***aiṇ.***
exaggerate, ***wadhāṇā.***
examin-e, -ation, in school, etc., ***imtihān laiṇā*** (***dā*** of person, subject) : be e., ***imtihān d.*** (***dā*** of subject) : e. books, ***paṛtāḷ*** or ***paṛtāl karnī*** (***dī***) : e. school, ***muāinā karnā*** (***dā***) : inspect (medical and in gen.) ***mulāhzā karnā*** (***dā***, U.) : cross-e., ***jahrā karnī*** : *see* pass, test.
examiner, ***imtihān laiṇwāḷā.***
example, ***namūnā***, m., moral, also pattern, sample : in grammar, etc., ***misāl***, f. : for e., ***maslan*** : make e. of, say ***dujjeā̃ nū̃ wī mat āwe.***
excavate, *see* dig.
exceedingly, *see* very.
excellent, *see* good : also ***baṛā abbaḷ***, ***baṛā ḍabal*** (strong, big), ***fasṭ klās***, ***baṛ umdā***, ***sohṇā*** (***baṛ*** for ***baṛā***).
except, ***de bājhō̃***, ***de suā***, ***nū̃ chaḍḍke***, ***de bagair*** (U.).
exception, ***kaide de k͟halāf.***
excess, ***bakāyā***, m. : ***jinnā waddhe*** : ***lōṛ tō̃ waddh*** : amount in e. or defect, ***wādhā ghāṭṭā***, m.
excessive, ***haddō̃ waddh*** : -ly, ***sak͟ht*** (for something undesirable) : *see* very.
exchange, ***waṭāṇā*** : *see* change : in e., ***ohde thā̃*** or ***badle*** : that may be e., ***waṭāwā̃.***
excise, v., ***waḍḍhṇā.***
excite, ***jōsh duāṇā*** (***nū̃***) : ***ghabrāṇā*** (confuse) : *see* incite, induce : be e.-ed, ***jōsh wicc auṇā*** : ***ghābbarnā*** (dismayed) :

halcal macṇī (tr. ***macāṇī***, lot of people).
excitement, ***jōsh***, m., ***hal cal paiṇī*** or ***macṇī*** among lot of people : *see* disturbance.
exclud-e, -ing, *see* except, expel
excommunicate, ***chēkṇā***, ***zātõ chēkṇā*** : ***hukkā pāṇī band karnā*** (***dā***, int. ***h.***) : remove ban, ***hukkā pāṇī kholhṇā***, (int. ***khulhṇā***).
excrement, *see* dung.
exculpate, ***barī k.*** : *see* acquit.
excursion, ***sail***, m. or ***sair***, m. or ***sail sapaṭṭe wāste jāṇā***.
excuse, v., from doing, ***muāf k.***, int. ***h.*** (***thõ***) : *see* forgive : n., ***uzar***, m. : you've no e., ***terā koī caṅgā uzar nehī̃*** : what e. have you ? ***wajhā kī e*** : a mere e., ***huṭṭar***, m., ***hīlā***, m., ***jugat***, f. (quibble) : *see* pretence.
execrate, ***nā̃ suṇke saṛnā*** : *see* curse.
execute (hang), ***phāhe d.*** (***nū̃***) ***phāhe lauṇā*** (***nū̃***) : *see* do, finish, behead.
executive, ***intizāmī***.
exempt, v. tr., ***muāf k.*** (int. ***muāf h.***, ***thõ***).
exercise, bodily, ***warzish***, f. (***k.***) : ***kasrat***, f. (***k.***) : practice, ***mashk***, f. : e. book, ***kāpī***, f.
exert, *see* effort.
exhausted, *see* faint.
exhibit, -ion, *see* show, spectacle.
exhort, ***nasīhat dēṇī*** (***nū̃***) : *see* incite, encourage.
exile, v.n. : *see* banish and add : ***mulkhõ paṛ mulkh*** (***karnā***, int. ***hōṇā***).
exonerate, *see* exculpate, acquit.
exorbitant, *see* dear.
exorcist, *see* magician.
expect, ***umēd***, f. (***h.***, ***k.***) : person, ***uḍīkṇā***.
expedient, *see* means, plan.
expedition, military, ***lām***, m. (***laggṇā***, sometimes f.).
expel, ***kaḍḍhṇā***, ***bāhr dhikkṇā***, ***banne saṭṭṇā*** : *see* turn out.
expend, *see* spend, expense.
expense, ***kharc***, m. : ***lāgat***, f. : *see* cost : at my e., ***mēre pēṭe***, ***mēre palleõ :*** G. 34 : M. 129. 20 : marriage expenses paid to inferior castes, ***lāg***, m.
expensive, *see* costly.
experience, ***tajrabā***, m. (***k.***, ***dā***).
experiment, science, ***tajrabā***, m. (***k.***) *see* test.
expert, *see* clever-, -ness.
explain, ***samjhāṇā***, ***bĕān karnā***, ***matlab dassṇā***, ***suṇānā***.
explicit-, -ly, ***sāf***, ***sāf saf***, ***safāi nāl***.
expression, favourite, constantaly used, ***takiā kalām*** m.
expressly, *see* especially, explicitly.
exquisite, ***ḍāhḍā sohnā*** : *see* excellent.
extensive, ***mōkḷā***, ***waḍḍā***.
exterminate, ***aslõ*** or ***mūḷõ kaḍḍhṇā*** : *see* destroy, annihilate, uproot.
extinguish, lamp, fire, ***bujhāṇā***, (int. ***bujjhna***) : for lamp also ***waḍḍā k.***, G. 113.
extort, *see* force, confess.

extraordinary, *see* strange, wonderful.
extract, v., ***kaḍḍhṇā*** : n., from book, ***ibārat***, f.
extraction, ***kāḍh***, f.
extravagance, ***fazūl kharcī***, f.
extravagant, ***fazūl kharc***.
extremity, of trouble, heat, etc., ***ākhar aī hoī e***.
exude, *see* ooze.
eye, ***akkh***, f. (pl. ***akkhīā̃***) : have bad eyes, ***akkhīā̃ auṇīā̃*** (***dīā̃***), M. 116. 1 : evil e. *see* evil : pupil of, ***dhīrī***, f. : healed ulcer in, ***phōllā*** (***paiṇā***), ***ciṭṭā*** (***paiṇā***).
eyebrows, ***bharwaṭṭe***, m. pl.
eyelash, ***pipṇī*** f.
eyelid, ***chappar***, m.
eye-witness, use ***akkhī ḍiṭṭhī gall***, f.: *see* witness.

F

fable, *see* story.
face, ***mū̃h***. m. : ***muhāndrā***, m. : *see* appearance : f. to f., ***mū̃h drūhī*** : ***āhmo sāhmṇe***, ***āhmṇe sāhmṇe*** : to his f., ***ohde mū̃h te*** : f. downwards, ***mū̃hdā***, ***mū̃hdre mū̃h***, ***mūhdre mū̃h*** : (fall) on f., ***mū̃h parne*** : faces, *see* grimace.
facilitate, words for easy w., ***karnā***.
fact, ***saccī gall***, f. : ***asl gall***, ***wākiā***, m. (U.).
fail, gen. ***ukkṇā*** : (exam.) ***fēhl h.*** (***wicc***) : other things, ***raih jāṇā***, ***kujjh nā baṇṇā*** : *see* bankrupt, deficient.
faint, ***behōsh h.***; feel f., ***dil chappṇā*** or ***chōṭā h.***, ***dil ghaṭṇā*** : M. 128.10 : exhausted through heat, thirst, etc., ***hussaṛnā***, ***ghābbarnā*** : adj., of colour, ***maddham***, ***phikkā*** : of light ***maddham***.
fair, complexion, ***gōrā*** : f.-haired, ***kakkā***.
faith, ***imān***, m. : *see* believe, trust, confide, reliance, religion.
faithful, ***namak-halāl***, ***imānwāḷā***.
fall, v., ***ḍiggṇā***, ***girnā*** : something big. ***ḍhaiṇā*** : house, ***ḍiggṇā***, ***ḍhiaṇā***, (collapse, ***baihṇā***) : hair, leaves, fruit, ***jharnā*** : evening, darkness, night, dew, drops of rain, ***paiṇā***.
fellow, ***peā hoeā***.
false, ***jhūṭhā*** : *see* deceitful : coin, ***khōṭā*** : forged, ***jāhlī*** : *see* mistake : f. story, ***gapp***, f. (***mārnī***).
falsely, ***kuṛī muccī***, ***jhūṭhī mūṭhī***.
fame, ***nā̃***, m. (na ne) : *see* famous.
familiar, too; cheeky, ***bhūhe h.*** or ***caṛhnā***.
family, ***ṭabbar***, m. : ***bāl bacce***, m. pl. : ***muṇḍe kuṛīā̃***, m. pl. : ***kabīlā***, m. (U.) : ***horī*** may be used, G. 82 : wide sense, ***khāndān***, m. : f.-man, ***bāl baccedār***, ***ṭabbarwāḷā*** : *see* tree.
famine, ***kāḷ***, m. : f.-allowance, ***maihṅgāī***, f. (pron. ***maṅghāī***), ***kaihtsāḷī***, f., ***kaiht***, m.
famous, ***mashāhūr***, ***manneā parwanneā***.
fan, ***pakkhā*** m. : *see* punkah.
fancy, silly, ***waihm***, m. : person w., ***waihmī***.

far, *see* distant : far side, *see* further.
fare, ***bhāṛā***, m. : ***karāyā***, m.
farewell, say f. to, ***widyā-k.*** (int. ***widyā h.***) : *see* leave, dismiss, salute.
farmer, (caste), ***jaṭṭ, jaṭṭ būṭ, zamīndār, wāhī karnwāḷā*** (actual farmer) : leg. ***kāshtkār.***
fast, *see* swift : tight, ***kasseā hoeā*** : of colour, ***pakkā.***
fast, n., ***rōzā***, m. (M.) : ***wart***, m. (H.) : keep f., ***rakkhṇā*** : break f. at wrong time, ***rōzā tōṛnā*** or ***bhannṇā*** ; at right time, ***rōzā kholhṇā.***
fasten, *see* tie, shut : button, ***bīrā*** or ***baṭaṇ mēḷnā*** or ***mārnā.***
fat, n., ***carbī***, f. : adj., ***mōṭā*** : *see* grease, corpulent.
fatal, ***marnwāḷā, jis thõ mar jāīdā e*** : *see* deadly.
fate, ***takdīr***, f. : ***kismat***, f. : ***nasīb***, m (all M.) : ***lēkh***, m. (H.).
fated, ***likheā hoeā.***
father, ***pyō, cācca*** : f. in law, ***sauhrā*** : married woman's f.'s house or family, ***pēke***, m. pl. (adj., ***pēkā***) : f. in law's f., ***dadiauhrā*** : f. in l.'s mother, ***dadēhas*** : f. in l.'s brother, ***patiauhrā, patrauhrā*** : ***patiauhrā's*** wife, ***patēhas*** : f. and mother of bridegroom are ***kuṛm*** and ***kuṛmṇi*** to f. and mother of bride, and vice versa.
fatigue, ***thakewā̃***, m. : *see* tired.
fault, ***kasūr***, m. : *see* mistake, defect, guiltless.
favour, ***ahsān*** (pron. ***as-hān***) m. : ***mehrbānī***, f. : out of deference to you, ***tērā lihāz karke*** : *see* grace.
favourtism, *see* partiality.
fear, n., ***ḍar***, m. : ***khauf***, m. : v., ***ḍarnā, saihmṇā*** : ***ḍar laggṇā*** or ***auṇā*** (***nū̃***) : (tr., ***ḍarāṇā***) : be afraid and confused, ***ghābbarnā***, (tr. ***ghabrāṇā***).
fearless, *see* venturesome.
feast, ***ziāfat***, f. : ***khāṇā***, m. : *see* festival, invitation.
February, ***farwarī***, f. : ***phaggaṇ***, m. (about Feb. 13 to Mar. 12).
fee, fees, ***fīs***, f. : entrance fee, ***dākhlā***, m.
feeble, ***māṛā, kamzōr*** : *see* weak, ill, delicate.
feed (v. tr.), ***khuāṇā*** (gen.) : poultry, int., ***cuggṛā*** (tr. ***cugāṇā***) : *see* graze. A.
feel, by touching, ***ṭohṇā, chohṇā, hatth lāṇā*** (***nū̃***) : *see* cold, hot, hunger, thirst : f. angry, etc., simply use *be* angry, etc. : f. pulse, ***nabz wēkhṇī.***
feeling, without f. in skin, etc., ***sunn*** : salvation not dependent on f., ***najāt es gall wicc nehī̃ pai sānū̃ baṛī khushī malūm howe yā̃ nā howe.***
fellow-countryman, ***watnī, mēre watan*** or ***dēs*** or ***piṇḍ dā.***
female, adj., ***zanānā*** : of sex (animals), ***madīn*** : *see* sex.
fence, *see* hedge, railing, enclose.
ferrel, at end of stick, ***shām***, f.
ferry, ***pattaṇ*** m. : f. -train, ***ṭhēllā***, m., ***ṭhehlā***, m.

fertile, *see* soil (good).
festival, ***id***, f. (M.) : ***tyohār***, m. (H.) : *see* holiday, keep.
fetch, *see* bring.
fetter, ***bēṛī***, f.
fever, ***kass***, f. : ***tāp***, m. : ***bukhār***, m. : get f., these words w ***caṛhnā*** (***nū̃***) : f. go off, ***laihṇā*** : f.-heat, ***bhakhā***, m. A.
few, ***thōṛe***, ***ṭā̃wā***, ***tāwā***, ***wirlā wirlā***, ***koī koī***, ***ghaṭṭ waddh*** (G. 28).
fez-cap, ***turkī ṭōpī***.
fiance, ***mangeā hoeā***.
fiancee, ***maṅg***.
fickle, *see* changeable, vacillate.
fie ! fie ! ***tobā tobā***.
field, ***paiḷī***, f. : ***khēt***, m. (U.) : part of, ***kiārā***, m. : division of arable land, ***waṇḍ***, f.
fierce, ***ḍāhḍī***, ***sakht***, ***waihshī***, ***ḍarāṇwāḷā muhāndrā*** (*see* face).
fife, ***wanjhḷī***, f. : ***bā̃srī***, f.
fifteen, ***pandrā̃*** : -th, ***pandhrawā̃*** : fifteen finger long shoe, ***pandhrī juttī*** : G. 19-24, 123.
fifty, ***panjāh*** : -one, ***ikwanjā*** : -two, ***bawanjā*** : -three, ***tarwanjā*** : -four, ***curinjā*** : -five, ***pacpach-wanjā*** : -six, ***chawinjā***, ***chiwanjā*** : -seven, ***salwanjā*** : -eight, ***aṭhwanjā*** : -nine, ***unāhṭh*** : ordinals add ***-wā̃***, 51 to 58 add also hightone h, ***ikwanjhawā̃***, etc., G. 19-24, 123.
fig, fruit, and tree, ***phagwāṛā***, m., ***phagwāṛī***, f., ***anjīr***, m.
fight, ***laṛnā*** : *see* quarrel : ***bhiṛnā*** (gen. of buffaloes) : n., ***laṛāī***, f.
figure, ***sūrat***, f. : ***shakl***, f. : in arithmetic, ***hinsā***, m. : *see* form, face.
file, n., ***rēṭī***, f. : v., ***rēṭṇā*** file papers, attach to file, ***natthī k.***
fill, ***bharnā*** : one's f., ***ḍhiḍḍh bhaṛke***.
filth, *see* dirt, dirty, rubbish.
final, ***chēkaṛlā***, ***ākhrī***, ***ōṛak dā***.
finally, ***chēkṛe***, ***chēkaṛ nū̃***, ***ōṛak nū̃***, ***nihait nū̃***, ***ākhar***.
find, ***labbh laiṇā*** : int. ***labbhṇā***, as ***menū̃ labbhā***, I. found it ; ***miḷṇā*** (***nū̃***) : f. out, *see* discover.
fine, n., ***ḍann***, m. : ***caṭṭī***, f. : ***jarimānā***, m. : impose, f., ***lāṇā***, int. ***laggṇā***.
fine, adj., *see* beautiful, good : not coarse, ***mhīn***, ***barīk*** : f. fellow (ironical) ***hazrat***, ***bātshāh***.
finger, ***uṅgaḷ***, f. : little f., ***cīccī***, f. : *see* thumb, toe.
finish, ***mukāṇā***, ***pūrā k.***, ***khatam k.***, ***nabēṛnā*** (settle) : ***bhugtāṇā*** (go through w.) : int. ***mukkṇā***, ***pūrā h.***, ***khatam h.***, ***nibbaṛnā***, ***bhugtṇā***. Also by adding to root of verb ***baihṇā***, ***raihṇā***, ***cukṇā***, ***haṭṇā*** ; G. 66 : or ***chaḍḍṇā***, ***dēṇā***, ***laiṇā***, ***suṭṭnā***, ***jāṇā***, G. 65, 110, 111 : it's all over, ***syāpā mukk geā***, ***khalāsī mukk gei*** : the food is finished, occ. ***waddh geā***, G. 114.
fire, n., ***agg***. f. : light f., ***agg bāḷṇī*** (int. ***baḷṇī***) : set on f., ***agglāṇī*** (***nū̃***, int. ***laggṇī***, catch f.) : *see* flame : slow fire, *see* slow.
fire, v., gun, etc., ***calāṇā*** : missile, ***mārnā***, ***calāṇā*** (bullet, arrow) : *see* stone, throw. A.

firefly, ***ṭaṭāṇā***, m. ***ṭanāṇā***, m.
fireplace, for fire or cooking, ***aṅgīṭhi***, f. : ***culhā***, m. fire wood, ***bāllaṇ*** (note ***l*** in ***bāḷṇā***, light).
fireworks, ***astbāzī***, f. : ***ātashbāzī***, f. : fire off f., ***calāṇā***, ***chaḍḍṇā***, int. ***calṇā***, ***chuṭṭṇā***.
firm, stand, fixed, ***ḍaṭṭṇā***.
first, ***paihlā*** : leader, ***āggū***, ***mohrlā*** : at f., ***paihlā̃***, ***paihlū̃***, ***paihle*** : at f. go off, ***paund***, ***paund saṭṭe*** : fr. the f., ***muṇḍhõ***, ***shurū tõ***.
firstborn, ***pahlēṭhī dā*** (pron. ***palēṭhi***, ***palēthi***).
fish, ***macchī***, f. : catch f., ***macchiā̃ phaṛniā̃***.
fisherman (water-carrying caste), ***māch-ī***, fem. ***-an*** (M.) : ***jhiūr-***, fem. ***-ī*** (H.).
fist, ***muṭṭh***, f., rarely ***muṭṭhī***, f. : close f., ***muṭṭh ghuṭṭnī*** : *see* handful
fit, v., key, *see* key : clothes, shoes, etc., ***pūrā auṇā*** or ***h.*** (***nū̃***).
fit, *see* able : f. for me, etc., ***de laik***, ***de jogā*** (G. 38) : ***de gōcrā*** (G. 38) : ***jogā*** w. infl. inf., G. 95 : *see* proper, suitable.
fitting, *see* suitable.
five, ***panj*** : fifth ***panjwā̃*** : G. 19-24 : fifth part, *see* time : two-fifths and three-fifths in land tenure, ***panj-duanjī***.
fix, in ground, ***gaḍḍṇā*** : f. day, date, *see* appoint.
flag, ***jhaṇḍā***, m. : small, ***jhaṇḍī***, f.
flame, ***lāṭ***, f. : ***lamb***, f. : ***bhāhm-baṛ***, m. : in lamp-chimney, ***lāṭ***, f. : flame up (lamp), ***lāṭ niklnī*** : fire, ***bhaṛk uṭṭhṇā***, ***bhāhmbaṛ uṭṭhṇā***.
flank, ***pāsā***, m. : of animal, ***wakkhī***, ***pāsā***.
flannel, ***falālain***, f.
flare up, *see* flame : get angry, ***gussā bhaṛknā*** (***dā***) : *see* angry.
flash, n., ***lishk***, f. : ***camak***, f. : ***jhalak***, m. : v., ***lishkṇā***, ***camkṇā***.
flat, ***caurā***, ***cairā*** : *see* level, plain.
flatter, ***cāplūsī karnī*** (***dī***).
flaw, *see* defect.
flax, ***aḷsī***, f.
flea, ***pissū***, m., ***pissū̃***, m.
fledgling, ***bōṭ***, m.
flee, *see* run.
flesh, ***mās***, m. ***gōsht*** or ***gōshat***, m. : for food, *see* meat, beef, mutton.
flexible, ***lifanwāḷā***.
flinch, ***sī karnī***.
float, ***pāṇī utte tarnā***.
flock, sheep, goats, ***ijjar***, m. : birds, ***ḍār***, m. : ***taraṇḍā***, m. : *see* herd, swarm.
flog, ***kōṭle mārne*** (***nū̃***).
flood, ***kāṅg***, f. : ***haṛh***, m. : Noah's f., ***Nūh nadī***, f. : ***Nūh dī parlō***, f.
floor, ***farsh***, m.
flour, *see* meal.
flourish, town, etc., ***baṛī rauṇak***, etc.
flower, ***phull***, m. : v., ***phullṇā*** of crops, vegetables, ***nissarnā***.
flower-bed, ***khēḷ***, f., ***kiarī***, f.
flower-pot, ***gamḷā***, m.
fluctuate, ***waddhṇā ghaṭṇā***.

fluent, ***far far karke boldā e.***
flute, ***wanjhḷī***, f. : ***bā̃srī***, f. : double f., ***jōṛī*** f.
flutter, ***phaṛkṇā*** : of distress, ***taṛafṇā.***
fly, ***uḍḍṇā.***
fly, n., ***makkhī***, f. : blue bottle, ***makkh***, m.
foal, ***wacherā***, m.
foam, ***jhagg*** f.
fodder, ***paṭṭhe***, m. pl. : ***paṭṭhā datthā***, m. : very common kinds, ***maiṇā***, m., ***sinjī***, f.
fog, ***dhundh***, f. (mist) : ***gaihr*** or ***ghaihr***, m. (haze).
fold, v., make f. in, ***bhann pāṇī*** (***wicc***), ***bhannṇā*** (***nū̃***) : f. in folds, ***taih-k.*** : roughly ***kaṭṭhā k.***, ***ṭhappṇā*** : f. double, ***dohrā k.***, treble, ***trehrā k.***, four fold, ***cauhrā k.*** : above four, ***ehde panj***, ***chetaih kar***, (or fem., ***ehdiā̃ taihā̃***), fold it five, six fold : f. up, ***waḷhēṭṇā*** : *see* wrap, single.
fold, n., in cloth, paper, ***bhann***, f. : sheep, etc., ***wāṛā***, m.
follow, ***magar jāṇā***, ***picche jāṇā*** : worryingly, ***magar paiṇā*** : f. Christ or relig. leader, ***pairwī karnī*** (***dī***) : f. Christ, ***Masīh de magar magar jāṇā.***
follower, ***murīd*** (M.) : ***cēllā*** (H.) ***mannaṇwāḷā.***
folly, *see* foolishness.
forment, limb, ***sēk karnā*** (***nū̃***), *see* toast (contrast word).
fond-, -ness, *see* like, desire.
fondle, ***lāḍ k.*** (***nū̃***) : ***pyār*** d. (***nū̃***) : *see* love, spoilt.
food, ***khāṇā***, m. : ***ṭukkar***, m. : ***ṭukkar cappā***, m. : ***rōṭī***, f. : ***bhōjaṇ***, m. (H.) : ***ann pāṇī***, m. : ***bhattā***, m. (midday meal taken to workers) : *see* diet : special for cattle, ***gutāwā***, m. (mixture of straw, chaff, oilcake, water, meal) : for horses, ***nihārī***, f.
fool, ***aihmak***, ***aihmakh̲***, ***bewakūf*** (last never to be used in address), ***balēllaṛ***, ***wāhyāt***, ***bā-*** or ***mat-*** or ***hōsh-*** or ***aklmāreā***, ***jhallā*** : *see* mad, ignorant, stupid.
foolishness, ***bewakūfī***, f. : ***jhallpuṇā***, m. : ***beaklī***, f. : ***nadānī***, f.
foot, ***pair***, m.. w. claws, ***panjā***, m. : *see* paw, claw : crooked footed, ***phiḍḍā*** : on f., ***ṭurdā***, ***paidal*** (U.) : fall at one's feet, ***carnī̃ diggṇā***, ***pairī̃ paiṇā*** : footfall, ***pairā̃ dā khaṛāk*** : f. of bed, ***puāndī***, f. : feet of bed, table, etc., *see* leg : f. of page, ***hēṭhḷā pāsā***, m.; *see* bottom : f. of 12 inches, ***fuṭ***, ***fiṭ***, m. : *see* rule, tiptoe, wts. and meas.
fop, ***bāṅkā***, ***shukīn***, ***jĕṇṭalmaiṇ*** : ***ākkaṛ kh̲ā̃.***
for, ***nū̃***, ***wāste***, ***laī***, ***kh̲ātar***, ***jogā***, ***gōcrā*** : *see* behalf, suitable, sake : gone for milk, ***duddh nū̃ geā*** : for of price, ***tõ***, ***thõ***, ***thī̃***, G. 89, or loc. G. 9,11, 78.
forbid, ***manā k.*** : *see* hinder, stop : forbidden food, etc., ***harām*** or use ***saũh***, oath : M. 107. 17-9.
force, n., *see* power, oppression, effort : by f., ***bado badī***, ***maḷo maḷī***, ***zōrī***, ***zōro zōrī***,

zabardastī, *majbur karke*, *majburī gall*, *kārī gall*, *dhakke nāḷ* : f.-ed. labour, *wagār*, f. *wagyār*, f. : f.-ed labourer, *wagārī*, *wagyārī*.
force, v. tr., *majbūr k.*, or causal, v.w. word for "by force," G. 110 : f. him to do. *oh de kōḷõ zōre karā*, etc. : *see* cause.
forenoon, about 8 or 9, *chāhwēḷā* : 10, *kūḷā bhattewēḷā* : 11, *bhaṭṭewēḷā* : 10 or 11, *rōṭī wēḷā* : *see* noon, morning.
forehead, *matthā*, m.
foreign, *horī mulkh dā*, *pardesī*, *ōprā*, *parāyā* : *see* strange.
foreknowledge, *see* prescience.
foremost, *āggū*, *mohrlā* : *see* first.
foresight, *dūrandesh-ā*, m., *-ī*, f.
forest, *ujāṛ*, m., *jaṅgaḷ*, m.
forged, *jāhlī*.
forgery, *jāhlsāzī*, f.
forget, *wisārnā*, *wissarnā*, *bhullṇā* ; last two mean forget of person, or be forgotten of thing. A.
forgetfulness, *see* mistake.
forgive, *muāf k.*, *bakhshṇā chaḍḍṇā*, *jāṇ d.*, *muāfī dēṇī*.
fork, for table, *kāṇṭā*, m. : f.-ed. stick, *dusāṅghī*, f. : f.-ed. tree, *dusāṅghā*.
form, *shakl*, f. : *ḍauḷ*, f. : outline of body, *but*, m. : *see* shape, face, appearance, system.
former, *see* previous.
formerly, *see* before.
fornicat-ion, -or, *see* adulter-y, -er.
fort, *kilhā*, m.
fortification, *kilābandī*, f.
fortress, *see* fort.
fortunate, *karmā̃wāḷā*, *caṅgeā̃ bhāgā̃wāḷā* (H.), *nasīb caṅge*, *kismat caṅgī* : *see* auspicious, unfortunate.
fortune, *see* fate : good f., *khush-kismatī*, f., *khush-nasībī*, f : *caṅge nasīb*, m. pl. : bad, *badkismatī* or *badnasībī*, f. : *bure nasīb*.
fortune-teller, *najūmī*, *ramḷī*, *jōtshī*, *majūsī*.
forty, *cāḷī* : -one, *iktāḷī* : -two *batāḷī* : -three, *tartāḷī* : -four, *cutāḷī* : -five, *paitāḷī* : -six, *chatāḷī* : -seven, *saitāḷī* : -eight, *aṭhtāḷī* : -nine, *uṇwañjā* : ordinals and *-wā̃* w. high tone h, *cāhḷīwā̃*, *iktāhḷīwā̃*, *uṇwañjhawā̃*, G. 19-24, 123.
forward, *agā̃*, *agge* : *see* before : cheeky, *athrā*, *ḍhīṭh* : *see* impertinent, familiar.
forwardness, *see* boldness.
foundation, *nī̃h*, f. : *bunyād*, f. (latter word also metaphorical)
founder, *bānī*.
foundling, *lawāris* (without owner).
fountain, *see* spring : artificial, *phuhārā*.
four, *cār* : -th, *cauthā* : fourth part, *see* time.
fourteen, *caudā̃* : -th, *cauhdawā̃* : G. 19-24, 123 : fourteen finger long shoe, *caudhī juttī*.
fowl, for table, *kukkaṛ*, fem. *kukkṛī* : *see* cock, hen, chicken.
fox, *lūmb-aṛ*, fem. *-ṛī*.
frame, for door, picture, *cugāṭh*,

f. : hanging f., for clothes, ***taṅgṇā***, m.
fraud, *see* deceit, clever.
free, adj., ***azād*** : v. tr., ***chuḍāṇā***, ***chaḍḍṇā*** *: see* leisure, gratis, liberty, release. A.
freeze, ***jammṇā*** : hands, feet, *see* cold
frequented, to be, of road, ***wagṇā***.
frequently, *see* often, repeatedly.
fresh, ***sajrā***, ***tāzā*** : green, ***harā***.
fretful, *see* irritable.
friction, *see* discord : use, ***aṛnā***, ***khaihke laṅghṇā***, ***ragoṛke laṅghṇā***.
Friday, ***jumā***, m. : ***sukkar***, ***shukkar***, ***sukkarwār***, ***shukkarwār***, (last four H.).
friend, ***sajjaṇ***, ***mittar***, ***dōst***, ***yār*** (only one man of another), ***bēlī*** : see companion.
friendship, ***dōstī***, f. : ***yārī***, f. (between men) : strong f., ***gūṛhī dōstī*** : make friends w., ***dōstī***, ***yārī***, ***pyār***, m., all w. ***pānā*** and ***nāḷ*** (int. ***paiṇā***, ***nāḷ***) : M. 120. 27 : 243. 5 : ***dōstī rakkhṇī*** (***nāḷ***), be friendly w.
frighten, *see* fear.
frill, ***jhālar***, f.
from, ***tõ***, ***thõ***, ***thī***, ***-õ***, G. 13, 36, 37, 88, 89 : fr. person, animal, ***koḷō***.
front, in, adv. ***agge***, ***mohre***, ***agēre*** : adj., ***mohrlā*** : prep. ***sāhmṇe*** : *see* face, forward, before.
frost, hoar, ***korā-kakkar***, m. : *see* freeze.
frontier, ***sarhadd***, f. : adj., ***sarhaddī***.
froth, ***jhagg***, f.
frown, ***treoṛhiā̃*** or ***ghurākiā̃*** or ***ghūriā̃***, all with ***waṭṭṇiā̃*** : ***ghūrke wekhṇā***, look angrily : *see* angry.
frozen, *see* freeze.
fruit, ***phaḷ***, m. : raisins, etc., ***mewā***, m.
fruitful ***phaḷwāḷā***.
fruitless, tree, ***apphaḷ*** : *see* useless, vain.
fryingpan, ***fraipān***, m. (***K.***), Indian, ***kaṛāḷī***, f.
fuel, *see* firewood.
fugitive, ***nasseā hoeā***.
fulfil, *see* finish.
full, ***bhareā hoeā*** : f. of Holy Spirit, ***Pāk Rūh nāḷ bhareī hoeā*** : f. brother, etc., ***sakkā***
fumigate, ***dhūkh*** or ***dhūf dēṇā*** : ***guggaḷ dhukhāṇā*** : ***gandhak*** (sulphur) ***dhukhāṇī*** : *see* disinfect.
fun, *see* entertainment.
funeral, ***janāzā***, m. (***paṛhnā***).
funnel (engine, steamer, brickkiln), ***cimṇī***, f.
fur, ***jatt***, f.
furious, ***baṛe gusse wicc***, ***bhakheā hoeā*** : *see* anger, rage.
furlong, ***farlāṅg***, m.
furnace (with boiler) ***bhaṭṭhī***, f. : for sugarcane juice, ***cumbā***, m.
furrow, including ridge, ***siār***, m. : ***raihḷ***, f.
furniture, ***mēz kursiā̃***, f. pl.,

asbāb, m. : old f.-seller, ***kuāṛiā***, ***kabāṛiā***.
further, ***zyādā dūr***, ***waddh dūr***, ***paiṇḍā waddh e*** : on far side, ***parlā***, ***pailā*** : ***parle*** or ***paile pāse*** : *see* distant : moreover, ***nāḷe***.
fuss, ***raṭṭā*** or ***rēṛkā pāṇā*** (int. ***paiṇā***) : *see* disturbance, quarrel.
future, ***agge nū̃***, ***agge wāste***.

G

gain, *see* advantage, profit, obtain, earn, reach, succeed, win.
gait, ***ṭōr***, f. : ***eāl***, f.
gale, *see* storm.
galled, be (horse ass, mule) ***lāggā laggṇā*** (***nū̃***) : M. 121. 14.
gallop, gentle, ***poīā turnā*** : vigorous, ***sarpaṭṭ turnā***. A.
gallows, ***sūḷī***, f. : *see* hang, crucify.
gamble, ***jūā khēḍṇā*** : gambling, ***jūā***, m.
gambler, ***juāria***, m.
game (gen.), ***khēḍ***, f. : single g. or match, ***bāzī***, f. : win g., ***bāzī jittṇī*** : lose g., ***bāzī hārnī***, ***bāzī ohde sir hōṇī***, ***bāzī caṛhnī*** (***nū̃***, M. 118. 24).
gaol, *see* prison.
gap, ***khappā***, m., ***witth***, f.
garden, ***bāg***, m. : public g., ***kaumpnī bāg*** : g.-walk, ***rāk***, m. : g.-bed, ***khēḷ***, f. : ***kiārī***, f.
gardener, ***māl-ī***, fem. ***-aṇ*** : caste, ***arāī̃***, fem. ***arain*** ; ***maihr-***, fem. ***-ī***.
garlic, ***thōm***, f.
garrulous, *see* talkative
gasp, in death, ***saihkṇā*** : *see* pant ; breath, out of.
gate, ***phāṭak***, m. : *see* door.
gather, *see* collect, infer.
gender, ***jiṇs***, f.
general, n., ***jarnail***.
general, adj., ***ām***, ***mamūlī***.
generally, ***aksar***, ***ām***, ***bauht karke***.
generation, ***pīṛhī***, f.
generosity, ***sak͟hāwat***, f. (U.).
generous, ***sak͟hī***.
genius, ***pujjke akl-wālā*** : *see* sense.
gentle, no good word, ***sharīf***, ***ashrāf***, ***bhalāmāṇas*** : animal, ***garīb***, ***sāū***.
gently, ***saihje saihje***, ***saihe saihe***, ***saihje nāḷ***, ***saihe nāḷ***, ***hauḷī hauḷī*** : *see* quitely, slowly : speak g. ***hauḷī***, ***nimmhī***.
gentleman, ***sāhb***, ***sharīf***, ***sharīf*** or ***ucce k͟hāndān dā*** : *see* gentle.
genuine, *see* real.
get, *see* obtain : g. something done, *see* cause.
ghee, ***ghyō***, m., occ. ***thindhā*** m., ***cōpaṛ***, m.
ghost, ***bhūt***, m., ***jinn***. m. (M.) : Holy Ghost : *see* spirit.
giant, no word, ***baṛā lammā***, etc.
gibberish, ***ẽwẽ bakṇā***.
gibe, *see* taunt.
giddy, *see* dizzy.
gift, to superior, ***nazr***, f., ***dhoā***, m., ***ḍāhḷī***, f. : to inferior, ***ināṃ***, m., ***bak͟hshīsh***, f.
gild, ***mulammā-k***. : ***gilṭ-k***.

ginger, ***adhrak***, f. : ***sundh***, f. (dry).
girdle, *see* belt, griddle.
girl, ***kuṛī***, ***kākkī***, ***jātkṛī***, ***laṛkī*** : occ. ***bālṛī*** : European, ***miss bāwā*** : *see* daughter.
girth, of saddle, ***taṅg***, m.
gist, ***khulāsā***, m. : ***matlab***, m.
give, ***dēṇā*** (pa. p. ***dittā***), ***bakhshṇā*** : g. in, admit defeat, ***hār mannṇī*** : lose heart, *see* discourage.
glad, ***khush***, ***rāzī***.
gladly, ***khushī nāḷ***, ***khush*** or ***rāzī hōke***.
glance, at book, letter, etc., ***nazr mārnī*** (***te***) : just a g., ***sarsarī nazr***, f.
glass, ***kac***, f. : ***shīshā***, m. : drinking g., ***gilās***, m. : *see* mirror, drinking vessel.
glimmer, ***thōṛī lishk*** or ***camak***, f.
glimpse, get g. of, ***zarā nazrī paiṇā*** (***ohdī***, &c.).
globe, of lamp, ***hāndī***, f.
glory, ***jalāl***, m. : *see* splendour.
glove, ***dastānā***, m. : G. 74.
glowworm, ***ṭaṭāṇā***, m., ***ṭanāṇā***, m.
glue, ***saṛēsh***, ***gūnd*** f. : v., ***sarēsh lāṇī***, ***sarēsh nāḷ jōṛnā*** : *see* gum, paste.
gnash teeth, ***dand pīhṇē*** : *see* frown.
glutton, *see* greedy.
gnaw, of rodents, ***kutarnā***, ***ṭukkṇā*** : bone (dog), ***khāṇā*** : crunch, ***kuṛkāṇā***.
go, ***jāṇā*** (pa. p. ***geā***), ***ṭurnā***, ***calṇā*** ; g. away, ***ṭur jāṇā wag jāṇā***, *see* rise : g. out, ***nikḷnā***, ***banne jāṇā*** : g. in, ***waṛnā*** : *see* start. walk. off.
goad, ox-, wooden, ***parāṇī***, f.: v., ***parāṇī nāḷ hujj mārnī*** (***nū̃***) ***ār lānī*** ; *see* prod : metaph., see incite, urge.
goal, football. -hockey, polo, etc., ***gōl***, m. : *see* aim, object.
goat, ***bakr-ā***, fem. ***-ī*** : long-haired, ***kāgānī bakrā*** adj., ***bākrā*** : *see* kid.
gobble, *see* devour.
God, ***Khudā***, ***Rabb***, ***Maulā*** (all M.) : ***Parmēshwar***, ***Ishwar***, ***Bhagwān*** (H.) : god, ***māhbūd***, m. (object of worship, M.), ***dēotā***, m. (H.).
goddess, ***dēwī***.
goitre, ***gillhaṛ***, m. : man w.g., ***gillhaṛwāḷā***.
gold, ***syōnā***, m. : ***sōnā***, m. golden, ***syōne dā***.
goldsmith, ***sunyārā***.
gong, *see* bell.
good, ***caṅgā***, ***acchā***, ***umdā***, ***wall***, ***baṛā waddhiā*** : ***kharā*** (genuine) : of character, ***caṅgā***, ***acchā***, ***nēk***, ***bhalāmānas***, ***ashrāf*** : of soil, *see* soil : coin, *see* coin : *see* excellent, very : interj., ***caṅgī gall***, ***kharī gall*** n., God seeks our good, welfare, ***bhalā***, m. : *see* welfare.
goodness, ***nēkī***, f. : ***bhaleāī***, f. : ***bhalmans-āī***, f., ***-aū***, m.
goodbye, *see* farewell.
goods, ***asbāb***, m. : ***laṭar paṭar***, m. : ***nikk sukk***, m. : *see* property bag and baggage.

gooseberry, cape, ***ṭipārī***, f.
Gospel, ***Injīl***, f. : ***Anjīl***, f. (the book) : G. message, ***najāt, dī khabar***, f.
gossip, *see* conversation, chatter.
govern, ***hukūmat karnī, bādshāhī karnī, rāj karnā.***
governor, ***hākim*** : Lieutenant G., ***lāṭ sāhb.***
grace, ***fazl***, m. (M.) : ***dayā***, f. (H.) ***kirpā***, f. (H.).
gradually, ***hundeā̃ hundeā̃, hundeā̃ hawāndeā̃.***
graft, n. (plant), ***pyōnd-karnā.***
grain, ***dāṇā*** m. : ***dāṇā phakkā*** : wheat and barley, ***gōjī***, f. : wheat, barley and gram, ***bērṛā***, m. : receptacle for, ***bhaṛohlā***, m., ***bhaṛohlī***, f. ***kōṭhī***, f.
gram, ***chōlle***, m. pl.
granary, *see* grain.
granddaughter, son's daughter, ***pōtrī*** : daughter's, ***dohtrī.*** *see* grandson
grandfather, paternal, ***dāddā*** : maternal, ***nānnā*** : ***dāddā's*** father, ***paṛdāddā*** : ***dāddā's*** mother, ***paṛdāddī*** : ***nānnā's*** father, ***paṛnānnā*** : ***nānnā's*** mother, ***paṛnānnī*** : ***dāddā's*** house or family, ***dādke***, m. pl. : ***nānnā's*** house or family, ***nāṇke***, m. pl. : adjj., ***dādkā nāṇkā.***
grandmother, paternal, ***dāddī*** : maternal, ***nānnī.***
grandson, son's son, ***pōtrā*** : daughter's son, ***dohtrā*** : ***potrā's*** son, ***paṛpōtrā*** : ***potrā's*** daughter, ***paṛpōtrī*** : ***dohtrā's*** : son, ***paṛdohtrā*** : ***dohtrā's*** daughter, ***pardohtrī.***
grant-in-aid, ***grāṇṭ***, f. : ***imdād***, f. : in receipt of g. (institution), ***imdādī.***
grant, *see* allow, give.
grape, tree and fruit, ***dākh***, m. : ***aṅgūr***, m.
grasp, ***hatth nāḷ phaṛnā*** or ***phagaṛnā.***
grass, ***ghāh***, m. : special kinds, ***khabbaḷ***, m. : ***ḍīḷā***, m. : ***dabb***, f.
grasshopper, ***triḍḍ***, m., ***triḍḍī***, f.
grateful, ***dā shukrguzār*** : *see* thank.
grating, small iron, ***janjriā̃***, f. pl., ***jhajjriā̃***, f. pl. : larger bars, ***jharne***, m. pl.
grat-is, -uitous, ***muft, mukhat, muft dā.***
grave, M. ***kabr***, f. : saint's ***khāngāh***, f. : H. ***marhī***, f. : ***samādh***, f.
grave, *see* serious, sober.
graveyard, ***kabristān***, m.
gravel, single stone, ***giṭī***, f. : collective, ***bajrī***, f., ***kaṅkrī***, f. : *see* pebble.
gravy, ***grēbbī***, f. (K.)
graze, v. int. ***cugṇā, chiṛnā*** (go out to g.) : tr. ***cārnā, cugāṇā, chēṛnā.***
grease, ***thindheāī***, f. : ***ciknāī***, f. (both words mean greasiness) : *see* fat.
greasy, ***thindhā, ciknā.***
great, of size, age, dignity, ***waḍḍā***, otherwise ***baṛā*** : *see* very : G. 34.
greed- -y; *see* covet-, -ous : ***ohdī nazr bhukkhī e.*** : great eater, ***baṛā khāū*** or ***khāṇwāḷā.***

green, ***harā.***
greengrocer (woman) ***araiṇ*** f. : *see* gardener.
greenhorn, ***aṇāṇā, siddhā, kaccā, allhaṛ.***
greenness, ***hareaul,*** f.
greet, *see* welcome, salute.
gregarious, ***kaṭṭhe raihṇwāḷe.***
grey, *see* brown : green grey, ***sāwā*** : of hair, *see* hair.
greyhound, ***tāzī kuttā.***
griddle, girdle, ***tawā,*** m. : ***tajāl,*** m.
grief, ***du͟kh,*** m. : ***jhorā,*** m. : ***afsōs,*** m. : ***gam,*** m. : ***ranj,*** m. (all w.h., ***afsōs*** also w. k).
grieve, ***jhurnā*** : (***dā***) ***dil du͟khī hōṇā*** : tr. ***dil du͟khāṇā*** (***dā***) : *see* regret.
grimace, make to annoy, ***cinghē lāṇe*** : ***ḍandīā̃ cinghāṇīā̃*** : bad taste in mouth, etc., ***bhaiṛā mū̃h banāṇā.***
grin, ***dand kaḍḍhṇe, mū̃h aḍḍṇā, guṭak paiṇā.***
grind, fine, ***pīhṇā*** (int. ***pīsṇā***) : coarse, ***dalṇā*** : g.-ing board, ***sīḷ,*** f. : roller, ***waṭṭā,*** m. : *see* mill, grindstone, pin.
grindstone (for knives, etc.) ***sāṇ,*** f. : v., ***sāṇ te lāṇā.***
grizzled, *see* hair.
groan, ***aṛāṇā hūṅgṇā.***
grocer, ***pasār-ī*** fem. ***-an.***
groom, ***sīs*** (often pron. w. low tone, ***s-hīs***).
groove, ***nāḷī,*** f.
ground, ***zamīn,*** f. (***zimī̃, jīwī̃, jiwī̃***) : on the g., ***bhuñē, bhūē*** : *see* soil, foundation.
groundless, ***ehdī bunyād koī nehī̃***
grow, ***waddhṇā*** : plants, ***uggṇā,*** begin to grow : *see* sprout.
growl, ***hūṅgṇā.***
grudge, *see* envy.
grudgingly, *see* reluctant.
grumble, ***ū̃ ū̃ karnī, kuṛhnā, buṛ buṛ*** or ***bhus bhus karnī.***
guard, ***rakhwālī*** or ***rākhī karnī*** : ***caukīdārī karnī*** : protect, ***hifāzat karnī*** (all ***dī***) : be on g. against, ***ohde wallō hushyār raihṇā*** : *see* preserve, save.
guard, in train, ***gāḍ,*** *see* sentry.
guardian, of things, ***rākkhā, rakhwālā, caukīdār*** : of persons, ***sarprast, walī wāris*** : leg. ***wāris,*** *see* saviour.
guess, ***tukk lāṇī*** : ***ṭewā lāṇā*** : g. prove correct, ***tukk ṭhīk wajjṇī*** : *see* calculate, estimate, approximately.
guest, ***parauhṇā,*** m.
guide, ***rāh dassṇā*** or ***wa͟khāṇā*** set one on one's way, ***rāhe pāṇā.***
guilt, ***jurm,*** m. : *see* fault.
guiltless, ***bēgunāh, bēkasūr,*** *see* innocent, acquit.
guilty, ***mujram, kasūrwār.***
guitar, ***sitār,*** f. : *see* plectrum.
gulf, ***k͟halīj,*** m.
gum, ***gūnd,*** f. : v., ***gūnd lāṇī, gūnd nāḷ jōṛnā*** : *see* paste, glue
gum (mouth), ***masūṛā, phaḍ,*** m. (gen. plur.).
gun, ***bandūk,*** f., (***calāṇī,*** int. ***calṇī***) : *see* fire.
gunpowder, ***barūd,*** m.

gush (water) ***zōr nāḷ wagṇā.***
gust, *see* storm.
gutter, *see* drain.
gyve, *see* handcuff.

H

habit, ***biṭlar***, f., ***gējh***, f. ***wādī***, f., ***ādat***, f., (all with ***paiṇī***) : *see* custom : make h. of, special verbal construction, G. 68, 69 : ***gazā pakk jāṇī*** (***dī***) : *see* accustomed.
haggle, ***mull dī bābat jhagaṛnā.***
hail, n., ***candrā***, m., ***gaṛā***, m., ***aihn***, f.
hair, ***wāḷ***, m. (single h.) : very fine hair on body, each hair, ***lū̃***, m. : fur, ***jatt***, f. (also goat's h. etc.) : long hair, ***chatte***, m. pl. : plaited lock, ***mēḍhī***, f., ***mēṇḍhī***, f. : curl, (special kind), ***kalam***, f. : Sikkh's hair, ***kēs***, m. : Hindu's lock, ***bōddī***, f. : white hair, ***dhauḷe***, (***auṇe***, M. 117. 10), ***ciṭṭe*** or ***bagge wāḷ*** : grey, ***karr barre*** or ***karṛ barṛ wāḷ***, m. pl. : do one's h. ***wāḷ suārne.***
hairless (on face) ***khōddā*** : beard, etc. not yet grown, ***alū̃*** : *see* bald.
half, ***addhā***, ***addh*** : h. and h., ***addh pacaddh***, approximately ; ***addho addh***, exactly : in land tenure, ***adhiāre te*** : h. way, ***adhwāṭe*** : 1½, 2½, *see* one, two : above 2, ***sāḍhe*** w. number, G. 23 : *see* halve.
hall, in school, etc., ***hāl***, m. : in house, ***hāl kamrā***, m.
halo, round moon, ***piṛ***, m., ***cann piṛ malleā hoeā e.***
halt, ***makām karnā***, ***rāt raihṇā.***
halter, esp. cattle, ***mohrak***, f. : horse, ***talihārā***, m.
halve, ***addho addh karnā.***
hammer, ***hathauṛā***, m. : wooden, ***muṅghlī***, f. : sledge h., ***wadān***, m.
hammer, v., pegs, nails, ***ṭhōknā*** : poles, ***gaḍḍnā.***
hand, ***hatth***, m. : without one or both h., ***ṭuṇḍā*** : h. of watch, clock, ***sūī***, f. : by h. ***dastī*** : *see* tie.
hand, v., ***phaṛāṇā***, ***dēṇā*** : ***leā*** (imperat. only).
handbreadth, ***cappā***, m.
handcuff, ***hatthkaṛī***, f., ***kaṛī***, f.
handful, single, ***lapp***, f. : double, ***bukk***, m. : fistful, ***muṭṭh***, f. rarely ***muṭṭhī***, f.
handkerchief, ***rumāl***, m.
handle, w. hole through it, of cup, dish, ***kuṇḍā***, m. : button of lid, ***ḍūḍḍaṇ***, m. : latch -h., ***lāṭū*** m. : others, ***hatthā***, m., ***hatthī***, f. : ***muṭṭh***, f. : ***dastā***, m. : cloth catch of ***chikk***, ***khūṭī***, f., ***khuṭṭī***, f.
handsome, *see* beautiful.
hand, v. tr., ***ṭaṅgṇā***, ***lamkāṇā*** (int. ***lamkṇā***) : h. person, ***phāhe*** d. (***nū̃***) : h. oneself, ***phāh laiṇā*** : h. -ing frame for clothes, ***ṭaṅgṇā*** m. : hanging, ***lamkdā***, ***ṭaṅgeā hoeā.***
happen, ***kōṇā***, ***bītṇā.***
happy, ***khush***, ***rāzī.***
harass, *see* annoy.

harbour, ***bandargāh***, f.
hard, ***ḍāhḍā***, ***sakht***.
hardly, *see* scarcely, difficulty.
hare, ***saihā***, ***sehā***, m. : also rabbit.
harm, *see* injure, loss, hurt.
harmless, *see* guiltless, innocent : also harm w. neg.
harmony, *see* tune, agreement.
harness, ***sāz***, m. (***lāṇā*** int. ***laggṇā***) : v., also ***jōṇā*** (int. ***juttṇā***, ***juppṇā***).
harrow, ***suhāggā***, m. (***phērnā***, int. ***phirnā***).
harsh, *see* hard, rough.
harvest, ***fasl.*** m. : *see* reap.
haste, n., ***kāhḷ***, f. : ***tāṛ***, f. : ***utauḷī***, f. : *see* impatien-ce,-t.
hasten, ***kāhḷ*** or ***chēti*** or ***shtābi*** or ***jaldī*** all w. ***karnī*** : ***kāhḷā*** or ***utauḷā ṭurnā*** : *see* headlong.
hasty, ***kāhḷā***, ***utauḷā*** : ***jaldbāz*** (bad sense).
hat, ***ṭōpi***, f.
hatch, ***bacce kaḍḍhṇe***.
hatchet, ***kuhāṛī***, f. : *see* axe
hate, ***wair rakkhṇā*** : ***dushmaṇī rakkhṇī*** : *see* dislike, disgust, envy.
haught-iness, -y. : *see* pride, proud.
haul, *see* pull.
have, ***de kōḷ h.*** : *see* keep : to h. to, inf. w. agent, G. 75, 97 : or inf. w. ***paiṇā*** or aux. v. w. ***hōṇā***, G. 96, 97 : have something done, *see* cause : *see* possession.
hawker, ***chābṛīwāḷā***.
haze, *see* fog.
he, ***eh***, ***oh*** : his her, ***ehdā***, ***ohdā*** : also ***s***, ***sū***, G. 82-6 : to him, her, ***ehnū̃***, ***ohnū̃***, also ***s***, ***sū***, G. 82-6.
head, ***sir***, m. : of inanimate things, ***sirā***, m. : sheep, goat, for eating, ***sirī***, f. : bed, ***sarhāndī***, f. : door, ***sērū***, m. : of canal ***hĕḍḍ***, m.
heading, *see* title.
headlong, on one's head, ***sir parne*** : h. flight, paraphrase, as ***khurī karke*** or ***annhe wāh*** or ***khiṭṭ dēke bhajj jāṇā***.
headman, ***caudhrī*** : of village, ***lambaṛdār*** : *see* lead-, -er.
headquarters, ***hĕḍkuāṭar***, m. : ***mukh-daftar*** of canal, *see* head.
headstrong, *see* obstinate
heal, *see* cure, treat.
health, ***tandrustī***, f. ***séht***, f.
healthy, ***wall***, ***caṅgā***, ***acchā***, ***tandrust***.
heap, ***ḍhēr***, m., ***ḍhērī***, f. : of sugarcane, straw, chaff, plastered over, ***dhaṛ***, f. : *see* wood.
hear, ***suṇṇā*** : ***suṇāī dendā e***, he, she, they, etc., can hear : M. 238. 19.
hearing, of lawcase, ***pēshī***, f.
hearsay, ***suṇī suṇāī gall***, f.
heart, ***dil*** or ***diḷ***, m. (lit. and gen.) : ***man***, m.
heartily, ***dilõ wajhõ hōke***, ***dil nāḷ***
heat, ***garmī***, f. : ***tā***, m. (of fire) : fever h., ***bhakhā***, f. : pungent heat, *see* hot : v. tr., ***garm k.***, ***tāṇā*** ; ***tā pāṇā***, put burning coal into fire : ***tā d.***, make coal burn up : become very hot (of fire),

see blaze and add tr. ***bhakhāṇā*** : *see* slow (fire), hot (fire).

heaven, ***bihist***, m. (gen.) : ***surg***, m. (H.) ***suwarg***, m.

heavy, ***bhārā***.

hedge, ***wāṛ***, f., *see* railing, enclose.

hedgehog, ***jhāh cūhā***, m.

heel, ***aḍḍī***, f.

height, ***ucāī***, f. : of person, ***ucāī***, ***lamāī***, f. : ***masātar***, f., height to tips of fingers above had (to estimate depth of water).

heir, ***wāris***, m.

hell, ***dozakh***, m. and ***jahannam***, m. (M.) : ***nark***, m (H.).

help, v., ***madat***, f. (***k.***, ***dī*** : ***d.***, ***nū̃***) : ***hatth pharnā*** (***dā***) : also caus. of v. w. dat. of pers. and acc. of thing. G. 109 : without assistance, by himself, without being told to, ***ā pū̃***, ***āpe***, ***āpī***, ***āpõ*** G. 88.

helper, ***wasīlā***, m. : ***madadgār***, m.

helpless, ***lacār***, ***wacārā***.

hemorrhoids, ***bawāsīr*** f., bleeding, ***khūnī***.

hemp, ***saṇ***, f. : ***saṇkukṛā***, m. : ***sūjjo-*** or ***sajjo-bhārā***. m. : intoxicating h., ***bhaṅg***, f., ***cars***, f.

hen, ***kukkṛī***, f.

hence, ***ētthõ***, ***ēttalõ***, ***edharõ***.

henceforth, ***edū̃ agge***, ***agge nū̃***.

her, *see* he.

herb, medicinal, ***būṭī***, f.

herd, cattle, ***wagg***, m. : *see* flock.

herdsman, ***wāggī***, ***chēṛū***, ***ḍāṅgrī***, *see* shepherd.

here, ***ētthe***, ***ēttal***, ***eddhar*** : ***ure*** or ***urhā̃*** (gen. of motion alone) : here it is, ***āh***, ***wekhā̃*** : h. and there, ***kitale kitale***, ***kite kite***, ***kidhare kidhare***.

hereditary, ***maurūsī***.

hero, ***bahādar*** : *see* brave.

hesitate, ***shakk wicc raihṇā***, ***ḍōlṇā***, ***ḍāwā̃ ḍōl raihṇā*** : *see* desire.

hiccup, ***hiḍkī laggṇī*** (M. 124. 50) or ***auṇī***, (both w. ***nū̃***).

hide, ***lukāṇā***, ***chapāṇā*** (int. ***lukkṇā***, ***chappṇā***) : hidden, ***gujjhā***.

hide, n., *see* skin.

hideous, *see* ugly.

high, ***uccā*** (gen.) : person, ***uccā***, ***lammā***.

hill, ***pahāṛ***, m. : small, ***pahāṛī***, f. : v. small, ***ṭibbā*** m. : range of small hills, ***pabbī***, f.

hilly, belonging to hills, ***pahāṛī***.

him, *see* he.

hinder, ***ḍakkṇā***, ***rōkṇā***, ***aṭkāṇā*** : *see* stop, forbid, obstruct.

hindrance, material, ***ḍakkā***, m. : abstract ***aṭkā*** m. ***bāndhā*** m. : ***rukāwaṭ***, f. (gen.).

hinge, ***kabzā***, m. : *see* pivot socket.

hint, ***ishārā***, m. (***k.***, ***de wall***) : *see* hit, point.

hip, ***lakk***, m. : h.-joint, ***cūknā*** m., ***cūḷā***, m.. ***cūkḷā***, m. : (carry) on hip, ***ḍhākke***.

hippopotamus, ***daryāī ghōṛā***, m.

hire, ***bhāṛā***, m. : ***karāyā***, m. : *see* wages.

hiss, (snake), ***shūkṇā***, ***shūkarnā*** :

n., ***shūkar*** f., ***shukāṭ***, f., (both ***pāṇī***).
history, ***tawārīkh***, f.
hit, int. ***laggṇā*** (stone, bullet, etc.) : *see* beat : h. at in speech, ***nōk lāṇī*** (***nū̃***, int. ***laggṇī***, ***wajjṇī***) : *see* hint, point.
hither, ***ure***, ***urhā̃*** : *see* here.
hoarse, become, ***saṅgh*** or ***wāz baihṇā*** (***dā***) : M. 117. 15 : ***wāz*** or ***awāz bhāṛā*** h. (***dā***).
hobble, v. tr., ***ḍhaṅgṇā*** : v. int., *see* lame.
hoe, ***gōḍṇā***, ***gōḍḍī karnī*** : n., small, ***rambā***, m. : large, ***kahī***, f.
hold, ***phaṛī rakkhṇā***, *see* haye, keep, seize.
hole, ***mōrī***, f., (***kaḍḍhṇī***) : ***chēk***, m. (***kaḍḍhṇā***) : in roof, ***maggh***, m. : in wall, made by rain, etc., ***gharl***, m. : in water-channel, ***ghukkā***, m. (these last three w. ***paiṇā***) : animal's burrow, ***khuḍa***, f. (***kaḍḍhṇī***).
holiday, ***chuṭṭī***, f. (leave) : *see* leave, festival.
hollow, ***pōllā*** (soft inside), ***khoḷā***, ***khōkhḷā*** (U.).
holy, ***pāk*** (M.) : ***pawittar*** (H.) : *see* pure : h. man (H.), ***sādhū***, ***sanyāsī***, ***gusāī̃***, ***jōggī*** : (M.) ***auluā***, ***sāī̃***, ***fakīr*** : *see* priest.
home, *see* house : at h., ***ghare*** : gone h., ***ghar geā***.
homesick, feel ***oddarnā*** (***mā̃ khuṇō̃*** or ***bājhō̃*** or ***thō̃***, for his mother).
homesickness, ***udrēwā̃***, m.
honest, ***dyānatdār***, ***imānwāḷā***.
honey, ***shaiht***, m., ***mākhyō̃***, ***mākhyō̃***, f. : *see* bee.
honeycomb, ***mākhyō̃*** (f.) ***dā khaggā*** or ***pakkhā*** or ***kharkṇā*** (or ***dī challī***).
honour, ***izzat***, f. (***k.***) : ***ādar***, f. (***k.***) : ***pat***, f., *see* esteem, respect.
honorary, ***bētankhāh*** : h. magistrate, ***ānararī majasṭrēṭ***, m.
hoof, ***khur***, m. (cloven) : ***sum***, m. (uncloven).
hook, ***kuṇḍā***, m. (gen.) : clothes, ***hukk***, f. : fish-h., ***kuṇḍī***, f.
hoop, boys', ***reṛhā***, m., ***cakkar***. m.
hoot, ***oe oe karnī*** : *see* clap.
hope, ***umēd***, f. : *see* expect : ***umēd***, expectation, seldom used for hope : I h. he will soon get well, ***Khudā*** (or ***Rabb***) ***kare shtābī wall ho jāe*** : I h. it did not hit him, ***wajj nehī̃ nā baiṭhā su*** ? I h. you will not get wet on the way, ***wāṭe bhijj nā jāe*** : I h. your horse does not jib now, ***huṇ te nehī̃ õ nā ghōṛā aṛdā*** ?
horn, ***sihng***, m. : -ed, ***sihngā̃ wāḷā***.
hornet, ***ḍehmū̃*** m. : *see* wasp.
horse, ***ghōṛā*** : ***waihtar***, m. (beast of burden, horse, mule ass).
horse-breaker, ***cābuksuār***, m.
horse-race, ***ghurdauṛ***, f.
hospital, ***haspatāḷ***, m.
hostile, *see* enemy.
hot, ***tattā***, ***garm*** : pungent in taste, ***garm*** (not ***tattā*** : n., ***garmī***, f.) : feel h., ***waṭṭ laggṇā*** (***nū̃***) : ***garmī laggṇī*** (***nū̃***) : ***baṛā hussaṛ e*** : cook at hot fire, ***tēz tā pakāṇā***.

hour, ***ghaiṇṭā***, m. : ***ghaṛī***, f. (strictly 22½ min.).
houri, ***parī***, f. : ***hūr***, f.
hourly, *see* repeatedly : ***ghaiṇṭe ghaiṇṭe picche***.
house, ***ghar***, m., ***kōṭhā***, m., ***makān***, m. : european, ***kōṭhī*** f., ***baṅglā***, m. : *see* home, hut : cow-h., ***kuṛh***, f. (for cattle) : pigeon -h., on pole, ***kābuk***, f. : in ground, ***ghumaiḷ***, f. : *see* roost.
housewife, ***gharwālī***, f.
how, ***kīka-ṇ***, ***-nā̃***, ***-r***, ***-rā̃***, ***kis tarhā̃***, ***kiñ***, ***kīkū̃*** : *see* somehow.
howl, ***rōṇā cilāṇā***, ***karlāṇā*** : of jackal, ***hawāṅkṇā***, *see* scream.
hubbub, *see* noise.
huff, take, ***russṇā***.
hug, *see* embrace. ***japhī***, f.
hum, *see* buzz.
humble, neg. of proud : h. oneself, ***apṇe āp nū̃ nīweā̃ k.*** : h. another, ***ohdī lamb kaḍḍhṇī***, ***ohdī ākkaṛ bhannṇī*** : be humbled, ***ohdī lamb*** or ***phūk nikḷnī*** : *see* humiliation.
humiliation, ***beiztī***, f. : ***namōshī***, f. : v., *see* humble, disgrace, dishonour, pride.
hunchbacked, ***kubṛā***, ***kubbā***.
hundred, ***sau***, ***sai***, ***saikṛā*** : -th, ***sauwā̃***, ***sauhwā̃*** : G. 20, 22, 93, 123 : *see* per cent.
hunger, ***bhukkh***, f. (***laggṇī***, ***nū̃***, G. 108).
hungry, ***bhukkhā***.
hunt, ***shikār*** k. and ***khēḍṇā*** : *see* search, prey.
hunter, ***shikārī***.
hurry, *see* hasten.
hurt (from blow, accident, etc.), ***saṭṭ*** f. (***laggṇī***, ***nū̃***) : *see* wound, pain, damage, injury : of new shoes, medicine, etc., ***laggṇā*** (***nū̃***) : *see* strike.
hurtful, ***nuksān*** or ***zyān*** (***jān***) ***karnwāḷā***.
husband, ***khasm***, ***gharwāḷā*** : h. and wife, ***miā̃ bīwī***, ***dowē̃ jī***, G. 122, M. 128. 16.
hush, *see* quiet; h. up, *see* screen.
husk, ***chill***, f. : v., ***chaṛnā*** : *see* peel.
hut, small house, ***kullī***, f. : ***jhuggī***, f. : thatched h. ***chappar***.
hydrophobia, *see* rabies.
hypercritical, be, ***ghutkḷā̃ cheṛ niā̃*** or ***kaḍḍhṇiā̃*** : *see* criticize.
hypocrisy, ***makārī***, f. : ***pakhaṇḍ***, m. : *see* deceit.
hypocrite, ***makār***, ***pakhaṇḍī*** : *see* decitful.

I

I, ***maĩ*** : people like me or us, ***hamātaṛ***, G. 28.
ice, ***warf***, f. : ***barf***, f.
idea, ***khyāl***, m. : *see* thought, believe, opinion.
idiom, ***muhāwrā***, m.
idiot, *see* mad. ***jhallā***.
idle, ***sust***, ***kamcōr*** : out of work, ***bekār***, ***wehlā***.
idol, ***but***, m. : ***mūrat***, f. (picture).
idolator, ***butparast***, ***butā̃*** or ***mūratā̃ nū̃ pūjjaṇwālā***.
idolatry, ***but parastī***, ***mūrat-pūjā***.
if, ***jē***, ***agar***, ***jēkar*** : ask or see if, ***pucch lai paī***, (never ***jē***, ***agar***).

ignite, *see* light.
ignorance, ***añāṇpuṇā***, m. : ***beilmī***, f. : ***nawākfī***, f. : *see* foolishness, stupid.
ignorant, ***beilm añāṇā***, ***jaihl*** : *see* stupid.
iguana, ***goh***, m.
ill, ***bamār***, ***wall nehī̃*** : ***māndā***, ***rōgī*** (habitually ill) : out of sorts, ***nimmā***, ***nimmo jhūṇā*** : of men, boys, animals, ***maḷeā hoeā***, ***ṭhaṅgreā hoeā***, ***hanēkeā hoeā***.
illegal, ***kanūn de khalāf*** : *see* unlawful.
illegitimate, child, ***harām dā*** : *see* illegal.
illfeeling, *see* envy (not distinguished).
illness, ***bamārī***, f. : ***auhr***, f. : ***rōg***, m.
illusion, ***waihm***, m. : *see* decit.
imagin-e, -ation, ***khyāl karnā***, ***farz karnā*** (suppose) : ***waihm***, m. (foolish fancy, ***h.***).
imaginary, ***khyālī gall***, ***farzī gall***.
imitat-e, ion, ***nakl***, f. (***k.***) : copy at school, ***nakl mārnī***, ***k.*** : of clown, ***nakl utārnī***, ***sāṅg utārnā*** : in i. of ***ohde wallõ wēkhke***, ***ohdī wēkhā wēkhī*** (U.) : *see* counterfeit, copy.
immediately, ***huṇe***, ***ese weḷe***, ***jhaṭ paṭṭ*** : past time, ***ōse weḷe***, ***owẽ***.
immodest, ***bēhayā***, ***besaram***.
immovable, ***nehī̃ halldā*** : *see* lasting.
impartial, be, ***raī nā karnī***, ***sabbhnā̃ nū̃ ikkī akkh nāḷ wēkhṇā***.
impassable, ***laṅghaṇwāḷā nehī̃***.
impatience, ***sauṛ***, f., ***kāhḷ***, f. (both ***paiṇī***), : *see* hast-e, -en.
impatient, ***kāhḷā***, or ***sauṛā*** (***paiṇā***), ***bēsabrā*** : ***sabr***, m., or ***hauslā***, m., ***nā k***.
impediment, *see* hindrance. ***rōk, atkaṇ*** f
imperfect, ***kaccā***, ***nākas***, ***mukkā nehī̃***.
imperfection, *see* defect, fault.
imperious, be, ***hukm cāṛhnā***, ***zōrāwarī karnī*** : adj., ***hākamānā***.
impertinent, ***gustākh***, ***shōkh*** : *see* forward, rude.
implore, *see* beseech.
important, ***bhārā***, ***zarūrī***.
impossible, ***namumkin***, ***unhōnī*** : as interj., ***mērī majāl e*** ? ***majāl gei e*** ? ***tōbbā*** !
impress upon, ***pakkī karnī*** (***nū̃***).
impression, ***nishān***, m. : on mind, ***asr***, m.
imprison, ***kaid-k*** : be -ed, ***bajjhṇā***, ***kaid-h*** : *see* prisoner.
improper, ***nāmunāsib***.
improve, int., ***suddharnā***, ***saurnā*** : tr., ***sudhārnā***, ***suārnā*** : *see* correct.
improvement, *see* progress : in disease, ***riait***. f., ***arām***, m., ***armān***, m.
imprudent, ***sōcdā nehī̃***.
impure, *see* dirty, unclean.
in, ***wicc***, ***andar*** : on the inside, ***andarwār*** : from inside, ***wiccõ***, ***andarõ*** : pass by way of inside, ***wiccõ*** or ***andarõ dī laṅghṇā*** : of place, often loc., G. 9, 10, 77 : in or after half an hour, three

weeks, ***addhe ghaiṇṭe*** (***triū̃h hafteā̃***) ***nū̃*** or ***picche*** : within half hour, etc., ***addhe ghaiṇṭe de andar*** : often loc., ***tinnī̃ haftī.*** in three weeks, so in the morning, evening. etc., G. 10, 34, 78.

inadvertently, *see* accidentally, carelessness.

inattentive, ***dhiān nehī̃ kardā.***

inauspicious, *see* auspicious.

inborn, ***zātī.*** A.

incantation, perform, ***hāl khēḍṇā, sir mārnā, mantar parhnā*** (H.).

incapable, incapacity, *see* able, worthless, useless.

incarnate, become, ***deh dhārī h.*** (H.) : ***autār dhārnā*** (H.) : ***mujassam h.*** (M.) : ***bandeā̃ dī sūrat shakl wicc auṇā.***

incense, n., ***dhūf,*** m., ***dhūkh,*** m.

incessant, *see* always, repeatedly, daily.

inch, ***incī,*** f. : *see* wts. and meas.

incite, ***cukkṇā, bhaṛkāṇā, macāṇā, paṭṭī paṛhāṇī*** (***nū̃***) : ***kann wicc phūkṇā*** (***de***) : *see* induce, excite, urge, seduce.

incitement, ***cukk,*** f.

inclined to, ***rūh*** or ***jī karnā,*** (e.g. ***cukkaṇ nū̃,*** to lift, etc.) : *see* desire, taste.

includ-ed, -ing, ***de saṇe, wicc pāke, shāmil karke, raḷāke.***

incoherent, ***bemaihṇe.***

income, ***āmdanī,*** f.

incompetent, *see* able, worthless, useless.

incomplete, *see* imperfect.

incomprehensible, ***samajh wicc nehī̃ aundā, kujjh piṛ palle nehī̃ peā.***

incongruous, ***raḍdā*** or ***phabbdā nehī̃.***

inconvenience, ***wakht,*** m. : ***taklīf,*** f. : ***bēarāmī,*** f.

inconvenienced, ***khajjal, khajjal khuār, aukkhā*** : *see* difficulty, trouble, straits.

inconvenient, ***sāḍḍe wāste mushkil e, eh wēḷā ṭhīk nehī̃*** : *see* convenience.

increase, int. ***waddhṇā, trakkī karnī*** ; tr., ***wadhāṇā, trakkī dēṇī*** (***nū̃***).

incredible, ***mannaṇwāḷī gall nehī.***

incubate, ***bacce kaḍḍhṇe.***

incurable, ***koī ilāj nehī, lāilāj.***

indebted, *see* debtor : acknowledge obligation, ***ahsān*** or ***ṭhāhrā mannṇā.***

indecent, of words, ***fohsh*** ; of persons, ***luccā.***

indeed, is it so ? ***halā sacc e*** ?

indefatigable, ***anthakk, thakkaṇwāḷā nehī̃.***

indefinite, ***ṭhīk patā nehī̃, ṭhīk faislā nehī̃, kuccī gall, kac pakk.***

independent, ***khudmukhtār, āpū̃ mālik e.***

index, ***firist,*** f.

indicate, *see* show. ***isārā karnā.***

indifferen-ce, -t, *see* carelessness. ***beparwāhī,*** f.

indigent, *see* poor.

indigestible, ***pacdā nehī̃.***

indigestion, ***badhazmī,*** f., ***unpācā,*** m.

indigo, ***nīl***, f.
indistinct, ***sāf nehī̃***, ***maddham.***
induce, ***manāṇā*** : *see* incite, urge.
indulge (child), ***lāḍ karnā*** (***nāḷ***).
industrious, ***mehntī.***
inevitable, ***zarūrī***, ***atall***, ***kismat nāḷ nehī̃ laṛidā***, etc.
inexperienced, ***añāṇā*** : ***kaccā*** : ***nā tajrabekār*** (U.) : ***tajrabā nehī̃***, ***allhaṛ.***
inexpert, ***añāṇā***, ***kaccā*** : *see* clever.
infant, ***kucchaṛ wicc***, ***duddh pīṇwāḷā.***
infer, ***natījā kaḍḍhṇā.***
infidel, *see* atheist : ***kāfar*** (M.).
infidelity, ***kufr***, m. (M.) : ***bedīnī***, f. : *see* adultery.
inflammation, ***sōj***, f. (swelling) : v., ***sujjṇā.***
influence, ***rōhb***, m. (half fear) : ***rusūkh***, m. : ***asr***, m.
inform-, -ation, ***itlāh dēṇī*** ; ***kaiṛ karnī*** : ***khabar dēṇī***, (all ***nū̃***).
ingenious, *see* clever.
ingenuity, ***hikmat***, f.
ingratitude, ***nāshukrī***, f. : ***kirt ghaṇī***, f. : *see* ungrateful.
inhabit, ***wassṇā***, ***raihṇā*** : being i.-ed, ***wassō̃***, f. : caus. v., *see* people.
inhabitant, ***raihṇwāḷā*** : *see* resident.
inherit, ***wāris h.*** : i.-ed, ***maurūsī.***
inheritance, ***wirsā.*** f. : ***mirās***, f.
inhuman, ***insān nehī̃***, ***bandā nehī̃*** : *see* cruel, oppression.
injure, ***traṭṭī cauṛ karnī*** (int. ***hōṇī***, both ***dī***) : *see* damage, hurt, loss.

injustice, ***bēinsāfī***, f. : ***bēniāī̃***, f. (H.).
ink, ***syāhī***, f. : coloured i., ***raṅg***, m.
inkstand, ***duāt*** f.
inn, ***sarā̃***, f. : European resthouse, ***ḍāk baṅglā***, m.
innings, ***wār.*** f. (both individual and side : ***laiṇī***, ***dēṇī***).
innkeeper, ***bhaṭhyārā.***
innocent, ***masūm*** : *see* guiltless, acquit.
innuendo, ***nōk lāṇī*** (***nū̃***) : ***ishārā k.*** (***de wall***) : i be apposite, ***nōk wajjṇī*** (***nū̃***) : *see* hint.
innumerable, ***aṇgiṇā***, ***bē-bahā***, ***-shumār***, ***-hadd.***
inoculate, ***ṭīkā lāṇā*** (int. ***laggṇā***, caus., ***luāṇā***) or ***ukhṇāṇā*** (int. ***ukkhaṇṇā***).
inquire, *see* ask, discover : i. after health, ***surt laiṇī*** (***dī***), ***patā karnā*** (***dā***), ***pucchṇā*** (***nū̃***).
inquirer, ***mutlāshī*** (or catechumen).
inquiry, investigation, ***takīkāt***, f. (***k.***, ***dī***).
insane, *see* mad.
insect, ***kīṛā***, m. (often snake) : large ants, ***kīṛe***, ***ḍhak makauṛe***, m. pl.
insensible, ***behōsh*** : *see* numb.
inside, *see* in.
insipid, ***bēsuādda***, ***phikkā*** : without sauce, etc., ***rukkhā***
insist, *see* obstinate : ***takrār karnā***, ***magar paiṇā*** (***de***) : ***gal paiṇā*** (***de***).
insistence, ***takrār***, m. : *see* obstinate.
insistent, ***khaihṛā nehī̃ chaḍḍā.***

inspection, school ***muāinā karnā*** (***dā***) : medical, etc., ***mulāhzā karnā*** (***dā***) : in gen. ***phērā mārnā*** (visit, etc.).
inspector, ***inspiṭṭar, inspĕkṭar.***
instalment (money), ***kisht,*** f. ***kisht.***
instance, *see* example.
instant, n., ***sakinṭ,*** m. : ***dam,*** m. : ***jhaṭ,*** m. : ***pall,*** m.
instead, ***de thā̃, de badle.***
instigate, *see* incite.
instinctively, *see* intuitively.
instruct-, -ion, *see* teaoh.
instrument, ***racch,*** m. ***hathyār,*** m. : ***kalā̃,*** f., ***kalā,*** f.. musical, ***wājā,*** m. : *see* play, tune, tool.
insult, *see* disgrace.
insure, oneself, etc., ***bimā,*** m. ***karāṇā*** (***dā***).
intelligent, ***siāṇā.***
intelligence, ***siāṇap,*** f. : *see* sense, clever.
inten-d, -ntion, ***manshā,*** f. : ***irādā,*** m. : ***niyat,*** f. : ***matlab,*** m. : ***dalīl,*** f. : ***pucchaṇ pucchaṇ kardā sā̃,*** intended to ask but hesitated, G. 112 : *see* object, desire.
intentionally, *see* deliberately, purposely. ***irāde nāḷ***
intercede, ***sifārish karnī*** (***dī***) ***shafāt karnī*** (***de-wāste***).
intercept, ***rāh wicc phaṛnā.***
intercessor, ***sifārish*** or ***shafāt karnwāḷā.***
intercourse, ***saṅgat,*** f. : ***sohbat,*** f. : ***wāh,*** m. : (*see* connection) : esp. eating, drinking, ***wartõ,*** f., ***wartāwā,*** m., ***wartṇā,*** m. : coming and going. ***auṇā jāṇā.***
interest (gen. monthly), ***byāj,*** m., ***sūd,*** m. : *see* advantage, profit, benefit : self-i., ***khudgarzī,*** f. : ***gaū,*** m. : *see* object, intention.
interested in, ***dilcaspi,*** f. (***menū̃ ehde nāḷ e***), ***ohdā shauk h.*** (***nū̃***).
interesting, ***suādḷā, dilcasp.***
interfere, ***dakhl dēṇā*** (***wicc***).
intermingle, mix : *see* mix.
internal, ***wiclā, wishkārlā, andarlā, andrūnī*** (U.).
interpose, *see* mediator, interfere, interrupt
interpret, ***tarjmā karnā*** (***dā***).
interpreter, ***tarjmā karnwāḷā, mutrajjim.***
interrupt, ***gall ṭukkṇī*** (***dī***), ***dī gall wicc gall karnī*** : *see* interfere.
interval, time, ***cir,*** m. : ***mohlat,*** f. (days of "grace") : ***wakfā,*** m. (U.) : space, ***paiṇḍā,*** m. : ***khappā,*** m., ***witth,*** f., ***wāṭ,*** f.
intervene, *see* interpose.
interview, ***mulākāt karnī*** (***nāḷ***).
intimate, ***pakkā dōst*** or ***yār*** : *see* friend.
intimidate, *see* fear.
intolerable, ***jehrā nā jareā*** (or ***saiheā*** or ***jhalleā***) ***jāe.***
intoxicant, ***nashā,*** m. : ***nashe wāḷī ciz,*** f.
intrench, ***khandak,*** f. or ***ṭoā,*** m. (***kaḍḍhṇā***).
intricacy, ***waḷ,*** m., ***pēc,*** m. : ***waḷ pēc,*** m.
intricate, ***pēcwāḷā, waḷ pēcwāḷā.***
intrigue, *see* plot. ***gunjhal,*** f.
introduce, person, ***miḷāṇā*** (***nāḷ***),

wākif karāṇā (***nāḷ***) : ***mēḷ karāṇā*** (***dā***) : law, custom, money, ***jārī karnā ṭōrnā, kaḍḍhṇā.***
intrude, *see* interfere interrupt.
intrust, *see* entrust.
intuitively, ***uñ, āpū̃ khyāl āeā, apṇī*** (***apṇe***) ***akl nāl, k͟hāhmak͟hāh.***
invade, ***mulk͟h wicc hamlā karke waṛnā, hamlā karnā***
investigation, *see* inquiry.
invincible, *see* unconquerable.
invisible, ***jehṛā nā disse.***
invit-e, -ation, ***saddnā, rōṭī ākhṇī*** or ***ṭhākṇī*** or ***warjṇī*** (***dī***), ***dāwat karnī*** (***dī***) : ***sāḍḍī ohde wall roṭī e.***
invoke, ***kise dī duhāī deṇī.***
involuntarily, ***k͟hāhmak͟hāh*** : *see* force.
iron, ***lohā***, m. : adj., ***lohe dā*** : (ironing) ***istrī***, f. : iron v. tr., ***istrī-k.***
irony, ***tāhnā mārnā*** (***nū̃***), ***nōk lāṇī*** (***nū̃***), ***mak͟haul nāḷ ākhṇā.***
irrecoverable, ***geā guātā.***
irregular-, -ity, ***bēkaid-ā*** (n. ***-agī***, f.) ***bēkanūn-*** (n. ***-ī***, f.), ***bētartīb-*** (n., ***-ī***, f.).
irrelevant, ***ehdā tallak nehī̃*** (***nāḷ***), ***bematlab***
irreligious, ***bedīn*** (M.) : ***bedharm*** (H.) : nouns add ***-ī.***
irremediable, ***dā ilāj nehī.***
irrigate, *see* water.
irritable, ***ciṛhnwāḷā, kiṛntwāḷā.***
irritate, *see* tease.
island, ***ṭāpū***, m. : ***jazīrā*** m.
issue, order, ***jārī-k., kaḍḍhṇā.***
it, *see* he, she.
itch, n., v., ***khurk***, f. (***h. paiṇī***).
item, ***gall***, f.
itinerary, ***safar***, m. : ***safarnāmā***, m.
ivory, ***dand khaṇḍ***, f.

J

jackal, ***giddar***, m.
jacket, ***kōṭ***, m : ***jākaṭ.*** m.
jail, *see* prison.
jam, ***jām***, m. (K., ***banāṇā***) : ***murabbā***, m. (***pāṇā***).
janitor, ***caprās-ī***, m. fem. ***-aṇ.***
January, ***janwarī***, f. : ***māhṅg, māh***, m. (about Jan. 13 to Feb. 12).
jar, *see* pot. ***martbān***
jasmine, ***cambā***, m.
jaw, ***khakhwāṛā***, m. : ***haṛbaccī***, f
jealous-, y, *see* envy, suspicious. ***sāṛewālā***
jeer, *see* mock.
jerk, *see* jolt.
jester (excess implied), ***mak͟haulīā, ṭokī, mask͟harībāz*** : professional ***bhaṇḍ*** : *see* joke.
Jesus, ***Yĕsū, Īsā, Hazrat Īsā*** (M.).
jet-black, v. black, ***kāḷā syāh, kāḷā shāh.***
Jew, ***Yahūd-ī***, fem. ***-aṇ.***
jewellery, ***gaihṇā***, m., ***gaihṇe***, m. pl. : each piece, ***ṭūmb***, f., also ***gaihṇā.***
jib ***aṛnā.***
jingle ***chaṇ chaṇ k.*** : *see* tinkle
join, ***jōṛnā*** (int. ***juṛnā***) : person, ***ralṇā*** (***nāḷ***), ***milṇā*** (***nāl, nū̃***) : army, ***bhartī h.***
joint, body, ***jōṛ***, m.

jointly, ***raḷke, miḷke, kaṭṭhe.***
joke, ***hāsse dī gall*** : ***jugat,*** f. (quibble w. slight sting) : rather objectionable, ***makhaul.*** m. : ***maskharī,*** f., ***mashkarī,*** f.
jokingly, ***hāsse nāḷ, makhaul nāḷ.***
jolt, ***hujjkā laggṇā*** (***nū̃***) : ***dhakkā khāṇā.***
journal, diary, ***rōznāmcā,*** m. (U) : ***ḍairī,*** f. : *see* newspaper.
journey, ***safar,*** m. (***k.***) : ***sair,*** m. or ***sail,*** m. or ***sail sapaṭṭā.*** m., j. for pleasure, walk, etc. : ***phērā,*** m. (***pāṇā mārnā,*** int. ***pāiṇā***), esp. visit, useless j.
joy, ***khushī,*** f.
joyful, ***khush.***
judge, n., ***jaj, munsuf*** (civil), ***tasīldār,*** (cirminal and executive) : *see* magistrate : v., ***faislā karnā.***
judgment-day, ***kiāmat dā din,*** m. (***kiāmat,*** f., really resurrection).
jug, water or milk, ***jagg,*** m. : *see* pot.
juggler, ***madār-ī,*** fem. ***-an.***
juice, ***ras,*** m.
juicy, ***raswāḷā.***
July, ***jaulāī,*** f. : ***julāī,*** f. : ***jaulā,*** m. : ***saoṇ,*** m. (about July 13 to Aug. 12)
jumble up, ***hēth ulā̃ k., rauḷā mārnā, gaṛbaṛī karnī.***
jump, ***ṭappṇā*** (over, ***nū̃*** : on to. ***utte***) : waves, water, ***uchaḷṇā*** : n., ***chāḷ,*** f. : ***chalāṅg,*** f. : ***phalāṅg,*** f. (all w. ***mōrnī***).
June, ***jūn,*** m. : ***hāhr,*** m. (about June 13 to July 12).
jurisdiction, ***ikhtiār,*** m.
just, ***insāfwāḷā, niāī*** : adv., ***zarā*** : j. now, ***huṇe.***
justice, ***insāf,*** m. : ***niā̃,*** f.

K

kedgery, food, ***khicṛī,*** f.
keen, on sthg., ***shukīn*** : *see* desire, sharp.
keep, ***rakkhṇā,*** in one's possession, ***apṇe kabze wicc rakkhṇā*** : animals ***rakkhṇā*** : k. seat, *see* engage : k. safe, ***sāmbhṇā*** : temporarily k. back money, wages, ***hẽth rakkhṇā*** (G. 91) : *see* detain, hinder : kept tame animal, ***rākhwā̃*** : k. feast, ***īd karnī*** ; *see* celebrated
keeper, *see* guardian, watchman.
keepsake, ***yādgār,*** f.
kernel, ***girī,*** f. : (cocoanut, ***garī***).
kettle, ***kētlī,*** f.
key, ***kunjī,*** f. : ***cābī,*** f. : fit, ***laggṇī*** (tr. ***lāṇī,*** try).
kick, by person, ***thuḍḍā lāṇā*** or ***mārnā*** (int. ***khāṇā, laggṇā***) : also ***thuḍḍī mārnā*** : football, ***kik mārnī*** : by horse, etc., ***dulattā mārnā.***
kid, ***bagrōṭā.***
kidney, ***gurdā,*** m.
kill, ***mār chaḍḍṇā*** or ***saṭṭṇā, thā̃ mārnā, jānō mārnā*** : for food, ***kohṇā*** : ***halāl-k.*** (M.) : ***takbīr paṛhnī*** (utte, M.) : ***jhaṭkā karnā*** (***dā, nū̃,*** H.).
kiln, ***bhaṭṭhā,*** m. : ***āwā,*** m. : ***āwī,*** f.
kilt, ***ghaghrī,*** f. : *see* skirt : k. -ed regiment, ***ghāghrā palṭaṇ,*** f.

kind, ***mehrbān.***
kind, n., ***jiṇs,*** f. : ***kism,*** f.
kindness, ***mehrbānī,*** f.
kindred, *see* relati-ve,-onship.
king, ***bādshāh*** : ***rājā, māhrājā, sultān.***
kingdom, ***bādshāhī,*** f. : ***saltanat,*** f. (rule, etc.) : ***rāj,*** m.
kiss, ***cummṇā*** : n ***cummā,*** m. : ***cummī.*** f. (all gen. w. bad meaning) : *see* caress.
kitchen, ***baurcikhānā,*** m. : village, ***culhānnī,*** f. (M.) : ***rasōī.*** f. (H) : H's square, ***caukkā,*** m., ***caũkā,*** m.
kite, boy's, ***guḍḍī,*** f.
kitten, ***bilūṅgā,*** m.
knack, ***jāc,*** f. : ***thauh,*** m.
knead, flour, ***gunnhṇā*** (pa. p. ***guddhā, gunnheā*** : int. ***gujjhṇā***) : clay w. hands or feet, ***gōṇā.***
knee, ***gōḍḍā,*** m. : -cap, ***cappṇī,*** f., ***chūṇī,*** f.
kneel, ***gōḍḍe niwāṇe*** or ***tēkṇe, goḍḍeā̃ bhār*** or ***parne baihṇā.***
knife, ***churī,*** f. : ***kard,*** f. : pen-k., ***cakkū,*** m. : large k., ***churā,*** m. : -board, ***takhtī,*** f.
knob, *see* handle.
knock, at door, ***kharkāṇā*** (lit. rattle) : k. down, ***ḍhāṇā, ḍēgṇā*** : k. against, gently, ***khaihṇā*** (***nāḷ***) : *see* collide : be k. -ed about, ***dhakke*** or ***bham-baḷbhūse khāṇe.***
knot, n., (tied or in wood) ***gaṇḍh,*** f. : v., ***gaṇḍhṇā gaṇḍh dẽṇī*** (***nū̃***) : open, ***kholhṇī.***
know, ***jāṇṇā, patā hōṇā*** (***nū̃***), ***malūm hōṇā*** (***nū̃***) : make known, ***patā dẽṇā*** ; spread abroad, ***dhumāṇā*** (int. ***dhummṇā***) : k. languages, ***jāṇṇā,*** adj., ***-dān, fārsī-dān,*** knowing Persian, etc.
knowingly, *see* purposely.
knowledge, ***ilm,*** m.
knuckle (hand or foot), ***gaṇḍh,*** f.

L

label, ***ciṭṭ*** f.
labour, ***mehnat.*** f. : *see* force, effort, labourer.
labourer, ***mazdūr,*** m. : fields, ***kāmmā*** : employer or employee, wages in kind, ***sēpī.*** fem. ***sēpaṇ*** : all-time employee. ***āthṛī*** : one of menial classes, ***kammī*** fem. ***kamṇeāṇī*** : condition of ***sepi, sēp,*** f. : *see* servant.
lace, boot, shoe, ***waddhrī,*** f. : ***tasmā.*** m. (U).
lack, n., ***thuṛh,*** f. : ***ghātā.*** m. : v. ***thuṛhnā ghaṭṭṇā*** (be insufficient).
ladder, ***pauṛī,*** f., ***paṛsāṅg.*** f. : *see* rung.
ladle, *see* spoon, ***kaṛchī,*** f.
lady (European) ***mēmsāb*** : unmarried ***miss sāb, miss.***
ladybird, ***kummhā kīṛā.*** m.
lake, ***jhīl,*** f., ***sar,*** m. ***ḍaḷ,*** m. : *see* pond.
lamb, ***lēllā,*** m.
lame, ***laṅgā, laṅgṛā*** : walk l., ***laṅgāṇā*** : *see* cripple.
lament, *see* mourn. weep.
lamp, ***lamp,*** m. : ***battī,*** f. : wall-

l., ***duālgīr***, m. : earthen, ***dīwā***, m.
lamppost, ***munnā***, m. : ***waḷā***, m.
lampstand, movable, ***dīurī***, f. : in wall, ***duākhā***. m.
lance, *see* spear.
land, ***zamin*** or ***zimī̃*** or ***jīwī̃*** or ***jiwī̃***, f. : *see* soil, country.
land, v. of ship, ***kaṇḍhe*** or ***dande laggṇā*** : of person, ***jahāz uttō utarnā***
landlord, ***mālik***, m.
lane, ***galī***, f.
language, ***bōlī***, f. : ***zabān***, f. : see speech.
lantern, ***lālṭaiṇ***, f., ***hatth battī***, f.
lap, ***gadd***, f. : *see* arm : ***jhoṭī***, f. (front of garment, for carrying things in).
large, *see* big, roomy, loose.
last, adj., ***chekaṛlā***, ***pishlā*** : year, week, month, *see* year, week, month : last night ***ajj rāt nū̃***, ***ajj dī rāt***, ***rātī̃*** : l. Monday, ***pishle suār nū̃*** : l. time, ***aglī wārī***.
last, v., boots, clothes, etc., ***haṇḍhnā*** : last 2, 3 days, of food, ***kaḍḍhṇā*** (***dō trai din***) G. 118 : M. 119. 45 : of join in furniture, machinery, ***khlōṇā***.
lasting, ***pakkā***, ***baṛā haṇḍhaṇ-wāḷā*** : *see* permanent.
lastly, *see* finally.
late, adj., ***cirkā***, ***carāhkā*** (but ***carōkṇā***, of a long time ago), ***pachētrā*** : be l., ***cir***, m., ***ḍēr***, f. (both w. ***lāṇā***. int. ***laggṇā***), ***paccharṇā*** : ***cirkā auṇā***, etc. (of train often ***lēṭ auṇī***) : late, deceased. ***marhūm*** (M., U.), ***bahishtī*** (M), ***surgi*** (H).
lathe, ***k̲h̲arād***. f. : v., ***k̲h̲arādṇā***. ***k̲h̲arād k.*** or ***cāṛhnā***.
laugh, ***hassṇā*** : ***hāssāauṇā*** (***nū̃***), inclined to laugh, (M. 117, 6) : ***guṭakṇā*** (giggle) : derisive words, ***mūh aḍḍṇā***, ***dand kaḍḍhṇe*** : *see* joke, ridicule.
law, ***kanūn***, m. : relig., ***sharā***, m. : ***shariat***. f. (both M.).
lawful, ***jāiz*** : ***halāl*** (M., esp. food, money) : *see* legal.
lawsuit, ***mukadmā***, m. : *see* case, lose, hearing : date of l., ***tārīk̲h̲***, f. : ***tarīk***. f.
lawyer, ***wakīl***, m. : ***bālishtar***, m. : the practice or work, ***wakālat***, f., ***bālishṭrī***, f. : his pay, ***mehntānā***. m.
lay, *see* place : eggs. ***dēṇā***.
layer, fold, ***taih***, m. f. : of bricks in building, ***raddā***, m. or ***radā*** m.
laziness, ***ḍhill***, f., ***ḍhill maṭṭh***, f. : ***sustī***, f.
lazy, ***ḍhillā maṭṭhā sust***, ***kamcōr***.
lead, ***sikkā***, m
lead, ***mohre calṇā***, ***agge calṇā***, ***lai calṇā***, ***āggū*** or ***mohrlā h.*** : *see* guide.
leader, ***sardar*** : *see* lead, headman.
leaf, ***pattar***, m. : of book, ***wurkā***, m. : of door, ***bhitt***, m.
leak, *see* drip, ooze
lean, adj., ***māṛā***, ***patlā***, ***lissā***.
lean on, ***de sahāre calṇā*** or ***khlōṇā*** : l. back, ***nāḷ ḍhāsṇā lāṇā***, ***ḍhoh lāṇī*** : *see* stoop.

leap, *see* jump, ***chāl mārnī***
learn, gen. ***sikkhṇā*** : study in gen., ***poṛhnā*** : lesson, ***pakāṇā, yād-k.*** (im. ***pakkṇā, yād h.*** or ***auṇā***, M. 117. 4).
learned, ***ālam, ilmwāḷā*** : ***maulwī*** (M.) : ***paṇḍat*** (H.) : *see* expert.
lease, ***paṭā***, m. : ***thēkā***, m. (contract) : v., ***paṭe*** or ***ṭhēke te dēṇā.***
least, ***sabbhnā̃*** or ***sāreā̃ tõ nikkā*** or ***ghaṭṭ*** : at l., ***ghaṭṭo ghaṭṭ, ghaṭṭ tõ ghaṭṭ.***
leather, ***camm***, m. : ***comṛā***, m. : untanned, ***khall***, f. : l. worker, ***mōc-i***, fem. ***-aṇ***, ***cameār-***, fem. ***-ī*** (fr. the U.P.)
leave, ***chuṭṭī***. f. (***laiṇī, dēṇī***) : take l. of, ***widyā -h., rukhsat -h.*** (send off, ***widyā -k., rukhsat -k***) : l. off, *see* abstain : l. off work, ***chuṭṭī karnī*** : *see* liberty.
leavings of food, ***jūṭhā***, any food once begun is ***jūṭṭā***, adj. : n., ***jūṭh***, m.
leaven, ***khamīr***, m.
lecture, ***dars***, m. (***d.***) : ***likoor***, m. (***d.***).
leech, ***jōk***, f.
left, ***khabbā*** : l.-handed, ***khabbā.***
leg, ***laṭṭ***, f. : ***ling***, m. : of furniture, ***pāwā***, m. : of mutton, ***lēk***, f. (K.) : *see* calf, shim. thigh, muscle.
legal, ***kanūn wallō jāiz*** : *see* lawful.
legend, ***kahāṇī***, f.
legitimate (child) ***halāl dā*** : *see* legal, lawful.
leisure, ***wehl***, f. : ***wāndak***, f. : ***wānd***, f. : ***fursat***, f. (U.) : *see* leave : at l., ***wehlā, wāndā.***
lemon, *see* lime.
lemonade, ***lomnēṭ***, m., ***miṭṭhā pāṇī***, m.
lend, money, ***udhār d.*** : *see* debt, borrow
lender, *see* money-lender.
length, ***lamāī***, f. : ***lām***, m. : ***lamittaṇ***, f. : l.-wise, *see* direction.
leopard, ***cittrā***, m.
leper, ***koṛhā***, fem. ***koṛhī.***
leprosy, ***koṛh***, m. : ***waḍḍā rōg*** or ***dukh.***
less, ***kamm, ghaṭṭ, kassā.***
lessen, ***ghaṭāṇā, ghaṭṭ k., kamm k.*** : (int. ***ghaṭṭ h., kamm h., maṭṭhā h.***) : price, ***riait karnī.***
lesson, ***sabak***, m. : *see* learn, teach.
lest, ***mate, cetā, ajehā nā howe pai.***
letter, ***ciṭṭhī***, f. : ***khatt***, m. (often postcard) : note, ***rukkā***, m. : ***parcī***, f. : offical l., ***rōbkār***, m. : of alphabet, ***harf***, m. : ***akkhar***, m. (H).
lettuce, ***salāt***, m. : ***salād***, m.
leucoma, *see* eye-ulcer.
level, ***padhrā, suāhrā, sāf, barābar*** : *see* flat, plain.
lever, ***tuḷ*** (***dēṇī***, l. up, raise).
liable, *see* prone.
liar, ***jhūṭhā.***
libel, action, ***izzat dā dāhwā*** : *see* slander, accuse.
liberal, *see* generous : thought, ***azād khyāl wāḷā.***
liberty, gen. ***azādī***, f. : l. to do

something, ***khullh***, f., ***ijāzat***, f : ***izn***, m. : take l., be familiar, *see* familiar : act without leave, ***ijāzat tõ binā karnā*** : (or ***bē*** or ***bilā ijāzat***).

library, ***laibrerī***, f. : room in house, ***daftar***, m.

licence, ***laisans***, f. (a written l.) : *see* liberty.

lick, ***caṭṭṇā***.

lid, ***ḍhakṇā*** m. : ***ḍhakkaṇ***, m. : for vessel, ***cappṇī***, f., ***chūṇī***, f., ***chūṇā***, m.

lie, tell, ***jhūṭh bōlṇā*** or ***mārnā***.

lie, down, ***lammā paiṇā***, G. 64 (tr. ***pāṇā***) : ***saūṇā*** (sleep) : remain lying, ***peā raihṇā A***.

lieutenant, ***lafṭain*** : L. - Governor, ***lāṭ sāb***.

life, (animal) ***jān*** : course of, ***hyātī***, f., ***zindagī***, f., ***jindṛī***, f. : eternal l., ***hamēshā dī zindagī*** : past l., ***guzrī hoī*** or ***pishlā zindagī*** : biography, ***hāl***, m., ***hawāl***, m. : conduct ***cāl caln***, m.

lifeless, ***bejān***.

lift, ***cukkṇā***, ***uṭhāṇā***, ***cāṇā*** : *see* carry.

light, n. ***lō***, f. : ***cānnaṇ***. m. : ***cānṇā***, m. : ***rōshnī***, f.

light, adj, not heavy, ***hauḷā*** : colour, ***hawāī, nīm***.

light, lamp, fire, ***bāḷnā*** (int. ***baḷṇā*** : begin to burn, ***baḷ paiṇā***) : *see* fire, burn.

lightning, ***baddaḷ***, ***lishkṇā*** : ***bijlī***, f.

like, adj., *see* similar.

like, v., ***caṅgā laggṇā*** (***nū̃***) : *see* desire, taste.

limbs, gen., ***naiṇ prāṇ***, m. pl. : ***hatth pair***, m. pl. : ***aṅg***, m. : *see* cripple.

lime, lemon, large kind, ***khaṭṭā***, m. : small, ***nimbū***, m. : (thin rind) ***kūgzī nimbū*** : sweet, ***miṭṭhā***, m. : small do, ***nārgī***, f. inferior l., ***galgal***, f., ***truñ***, f., ***kimb***, m. : eat l., ***cūpṇā***.

lime, building, ***cūnā***, m.

limestone, ***rōṛ***, m.

line, ***līk***, f. : ***lakīr***, f. : in book, ***satar***, f. : of poetry, ***misrā***, m. : railway, ***laiṇ***, f. : of boys, etc., ***katār***, f. (U.) : draw l., ***khiccṇā*** : a few lines (letter) ***dī*** or ***cār harf***, m. pl.

lineage, ***nasabnāmā***, m. (genealogy) : *see* descendants. tree.

lining, ***ḷailaṇ***, f.

link, of chain, ***kuṇḍī***, m. : ***saṅglī***, f. (rare).

linseed, ***aḷsī***, f.

lion, ***shēr babar***, ***babar shēr***, m.

lip, ***bull***, m. : ***hōth***, m.

lisp, nearest word "stammer."

list, ***firist***, f.

listen, ***sunnā*** : attentively, ***kann lāke*** or ***dhyān karke*** or ***lāke sunnā*** : l. for, ***kair laiṇī*** (***dī***).

literal, meaning, ***lafzī***.

literary, ***kitābī***.

literature, ***kitābā̃***. f. pl.

litigious, ***mukadmebāz***.

little, size, *see* small : quantity, ***thōṛā jehā***, ***zarā ku***, ***kujjh kujjh***, ***ghaṭṭ waddh*** (G. 28) : v. l., ***ruāḷ***, as ***ruāl ku āṭā***, v. l. flour : too l., ***kassā***, ***thōṛā***.

live, ***jyūṇā*** (pa. p. ***jiweā***) : dwell, ***raihṇā*** : l. good life, ***cāl caln acchā e*** : l. in ease, ***arām wicc*** or ***nāḷ raihṇā***.

livelihood, ***rozī***, f. : ***rōzgār***, m. : ***guzārā***, m.

liver, ***kalejā***, m. : of animal, ***kalejī***, f., ***kalejā***, m.

livery, ***wardī***, f.

living, *see* alive, livehood.

load, ***bhār***, m. (***laddṇā***) : ***bōjh***, m. (U.) : *see* wts. and mess.

loaf, Indian, ***rōṭī*** f. : ***capātī***, f. : ***parauṇṭhā***, m. : small, ***gullī***, f. : European, ***ḍabal rōṭī***, f. : *see* bread.

loafer, ***awārā***, fem. the same.

loan, *see* lend.

loathsome, ***ghinaoṇā*** : words for disgust.

lock, ***jandrā***, m. : ***tāḷā***, m. (both w. ***mārnā***, ***lāṇā***, int. ***laggṇā***, ***wajjṇā***) : unlock, ***jandrā lāhṇā*** (int. ***laihṇā***).

lock, hair, *see* hair : Hindu's, ***bōdī***, f.

locust, ***makṛī***, f.

log, ***gēllī***, f. v. short, for fuel, ***mōchā***, m. (***pāṇā***, int. ***paiṇā***) : *see* sleeper.

logic, ***mantak***, f.

loincloth, ***laṅgōṭī***, f.

loins, *see* waist.

lonel-y, -iness, use ***kallā***, alone, and *see* homesick.

long, adj., ***lammā*** : l. time, ***cir***, m. : fr. l. time ago, ***kadōkṇā***, ***carōkṇā***, ***jū̃*** : *see* delay : longways, *see* direction : as long as, ***jinnā cir***, ***jicar***, ***jicar tikar*** : long days (summer), *see* day.

long for, ***taṛafṇā*** (great unrest) : ***saihkṇā***, (***nū̃***), ***tarsṇā*** : cause to l. f., afflict, ***tarsāṇā***.

long-lived, ***waḍḍī umr dā*** : *see* old.

look, ***wēkhṇā*** (pa. p. ***ḍiṭṭhā***, ***wekheā***), ***takhṇā*** : glance, ***nazr mārnī*** (***utte***) : l. stealthily, ***jhātlī mārnī*** : *see* frown, search : l. after, ***sāmbhṇā***, ***sambhāḷṇā*** : *see* watch, protect.

loom, ***khaḍḍī***, f. : warp. ***tāṇī***, f., woof, ***pēṭā***, m.

loose, ***ḍhillā*** : get loose, machinery, masonry, ***ukkhaṛnā*** (tr. ***ukhēṛnā***, *see* piece) : clothes, ***mōklā***.

lopsided, *see* weight, ***puthā-siddhā***

loquacious, *see* talkative.

lord it over, lordly, *see* imperious.

lose, ***guāṇā***, ***khaṛāṇā***, ***gum-k.*** (U.) : int. ***guācṇā***, pa. p., ***guātā*** or ***guāceā*** : ***khaṛācnā***, pa. p. ***khaṛātā***, ***khaṛāceā*** : ***gum-h.***, (U.) : also ***jāndeā raihṇā*** : l. game, *see* game : l. law-case, ***ohdī*** or ***ohde-sir digrī hōṇī***. ***mukadmā khārij hōṇā*** (***dā***), ***mukadmā hārnā*** (***dā***).

loss, damage, ***nuksān***, m., ***jān***, m., ***zyān***, m., all w. ***h.*** : financial, ***mōs***, f., ***ṭoṭṭā***, m., both w. ***laggṇā***, ***khāṇā***, ***paiṇā*** : ***harj***, m. (h.), ***caṭṭī***, f. (***paiṇī***) : ***ghāṭā***, m. (***khāṇā***, ***paiṇā***) : make up l., ***ṭoṭṭā*** or ***ghāṭā pūrā k.*** : ***kasr kaḍḍhṇī*** : pay for l., ***nuksān bharnā*** : *see* damage.

lot, *see* fate : lots, draw, ***guṇe pāṇe***.

lottery, ***lāṭarī***, f.
loud, ***sōr dā***.
loudly, ***uccī uccī***, ***uccī dittī***, ***dabbke***, ***zōr nāḷ***, ***kaṛakke*** (angrily) : *see* aloud.
louse, ***jū̃***, f.
love, ***mhabbat***, f. : (***rakkṇī*** or ***k.***, ***nāḷ***) : ***pyār***, m. (k. ***nū̃***, ***nāḷ***) : *see* fondle, indulge : ***ishk***, m., ***āshik h.*** (***utte***) : *see* lover.
lover and loved one, ***āshik mashūk*** : words ***ishk***, ***āshik***, ***mashūk*** gen. bad meaning.
low, adj., ***nīwā̃*** : -er, ***hēṭhlā***, ***uīwā̃*** : speak low, *see* gently : *see* mean.
low, cattle, ***aṛiṅgṇā aṛāṇā***.
loyal, ***khairkhāh***, ***namakhalāl***.
luck, *see* fate, fortune.
lucky, *see* fortunate, rich.
lucrative, ***baṛī khaṭṭī wālā***.
luggage, *see* baggage : -receipt, ***bilṭī***, f.
luggage-van, *see* brake.
lukewarm, *see* tepid.
lump, of earth, ***dhehm***, f. : in flesh, ***gilhṭ***, m. : ***sunḍhā***, m. : *see* boil (I) : of meat, *see* piece.
lunch, ***tipan***, m.
lung, ***phēphṛā***, m.
lust, ***lucpuṇā***, m. : ***shaihwat***, f. (U.).

M

macaroni, ***makrūnī***, f.
machine, ***mashīn***, f. : ***kalā̃***, f. (mechanical device).
mad, ***jhallā***, ***pāgal***, ***kamḷā***, ***shudāī***, : ***bā*** or ***mat*** or ***hōsh mārī jāṇī***, hence adj., ***bā mārеā***, etc. : *see* fool, foolishness : m. dog, ***haḷkā kuttā*** : *see* rabies.
magic, ***jādū***, m. : ***mantar***, m.
magician, ***jādūgar-***, fem. ***-nī*** : *see* witch.
magistrate, ***majasṭrēṭ*** : *see* honorary.
magnet, ***miknātīs***, f.
magnificence, *see* splendour.
maiden, *see* girl, virgin, young.
mail, ***ḍāk***, f. : m. train, ***ḍāk gaḍḍī***, f. : Bombay, Calcutta m., ***bambā*** or ***kalkattā mēl***, f.
maimed, *see* limb, cripple.
maintain, ***pāḷṇā***, ***parwarish karnī*** (***dī***) : ***khare dēṇā*** (***dā*** or ***nū̃***) : *see* assert.
maintenance, ***rōṭī kapṛā***, m. ***kharc***, m., ***parwarish***, f.
maize, ***makaī***, f. : *see* cob.
make, ***baṇāṇā*** (int. ***baṇṇā***) : *see* force, cause : ready-made, ***baṇeā battreā***.
make-weight (for scales), ***pāskū̃***, m. : *see* patch.
male, of animals, ***nar*** : adj., (men), ***mardānā***.
malice, *see* envy. ***sāṛa***, m.
mallet, ***muṅglī***, f.
man, gen. ***bandā***, ***ādmī***, ***insān***, m. : m. -kind, ***iṅsān*** : m., not woman, ***jaṇā*** : my good m., ***whaī***, M. 130. 32 : G. 125.
manage, *see* arrange : get along, ***guzārā karnā***.
manager, ***mainajar*** : of land, ***gumāshtā***.
mane, of horse, ***jāddā̃***, f. pl.
manger, ***khurlī***, f.

mango, ***amb***, m. (tree and fruit) : eat m., ***cūpṇā***.
manifest, *see* evident.
manner, ***tarhā̃***, f. : ***tarīkā***, m. : ***ḍhaṅg***, m.
mansion, ***mahall***, m. : ***hawēlī***, f. : ***waḍḍā makān***.
manufacture, *see* make.
manure, ***mallhar***, m. (***pāṇā***, int. ***paiṇā***).
manuscript, ***nuskhā***, m.
many, plur. of much : *see* much.
map, ***nakshā*** (***banāṇā***, ***khiccṇā***).
marble, ***saṅg marmar***, m.
March, ***mārc***, ***mārac***, m. : ***cēttar***, m. (about Mar. 13 to Apr. 12).
march, v., ***kūc karnā*** (U.) : ***painḍā mārnā***.
mare, *see* horse, pony.
margin, book, ***hāshiā***, m. : *see* edge.
marine, ***baibrī***, ***samundar dā***.
mark, ***nishān***, m. : exam.. ***nambar*** : beating leaving no m., ***gujjhī mār***, f. : Hindu m., ***ṭikkā***, m., ***tilak***, m.
market, ***bazār***, m. : for special goods, ***manḍī***, f : *see* purchases.
marriage, whole celebration, ***shādī***, f., ***wiāh***, n. : actual m., ***nikāh***, m. (M.) : *see* marry
marriage procession, ***jañ***, f. : gathering, ***mēḷ***, m. : member of ***jañ***, ***jāñī*** : of ***mēḷ***, ***mēḷī*** : m. -gift, ***neōndrā***, m. : ***bhāñī***, ***bhānjī***, f. : m. settlement, maihr, m. (M.).
marrow, ***mikkh***, f.
marry, M. ***shādī k***.. ***wiāh k***., ***nikāh paṛhāṇā*** (all w. ***nāḷ***) : of priest, ***nikāh paṛhnā***. H., ***lāwā̃ laiṇiā̃***, ***phere laiṇe*** : ***wiāh k***., ***manḍū paṛhnā*** (both w. ***nāḷ***) : of priest, ***wiāh karāṇā*** (***dā***), ***wiāh paṛhnā*** (***dā***) : widow remarriage, ***cādar pāṇī***, ***cādrā pāṇā*** (***nāḷ***), ***karēwā***, m. (H.)
Gen. words, ***khasm karnā*** (marry husband), ***zanānī karnī*** (wife), or ***karnā*** w. person's name : ***ghar wassṇā*** (***dā***) : man married second time, ***duhājū*** (no word for woman).
marsh, ***jhīl***, f. (also lake).
martyr, ***shahīd***, m.
martyrdom, ***shahīd*** h.
masculine, ***muzakkar***.
mason, ***rāj***, m.
massage, *see* shampoo.
mast, ***mastaul***, m.
master, *see* owner, teacher, clever.
masterless, *see* ownerless.
mat, straw, ***phūhṛ***, m. : ***catāī***, f. : small ***phūhṛī***, f. : for prayer, ***masallā***, m. (M.) : *see* rug, sack.
match (lucifer), ***tīllī***, f. : collective, ***mācas***, m. : m.-box, ***ḍabbī***, f.
match, game, ***maic***, m.
match, v., ***raḷāṇā***, int. ***raḷnā***.
matchless, ***sabbhnā̃ tō caṅgā***, ***waḍḍā***, etc. : *see* unique.
mate, ***jōṛīdār***, ***sāthī*** : *see* companion.
materials of house, ***malbā***, m. : minor m. for building, ***masālā***, m.
mathematics, ***hisāb***, m. : ***riāzī***, f.

matter, *see* affair, pus : no m., ***oh jāṇe, koī ḍar nehī̃, koī parwāh nehī, jāṇ dē*** : *see* right (2).

matting, *see* mat.

mattress, ***tulāī***, f. : ***gadēlā***, m. : *see* quilt.

mature, ***pūrī umr dā, pakkā***.

maund, ***maṇ***, m. : *see* wts. and meas.

May, ***maī***, f. : ***mĕī***, f. : ***jēṭh***, (about May 13 to June 12).

maxim, opinion, ***maslā***, m.

maximum, ***waddh tõ waddh*** marks, ***pūre nambar***.

me, ***menū̃***.

meal, a, ***khāṇā***, m. : one of two daily meals, ***daṅg***, m. : flour, coarse, ***āṭī***, m. ; fine, ***maidā***, m.

mean, ***kamīnā*** : stingy, ***shūm, kaṇjūs*** (U).

mean, v. *see* signify.

meaning, of word, ***maihṇe***, m. pl. : sense, intention, ***matlab***, m.

meanness, ***kamīnā kamm***, m. : stinginess, ***shūm puṇā***, m.

means, ***wasīlā***, m. : *see* income, livelihood : by m. of, through, ***oh de wasīle. ohdī rāhī*** : by all m., *see* certainly : you're welcome. ***jam jam, jī sadke, sir matthe te***.

meanwhile, ***inne*** or ***ōnne wicc, hālī, hālā̃, ucarā̃ nū̃, icarā̃ nū̃***.

measles, ***khasrā***, m. : (***nikḷṇā, nū̃***).

measure, v., ***miṇṇā, kacchṇā, mēcṇā*** : be m.-ed. by tailor, shoemaker, ***nū̃ mēcā dēṇā*** : n., ***nāp***, m. : ***mēcā***, m. : ***pamaish***, f (***k.***).

measuring-tape, ***fītā***, m.

meat, for food, ***mās***, m. : ***gōshat, gōsht***, m. : ***tarkārī***, f. : ***lauṇ***, m. : *see* mutton, beef, flesh.

meat-safe, ***ḍōllī***, f.

mechanical, ***kalā̃ nāḷ***.

mechanism, ***kalā̃, kalā***, f. : *see* machine.

medal, ***tagmā***, m. : ***takmā***, m.

meddle, *see* interfere.

mediator, ***wicōlā*** : referee, ***tarfain*** : *see* umpire.

medicine, ***duāī***, f. : ***dārū***, m.

mediocre, *see* average, and add ***mamūlī, aust darje dā***.

meditation, ***dhiān***, m., ***giān dhiān***, m

meek, use "not proud."

meet, ***milnā*** (***nū̃***) : ***ṭakkarnā*** (***nū̃***, by accident) : ***mulākāt karnī*** (***nāḷ***, interview) : go to meet, ***ohnū̃ aggõwāḷī*** or ***aggalwāhndī milnā, ohdī aggalwāhndī nū̃ nikḷṇā, aggō laiṇ jāṇā***.

meeting (someone), n., ***ṭākrā***, m. : ***mulākāt***, f. : relig. m., ***miṭiṅ***, f. : *see* assembly.

melody, *see* tune.

melon, musk, ***khakkhṛī***, f. : water, ***haduāṇā***, m. : Kabuli, ***sardā***, m.

melt, v., int., ***gaḷṇā*** (also meat, rice, etc., getting too soft : tr. ***gāḷṇā***) : ***pagharnā*** (esp. fat before fire : tr. ***paghrāṇā***) : dissolve, as salt, sugar in water, tr. ***ghōḷṇā, khōrnā*** (int. ***ghuḷṇā, khurnā***).

member, ***sharīk***, m. : ***mimbar***, m.

memorial, ***yādgār***, f. : *see* memory.
memory, faculty. ***cētā***, m. : (or ***hāfzā***, m., U. : never ***yād***) : bad m., ***cētā kharāb*** : within my m., ***mērī hōsh sambhāḷ wicc*** : *see* remember : in m. of, ***dī yādgārī wāste***, or ***wicc***.
mend, *see* repair, shoe.
menial, member of lower caste, shoemaker, barber, carpenter, sweeper, etc., ***kam-mī***. fem. ***-ṇeāṇī*** : *see* servant.
mention, ***dā zikr k.***, ***dā nā̃ laiṇā***, ***dī*** (or ***dā***) ***carcā k.***
mercantile, ***sudāgarī dā***, ***tajārat dā***.
merchandise, ***saudā***, m. : ***saudā sūd***, m. ***māl***, m.
merchant, ***sudāgar***, ***byōpārī***, ***tajārat karnwāḷā***.
merciful, *see* compassionate, mercy.
mercury, ***pārā***, m.
mercy, ***raihm***, m. (***auṇā*** or ***k.***, ***utte***) : *see* pity.
merely, ***nirā***, ***sirf*** (not ***khālī***).
merrymaking, ***khushī karnī***.
message, verbal, ***sanēhā***, m. : ***sanāh***, m. : work, ***kamm*** m. : ***buttī***, m. : ***wiḍḍī***, f.
messenger, use "man."
metal, ***dhāt***, f.
method, ***tarīkā***, m., ***kaidā***, m., *see* manner.
metempsychosis, ***awāgaū***, m. : ***āwāgauṇ***, m. : ***curāsī***, m. (all H.).
mew, cat, ***miaūkṇā***.
midday, *see* noon.
middle, ***wishkār***, m. : ***addh wishkār***, m. : adj., ***wiclā***, ***wishkārlā***.
middle-aged, ***adhkaṛ***.
middleman, ***dalāl***.
middling, *see* average, mediocre.
midnight, ***addhī rāt***, f.
midwife, ***dāī***.
might, *see* power, strength, strong.
milch, ***lawērī*** (cow or buffalo).
mild, person, ***halīm***, ***narmdil***, *see* kind, compassionate, merciful.
mildness, ***halīmī***, f. : ***narmdilī***, f.
mile, ***mīl***, m. : 1½ m., ***kōh*** : m., roughly, ***kuhāṭrā***, m. : *see* wts. and meas.
milestone, ***mīl dā pathar***, m.
milk, n., ***duddh***, m. : for first few days after calf born, ***bauhḷī***. f., ***bauhḷā***, m. : butter-milk, ***lassī***, f. : v., ***dhār kaḍḍhṇī*** (***dī***) ; ***cōṇā*** (obj. both milk and cow) : cow, etc. let herself be milked, ***gā̃ milṇī***, M. 125. 1.
milkman, ***dodh-ī***, fem. ***-aṇ*** ; ***duddhwāḷā***.
mill, hand-, ***cakkī***, f. : oxen, ***khrās***, m. : water, ***ghrāṭ***, m. : *see* millstone.
millet, ***juār***, f. : ***bājrā***, m.
million, ***das lakh*** : ten m., ***karōṛ***, m. : ordinals, ***das lakhwā̃***, ***karōṛwā̃***.
millionaire, ***lakhpatī***, ***karōṛpatī***.
millstone, ***puṛ***, m. : to roughen m., ***rāhṇā***.
mimic, *see* imitate, jester, grimace.

mince, ***mins***, m. (***k.***, K.) ; ***kīmā***, m. (***k.***).
mind, ***dil***, m. : ***jī***, m. : ***man***, m. : *see* sense, intelligence : never m., *see* matter : not m. him, ***ohdī parwāh nā karnī.***
mine, n., ***khāṇḍ***, ***khāṇ***, f. : *see* tunnel.
mingle, *see* mix.
mint, herb, ***pūdnā***, m.
mint, for coin, ***ṭaksāl***, f., ***taṅgsāl***, f.
minute, n., ***minṭ***, m.
minute, fine, *see* fine.
miracle, ***karāmāt***, f. : ***mohjzā***, m.
mirror, ***shīshā***, m.
mischief, ***sharārat***, f.
mischievous, ***sharārtī***, ***sharīr*** (last three words applied to grown-up people mean wicked-, -ness).
miser, ***shūm***, ***kanjūs***, nic.
miser-able, -y, *see* poor, straits.
miserliness, ***shūmpuṇā***, m. : ***kanjūsī***, f.
misfortune, ***badkismalī***, f. : ***badnasībī***, f. : *see* calamity.
misjudge, ***galt khyāl karnā*** (***dā***, ***dī bābat***).
mispronounce, ***galt talaffaz bōlṇā*** (***dā***)
mislay, ***rakkhke bhull jāṇā.***
miss (aim), ***ukkṇā***, ***wār ẽwẽ jāṇī***, ***nishānā ẽwẽ jāṇā***, ***gōlī*** etc., ***nā laggṇī*** or ***khunjh jāṇī*** ; m. train, ***gaḍḍīõ khunjhṇā*** or ***ghussṇā*** or ***raih jāṇā*** : m. way, ***rāhõ khunjhṇā*** or ***ghussṇā*** : feel person's absence, ***ohde khuṇõ*** or ***bājhõ dil õddarnā*** : m. day, ***diṇ chaḍḍṇā diṇ khālī jāṇā.***
mission, ***mishn***, f.
missionary, ***mishnarī***, ***pādrī sāb*** : lady m., ***mishn dī miss snb.***
misstate, ***galt beān karnā*** (***dā***).
mist, *see* fog.
mistake, ***galtī***, f. (***k.***, ***h.***) : ***bhull***, f. (***h.***), ***bhull cukk***, f. : ***bhulēkhā***, m. (***laggṇā***, ***nū̃***) : ***khunjhṇā***, ***ghussṇā.***
mistress, *see* teacher.
misunderstanding, ***galtfaihmī***, f. (U.)
mix, v. tr., ***raḷāṇā***, ***miḷāṇā*** (int. ***raḷṇā***, ***miḷṇā***) : int. ***āpe icc miḷde juḷde*** (or ***giḷde***) ***ne.***
mix-ed, -ture, ***raḷā miḷā*** : ***khicṛī***, f., *see* adulterate., -d.
moan, *see* groan.
mock, *see* imitate, jester.
mocker, *see* jester.
model, *see* pattern.
moderate, *see* average, mediocre.
modern, ***inhā̃ diṇā̃ dā***, ***ajj kall dā***, ***hāl de zamāne dā*** : *see* new.
modest, ***nēkbakht***, or *see* good.
moist, moisten, *see* damp, wet.
moisture, *see* damp : in soil for ploughing, ***wattar.*** m., G. 122 : M. 129. 26.8 : ***wattar hō geā***, rain has wet soil enough for ploughing : ***jīwī̃ wattar ā gei***, (after v. heavy rain) soil dried enough to be ready for ploughing : ***hēṭhlā utlā wattar raḷ geā e***, the m. from rain has reached down to the soil m. : ***rēj***, m. (m. in earth of house after rain).
Monday, ***suār***, m. : ***somwār***, m.

money, ***rupayyā paisā***, m. : *see* wealth.
money-lender, ***sāhūkār***, ***shāhūkār***, ***shāh***.
mongoose, ***neōḷa***, ***nyōḷa***, m.
monkey, ***bānd-ar*** fem. ***-rī***.
monotheis-m, -t, ***ikko Khudā nū̃ mann-ṇā***, ***-aṇwāḷā***.
month, ***mahīnā***. m. : last m., ***pishle mahīne***. *see* next.
monthly, ***mahīne dā***, ***mahīne de mahīne***.
moon, ***cann***, m. : full m., ***pandhrawī̃ rāt dā cann*** : light night, ***cānnī rāt*** f : *see* rise, set.
morals, ***cāl caln*** m.
more, ***waddh***, ***wadhīk***. ***hōr***, ***zyādā***, ***wadhērā***.
moreover, ***nāḷe***, ***te nāḷe***
morning, ***subā***, f. : ***waddewelā***, m. : ***sarghī weḷā***, ***parbhāt weḷā***, 1½ hrs. before dawn : ***namāz weḷā***, ¾ hour before dawn : ***jhucmusṛā***, m., ***muhānjlā***, m., ***mū̃h anhērā***, m., morning twilight : ***dhammī weḷā***, m., time of dawn : ***jhalānghe***, at sunrise : ***fajr***, f., early m. : *see* forenoon.
morsel, *see* mouthful.
mortal, ***fānī*** : *see* deadly, fatal.
mortar for pointing, pink, ***cūnā***, m. : black, ***simīlṭ***, m. : ***simīnṭ***, m. : *see* point (4), pestle.
mortgage, v., ***gaihṇe pāṇā*** : *see* pawn.
mosque, ***masīt***, f.
mosquito, ***macchar***, m. : ***guttī***, f. : -net, ***machairī*** f., ***jāṭī*** f., do. w. rods, ***macchardānī***, f.
most, ***sabbhnā̃*** or ***sāreā̃ tõ waddh***, ***waddh tõ waddh***.

moth, ***bāhmaṇ baccā***, m.
mother, ***bēbbe***, ***mā̃***, ***māī***, ***wāldā*** (U.) : m. in law, ***sass*** : m. in law's father, ***naniauhrā*** (his wife, ***nanēhs***) ; m. in law's brother ***maliauhrā*** (his wife, ***malēhs***) : mothers of bride and bridegroom are ***kuṛmṇī*** to each other.
motion, ***harkat***, f. : in meeting, ***mōshn***, f. : ***rā*** f. : *see* move.
motive, ***matlab***, m. : ***wicclā matlab*** ; ***garz***, f
mould, bricks ***saccā***, m. : pudding ***sāncā***, m. (K.) : v. tr., ***sacce wicc ḍhāḷṇā*** (int. ***ḍhaḷṇā***).
mould (green), ***ullī***, f. (***lagg- ṇī***, ***nū̃***).
mound, ***ṭibbā***, m. : ***ḍhērī***, f.
mount, ***utte carhnā*** (tr. ***cārhnā***) : m. animal or vehicle, ***suār h.*** (tr. ***k.***).
mountain, ***pahār***, m. ***parbat***, m. : *see* hill.
mountainous, belonging to mountains, ***pahārī***.
mourn, ***mātam-k.***, ***karlāṇā***.
mourners, collective, ***mukān***, f.
mourning, united, ***mukān***, f.
mouse, ***cūhi***, f. (no word for male) : *see* rat
mouse-trap, *see* trap.
moustache, ***muochā̃***, f. pl. : beard and m., ***dārhī mucch***, f.
mouth, ***mū̃h***, m. : at his m., through him, ***ohdī zabānī***, G. 36, 37 : corner of m., ***warāch***, f. : get sore m., ***mū̃h pakk jāṇā*** (***dā***) : do. horse, cattle, etc. ***mū̃h***

auṇā (*dā*), M. 117. 9 : ***mū̃h pakk jāṇā***.
mouthful, liquid, ***ghuṭṭ***, m. : solid, ***barkī***, f., ***burkī***, f., ***garāh***, m., ***garāhi***, f.
move, ***hallṇā*** (tr. ***halāṇā***) : m. away, ***haṭṇā*** (tr. ***haṭāṇā***) : m. a motion, ***pēsh-k.*** : without moving, gently, ***aḍōl***, ***malkṛī***.
moving, *see* pathetio, motion.
mow, grass, ***ghāh mārnā*** or ***waḍḍhnā***, *see* reap.
much, ***cōkhā***, ***bāḷā***, ***bauht***, ***bathērā***, ***ām***, ***wāfar*** : *see* more : many, use plur. of much : as m. as I, ***mēre jinnā***, G. 91 92 : *see* number.
mucus, ***balgam***, m
mud, ***cikkar***, m., ***cikkar***, ***cambhar***, m. : half-dry, ***khobhā***, m. : cake of m., ***carēpṛī***, f. : m. for building, w. straw, ***ghāṇi***, f. : without straw, ***gārā***, m. get covered w. m., ***bharnā***, ***miṭṭī nāḷ bharnā*** : M. 118. 22.
muddy (water), ***gandhḷeā hoeā***, ***gandhḷā***.
muffler, *see* tie (2).
mug, ***magg***, m.
mulberry, tree and fruit, ***tūt***, m. : large-fruited, ***shatūt*** m.
mule, ***k͟hac-rā***, fem. ***-car*** (masc. rare) : ***wáihtar***, m. (also horse, ass). man in mule corps, ***k͟haccarpātrī***.
multiply (educ.), ***zarb dēṇi*** (***nū̃***, ***nāḷ***) : *see* increase : multiplication table, ***pahāṛā***, m.
multitude, *see* crowd.
murder, ***k͟hūn***, m. (***k.***, ***dā***).
murderer, ***k͟hūnī***.
murmur, ***hauḷī bōlṇā***, *see* gramble.
muscle, no word, use ***mās***, m. : ***gōsht***, ***goshat***, m. : m. of forearm, ***bā̃h dī machḷī***, f. : of lower leg, ***pinnī dī machḷī***. f. : m. to right and left of aesophagus, ***rag***, f. : *see* biceps.
museum, ***ajaib ghar***, m.
mushroom, ***khumb***, f. : toadstool, ***padd bhairā*** m.
music, *see* tune, play, instrument.
musician, professional and gen. disreputable, ***mirās-ī***, fem. ***-aṇ*** : ***ḍūm-***, fem. ***-ṇī*** : singer (good meaning), ***gawayyā***, (no fem.); ***gauṇwālā***.
musk-rat, ***cakcūhndar***, m.
muslin, ***malmal***, f.
mustard, ***rās***, f., ***auhr***, f. : growing, ***sarhō***, ***sarheō***, f. : ***tārāmirā***, m.
mutineer, ***bāgī***.
mutiny, ***bagāwat***, f. (***k.***) : ***gadr***, m. (***k.***).
mutter, *see* murmur, grumble.
mutton, word for meat w. ***nikkā***, small, or ***bākrā***, of sheep or goat, prefixed ***maṭaṇ***, m. (K.).
muzzle, *see* snout, halter.
my, ***mērā***.
mvitery, *see* secret

N

nail, finger, toe ***nauh***, m. : smali iron, ***brinī***, f. : ***prēk***, f. : large, iron or wood, ***killī***, f. : ***kill***, m. : ***mēk͟h***, f. : *see* hammer.

naked, ***naṅgā.***
nakedness, ***naṅg,*** m.
name, ***nā̃*** m. : ***nā̃wa,*** m. (esp. in list) : v. tr., ***nā̃ rakkhṇā*** or ***dharnā*** : *see* call : get a n. for, ***all paiṇī*** (***dī***) : getting bad n., ***bhaṇḍī, badnāmī,*** f. (both w. ***h., dī***) : *see* named.
named, ***musamm-ī,*** fem. ***-āt*** : be called Kammo, ***Kammo akhwāndī*** or ***sadāndī e,*** G. 109 : ***Kammo, Kammo karke saddde ne.***
nape, *see* neck.
napkin, ***mēz dā tauliā,*** m. : for infant, ***nāpkin.*** m.
narrate, *see* relate.
narrow, ***sauṛā, bhīṛā, taṅg*** : ***ghatt cauṛā e*** : of cloth, ***bar chōtā e.***
native, ***dēsī*** (Indian) : n. language, ***mādrī bōlī*** : *see* country.
natural, ***kudratī***
naturally, ***uñ ī.***
nature (around) ***kudrat,*** f. : *see* disposition.
naughty, *see* mischievous.
navel, ***dhunnī,*** f.
navigable, ***jitthe kishtiā̃ yā̃jahāz jā sakaṇ.***
navy, ***jahāz,*** m. : ***jaṅgī jahāz*** (in plur.).
near, ***nēṛe, kōḷ, koḷe, nāḷ, karīb*** : *see* distance : adj., ***nāḷ dā, nēṛe dā, urlā,*** fr. n., ***nēṛeō̃, koḷō̃, nāḷō̃*** : pass by n., ***neṛe dū̃, nāḷdū̃*** or ***nāḷō̃ dī, kōḷdū̃*** or ***koḷō̃, dī*** (***laṅghṇā, jāṇā***).
nearly, ***karīban, karīb, kujjh ghaṭṭ*** : *see* approximately.
necessary, ***zarūrī, lāzarūrī*** : ***lō̃ṛīdā*** or ***cāhīdā,*** G. 67, 96 : *see* have to.
necessaries, ***sorūrī cizā̃, lō̃ṛwā ḷiō̃ cizā̃.***
necessity, ***lō̃ṛ*** f. : ***zarūrat,*** f.
neck, nape, ***gicī,*** f. : ***dhauṇ,*** f. : ***gāṭā,*** m. : ***muṇḍī,*** f. : ***garden.*** f. : front, ***gaḷ,*** m. : *see* throat, Adam's apple, aesophagun
necklace, ***haikaḷ,*** f. : ***hassī.*** f. : ***hass,*** m. : ***hasīrā,*** m. : etc.
necktie, ***nakṭāī,*** f.
need, *see* necessity
needle ***sūī,*** f. : large, ***sūī,*** m.
neglect, ***lāparwāhī,*** f. : ***gaflat,*** f., ***gāftī,*** f. (all ***k.***).
negotiation, ***gall katth,*** f. (***k.***).
negro, ***habsh-ī,*** fem. ***-aṇ.***
neigh, ***hiṇakṇā.***
neighbour, ***guāhṇḍ-ī,*** fem. ***-aṇ.***
neighbourhood, ***guāhṇḍ,*** f. : ***āhṇḍ guāhṇḍ,*** f.
neither, ***dohā̃ wiccō̃ koī nā*** : n ...nor, ***nā.. nā*** : ***nā te.. te nā*** : ***nā.. te nā.***
nephew, brother's son, ***bhatriā*** : sister's son, ***bhaṇēwā̃, bhaṇeā*** : n.'s wife, ***bhatriō̃ nū̃h bhaṇeweō̃ nū̃h.***
nest, ***ālhṇā,*** m.
net, fishing, ***jāḷ,*** m. : tennis n., ***jāḷī,*** f. : for straw, chaff, ***traṅgaṛ,*** m. : wire netting, ***jāḷī*** : *see* mosquito.
never, ***kadī nā*** : never ! interj. ***majāl e, tōbbā tōbbā*** : of incredulity, ***hēkkhā̃,*** (the reply is ***hēkkhā̃ kī ?)***
new, ***nawā̃*** : fresh, ***sajrā*** : n. or

unwashed cloth, unused paper, waterpot, ***kōrā***.

news, ***khabar***, f. : incorrect, ***gapp***, f.

newspaper, ***akhbār***, f.

next, ***nāl dā***, ***dujjā***, ***aglā***, ***aglā*** : n. week, month, year, ***agle***, ***aunwāle hafte***, ***mahine sāl*** : ***aunde sāl*** : this day n. week, ***ajj de*** or ***ajōke dihāre***.

nib, ***cunjh***, f. : ***par***, m.

nibble, ***kutarnā*** : *see* gnaw.

nice, *see* good, tasty.

niche, ***ālā***, m.

nickel, ***cittā trāmmā***, m.

nickname (to annoy) ***cēṛh***, f. (***paiṇī***) : otherwise, say ***nā̃ pai geā***.

niece, brother's daughter, ***bhatrī***, sister's, ***bhaṇēwī̃***, ***bhaṇei***. niece's husband, ***bhatrīõ*** or ***bhaṇewīõ jawāī***.

night, ***rāt***, f. (***paiṇī***) : by n., ***rātī̃*** n. and day, ***rātī̃ diṇe***, ***dēh rātī̃*** : to-n., last n., ***ajj rāt nū̃***, ***ajj rātī̃*** : n -clothes, ***rāt de kapṛe***, m. pl. : *see* bedding.

nightmare, ***ḍaraonī khāb***, f.

nine, ***naū̃*** : ***-th***, ***nauā̃***, ***nāwā̃***.

nineteen, ***unnī*** : ***-th***, ***unnhīwā̃***, G 22.

ninety, ***nawwe***, ***nabbe*** : -one, ***ikānwe*** : -two ***bānwe*** : -three, ***tarānwe*** : four, ***curānwe*** : -five, ***pac-*** or ***panj-ānwe*** : -six, ***cheānwe*** : seven, ***satānwe*** : -eight, ***aṭhānwe*** : -nine, ***naṛinwe*** : ordinals add ***-wā̃*** and high tone ***h***, ***nabbhewā̃***, ***ikāhnwewā̃***, etc. :

nipple, baby's indiarubber, ***cūsṇī***, f., ***cūpṇī***, f.

nitre, ***shōrā***, m.

no, ***nā***, ***nehī̃***, ***āhā̃*** (w. glottal stop at end) : *see* nothing, nowhere.

no one, ***koī nehī̃***.

nobility, ***sharāfat*** f. : *see* noble.

noble, rank, ***sharīf khāndān dā***, ***āhlā rais***.

nod, *see* sleepy.

noise, ***rauḷā***, m. : ***khapp***, f. : ***ḍaṇḍ***, f. : ***raṭṭā***, m. : ***rēṛkā***, m. (all ***pāṇā***, int. ***paiṇā***) : ***shōr***, m. (***k.***), ***awāz***, f. (***aunī*** : ***mārnī***, call) : ***khṛāk***, m. (***auṇā***, of footsteps, cart, etc.) : *see* splash, disturbance.

nomad, ***pakkhīwās-***, fem. ***-aṇ*** : ***ṭaprīwāḷā***, *see* tent.

nominal, ***nirā nā̃ ī e***.

nominate, ***nā̃ pēsh karnā*** (***dā***).

nonsense : *see* never : ***wāhyāt gall***, f. : ***bakwās***, f. : ***wāfrī***, f. : ***wāfar gall***, f. (all ***k.***) : ***yabbhā̃***, f. pl. (***mārniā̃***) : ***fazūl*** or ***wāfar gallā̃***, f. pl. (***k.***) : ***gappā̃***, f. pl. (***mārniā̃***) : talker of n., ***bakwās-ī***, fem. ***-aṇ***.

noon, ***dopaihr***, f. : at n., ***dopaihrī̃*** : *see* afternoon, forenoon.

nor, *see* neither.

north, ***pahāṛ***, m. : ***parbat***, m. : n.-wards, ***pahāṛ*** or ***parbat pāse*** or wall : n.-east, ***pahāṛ te caṛhde dī guṭṭh*** : n.-west, ***pahāṛ te laihnde dī guṭṭh***.

nose, ***nakk***; flat-nosed, ***phīhnā*** : blow n., ***nakk suṇknā***.

nostril, ***nās***, f.

not, ***nā, nehī̃.***
note, *see* letter : bank-n., ***nōṭ,*** m. : make n. of, ***likkṇā, nōṭ k.***
notebook, ***kāpī,*** f. : ***nōṭbuk.*** f.
noteworthy, ***sōccaṇ*** or ***suṇaṇ*** or ***yād rakkhaṇ jogā.***
nothing, ***kujjh, nehī̃*** : n. at all, ***kakkh wī nehī̃*** : come to n., ***guggaḷ jāṇā.***
notice, n., ***ishtihar,*** m. : v., ***khyāl karnā*** (***dā***) : ***dhiān karnā*** : *see* advertisement.
notwithstanding, ***bhāwẽ.***
nourish, *see* maintain.
novel, *see* new : book, ***nāwal,*** m.
November, ***nawambar,*** m. : ***magghar,*** m. (about Nov. 13 to Dec. 12).
now, ***hun, huṇe*** : at present, ***hālī, hālī*** : only n., ***aje huṇe*** : now now !, interj. (rebuke), ***hāẽ, āhẽ.***
nowhere, ***kitale nā,*** or ***nehī̃.***
noxious, *see* injure, loss, hurt.
numb, ***ṭhareā hoeā*** (through cold, v. cold) : ***sunn*** (also limb asleep).
number, *see* figure : ***nambar,*** m., of page, house, regiment, etc. : ***tedād,*** f., of people, etc. : what page ? ***kinnawā̃ safā̃*** ? (so ***jinnawā̃, innawā̃, ōnnawā̃***), also ***kinnā, kehṛā.***
nurse, ayah, ***āyā,*** f. : European n., ***nais miss sāb*** : midwife, ***dāī.***
nursery, of plants, ***zakhīrā.***
nut, pistachio, ***pistā,*** m. : *see* walnut.

O

O, calling : woman to woman, ***nī̃, aṛīe*** : woman to man, ***wē*** : man to man, ***ō, ōe*** : man to woman, ***ē*** : all imply "***tū̃***" : *see* oh.
oar, ***cappū,*** m.
oath, ***saũh,*** f. : ***kasm,*** f. (both ***khāṇī, cukkṇī***) : ***Kurān cukkṇā,*** take o. on Quran : administer o., ***duāṇī, cukāṇi*** (***nū̃***) : be v. unwilling to, lit, take o. against, ***eh kamm karn dī saũh hōṇī*** or ***cukkṇī*** : M. 107. 17-9.
oats, ***gaṇḍhaiḷ,*** f.
obey, obedience, ***tābedārī karnī*** (***dī***); ***ākkhe laggṇā*** (***de***); ***hukm mannṇā*** (***dā***).
object, ***garz,*** f. : *see* intention, sim : secure o., ***kamm*** or ***matlab kaḍḍhṇā.***
objection, ***ehtrāz,*** m. (***k.***) : ***uzr,*** m. (***k.***), excuse.
obligation, favour, ***ahsān,*** m. (pron. ***as-hān***) : ***ṭhāhrā,*** m. : admit o., ***ahsān*** or ***ṭhāhrā mannṇā*** (***dā***) : trade on another's o. to one, ***ahsān*** or ***ṭhāhrā cāṛhnā*** (***utte***) or ***manāṇā*** : *see* benefit.
oblige, *see* force, cause : *see* obligation.
obliterate, *see* delete, efface.
obscene, ***gandā, fohsh.***
obscure, *see* dark, ambiguous : ***matlab sāf nehī̃.***
observe, *see* notice, attend.
obstacle, *see* hindrance.
obstinacy, ***zidd*** (***bannhṇī***) : ***khaih*** (***rakkhṇī***) : ***hatth,*** m., ***aṛī,*** f., ***kabbpuṇā,*** m. (all w. ***k.***).

obstinate, ***ariyal, ziddī.***
obstruct-, -ion, *see* hinder, hindrance, and add ***arekā***, m. : ***mushkil***, f. : ***arikk*** or ***aricc***, f. (all w. ***pāṇā*** : also ***aricc ḍāhṇī***).
obtain, ***labbh laiṇā, laiṇā*** : ***menū̃ labbhā*** or ***mileā, mēre hatth āeā*** : *see* secure, supply, produce.
obvious, *see* evident.
occasion, ***maukā***, m. : *see* opportunity.
occur, take place, *see* place.
occurrence, ***gall***, f.
ocean, *see* sea.
o'clock, what o ? ***kī wajeā e, kinne waje ne*** ? one o., ***ikk wajeā e*** : at 1 o., ***ikk waje, ikk waje nāḷ*** (about one) : M. 61.
October, ***aktūbar***, m. : ***kattē̃***, m. (about Oct. 13 to Nov. 12).
octroi, *see* tax. ***cungī***
odd, not even, ***tāk*** : *see* strange.
of, ***dā*** : material, ***dā*** : of himself, of his own accord, *see* help.
off, *see* o. see farwell : send o., *see* send : go o., ***Allā Bēlī h., alī panj h.***
offence, stumblingblock, ***thohkar*** (***laggṇī, nū̃, lāṇī***) : take o., ***burā mannṇā*** (at, ***nū̃***) : *see* stumble, resent.
offer, ***pēsh-k., agge rakkhṇā*** : sacrifice, ***cāṛhnā, caṛhāṇā.***
offering, ***caṛhāwā***, m. ***nazr***, f. (both at shrine) : *see* gift, sacrifice.
office, room, ***daftar***, m.
officer, ***afsar*** (military or any superior in office).
official, adj., ***sarkārī*** : n., ***afsar, ohdedār.***
officiat-e, -ing. : ***iwzī, kaim makām, ohde thā̃ kamm karnā.***
often, ***aksar*** : *see* repeatedly.
oh, pain, ***hāl oe, hāe hāe*** : displeasure, ***hāẽ, āhẽ*** : surprise, ***halā***, *see* astonishment : protest, ***tōbbā, lai***, *see* never.
oil, ***tēl***, m : paraffin, ***miṭṭī dā tēl*** : for food, for rubbing, ***miṭṭhā*** or ***kauṛā tēl*** (sweet or bitter, according to origin).
oilman, caste, ***tēl-ī***, fem. ***-aṇ.***
ointment, anoint, ***malham***, f. (***lāṇī***, int. ***laggṇī***) : ***lēp karnā***, without bandage : ***phāh lāṇā***, w. bandage (int. ***laggṇā***) : *see* anoint.
old, ***buḍḍhā, buḍhrā, waḍḍā bandā*** ; *see* great : ancient, ***purāṇā*** : three years old, ***triũh sālā̃*** or ***warheā̃ dā*** become o., ***umar ḍhaḷṇī*** (***dī***) : o. age, ***pishlī umr, baṛī umr, buḍhēpā***, m.
old-fashioned, ***purāṇe faishn*** or ***ḍhaṅg*** or ***namūne dā.***
oleander, ***kanēr***, m.
olive, ***kaū***, m
omen, ***sagaṇ***, m. : random sentence in sacred book, ***fāl***, f. (***kholhṇī, kaddhṇī pāṇī***) : *see* auspicious.
omit, ***chaḍḍṇā*** : miss a day, *see* miss.
omniscient, God, ***sabbho kujjh jāṇdā e, ālam ul gaib*** : man, ***auliā*** (M.).
on, *see* upon.
once, ***ikk wārī, ikk ḍaṅg*** (*see*

meal) : at o., *see* immediately : all at o., *see* suddenly.

one, ***ikk*** ; G. 21 : all at o. time, adv., ***ikko ṛikkī*** : adj., ***ikko ṛikkā*** : 1½ ***ḍēḍh, ḍūḍh*** : adj. from these, ***ḍeoḍhā, ḍeoṛhā***.

onion, ***ganḍhā***, m.

only, ***nirā, sirf*** : *see* emphasis : o. son. no word in nom., obl. ***ikkse*** : for "***ikḳo***" *see* son.

ooze, ***simmṇā, nikḷnā*** : *see* drip, trickle.

open, v. tr., ***kholhṇā*** (gen. : int. ***khulhṇā***) : door, window, lock, ***lāhṇā*** (int. ***laihṇā***) : eyes, ***ughēṛnā*** (int. ***uggharnā***) : mouth, ***aḍḍṇā*** : w. open doors, *see* door : o. school, shop, ***kholhṇā***.

openly, ***khulham khulhā, sāf sāf, khulhī gall*** : *see* publicly.

operation, surgical, ***aprēshan***, m. (***k.***).

ophthalmia, *see* eye.

opinion, ***rā, rai***, f. : ***khyāl***, m. : ***kiās***, f. m. : in his o., ***ohde agge***. G. 91, ***ohde bhāṇe, ohde wanḍe dā, ohde bhā dā*** M. 127. 4-6.

opium, ***afhīm***, f. : ***pōst***, m. (poppy).

opium-eater, ***afīmī, pōstī***.

opponent, ***mukhālaf***, *see* enemy.

opportunity, ***maukā***, m. : ***tāṅg***, m. (both w. ***laggṇā***, get) : seek o., ***maukā wēkhṇā*** or ***jācṇā*** or ***tāṛnā***.

oppose, ***mukāblā karnā*** (***dā***) : ***mukhālfat karnī*** (***dī***) : *see* enemy.

opposite, prep., ***de sāhmṇe*** : *see* face : the o. of, ***ohdā uḷṭ***, M. 279. 18.

oppression, ***zulm***, m. : ***sakhtī*** f. : ***ḍāhḍpuṇā***, m. : ***taddī tōrī***, f. : ***jabr***, m. f. : ***sikkhā shāhī***, f. : (all w. ***k.***, ***utte*** or ***nāḷ***) : *see* violence, confess.

option, ***ikhtiār***, m. : ***marzī***, f.

optional, ***ikhtiārī***.

or, ***ke, yā̃*** : *see* either.

oral, ***zabānī***.

orally, ***mū̃hzabānī*** : heard o. fr. him, ***ohdī zabānī suṇeā***.

orange, Indian, ***santarā***, m. : Maltese, ***māḷṭā***, m. : eat o., ***cūpṇā***.

orange, adj., ***guṭaī***.

ordain-, -ed, *see* preacher.

order, written, ***parwānnā*** (for supplies, etc.) : *see* command, method, class, rank, arrange : in o. to, ***ēs wāste pai, pai, tā̃ jo*** : also inf. w. ***wāste, laī, nū̃***, etc. (G. 95), or simple inflec. inf : in line 17 of G. p. 95, for "in the past tenses of verbs" read "in the case of trans. verbs". Out of o. (machine, cart, well, etc.) ***hanēkeā*** or ***wingṛeā hoeā*** *see* disorder.

orderly, n., ***ardalī, capṛasī***.

orders, holy, *see* preacher.

ordinary, *see* common : every day, affair, ***rōz dī gall***.

organ, ***wājjā***, m. : play, ***wajānā***.

origin, ***asl***, f. : *see* beginning.

ornament, *see* adorn.

orphan, without father, ***yatīm, pyō mhaiṭar*** : without mother, ***mā̃ mhaiṭar***.

orthodox, gen. ***pakkā*** : Hindu, ***sanātanī.***
ostensible, ***zāhrī*** : only outwardly, ***uttō̃wāḷī.***
ostentation, *see* show.
ought, *see* necessary, advisable, duty, require, have to.
other, ***hōr, dujjā.***
otherwise, ***nehī̃ te*** : or use "lest."
out, *see* outside.
outbid, ***wadhke bōlī dēṇī.***
outhouses, ***naukarā̃ de ghar*** : *see* stable, cowhouse.
outpost, ***caukī***, f., ***caũkī***, f.
outside, ***banne, bāhr*** : fr. o., ***banneō̃, bāhrō̃*** : by way of o., ***banneō̃ dī, bāhrō̃ dī*** : on the o., ***bāhrwār.***
outwardly, *see* ostensible.
oven, ***tanūrī, tandūrī***, f. : ***bhaṭṭhī***, f., ***tandūr***, m.
over, *see* above, upon, finish.
overawe, *see* threaten : be o.-ed, ***dabbṇā.***
overcoat, ***waḍḍā kōt***, m. : ***brāṇḍī***, f. (waterproof).
overcome, *see* conquer.
overflow, in vessel, ***ucchaḷṇā*** : boil over, ***ubbaḷ jāṇā, ubbaḷke paiṇā*** : river, ***ucchaḷṇā.***
overhear, deliberately, ***cōrī*** or ***malkṛī suṇṇā*** : accidentally, ***shabb nāḷ*** or ***ẽwẽ suṇṇā.***
overlook, ***nā khyāl karnā*** (***dā***).
overseer, of labourers : *see* superintendent.
overshadow, *see* shade, shadow.
overtake, ***jā raḷṇā*** or ***phaṛnā*** (***nū̃***) : ***kōḷ appaṛnā, agge laṅghṇā.***
overturn, *see* upside down.
owe, he owes, ***ōs dēṇā e.*** he is owed, ***ōs laiṇā e, ohnū̃ aundā e*** : *see* debt.
own, adj., ***apṇā.***
own, owner, ***kih dā e, ehdā mālik kauṇ e.***
ownerless, ***lawāris, nikhasmā*** : of animal temporarily separated fr. its owners, ***luggā.***
ownership, ***mālkī.***
ox, *see* bull : pair for ploughing, ***haḷ***, m., ***jōg***, f.

P

pace, ***kadam***, m. : *see* walk.
pacify, ***rāzī-k.*** : ***sulhā karāṇī*** (***dī***) : *see* calm (2), appease.
pack, ***asbāb teār-karnā*** or ***bannhṇā*** : shove in, ***tunnṇā.***
packet, postal, ***pākaṭ, paikaṭ*** m. : *see* bundle, pareel.
pack-horse, ***lāddū ghōṛā.***
pack-saddle, ***sūṇḍkā.***
pad, on head, ***innū̃***, m.
padlock, *see* lock.
page, ***safhā***, m. : one double p., ***warkā*** (a leaf) : *see* sheet, paper.
pain, ***pīṛ***, f. : ***dard***, m. : griping, ***waṭṭ*** (***paiṇā***) : shooting, ***trāṭ***, f. (***paiṇī***) : *see* grief, hurt.
painful, ***dukhdā e, pīṛ kardā e.***
paint, ***raṅg***, m. : (***lāṇā, nū̃, k., dā*** or ***nū̃***, int. ***laggṇā***).
painter, ***taswīrā̃ baṇāṇwāḷā.***
pair, ***jōṛā***, m. : of oxen, etc., ***jōg***,

f. : ***hal***, m. (for ploughing) : the p. or fellow, ***ehde nāḷ dā***.

palace, ***mahall***, m.

palate, ***tālū***, m.

pale, ***pīḷā*** (***painā***, ***h.***) : ***raṅg laihṇā*** (***dā***) : ***bhussā***, p. ill : of colour, *see* light.

palm, hand, ***taḷī***, f. : date-p., *see* date (1).

palpitate, fear, ***dharaknā*** : excitement, longing, ***taṛafṇā***.

palpitation, ***dhaṛkī***, f.

palsy, ***adhraṅg***, m. : man w. p., ***adhraṅgī***.

pamphlet, ***rasālā***, m.

pankha, *see* punkah.

pannier, donkey's saddle-bags, ***chaṭṭ***, f.

pant, ***chetī chetī sāh laiṇā*** : *see* breath, out of; gasp.

pantry, ***bōtalkhānā***, m.

paper, ***kāgaz***, m. : sheet, ***tā***, m. : *see* news-p., page.

paragraph (educ.) ***pairā***, m.

paralysis, *see* palsy.

paramour, ***yār***.

parapet, ***banērā***, m.

parcel, ***pārsal***, m. : *see* packet.

parch, v. tr., ***bhunnṇā*** : int. ***bhujjṇā*** : grain-parcher, ***bhaṛbhūjā***.

pardon, *see* forgive. ***māfī***, f.

pare, peel, fruit, vegetables, ***chillṇā***, ***chill lāhṇī*** (int. ***laihṇī***, ***dī***) : nails, ***lāhṇā***, gen. ***luhāṇā***, get them done (A.).

parents ***māpe***, ***mā̃ pyō***, ***wāldain***.

part, n., ***hissā***, m. : take p. in, ***raḷṇā***, ***sharīk*** or ***shāmil h.*** (***wicc***) : fifth p., sixth p., etc., *see* time.

part, v., *see* divide.

partake, *see* part, share.

partially, as p. blind, ***kujjh annhā*** : *see* partly, partiality.

partiality, ***rai***, f. : ***tarfdārī***, f.: ***lihāz***, m. (all w. ***k.*** and ***dā***, ***dī***).

particular, *see* special : -s, *see* detail.

partition, *see* part, divi-de, -sion.

partly, ***kujjh te eh . . te kujjh eh***, ***abbaḷ te . .*** or ***ikk te . . te phēr***.

partner, ***sīrī***, ***sānjhī***, ***panjhāḷ***, ***sāthī***, ***jōṛīdār***, ***hissedār*** : half and half p., ***ādhī***.

party, ***farīk***, m. : ***dhir***, f. : ***pāssā***, m. : quarelling clique, ***dhaṛā***, m., *see* sect.

pass, ***laṅghṇā*** (tr. ***laṅghāṇā***) : p. money, ***lāṇā***, ***calāṇā*** (int. ***laggṇā***, ***calṇā***) : p. exam., ***pās h.*** or ***k.*** : p. time ***weḷā ṭapāṇā*** (int. ***ṭappṇā***), ***jhaṭ*** or ***wakat laṅghāṇā*** (int. ***laṅghṇā***).

passage, in book, ***ibārat***, f. : *see* tunnel.

passenger, ***suārī***, f. : p.-train, ***suārī gaḍḍī***, f. : *see* traveller, train (2).

passport, ***pās***, m. : ***rāhdārī***, f.

past, ***jehṛā zamānā laṅgh geā e.*** : ***purāṇā zamānā***.

paste, ***lēwī***, f. (for gumming : ***lāṇī***, int. ***laggṇī***) : for pudding, ***krās***, m. (K.) : *see* gum, glue.

pasture, *see* graze.

pat, v. tr., ***thāpṛī mārnī*** or ***dēṇī*** or ***lāṇī***, (also ***thāpṛā***, m.).

patch, cloth, leather, ***ṭākī*** (***lāṇī***, int. ***laggṇī***) : metal, ***ṭāṅkā*** (***lāṇā***, int. ***laggṇā***) : not a p. on him, ***ohdā pāskū̃ wī nehī̃***.

path, ***paihā***, m. : ***rāh***, m. : v. narrow (between fields, *see* boundary), ***bannā***, m. : track, ***ghāssī***, f. : *see* rosd, way.

pathetic, ***rōṇ-*** or ***ruāṇ-wāḷī gall***, f. : *see* sad, touching.

patience, ***hauslā*** m. : ***sabr***, m.

patient, adj., ***hausle*** or ***sabr wāḷā*** : n., ***bamār***, ***marīz*** (U.).

patriotism, ***watan dī mhabbat***, f.

pattern, ***namūnā***, m.

paucity, ***thuṛh***, f. : ***ghāṭā***, m. : ***kamī***, f. : *see* deficient.

paw, ***panjā***, m. : p. ground (horse), ***khauṛū kaḍḍṇā***.

pawn, v. tr., ***gaihṇe*** or ***bandhe pāṇā*** or ***rakkhṇā***.

pay, ***tankhdh***, f. (***tārnī***, ***dēnī*** : int. ***tarnī***, ***miḷnī***) : p debt, ***dēṇā***, ***lāhṇā*** (int. ***laihṇā***) : p. fine, ***bharṇā*** : *see* strike off.

peace, between parties, ***sulhā***, f. : in country, ***aman***, m. : rest ***arām***, m. : cf mind, ***tsallī***, f., ***taslla***, f. : M. salutaion, (***as-***) ***salām alaikum*** : reply, ***wā alaikum*** (***as-***) ***salām***.

peacemaker, ***sulhā karāṇwāḷā***.

peach, ***ārū***, m (tree and fruit).

peak, of countain, ***cōṭī***, f. : ***sirā***, m. : ***tīshī***, f.

pear, ***nākh***, f (tree and truit).

pea, ***maṭar***, m.

pearl, ***mōtī***, m.

peasant, *see* farmer, villager.

pebble, ***giṭī***, f. : ***giṭā***, m.

peck, ***cunjh*** or ***cinjh mārnī***, ***ṭhūngā mārnā*** : eat grain, etc., ***cuggṇā***.

peculation, ***gaban karnā***.

peculiar, *see* strange.

pedlar, *see* hawker.

pedigree, ***nasabnāmā***, m. : tree, ***shajrā***, m.

peel, ***chill*** f. : v., *see* pare.

peep, ***jhāttī mārnī***.

peepul tree, ***pippaḷ***, m.

peerless, ***sāreā̃ tõ wadhīā*** or ***awwaḷ***, ***ohde jehā*** or ***barābar koī nehī̃*** : ***bēnazīr*** (U.) ; ***lāsānī*** (U.), *see* matchless.

peevish, ***shtābī ciṛhnwāḷā***.

peg. *see* nail.

pellet, (small for ***gulēl***), ***gulēlā***, m. : (large, for ***kubhāṇī***), ***ḍhīṇḍhā***, m. : *see* sling. pebble.

pen, ***par***, m. : ***kalam***, f. : *see* nib : p. and ink, ***kalam duāt***, f. : p.-tray, ***kalamdān***, m.

pencil, ***pinsal***, f. : ***pilsaṇ***, f. ***rūl***, f. m.

penetrate, *see* enter, pierce. sink.

penknife, ***cakkū***, m.

penman, *see* caligraphist.

pension, ***pinshan***, f.

Pentateuch, ***taurēt***, f.

people, ***lōk***, m. pl. : ***lōkī***, m pl. : Tom, Dick and Harry ***jaṇā khaṇā***, ***hamā shamā*** : *see* common, everyone, all.

people, v. tr., ***abād - k*** (place) : ***wasāṇā***, settle p. in a place

pepper, black, ***kāḷī marc***, f. ***gōḷ marc***, f. : red, ***lāl marc***. f.

per, ***picche***, ***sētī*** (both after infl. noun) ; ***ṭī*** (before noun, U.) : in prices often loc., G. 78 : per man, ***jaṇe sētī*** : per house, ***ghar picche*** : at 6/- a maund, ***chī̃ rupaī̃ maṇ*** : *see* rate.
per cent, ***saikṛā*** (5%, ***panj rupayye saikṛā***) : ***jī sadī*** : -age given to lambardar, zaildar, ***panjōtrā***, m.

peremptory, *see* imperious, urgent.

perennial, ***jehṛā sārā sāl rawhe***.

perfect, ***kāmal***, ***pūrā*** : *see* complete, guiltless.

perfection, ***kamāl***, m.

perfid-ious, ***-y***, *see* treacherous treason. ***dagābāz***

perform, *see* do, finish.

perfume, ***acckī bō***, f. : ***khushbō***, f. (in villages this may mean also bad smell) : ***caṅgī khushbō***, f. : *see* smell.

perfunctory, ***kamm taraṅgarnā***.

perhaps, ***shaid***, ***shait***, ***ho sakdā e***.

period, ***zamānā***, m. : fixed p., ***miād***, f., ***mohlat***, f. long time, ***cir***, m. : ***muddat***, f. : ***bāmuddat***, d.

perish, ***nās-h.***, ***barbād-h.*** : *see* destory, downfall : perish !, ***bēṛā ri ṛhī*** (abuse).

perjury, ***jhūṭhī saũh*** or ***kasm***, f. : *see* oath.

permanent, *see*, lasting : service, ***mustakil***, ***pakkī*** (***naukrī***).

permissible, ***jāiz***, ***hukm***, m., or ***ijāzat***, f., ***haiwe***.

permi-t, -ssion, *see* allow, liberty.

perpendicular, ***siddhā***, (straight) : ***khaṛā***, steep.

perpetual, ***hamēshā dā*** or ***wāste***.

perplex, ***gallā̃ nāḷ phasāṇā*** (int. ***phasṇā***) : *see* confuse.

perquisite, ***dastūrī***, f., on purchases : ***kamīshan***, m.

persecut-e, -ion, *see* oppression.

persevere, ***khaihṛā nā chaḍḍṇā***, ***chaḍḍū nehī̃***, ***pakkā***.

persist, *see* persevere. obstinacy, -te.

person, *see* man, etc. : in p., ***āpū***, ***āpe*** : *see* self : the Spirit is a p., ***nirā asr nehī̃***, ***Rūh we***.

personal, ***zātī*** ; not used for "my p. Saviour,", which is ***mērā apṇā***, ***mērā ī*** : p. work ***jaṇe jaṇe nāl gall karke***, etc.

perspiration, ***muṛhkā***, m. (***wagṇā*** w. ***dā***, ***auṇā*** w. ***nū̃***) : ***trēḷī***, f. (through weakness or fear, ***auṇī***, ***nū̃***).

persuade, ***manāṇā***, ***samjhāṇā***.

perturb-, -ation, *see* perplex, confuse.

perverse, ***puṭṭhā***, ***ulṭā***.

pervert, v. tr., ***wagāṛnā***, ***gumrāh-k*** (int ***wigaṛnā***, ***gumrāh-h.***) : *see* excite, incite.

pervert, n., ***murtadd***.

pestilence, ***bamārī***, f. : *see* plague.

pestle and mortar, ***daurī ḍaṇḍā***, m. : ***caṭṭū waṭṭā***, m. : ***hamām dastā***, m. : in ground, ***ukhḷī mūhḷī***, f.

pet, child, ***lāḍlā*** (spoilt). ***pyārā*** : animal, kept, ***rākhwā̃***, ***pāltū***.
petal, ***patti***, f. : ***phull dī patti***.
petition, ***arz***, f., ***suāl***, m : leg., ***arzī***, f. (written).
petticoat, ***ghagghrī***, f. : ***pēṭikōṭ***, m. : *see* skirt, kilt.
pewter, ***jist***, m.
philosopher, ***failsūf*** (U.).
philosophy, ***taswīr***, f. : ***fōṭō***, m. f. (both ***khiccṇā***).
phthisis, ***tap dikk***, m.
physician, *see* doctor.
piano, ***wājjā***, m. : play, ***wajāṇā***.
pice, ***paisā***, m. : half p., ***dhēllā***, m. : quarter, ***damṛī***, f. : third, ***pāī***, f. : two p., *see* anna.
pick, flowers, fruit, ***khohṇā*** (int. ***khussṇā***), ***cuṇṇā*** : p. off sticky things, ***lāhnā*** (int. ***laihṇā***) : p. up, ***cukkṇā*** : *see* peck.
pick, tool, ***gainti*** f.
pickle, ***acār***, m. (***pāṇā*** ; of, ***dā***).
picture, ***taswīr***, f. (***baṇāṇī***).
khiccṇij, mūrat, f. (***baṇāṇī***).
piebald, ***dabbā***, ***ḍab khṛrbbā***.
piece, ***ṭōṭā***, m. : ***ṭukṛā***, m. : of meat, ***bōṭī***, f. : ***ḍakkrā***, m. : take to pieces, undo, machinery, bed, masoury, ***ukhēṛnā*** (int. ***ukkhaṛnā***) : *see* loose.
pierce, make hole, *see* hole : needle, thorn, *see* prick : pierce ears, nose, ***winndṇā*** (pa. p. ***widdhā*** : int. ***wijjhṇā***).
piety, *see* pious.
pig, ***sūr***, fem. ***sūrnī*** : ***bāhrlā***, ***bāhr dī shai*** : G. 114.
pigeon-house, *see* doveoot. ***kabūtarkḥānā***
pigmy, *see* dwarf.
pigtail, *see* hair.
pile, *see* heap.
piles, ***bawāsīr***, f., (also ***mohkā***, m.) : bleeding, ***khūnī***.
pilgrim, to Makkah, ***hājī*** ; Hindu, ***tīrthī***, ***jātrī***.
pilgrimage, to Makkah, ***hajj***, m. (***k.***) : to Muslim shrine, ***siārat***, f. : to Hindu shrine ***tīrath***, m. : ***jātrā***, m. (all ***k.***).
pill, ***gōḷī***, f. ; ***ṭikkī***, f. (flattened).
pillar, masonry or wood, ***thammh***, m. : small, ***thammhī***, f. (wood) : of brick, in house, ***kauḷā***, m. : *see* support, boundary.
pillow, ***sarhāṇā***, m. : ***takiā***, m. : p.-slip or case ***takīe dā uchāṛ*** m.
pimple, ***phimhṇī***, f.
pin, ***pinn***, m. : rolling-p., ***wēllaṇ*** or ***wēlṇā*** m. : *see* rolling-board.
pincers, ***sannhī***, f. : *see* tongs.
pinch, ***cūṇḍhī waḍḍhṇī*** or ***bharnī*** (***nū̃***).
pine, ***diār***, m. : ***biār***, m. (both cedar) : pinus longifolia or excelsa, ***cīhṛ***, f. : ***cīhṛ***, f. : ***cīhl***, f.
pinion, arms (tie), ***mushkā̃ bannhṇīā̃*** (***diā̃***).
pink, ***gulābī***, adj : *see* red.
pinnacle, of building ***kiṅgrā***, m. : *see* peak.
pious, ***khudā-parast***, ***dīndār***, ***parhēzgār***, ***bhagat*** (H.).
pipe, ***kukkā***, m. : ***paip***, m. (European).
pirate, ***daruāī cōr***, ***baihrī cōr***.
pistol, ***pistaul***, m. ***tamāncā***, m. (both ***calāṇā***, ***mārnā***) : *see* shoot.

pit, ***ṭoā***, m. (also ditch, ***kaḍḍhṇā***): ***khāḍḍā***, m. (***lāṇā***, int. ***laggṇā***) : ***khāttā***, m. (gen. an old ***khāḍḍā***).

pitch, tar, n., ***lukk***, f. : *see* tune.

pitch, tents, ***lāṇā*** : *see* strike.

piteous, *see* pathetic.

pith, ***girī***, f.

pitiful, *see* compassionate, pathetic. ***garībaṛā***

pity, ***tars***, m. (***auṇā***, ***k.***, ***utte***) : *see* mercy, compassionate : it's a pity that, ***afsōs a paī***.

pivot, ***cūthī***, f. : of bed, ***cūl***, m. : *see* socket.

place, n., ***thā̃***, m. f. : ***jaghā***, f. : out of p., ***kuthā̃-***, ***-e***, ***kojhā*** : in right p., ***thā̃ sir*** : *see* instead, awkward.

place, v., ***rakkhṇā***, ***dharnā*** : p. bed, chair, water (before animal), ***ḍāhṇā*** (int. ***ḍaihṇā***, pa. p. ***ḍaṭṭhā***) : *see* put A.

plague, ***tāūn***, f. : *see* pestilence.

plain, adj., ***sāf*** : *see* eviden : simple, (both simple-minded and unornamented), ***sādā***, ***siddhā sādā*** : *see* flat, level.

plain, n., ***madān***, m. : open space, no crops, ***raṛā thā̃***, m., ***raṛā***, m.

plainly, ***sāf sāf***, ***safāī nāḷ***.

plaintiff, ***mudaī***.

plaintive, *see* pathetic, sad.

plait, v., ***gundṇā*** : rope, ***waṭṭṇā*** : n., *see* hair.

plan, ***tajwiz***, f. : ***hikmat***, f. (both k.) : *see* arrange : of building, etc., ***nakshā***. m. (***baṇāṇā***).

plane, ***randā***, m. (***phērnā***) : v., ***randṇā***.

plank, *see* board. ***phaṭṭā*** m.

plant, n., ***būṭā***, m. : ***būṭī***, f. : young for replainting, ***panīrī***, f. (all w. ***lāṇā***, int. ***laggṇā***) : w. long tendrils, creeping, climbing, ***wēl***, f. : ***wall***, f.

plantain, *see* banana.

plaster, n., *see* mortar, mud : v., ***limbṇā*** : ***lēmbī*** or ***lapāī karnī*** (***dī***), ***plastar karnā*** (***dā***) : *see* mud, smear.

plate, gen. ***bhāṇḍā***, m. : large, ***plēṭ***, f. : smaller, ***hāfplēṭ***, f.: still smaller, ***kuāṭar***, m. : soup-p., ***suplēṭ***, f. : Indian, ***prāt***, f., ***thāḷ***, m. : ***thāḷī***, f. : *see* dish, drinking-vessel.

platform : ***thaṛhā***, m. : ***cabūtrā***, m.

play, n., ***khēḍ***, f. : drama, ***nāṭak***, m.

play, v., ***khēḍṇā*** : music, ***wajāṇā*** (int. ***wajjṇā***).

player, ***khaḍārī***.

playfellow, *see* companion.

pleader, ***wakīl***.

pleasant, ***dil nū̃ caṅgā laggṇā*** : *see* good, tasty.

please, v. tr., ***k͟hush-k.***, ***rāzī-k.*** : int. ***k͟hush*** h., ***rāzī*** h. : p. do it, ***mehrbānī karke*** (very emphatic), ***zarā*** ; gen. omit : p. God, ***in shā Allā***.

pleasure, ***k͟hushī***, f. : ***marzī***, f. : w. p., *see* means.

plectrum, ***mizrāb***, m.

pledge, *see* mortgage, pawn, promise.

plentiful, *see* much.

plenty, not famine, ***sukāḷ***, m. : *see* much.

pliable, pliant, of thing, ***lifaṇwāḷā, kūḷā*** : person, ***jaldī mannaṇwāḷā, jehṛe pāse bhuāīe bhaundā e*** : *see* changeable, vacillate.
plinth, ***kursī,*** f.
plot, ***garmathā,*** m. or ***gall,*** f. or ***matā,*** m. (w. ***pakāṇā*** : int. ***pakkṇā***), M. 125. 16.
plough, ***wāhṇā, haḷ wāhṇā*** (int. ***waggṇā***) : each ploughing, ***sī̃ lāṇī*** (int. ***laggṇī***) : *see* cultivate, train (1) : p.-ed land, ***warihāḷ,*** f. : ***wāhṇ,*** f. : *see* fallow.
ploughman, ***hāḷī, wāhk*** (plougher) : *see* farmer, cultivator.
pluck, *see* pick.
plug, ***ḍaṭṭ,*** m. (***lāṇā,*** int. ***laggṇā***).
plum, ***alūcā,*** m. : (tree and fruit) : small, tree, ***bērī,*** f.; fruit, ***bēr*** m. : large grafted ***bēr*** (fruit or tree), ***syō bēr*** : small ***kāṭhā bēr*** ; ***bēr*** bush, ***maḷhā,*** m.
plunder, *see* rob, steal ***luṭ-mār***
plural, ***jamhā̃,*** f.
P.M. *see* A.M.
pocket, ***bojhā,*** m. : ***jēb,*** m.
pocket-book, ***pākaṭ buk,*** f.
pocket-money, ***jēb kharc,*** m.
pod, ***phaḷī,*** f.
poem, ***nazm,*** f. : ***shēhr,*** m.
poet, ***shairī, nazmā̃ likkhaṇwāḷā, shāir*** (U.).
poetry, *see* poem.
point, ***nōk*** f. : p. of letter like ***sīn*** or ***shīn, dandā, kiṅgrā,*** m. : p. of story, etc., ***matlab,*** m. : be on the p. of, verbal form in ***-wāḷā,*** G. 98, 99 ; root of verb w. ***caleā*** G. 67 : *see* desire.
point, v., ***ishārā karnā*** (***de wall***) : *see* hit at.
point a building, ***ṭīp karnī*** (***dī***).
poison, ***mauhrā,*** m. : ***zaihr,*** m. : ***wiss,*** m.
poisonous, ***zaihrī.***
poke, w. stick, goad, ***hujj mārnī*** (***nū̃***) : *see* goad.
poker, wooden, ***kuḍḍhaṇ,*** m.
pole, north ***kutab,*** m. : polestar, ***kutab tārā,*** m.
pole, ***ḍaṇḍā,*** m., ***bā̃s,*** m. : *see* stick, post.
police, gen., ***puls,*** f. : ***polīs,*** f. : -man, ***pulswāḷā, kansṭebal*** : p.-station, ***thāṇā,*** m. : -post, ***caukī,*** f., ***caũkī,*** f.
polish, ***pālash,*** m. (esp. boot-p blacking, ***syāhī,*** f. both ***lāṇā,*** int. ***laggṇā***) : *see* varnish.
polite, ***shaistā*** : *see* courteous.
pollute, *see* dirty, defile, unclean.
polytheist, ***mushrik.***
pomegranate, tree and fruit, ***anār,*** m.
pomelo, tree and fruit, ***cakōdhrā,*** m.
pomp, *see* show.
pond, ***chappaṛ*** m. : ***chappṛī,*** f. (small, often dry) : ***ḍhāb,*** m. (big depression) : *see* lake.
ponder, ***sōcṇā*** (***nū̃***) : ***gaur karnā*** (***utte***).
pony, small, ***ṭaṭṭū,*** fem. ***ṭair.***
polo, ***pōlō,*** m.
pool, *see* pond.
poor, ***garīb, muthāj*** (seeking help), ***maskīn, wacārā*** (p. fellow) : ***mārā*** (feeble, poor) : ***daliddarī*** (wretched) : *see* straits

: of land, ***niras***, ***māṛī***, ***raddī***, ***maṭṭhī***, ***narm*** : *see* soil, waste : p. Panjabi, ***ṭuṭṭī bhajjī*** or ***māṛī mōṭī Panjābī***, f., *see* smattering.
popcorn, ***dhāhṇā̃***, f. pl. (barley).
poppy, ***pōst***, m.
popular, ***lōk baṛe khush ne ohde nāḷ*** or ***cāhnde ne*** (***nū̃***) or ***caṅgā jāṇde ne*** (***nū̃***).
population, ***abādī***, f.
populated, ***abād.***
populous, ***baṛī abādī***, ***baṛe lōk***, ***baṛā abād***, etc.
porcelain, ***cīnī***, f.
porridge, ***daḷīā***, m.
porter, ***kulī.***
portion, *see* part.
portmanteau, ***thailā***, m.
possess-, -ion, get p. of, ***kābūk.***, ***mallṇā*** : keep in p., ***apṇe kabze wicc rakkhṇā*** : *see* have.
possible, ***mumkin***, ***hō sakdā e*** : *see* able.
post (mail), ***ḍāk***, f. : by post, ***ḍāk wicc*** : p. letter, ***ḍāke*** or ***ḍāk icc pāṇā*** (int. ***paiṇā***) : travel post, ***ḍāk bannhke safar karnā.***
post, telegraph-, ***waḷā***, m. : short p., ***munnā***, m. : lamp-p., ***waḷā***, ***munnā*** : *see* pillar.
post, situation, ***asāmī***, f. : vacancy, ***asāmī khālī e*** : service, ***naukrī***, f.
postage, ***masūl***, m. : ***ḍāk dā masūl.***
postman, ***ḍākwālā***, ***ciṭṭhī rasān*** (U.) : ***halkārā***, runner.
post-office, ***ḍāk khānā***, m.
posterity, *see* descendants.
postpone, ***multawī-k.***, (U.) : p. a week, ***aṭṭhā̃ diṇā̃ te gall pā dittī***, ***aṭṭh din pāe*** : *see* respite.
pot, earthenware, ***ghaṛā***, m. : ***jhajjar***, f. : large, ***maṭṭ***, m., ***cāṭī***, f. : long-necked, ***surāhī***, f. : for cooking (earthen) ***hāṇḍī***, f., ***tauṛī***, f., ***kunnī.*** f. : at well, ***ṭiṇḍ***, f. : pot-stand (wooden), ***ghaṛwanjī***, f., ***ghaṛēthṇī***, f. : metal pots, v. large, ***kaṛāh***, m. ; smaller, ***kaṛāhī***, f., ***dēg***, f. ; small, ***dējkī***, f. ; ***gāgar***, f. (for water) : put on pot, ***cāṛhnā*** (int. ***caṛhnā***).
potato, ***ālū***, m.
potsherd, ***ṭhīkrā***, m. : small, ***ṭhīkrī***, f.
potter, ***kumbyār-***, fem. ***-ī.***
pound, ***kuṭṭṇā***, ***ghōṭṇā*** (w. liquid) : (p. and husk) rice, grain, etc., ***charnā*** : *see* grind, bettle, pestle, rolling-board.
pound, n., for cattle, ***phāṭak***, m. : coin, ***pauṇḍ***, m. : weight, *see* w s. and meas.
pour, ***lhṇā*** (int. ***ḍulhṇā***) : ***luddṇā*** : p. out, ***roṛhnā*** (int. ***ruṛhnā***) : *see* spill.
poverty, ***garībī***, f. : ***muṭhājī***, f. (seeking help, k., ***dī***) : ***maskīnī***, f. : ***taṅgī***, f. : *see* poor, difficulty, straits.
powder, gun-p, ***barūd***, m. : ***dārū***, m. : medicine, ***puṛī***, f., ***phakkī***, f. : no word for p. in gen.
power, ***was***, m. : ***mērī majāl e*** ? what p. have I (to do that) ? *see* authority, strength : p. of attorney, ***mukhtār-nāmā***, m.
powerful, *see* strong, strength.
practi-ce, ***-se***, ***mashk***, f (***k.***), ***jāc***, f (***knack***, ***auṇī***, ***nū̃***) : *see* use.
praise, ***waḍeāṇā***, ***salāhṇā***, ***waḍcāī***

k. (*dī*), *tarīf k.* (*dī*), *hamad karnī* (*dī*, only of God).

praiseworthy, *baṛā laik* : *see* good, excellent.

pray, prayer, gen., *duā maṅgṇī* or *karnī* : *namāz paṛhnī* (M.) : *prārthnā karnī* (H.) : prayers, *bandgī karnī*, *namāz paṛhnī* : p. for person, *duā dēṇī* (*nū̃*) ; gen, *de wāste duā karnī* or *maṅgṇī* : call to p., *bāṅg dēṇī* (M.) : *see* ask, beseech.

preach, in church, *wāhz* or *wāhd kar-nī* or *-nā* : to non-Christians, *manādī karnī*.

preacher, *pujārī*, *wāhz* or *wāhd karnwāḷā*, *pādrī*, *girjā karāṇwāḷā* : ordained person, *pādrī* ; ordain, *pādrī baṇāṇā* (int. *baṇṇā*) : *see* priest.

precaution, *khabardārī*, f. : *hōsh*, f., *ehtiāt*, (U.), all w. *k.*

precedent, *dastūr*, m., *rawāj*, m. : no p., *eñ kadī nehī̃ hoeā* : *see* custom, unexampled.

precept, *maslā*, m. : *see* advice.

precious, *pyārā* : *see* costly, good, excellent.

precipice, *khaḷā pahāṛ*, m. : *baṛī khaḍḍ*, f.

precipita-ncy, -te, -tion, *see* haste.

predestined, *rabb dī marzī nāḷ* or *de hukm nāḷ* : *see* fate, fated.

preemption, right of, *hakk shufā*, m. (*k.*).

prefer, *eh menū̃ ohdū̃ caṅgā laggdā e* : *see* desire, like.

preganant, woman, use *ohnū̃ umēdwārī e* : animals, *sūṇwāḷī*, *wakkōdī* (cattle).

prejudice, *tassab*, m. : *see* partiality.

prejudiced, *tassabī* : *see* partiality.

premature, *wakat tō paihlā̃*.

prepar-e, -ation, *teār-k.* (*nū̃*) : *teārī karnī* (*dī*) : *see* ready.

prescience, supernatural, *gaibdānī*, f., *gaib dā ilm*, *ilhām*, m.

prescription, medical, *nuskhā*, m.

presence, *hāzrī*, f. (not absence) : of superior, *huzūrī*, f. : *see* face, before : in p. of God, *khudā dī huzūrī wicc*, *khudā dī dargāh wicc*.

present, adj., *hāzar* (esp. of inferior) : *majūd*, (not absent) : p. time, at p., *hāl dā zamānā*, m. : *hālī*, *hālā̃*.

present, v., *dēṇā*, *pēsh-k.*

present, n., *see* gift.

presentiment, *mēre dil wicc agdū̃ eh gall āī sī* or *eh khyāl sī*.

preserve, *hafāzat nāḷ* or *sāmbhke rakkhṇā* : *see* jam : -d fruit, *murabbā*, m. (v., *pāṇā*).

press, n., for books, clothes, plates, in wall or otherwise, *almārī*, f. : v. small in wall, *āḷā*, m. : for sugarcane, *wēlṇā*, m. : binder's p., *shakanjā*, m. : oil-p., *kolhū*, m.

press, v., *dabāṇā* (int *dabbnā*) : *see* incite, urge, pressure, emphasise.

pressure, moral, etc., *dabā*, m. ; *rōhb*, m. (both w. *pāṇā*, *utte*).

pretence, *bahānā*, m., *khēkhaṇ*,

m., ***hīlā***, m., (all w. ***k.***) : *see* ostensible, put off, trifle.
pretty, ***sōhṇī*** *see* beautiful.
prevail, ***phailṇā*** (spread) : *see* conquer, persuade.
prevaricate, ***bahāne karnā*** *see* put off, trifle.
prevent, *see* stop, hinder, forbid.
previous, ***aglā***, ***paihlā***.
previously, *see* before.
prey, ***shikār***, m. : dupe, v. tr. ***jāḷ*** or ***shikār wicc phasāṇā***, (int. ***phasṇā***), ***shikār-karnā*** (int. ***hōnā***) : *see* hunt, shoot.
price, ***mull***, m., ***kīmat***, f. : *see* rate, cost, expense, spend.
priceless, use v. costly.
prick (needle, thorn), ***cubbṇā*** (tr. ***cōbhṇā***) : tr., ***sūī mārnī***, p. w. needle : p. up ears, ***kann khaḷe karne*** or ***khalhārne***.
prickly-heat, ***pitt***, f. ; come out, ***nikḷṇī*** ; subside, ***marnī***.
pride, (good) ***fakhr***, m. : (bad) ***magrūrī***, f., ***shekhī***, f., ***ākkaṛ***, f., ***mizāj***, f., ***damāg***. m. : *see* proud, airs, conceit, take down p., *see* humble.
priest, Christian, ***pādrī*** ; ***fādar*** (Rom. Cath.) : M., ***malwāṇā***, ***miyyā̃*** : H., ***prōhat*** : Cuhra, ***gyānnī***, ***fakīr*** : Jewish, ***kaihn***.
prince, ***shāhzād-ā***, fem. ***-ī***.
print, of printer, ***chāpṇā*** : caus. ***chapwāṇā*** : be p.-ed, ***chapṇā***.
prison, ***kaidkhānā***, m., ***jēhlkhānā***, m. : *see* imprison.
prisoner, war or prison, ***kaid-ī***, fem. ***-aṇ*** : *see* imprison.
private, ***sāḍḍī apṇī gall***, ***prāiwēt***, ***paṛde dī gall*** : in p., ***pasitte hōke***, ***nawēkḷe hōke***.
privet, ***sanatthā***, m.
privilege, ***hakk***, m. (right) : ***ijāzat***, f. (permission) : ***riait***, f. (easement).
prize, ***inām***, m. : v., *see* value.
probably, ***wīh wiswe***, ***umed e paī***.
probe, a matter, ***phōlṇā***.
procla-im, -mation (causal) ***ḍaunḍī piṭwāṇī***, ***ḍhanḍōrā duāṇā***, ***manādī karāṇī*** : of actual crier, ***ḍhanḍōrā d.*** : make known, ***dhumāṇā***, ***suṇāṇā***.
procrastinate, ***ṭālṇā***, ***ṭālde jāṇā*** *see* delay, put off.
procurable, ***miḷdā e***.
procure, ***labbh laiṇā***, *see* obtain, produce (2).
prod, w. stick or knuckles, ***hujj mārnī*** (***nū̃***), *see* goad.
produce, n., ***paidāwārī***, f. (of land), *see* crop: ***jo kujjh baṇdā e***.
produce, v., ***paidā-k***, ***baṇāṇā*** : *see* secure, supply, obtain.
profan-e, -ity, ***kufr bakṇā***.
profession, ***kamm***, m. (men or women) : ***pēshā***. m., ***kasab***, m. (these two not of women).
professor, ***ustād***, ***profēsar***.
proficient, *see* clever, able, intelligent.
profit, ***khaṭṭī***, f., ***labhat***, f., ***nafā***, m : for his own advantage, ***apṇe gaū̃ nū̃*** : p. and loss, ***nafā nuksān***, m : *see* advantage, excess.
profligate, ***luccā***, ***badkār***.
progress, ***trakkī***, f. (***k.***) : *see* advance.
prominent, ***mashoohr*** *see* famous, conspicuous.
promise, ***wāhdā***, m., ***sukhan***, m., ***karār***, m., ***gall***, f., ***zabān***, f. (all

w. k.) : break p., ***apṇe wāhde, sukhan***, etc., ***dā*** or ***thõ jhūṭhā h., wāhdā troṛnā*** : fulfil p., above words w. ***pūrā k.*** : *see* word.

promote, ***trakkī dēṇī*** (***nū̃***) : a scheme, ***calāṇā, madat dēṇī*** (***wicc***).

prone, on face, ***mū̃hdā, mū̃hdṛe mū̃h, mū̃h parne*** : p. to, liable to, use ***-wāḷā*** ; p. to forget, ***bhullaṇwāḷā*** : p. to fall, ***digganwāḷā*** : to sickness, ***bamar hōṇwālā.***

pronounce, letter, word, etc., ***bōlṇā***, bulāṇā : be p.-ed, ***bōlṇā, bōleā jāṇā, bulāeā jāṇā.***

pronunciation, ***talaffaz.*** m., (***bōlṇā***).

proof, ***sabūt*** (***dēṇā, dā***) : ***dalīl***, argument, ***dēṇī, dī***) : *see* prove.

prop, ***sahārā***, m. (***d.***, *see* lean) : for tress, ***thūhṇī***, f. : *see* support, pillar.

proper, ***munāsib, ṭhīk***, *see* suitable, right (2), advisable.

property, ***māl***, m., ***māl asbāb***, m. : estate, ***jāēdāt***, f., ***jāedād***, f. : ***hasīat***, f., wealth : *see* wealth, rich.

prophecy, ***nabuwwat***, f. (***k.***) : ***pēshīgoī***, f. (***k.***).

prophet, ***nabī, pakambar, pagambar.***

propitiat-e, -ion, *see* conciliate, atone.

propos-e, -al, ***rā*** or ***rai dēṇī, dassṇī*** : in meeting ***rā*** or ***mōshn pēsh karnī*** : *see* opinion, advise.

prose, ***nasr***, f.

prosecute, ***mukadmā karnā*** *see* case.

prosper-, -ous, *see* advance, progress, rich : or say ***ohdā kamm wāh wā caldā e.***

protect, *see* guard, preserve, save.

protector, *see* guardian, saviour.

protrude, ***nikḷnā, wadhṇā*** : -ing, ***nikḷeā*** or ***wadheā hoeā.***

proud, ***magrūr, mizāj-*** or ***damāg-*** or ***ākaṛ-*** ***-wāḷā*** : *see* pride.

proudly, words for pride w. ***nāḷ.***

prove, ***sābit-k.*** : *see* proof.

proverb, ***masāl***, f. : ***akhāṇ***, m.

provide, *see* obtain, supply, produce (2), secure.

provident that, ***jē*** or ***agar*** (if) : ***jē te, hā̃ par jē te*** : *see* condition.

province, ***sūbā***, m.

provision, rations, ***rasad***, f., ***rāsn***, f.

provo-ke, -cation, *see* annoy.

proxy, ***wakīl***, m.

prune, v. tr., ***chāngṇā, changāī karnī*** (***dī***).

pry, *see* peep.

psalm, ***zabūr***, m.; book of P., ***zabūrā̃ dī kitāb***, f., ***zabūr***, m. pl.: a volume containing the Ps., ***zabūr***, f.

publicly, ***khulham khulhā, khulhā, khulhā ḍulhā, lōkā̃ de sāhmṇe*** : *see* openly.

publish, ***chapwāṇā jārī karnā*** : be p.-ed, ***nikḷṇā, chapṇā*** : *see* print, proclaim.

pudding, ***puṭīn***, f.: ***phuṭīn***, f.

pull, ***khiccṇā*** : punkah, ***khiccṇā*** :

p. out hair, weeds, and other small things, ***puṭṭṇā*** : *see* drag.

pulley, ***garāri***, f.: for well, ***carakhṛī***, f.

pulpit, ***mimbar***, m., ***mēz***, ***mēc***, m.

pulse, ***nabz***, f. (***wēkhṇī***, caus. ***wakhāṇī***, also ***bā̃h***, f.).

pump, ***naḷkā***, m.: railway, etc., ***pamp***, m., ***papp***, m.

pumpkin, ***kaddū***, m.

punctual, ***weḷe sir auṇā*** : ***wakat dā paband*** (U).

puncture, (bicycle) ***pancar***, m. (h., ***nū̃***).

pungent, in taste, *see* hot.

punish-, -ment, ***sazā***, f. (***d.***) : capital p., ***phāhe*** or ***phā̃sī*** or ***maut dī sazā***.

punkah, ***pakkhā***, m.: to fan, ***pakkhā jhallṇā*** : pull p., ***khiccṇā*** ; p-coolie, ***pakkhewāḷā***.

pupil, of eye, *see* eye : of wrestler, ***paṭṭhā***, m.: *see* disciple, scholar.

puppy, ***katūrā***, m.

purchases, ***saudā***, m.: ***saudā sūd***, m.: *see* buy, obtain.

pure, ***khālas*** *see* clean : ceremonially, *see* holy :unadulterated, ***nakhākhrā***, ***khālas*** : pure Panjabi, etc., ***ṭhēṭh***.

Purgative, ***julāb***, m. (***laiṇā***, ***d.***). A.

purify, words for clean, pure, holy, w. ***k.***: *see* wash.

purity, ***pakīzgī***, f. (U.) : *see* cleanliness.

purple, ***kāshnī*** (violet), ***kirmzī kirmcī*** (red purple or crimson) : purplish, *see* somewhat.

purpose, *see* aim, object, intention : for the p of, *see* order : to no p., ***dhigāṇe***, ***ẽwẽ*** : *see* useless.

purposely, ***ucēcā***, ***jāṇke***, ***samjhke*** : *see* deliberately.

purse, ***guthlī***, f., ***gutthī***, f., ***thailī***, f., ***baṭūā***, m.

pursue, ***magar bhajjṇā***.

pus, ***pāk***, f.

push, ***dhikkṇā***, ***dhakkā dēṇā*** (***nū̃***).

put, ***rakkhṇā***, ***dharnā*** : *see* place: p. in, ***pāṇā*** (int. ***paiṇā***): p. away w. care, ***sāmbhṇā*** : p. off, *see* delay : p. off w. excuses, promises, ***lāre*** or ***lāre lappe dēṇe***, ***ṭālṇā*** (int. ***ṭalṇā***), ***ṭāl maṭolā karnā***, ***ṭāl ṭapoḷe karne*** : p. off w. semi-jocular remarks, ***jugtā̃ karnīā̃*** : p. on clothes, on to oneself or child, ***pāṇā*** ; to oneself, ***utte laiṇā*** : a shawl round one's head, ***bukkaḷ mārnī*** : make someone p. on clothes or let him put them on to oneself. ***puāṇā*** : *see* wear : p. out, *see* extinguish, annoy, eject.

putrid, ***bō mārеā*** *see* rotten, bad.

putty, ***puṭīn***, f., ***phuṭīn***, f.

Q

quadruple, ***cauṇā***, ***cār guṇā*** : in four folds, ***cauhrā*** : *see* fold, time.

qualification, ***liākat***, f.: ***kī pās e***, what has he passed ?

quality of mind, ***sift***, f. (also Divine attributes, attributes of mind) : q. of thing, ***darjā***, or simply good, bad, etc.

quantity, ***kinnā***, how much ? ***ēnnā***, ***ōnnā***, ***jinnā***.

quarrel, ***takrār***, m., ***jhagṛā***, m., ***laṛāī***, f. (all ***k.***, ***h.***): mild q., ***āpe icc rinj rāzī h.***: *see* disturbance, discord.

quarrelsome, ***jhagṛnwāḷā***, ***laṛākā***, ***takrārī***.

quart, about ***ikk sēr panj chaṭākiā̃***.

quartan fever, ***cauthā***, m.

quarter, G. 23, ***paūā cauthāī***, f.: ***cuhāī***, f. (esp. land) : ***cauthā hissā***, m.: ***pā***, m. (of ***ser***, *see* wts, and meas.) : q. more than, ***sawā***, as 3¼, ***sawā trai*** : adj., ***suāyā***, used for one and q.: q. less than, ***pauṇe***, as 1¾, ***pauṇe dō*** : q. of orange, etc., *see* section : ¾ of, ***munnā***.

queen, ***rāṇī***, ***malkā***, f.

quench, fire, ***bujhāṇā*** ; int., ***bujjhṇā*** : thirst, *see* slake.

question, ***suāl***, m. (***k.***) *see* ask.

quibble, ***jugat***, f. (***k.***), ***huṭṭar***, m. (***k.***), ***hujjat***, f. (***k.***) : *see* argument, excuse.

quick, *see* swift, quickly.

quickly, ***shtābi***, ***chētī***, ***jabde***, ***jhabde***, ***jhaw***, ***shapāshapp*** of action ***hallke hīlā karke***, ***wat tag*** : go q., ***khurī karnī***, ***khiṭṭ dēṇī*** or ***mārnī***.

quicksilver, ***pārā***, m.

quiet, ***cup***, ***cupkītā***, ***cup cupītā***, ***sun munn.***: keep q., ***aman karnā***, ***sāh laiṇā***, ***ḍaṇḍ nā pānī***, etc. (noise w. neg.). ***cup k.***; *see* screen.

quietly, ***malkṛī***, ***aḍōl***, ***aṇchōp*** : *see* gently, slowly.

quilt, ***lēf***, m., ***jullā***, m., ***razāī***, f., ***gudṛī***, f.: *see* mattress.

quince, fruit and tree, ***bahī***, f.

quintuple, ***panj guṇā***, ***panjauṇā*** : *see* fold, time.

quire, ***dastā***, m. (24 sheets).

quite, ***bilkul*** *see* absolutely, altogether.

quiver, *see* tremble, shake.

quorum, ***kōram***, m.

Quran, ***kurān***, m.: one who knows by heart, ***hāfaz*** : for ***hāfaj*** *see* blind : Q-stand. ***rehl***, f.

R

rabid (dog, etc.), ***haḷkā***.

rabies, ***haḷak***, m. (get, ***kuddṇā***, ***nū̃***).

race, ***dauṛ***, f.: horse-r ***ghuṛdauṛ***, f.

racquet, tennis, racquets, ***ballā***, m.

radish, ***mūḷī***, f.

raft, ***bēṛā***, m.

rag, ***līr***, f.: ***cithṛā***, m.

rage, get into r., ***agg laggṇī*** (***nū̃***): be angry inwardly, ***lūsṇā*** : *see* anger enrage.

ragged, garment ***pāḷā hoeā*** : man, ***pāṭeā̃ kapṛeā̃ wāḷā***, ***līrā̃ patīrā̃ wāḷā***.

railing, ***jaṅglā***, m.: *see* hedge, enclose.

railway line, ***laiṇ***, f.; ***rēl dī***

sarak ; sometimes ***pakkī sarak*** (also Grand Trunk Road) : *see* station train.

rain, ***mīh̃***, m. (***wassṇā***): ***jhaṛī***, f., (continued r., ***laggṇī***): ***pāṇī***, m. (***paiṇā***) : ***kaniā̃***, f. pl. (***paiṇiā̃***): ***kaṇī muṇī***, f. (***h.***) : ***kaṇman***, f. (***laggṇī***); last three words mean slight rain : ***bārish***, f. (U., continued r., h.): *see* drizzle, storm.

rainbow, ***piṅgh*** f., ***guḍḍī guḍḍe dī piṅgh***, f. (***paiṇī***).

raise, ***cukkṇā***, ***uṭhāṇā*** (int. ***uṭṭhṇā***): r. stick, ***uggarnā*** : r. wall, ***usārnā*** (int. ***ussarnā***) : r. dead, ***jawāḷnā***.

raisin, ***sauṅgī***, f., ***mewā***, m., (collective).

rake, ***jandrā***, m. (***lāṇā***): r. up a matter, ***phōlṇā***.

ram, ***chatrā***, m.

rampart, ***duār***, f., ***duāl***, f., ***fasīl***, f.

ramrod, ***gaz***, m.

rancid, *see* bad, rotten, smell.

random, at, ***uñ***, ***ẽwẽ***, ***bin sōceā̃*** ; *see* guess, reason.

rank, ***darjā***, m., ***ohdā***, m.: *see* line.

rankle, ***dil icc khaṭakṇā***.

ransom, ***fidyā***, m.: *see* save.

rap, *see* knock.

rapid, *see* swift.

rare, ***ghaṭṭ wēkhīdā e*** or ***miḷdā e***.

rash, ***jaldbāz*** (U.) : *see* hasty.

rashness, ***jaldbāzī***, f. (U.): *see* haste.

rasp, *see* file.

rat, ***cūhā***, m. (no word for female) : *see* mouse.

rat-trap, ***pinjarā*** *see* trap.

rate, ***bhā***, m., ***nirkh***, m.: at r. of, ***caũh ānnī̃ waṭṭī***, 4 lbs. for 4 annas, G. 78 : ***rupayye dā cār ser***, 4 ser a rupee : *see* tariff, per.

rather, *see* prefer, than : r. white, etc., ***eiṭṭā jehā***, G. 27, 92; or add ***-ērā***, ***waḍērā***. biggish : G. 18 : *see* somewhat : rather than, ***nāḷõ***.

ratify, ***tasdīk karnī*** (***dī***): *see* confirm.

rations, ***rāsn***, f., ***rasad***, f.

rattle, v. int., ***kharkṇā***, ***khaṛ khaṛ-k.***, tr. ***khaṛ kāṇā***.

rattle, toy, ***chaṇkṇā***, m.

raw, ***kaccā*** : *see* uncertain.

ray, of sun, ***kirn***, f. (U.)., ***rashm***, f. (U.), also of cloth.

raze, ***ḍhā chaḍḍṇā***.

razor, ***ustrā***, m.

reach, ***apparṇā***, ***paũhoṇā*** : ***hatth nehī̃ appardā***, cannot reach it : *see* obtain.

read, ***paṛhnā*** : r. it out, ***paṛhke suṇāṇā***.

readmit, to rel. privileges, *see* excommunicate.

ready, ***teār*** : r. to do. ***karn nū̃ teār*** : r. made, ***baṇeā battreā*** : *see* prepare.

real, ***aslī*** : r. gold, silver, ***succā*** : r. reason, ***wiclā matlab***, ***asl gall***, f.

reality, ***hakīkat***, f., ***asliat***, f.: in r., ***asl wicc***, ***hakīkat wicc*** : *see* root.

really, ***saccī***, ***sac-muc*** *see* reality.

reap, ***waḍḍhṇā, wāḍhiā̃ karniā̃, lāiā̃ karniā̃*** or ***lāṇiā̃.***
reaper, ***wāḍhā.***
reaping-hook, sickle, ***dātrī,*** f.
rear, v. tr., ***pāḷṇā, parwarish karnī*** (***dī***).
rear, of horse, ***sikhpā-h.***
rear, n., ***pishlā pāsa.***
reason, ***dalīl*** (argument) : *see* cause, purpose, therefore. without any reason, ***bēsbabb, uñ, ẽwẽ, dhigāṇe*** : *see* random.
reasonable, ***mākūl.***
rebel, ***bāgī*** ; ***sarkash*** rebellious (U).
rebellion, ***bagāwat,*** f., ***gaar,*** m.: *see* riot.
rebuke, *see* reprimand, forbid.
receipt, ***rasīd,*** f. (***likhnī, dēṇī***) : railway r., ***bilṭī,*** f.
receive, ***miḷṇā*** (***nū̃***), also for r. visitors.
receiver of stolen goods, ***cuṅg cōr.***
recent,-ly, ***jabde, jhabde, jhaw jhaw, nawā̃, ajj kall dā, huṇ dī gall, thōreā̃ dihāṛeā̃ dī gall, thoṛā cir hoeā.***
reciprocal, ***āpe icc.***
recite, ***ākhṇā suṇāṇā.***
reckless, ***lāparwāh.***
reckon, *see* count, estimate.
recluse, ***gōshā-nishī̃,*** (M. relig. term).
recognise, ***sihāṇṇā, sañhāṇṇā, pachāṇṇā*** (pa. p. ***sihātā, sāñhātā, pachā-ttā*** or ***-ṇeā***).
recognition, ***sihāṇ,*** f., ***soñhāṇ,*** f., ***pachāṇ,*** f.
recoil, ***pishā̃ haṭṇā*** (go back).
recollect, ***yād karnā*** *see* remember.
recommend, no exact word, ***safārish karnī,*** beg for (***dī***) : ***cāl caln dī ciṭṭhi dēṇī*** give letter of character : *see* advise.
recompense, ***badlā,*** m., ***iwzānā,*** m. (both ***d.***) : *see* damage.
reconcile, ***sulhā karāṇī*** (***karnī, hōṇī***), ***rāzī-k.*** : be r., ***āpe icc rāzī h.***; ***huṇ-rāzī e koī shikait nehī̃ kardā*** now r.-ed, no complaint.
record, ***likhṇā*** : n., ***sanad*** (f.) ***rawhe,*** that there may be a r
recover, get back, ***phēr milnā, phēr laiṇā*** : get well, ***wall*** or ***caṅgā h.***: r. oneself, ***sambhaḷnā.***
recruit, ***raṅgrūṭ*** : *see* enlist.
red, ***lāl, sūhā, rattā*** : v. red, ***lāl sūhā*** : of cattle, ***gōrā.*** A.
redeem, ***chuḍāṇā*** (from pawn, seizure, etc.) : rel., *see* save.
Redeemer, ***rākhā*** *see* Saviour.
reduce, ***ghaṭauṇā*** *see* degrade.
reduction in price, ***riait,*** f.
reed, ***kānnā,*** m.: various kinds, ***kāhī,*** f., ***naṛ,*** m., ***sarūf,*** m., ***sirkīm*** f., ***ḍibb,*** f.: ***dabb,*** f. (v. long grass).
reel, ***ḍōḷnā, ḍōldeā̃ jāṇā.***
reference, ***hawālā dēṇā*** (***dā***).
refined, ***shāistā*** (mauners).
reflection, in mirror, ***parchāwā̃,*** m. (***paiṇā***) : *see* thought, shadow.
reform, v. tr., ***sudhārnā,*** int., ***suddharnā.***
refrain, ***parhēz karn-ī*** or ***-ā*** (***tõ***): leave off, give up idea of,

muṛnā (***tõ***), ***chaḍḍṇā*** : *see* abstain.
refuge, ***panāh***, f.: *see* shelter.
refuse-e, -al, ***mukkarnā***, ***namukkarnā***, ***inkār karnā*** (***dā***), ***inkārī karnī*** (***dī***), ***nā̃h karnī*** : one who refuses to give leave *see* reject : receive refusal. ***juāb milṇā*** (***nū̃***): flat refusal ***sukkā juāb*** :
refuse, n., *see* rubbish.
refute, ***jhūthā sābit-k.*** ***radd-k.*** or ***raddṇā*** (***ohdī gall nū̃***) : *see* reject.
regard, *see* esteem, consideration, honour, respect.
regeneration, *see* conversion.
regiment, ***palṭan***, f.: cavalry ***rasālā***, m.: artillery, ***tōpkhānā***.
register, v. tr., ***rajistrī karāṇi*** (***dī***, said of sender: ***karnī***. of clerk): ed letter, ***rujisṭrī***, f.
regret, ***pachtāṇā***, ***afsōs***, m. (***k.***), sorrow in gen.: *see* grief repent, remorse.
regrettable, ***afsōs dī gall***, or words like, ***burī gall***, etc.
regular, ***kaide nāḷ***, ***kaide dī ga***,, etc.: a.r. thief, ***pakkā cōr***.
regulation, ***baidā***, m., ***hukam***, m.
regin, ***saltanat***, f., ***rāj***, m.
rein, ***wāg***, f.
reinstate, ***bahāl-k.***, ***phēr rakkhnā***. eject, ***radd-k.***, ***raddṇā***, ***raddī-k.***, ***nāmanzūr-k.***: *see* refuse (1), refute.
rejoice, ***khushī karnī*** (***dī*** of cause): *see* delight.
relate, ***bsān karnā*** (***dā***), ***suṇāṇā***.
relationship, ***sākādārī***, f., ***rishtedārī***, f.
relative, n. ***sāk***, ***rishtedār*** : *see* full : be related to, word for relative w. verb subst. or ***hōṇā***. G. 119, M. 121. 11
release, ***chaḍḍnā***, ***azād-k.*** (U.): *see* acquit, free.
relent, *see* pity, mercy, compassionate.
reliable, ***mohtbar***, ***pakkā***, ***imānwāḷā*** : A : *see* untrust worthy.
reliance, ***wasāh***, m., ***mān***, m. (both w. ***k.***, ***dā***): *see* confide, trust, faith, untrustworthy.
relief, *see* ease, rest: military, ***badlī***, f.
relieve, *see* ease, rest.: of one's duty, ***ralīw-k.*** (int. ***ralīw-h.***), ***kamm chuḍāṇā*** (***koḷõ***).
religion, ***mazhab***, m. (gen.): ***dīn***, m. (M.): ***dharm***, m. (H.).
religious, ***dīndār*** (M.), ***namāzī*** (praying much, M.): ***dharmī*** and ***bhagat*** (H.).
relinquish, *see* abandon.
relish, *see* enjoy, like, taste.
relucatant, use not wish, not desiro, ***rūh nehī kardā*** : *see* wish, cath, desire, sick of.
rely, ***āsre raihṇā*** *see* reliance, trust, confide.
remain, be left over, ***bacnā***, ***wadhṇā***, ***bākī raihṇā*** : r, behind, ***picche raihṇā*** : r. in one place, ***ṭikṇā*** : *see* stay.
remainder, financial, mathematics, ***bakāyā***, m.: gen., ***jehṛā bākī e***.

remedy, *see* treat, cure, recompense.

remember, not forgot, gen., ***cētā***, m. (***auṇā***, ***raihṇā***, ***nū̃***, M. 117, 11) : ***thauh***, m. (***raihṇā***, ***nū̃***), ***yād-raihṇā*** (***nū̃***), M. 117. 4. r. is also ***yād rakkhṇā*** or ***karnā*** : note ***yād rakkhṇā*** is keep in mind : ***yād karnā*** is (1) r. a person. think of him : (2) used speaking respectfully of calling someone. (3) learn lesson : (4) r. after an interval : *see* memory.

remembrance, ***yād*** *see* memorial, memory.

remonstrance, ***phaṭkār*** *see* objection, reprimand, reproach.

remiss, *see* lazy, delay.

remorse, ***pachtāwā***, m. (***laggṇā***, h., ***nū̃***), ***afsōs***, m. (***auṇā nū̃***, ***k.***): *see* regret.

remote, ***dūr, parāyā*** *see* distant.

remove, v. tr., ***dūr-k.***, ***laiṛāṇā***, ***kharnā***, ***haṭāṇā*** : int., to another house, city, ***uṭṭh jāṇā***.

renegade, ***murtadd*** (M., rel.): *see* treacherous.

rennet, ***jāg***, f. (***lāṇī***, int. ***laggṇī***) ***khaṭṭā launā*** : tablet of r., ***ṭikkī***, f.

renounce, *see* abdndon : r. claim, ***dāhwā chaḍḍṇā*** (***dā***). A.

repair, ***marammat karnī*** (***dī***) : *see* shoe, require.

repeal, laws (of God), ***mansūkh-k.*** (M.) *see* abolish, cancel.

repat, ***phēr ākhṇā*** : r. after me, ***mēre picche picche ākh***, ***mērī gall durhāndā jā***, ***jo mai ākhā̃ tū̃ wī ākhdā jā*** : r. or recite poetry, etc., ***ākhṇā***, ***paṛhnā***.

repeatedly, ***bhaũ caũ***, ***jhaṭe binde***, ***ghaṛī ghaṛī***, ***ghaṛī muṛī***, ***jhaṭe jhaṭe***, ***bauht wārī***, ***baṛī wārī***, ***kinnī wārī*** (for ***wārī*** also ***wērī***) : do thing repeatedly, special verbal construction, *see* G. 68, 69.

repent, ***tobā karnī*** (***dī***, ***tõ***): ***pachtāṇā*** (***tõ***): ***kannā̃***) ***nū̃ hatth lāṇā***, ***nakk nāḷ līkā̃*** (or ***hadīsā̃***) ***kaḍḍhṇiā̃*** (caus. ***kaḍhāṇiā̃***).

repentance, ***tobā***, f.: ***pacchōtāp***, f. (***k.***).

repetition, ***dohrāṇā*** *see* repeat, repatedly.

report, ***khabar***, (***d.***, ***dī***) : ***rapōṭ***, f. (***d.***, ***dī***).

representative, *see* ambassador, delegate.

reprieve, *see* forgive, respite.

reprimand, ***jhiṛak***, f., ***jhār***, f., ***taṛī***, f., ***ghurkī***, f. (all w. ***d.***, ***nū̃***): also ***ohnū̃ jhāṛ kītī*** or ***pāī***, or ***ohdī jhāṛ kītī*** : ***jhārnā***, ***jhiṛkṇā***, ***ghurkṇā***, ***dābbā cāṛhnā*** or d. (***nū̃***), ***ṭhākṇā*** : *see* reproach, sit upon.

reproach, ***ulāhmā dēṇā*** (***dā*** of cause, ***nū̃*** of person): ***phiṭkā̃ dēṇiā̃*** (v. mild abuse).

reprove, *see* reprimand.

republic, ***jihde wicc kamēṭī kamm calāndī e***, ***bādshāh koī nehī̃*** : (U., ***jamhūrī riāsat***, f.).

repudiate, *see* renounce, refuse (1), abandon.

request, ***minnat,-karnī*** *see* ask, beseech.

reuqire, *see* ask, desire, advisable, necessary : r. to be done, often verbal part. in *-wāḷā, juttī gaṇḍhaṇwāḷī e,* shoes r. to be repaired, G. 45.
resemblance, *ape icc raḷde ne, ikko jehe ne, miḷde juḷde ne* : of face, *muhāndrā raḷdā e* : *see* same.
resent, *burā mannṇā* (*gall nū̃*) : *see* offence.
reserve, *rakkh chaḍḍnā.*
resident, *raihṇwāḷā* : *wassanwāḷā* : leg. *sākan,* fem. *saknā* : *see* dwell, inhabit.
resign, *istīfā dēṇā* (*kamm tõ*) : *kamm chaḍḍṇā,* sometimes *chuṭṭī mangṇī.*
resin, *gūnd,* f., *rāḷ,* f. : *see* gum,
resist : oppose, objection, fight.
resolute, *ḍāhḍā, rāṭh, pakkā.*
resolution, *faislā,* m. (decision) : firmness, *ḍāhḍpuṇā,* m., *ḍaḍhippaṇ,* m. : *see* intend.
resolve, *see* decide : in meeting, *faislā karnā* (int. *hōṇā*) : *tajwiz karnī* (int. *hōṇī*).
respect, *adab,* m., *izzat,* f., *ādar,* f., (all w. *k.* and *dā, dī*) : word of respect, *hori,* m. pl., G. 27, 73, 82.
respectable, *izzatdār, sharif* and words for good.
respectful, *adab wāḷā, adab nāḷ kūṇā.*
respite, give r. of two months, *do mahine pāe* ; M 126. 23 : *mohlat,* f., (U) : *see* postpone. forgive.
responsible, *zimmewār* : make oneself r. for, *zimmā cukkṇā,* (*dā*), *zimmewārī cukkṇī* (*dī*), *bīṛā cukkṇā* (*dā*) : hold someone r. for, *ohde peṭe pāṇā,* G. 34 : *ohde zimme lāṇā* : *ohde matthe lāṇā* (blame for).
rest, *arām,* m. (*k.*), *cain,* m. (of mind, U.) : *tsallī,* f. (mind) : take a r., *sāh laiṇā* : give person r. by doing his work for short time, *sāh kaḍhāṇā* (*nū̃*) : let animal r., *sāh duāṇā* (*nū̃*) : for these three *see* G. 122, 109; M. 129. 22; 118. 32 : give person r., also *chaḍḍnā* : *see* ease, convenience.
resthouse, *banglā,* m. or *ḍākbanglā* : village, *dārā,* m. : a serai, *sarā̃,* f.
restless, *bēkarār,* troubled in mind ; *becain,* uneasy (both U.).
restlessness, *cintā, bēkarārī,* f. (U.). *becainī,* f. (U.) : *bēarāmī,* f.
restrain, *rōknā, thamhnā see* stop, forbid, hinder.
resurrection, *jī uṭṭhṇā, kiāmat,* f. (often used for judgment-day) *see* rise.
retail, *parcūn see* wholesale.
retinue, *nāḷ de bande, nāḷ de suār.*
retire, go back, *pishā̃ haṭṇā* : *naukrī chaḍḍnī, raṭair hō jāṇā* (*tõ*).
return, v. int., *partṇā, part jāṇā, part auṇā, muṛnā, pishā̃ muṛnā* : v. tr., *partāṇā, pishā̃ mōṛnā, mōṛnā* : article that may be returned, *mōṛwā̃* : r. fare, *wāpsī*

karāyā, m. : r. post, ***wāpsī ḍāk***, f. : *see* turn back.
revenge, ***badlā laiṇā*** (***de koḷõ***, ***gall dā***) : ***sijjhṇā*** (***nū̃***).
revenue, ***āmdaṇ***, f.
revere, ***adab karnā***, ***ādar karnā*** *see* acknowledge, respect, honour.
reverse, v. tr., ***puṭṭhā-k.*** ; turn back, ***pisehā̃ bhuā̃nā*** : *see* upside down, defeat.
revile, ***burā akhṇā*** (***nū̃***), ***gāhḷā̃ kaḍḍhnaā̃*** (***nū̃***).
revise, lesson, etc., ***durhānā***, ***rawaiz-k.*** (***nū̃***) : look over again, ***nazr sānī karnī*** (***dī***, U.).
revive, ***jān wicc jān auṇī***, ***hōsh auṇī*** (***nū̃***).
reward, ***inām***, m. : ***ajar***, m. (of God, U.).
ryhme, ***kāfyā***, m. (***bannknā***, int. ***bajjhṇā***).
rib, ***pasḷī***, f : I'II break your ribs, ***babbar bhannū̃gā***.
ribbon, ***fitā***, m. : ***rēshmī fitā***, silk r.
rice, growing, ***munjī***, f., ***dhāṇ***, m. : grain, cooked or not, ***cauḷ*** m. pl. : r. cooked w. milk, ***khīr***, f. : cook r..***rinnhṇā*** (pa. p. ***riddhā*** : int. ***rijjhṇā***) : get soft in cooking, ***baihṇā***.
ricrochet, ducks and drakes, ***tatto tārī***, f. (***khēḍṇī***).
rich, ***amīr***, ***bakhtāwar***, ***saukhā***, ***paise-wāḷā***, ***hasiat-wāḷā***, ***dhaṇī*** (H.), ***daulatwand***.
riches, *see* wealth.
riddle, ***kahāṇī*** (***pāṇī***) : ***bujhārat*** (***pāṇī***) : *see* secret.
ride, ***suār h.***, ***suār hōke jāṇā***, ***ghōṛe te jāṇā*** : get ride, carriage, boys' back, anywhere ***hūṇte laiṇe*** (***de***).
ridicule, mock, ***makhaul karnā*** (***nū̃***) : ***hujtā̃ karniā̃*** (***nū̃***) : milder, ***jugtā̃ karniā̃*** (***nū̃***) : ***kise diā̃ maskhriā̃ karniā̃*** (also means laugh w. pleasure) : ***chnū̃ tauṛī mārnī*** : *see* taunt, imitate, laugh, jester, clap.
rifle, ***rafal***, f., ***bandūk***, f.
right, not left, ***sujjā*** : r.-handed, ***sajjā***.
right, not wrong, ***thīk***, ***durust*** : and words for good, etc. : all right, ***khair sallā***, ***khair mehr e***, ***caṅgā***, ***halā*** : *see* matter.
right, n., ***hakk***, m. : person w. a.r, ***hakdār***.
righteous, ***nēk*** : *see* religious, good.
rigid, ***sakht***, ***dāhḍā***, ***jehṛā nā life***.
rind, *see* peel, pare.
ring, n., large or small without stone, ***challā***, m. : small w. stone, ***mundrī***, f., ***chāp***, f. (see stone) : ear-p., ***wālī***, f., ***murkī***, f. : thumb-r., ***ārsī***, f.
ring, v. tr., small bell, etc., ***chaṇkāṇā*** (int. ***chaṇaknā***) : large bell, gong, coin or pot to see if sound, ***wajāṇā*** (int. ***wajjṇā***) : also ***bulāṇā***, ***khaṛkāṇā*** : coin, etc., rings, ***wajjdā e***, ***bōlā e***. ***nehī bōldā e*** : does not r., ***bōlā e***. ***nehī bōldā***, or ***wajjdā***, ***ḍorā e***.
ringworm, ***dhaddar***, ***daddar***, m.
rinse, month, ***kurlī karnī*** : vessel, etc., ***haṅgāḷṇā***.

riot, ***balwā***, m. (***k.***, int. ***h.***) : *see* disturbance.
rip, *see* undo.
ripe, ***pakkā*** : half r., ***āhbū*** ; ***ḍaḍḍrā*** (also half cooked).
rise, ***uṭṭhṇā*** : note following pairs : ***uṭṭhke bauh***, get up into sitting posture : ***uṭṭh bauh***, get up (gen. implying "and go away") : ***uṭṭhke khlō***, (also ***khlō jā***), stand up : ***uṭṭh khlō*** rise (and move away) : ***uṭṭhke geā***, he rose and went away : ***uṭṭh geā***, he removed (to another house) : r. fr. dead. ***jyū paiṇā***, ***jī uṭṭhṇā*** (***murdeā wiccō̃***).
rise, sun, moon, stars, ***carhnā***, ***nikḷnā*** : r. late, of moon on 15th day, ***gōḍḍā mārnā*** or ***lāṇā*** (int. ***gōḍḍā laggṇā cann nū̃***), G. 119 : M. 121. 17.
rise, of price, ***wadhṇā*** : dearness, ***manghāī***, f., ***maihṅg***, f., ***tēzī***, f., ***pyār***, m. : *see* dear.
rise, of wind, ***wagaṇ lagī e***.
rise, originate, ***shurū-h***.
risk, ***khatrā***, m.
rites, ***rīt rasm***, f. (***pūrī karnī***).
rival, ***jehṛā mukāblī kare***.
river, ***daryā***, m. : *see* stream.
rivet, ***kāblā***, m. : r.-screw, ***ḍhibrī***, f. : *see* patch.
road, metalled, ***pakkī zarak*** : unmetalled, ***kaccī sarak***, f. : village, ***paihā***, m. : *see* path, way : centre of metalled r., ***goḷā***, m. : sides, ***paṭrī***, f. : dip in metalled r. for water-flow, ***gaib***, f. : *see* roughness.
road-metal, ***rōṛ***, m.
road-mender, ***māhwāriā***, m.
roar, of animal, man in anger, ***gajjṇā***.
roast, ***bhunnṇā***, int. ***bhujjṇā*** : r.-meat in bazar, ***kabāb***, m. : r. vegetables or rice, ***bhujiā***, m.
rob, ***luṭṭnā***, ***dhārā mārnā***, ***luṭṭ mārnī*** or ***macāṇī*** : metaph. ***ṭhaggṇā*** : *see* steal.
robber, ***ḍākū***, ***dhārwī***, ***luṭērā*** (esp. metaph.).
robbery, ***ḍākā***, m. (***mārnā***, int. ***paiṇā***).
robust, ***tagṛā*** : *see* strong.
rock, no word, ***caṭān***, f. (U.), *see* stone.
rocket, ***hawā̃***, f. (***calāṇī***, ***calṇī***).
rod, *see* stick : iron r., ***kandḷā***, m., ***sīkh***, f.
rogue, *see* blackguard.
roll, call, *see* attendance and call.
roll, v. int. ***riṛhnā*** (tr. ***reṛhnā***).
roller, iron, ***rūl***, m., ***rōlar***, m.
rolling-board, ***phaṭṭā***, m. -pin, ***wēlṇā***, m. ; of stone, for grinding, ***sil*** f., ***waṭṭā***, m.
roof, ***chatt***, m., ***kōṭhā***, m. : v. tr., ***chattṇā***.
room, ***kamrā***, m. : in village house, ***kōṭhṛī***, f. : front r. in do., ***pasār***, m. : spare-r., ***musāfar kamrā*** or ***khānā***, m. : r. on roof, ***cubārā***, m. : *see* bath-, bed-, dining-, drawing-r.
room, space, ***thā̃*** m. f., ***jaghā***, f., ***gunjaish***, f.
roomy, ***mōklā*** : non-r., ***saurā***, ***taṅg***.

root, ***jaṛ***, f. : *see* uproot : get to root of thing, ***kuṇh kaḍḍhṇī*** (***dī***), ***asliat*** or ***hakīkat dā patā lāṇā***.

rope, ***rassā***, m. : for drawing water, ***lajj***, f. : round the ***baiṛ***, ***baraṛ***, m.. round ***baiṛ*** for ***tiṇḍā̃***, ***māhl***, f. : for well, gen., ***khabbaṛ***, m., ***chillaṛ***, m. (also ***dullaṛ***, ***tillaṛ***, m.) : for horse's heels, ***pachāṛī***, f. ; for his forelegs, ***agāṛī***, f. : *see* string, thong.

rosary, ***tasbī***, f. (M., ***phērnī***, ***raḷṇī***) : ***māḷā***, f., (H., ***phērnī***, ***simarnī***, ***raḷṇī***).

rose, ***gulāb***, m. : colour, ***gulābī***.

rot, decompose, ***trakkṇā*** : b gir to r., ***bō chaḍḍṇī*** : get soft, ***gaḷṇā*** : allow to rot, decompose, ***tarkāṇā***.

rotten, *see* rot, bad.

rough, ***kharhwā*** : r. work, ***mōṭā kamm*** : r. and ready, ***jaṭkā***, ***jaṭkā hisāb***, m. : ***dagg jehā*** : r. road, *see* roughness.

roughness, unevenness, in ground, ***aḍḍokhōṛā***, m., ***khṛappā***, m., ***khṛōc***, m.

round, adj., ***gōḷ*** : adv. ***duāḷe***, ***āḷe duāḷe***, ***cufere***, ***cār cujere***, ***cāre pāse***, ***sabbhnī̃ pāsī̃***.

prep., ***de duāḷe***, ***de āḷe duāḷeõ de cufēr***, ***de cār cufēre***. ***dī caūh pāsī̃***.

pass by way of round, ***duāḷeõ***, ***dī langhṇā***, pass beyond and round, ***waḷṇā*** : go r. and r., esp. involuntarily, ***cakkar khāṇā***.

round, n., a long round, ***waḷā*** (***paiṇā***, ***nū̃***): ***waḷe wāḷā rāh*** : ***cakkar laggṇā*** (***nū̃***) : of ladder, *see* rung.

roundness, ***guḷeāī***, f.

rouse, ***jagāṇā***, ***bhaṛkāṇā*** *see* wake, incite, excite, urge.

rover, ***awārā*** (bad sense), fem. the same : *see* nomad.

row, ***katār*** *see* line.

royal, ***bādshāhī***, ***shāhī***.

rub, ***malṇā***, ***mālish karnī*** (***nū̃***); ***ragaṛnā*** (roughly) : gently in passing, ***khaihṇā*** (***nā***) : skin get rubbed and sore, ***ucchṇā ambṇā*** : *see* chafe; rubbed off, ***chill ghattṇā*** : anything get rubbed, ***ghasar laggṇī*** (***nū̃***): get rubbed, away, ***gass jāṇā*** : r. out, *see* delete.

rubber, ***rabaṛ***, m., ***rabaṭ***, m.

rubbish, refuse, ***kūṛā*** m. : r.-heap, ***rūṛī***, f. : *see* nonsense.

ruby, ***lāl***, m.

rude, *see* impertinent, forward : answer back, ***gall partāṇī***, ***aggõ bōlṇā*** : rough and r., ***waihshī*** ; *see* rough and ready.

rudeness, ***gustā<u>kh</u>ī***, f., ***shō<u>kh</u>ī***, f. : *see* rude.

rug, ***galīcā*** m., ***namdā***, m.

ruin, *see* destroy, downfall, perish: add ***tabāhī***, f., ***<u>kh</u>arābī***, f.

ruins, of house, only walls, ***khoḷe***, m. pl.

rule, ***kaidā***, m., ***kanūn***, m. (both ***baṇāṇā***): ***tarīkā***, m. (method) : *see* custom, govern.

rule, foot-rule, ***dufaṭṭā***, m. ***fuṭṭā***, m.

ruler, ***hākim***, m.
ruler, wooden, ***rūl***, f. m.
rumble, of wheels, etc., ***khṛāk auṇā*** : noise of ***hukkā***, camel, ***buṛhkṇā***.
ruminate, ***chew cud***, ***ugālī karnī***.
rumour, ***afwāh***, f. (***uḍḍṇī***, tr. ***uḍāṇī***) : *see* spread.
run, ***bhajjṇd***, ***daurnā*** (caus. ***bhajāṇā***, ***duṛāṇā***) : r. away ***bhajj jāṇā***, ***maḷ***, ***jāṇā***, ***nass***, ***jāṇā*** (caus. ***nasāṇā***), ***khiskṇā*** (caus. ***khaskāṇā***) : go off quickly, ***wag jāṇā*** (caus. ***wagāṇā***) ; *see* swift : run, of water, ***wagṇā*** : run of sore, nose, ***wagṇā*** : of eyes, ***akkhiā̃ wiccõ pāṇī wagdā e***.
rung of ladder, ***ḍaṇḍā*** e.
rupee, ***rupayyā***, m., ***rupeā***, m., jocular, ***chill***, f., ***chillar***, f.: r.'s worth of change, ***rupayye dā bhanghaṛ***, or ***bhān*** : but bring back the change, ***bākī lai ā***.
ruse, ***dā***, m., (***lāṇā***, int. ***laggṇā***, ***khāṇā***) : *see* deceit, trick.
rush at, ***ṭuṭṭke paiṇā*** (***nū̃***) : ***hatthī̃ paiṇā*** (***oh dī***): ***mārn paiṇā*** (***nū̃***).
rust, n., ***jaṅgāḷ***, m.: v., ***jaṅgāḷ laggṇā*** or ***khāṇā*** (***nū̃***).
rut, of wheels, ***gail***, f.: metaph., paraphrase w. habit, custom.

S

sabre, ***teg***, ***talwār*** *see* sword.
sack, ***bōrā***, m. : ***bōrī***, f. : ***gūṇī***, f. : -cloth, ***trappar***, m. : *see* pannier.
sacred, ***pawittar*** (H.) : ***pāk***, ***mukaddas*** (M.).
sacrifice, n., ***kurbānī***, f. (M.) : ***balidān***. m. (H.) : v., ***kurbān-k.***, ***balidān-k***.
sad, ***udās***, ***nimmo jhūṇā***. *see* sorry, grief.
saddle, ***zīn***, f., ***kāṭhī***, f. (wooden) : put on 8., ***pāṇī*** : to s. something on anyone, *see* responsible.
saddle-bags, *see* pannier.
sadness. ***udāsī***,f. : ***gacc***, m. (***auṇā***), almost weeping.
safe, ***salāmat***, ***sahī salāmat***. A:
safety, ***salāmtī***, f., ***bacā***, m.: *see* guard, preeserve, save.
sago, ***sāgū***, m.
sail, n., ***bādbān***, m. : v., ***jahāz wice sail*** or ***safar karnā***.
sailor, ***berīwālā***, ***malāh***.
saint, *see* holy and add ***pīr***, (M.) : ***rishī***. ***muni***, ***warāgī*** (H.).
sake, ***de wāste***, ***de wāte***, ***de laī***, ***dī k͟hātar*** : in prayer ***Masīh dī k͟hātar***.
sale, ***wikrī***, f., ***farōk͟ht***, f. (U.).
saliva, ***thukk***, m. : ***lab***, m.
salt, ***lūṇ,*** m., ***namak***, m. (U.) : s.-cellar. ***lūṇ-*** or ***namak-dān***, m. : s. water, ***khārā pāṇī***, m. : s. opposed to sweet in food, ***salūṇā*** : without s., of something which should have s., ***phikkā*** (see insipid) : s. meat, ***namkīn*** : to s., ***namkīn-k***.
saltpetre, ***shōrā***.
salute, salutation, ***salām***, f. m. (***k.***) : ***bandgī***, f. (***k.***) : acknowledge s., ***salām dā juāb d.*** : s. with guns, ***salāmī***, f.
salvation, ***najāt***, f. (M.) : ***muktī***, f. (H.).

same, ***īho***, ***īhoī***, ***ūho***, ***ūhoī***, ***oh ī*** : ***ose*** or ***ese tarhā̃ dā***, ***eho-*** or ***ūho-jehā*** : of same age, *see* equal : *see* resemblance.
sample, ***namūnā***, m.
sanction, ***manzūri***, f. : obtain, ***laiṇi*** : grant, ***deṇī***, also ***manzūr-k.***
sand, ***rēt***, f : stretch of s. in water, ***barēt-ā***, m., ***-ī***, f.
sandy, ***rētlā***.
sarcasm, ***méhṇā*** *see* taunt.
Satan, ***shatān***.
satiat-e, -ed, -y, *see* satisfy, etc., appease (hunger) in A.
satin, *see* silk.
satisfaction, ***tsallī***, or ***tsallā***, f. (comfort) : ***rāzī*** or ***khush h.*** : having had enough food, drink, water (said of land, trees, people, cattle), of someone's society, etc., ***rajj***, f. : *see* satisfy, satiate.
satisfactor-y, -ily, ***khātarkhāh*** : *see* good.
satisfy, ***rāzī*** or ***khush k.***, (int. ***h.***), ***tsallī*** or ***tsallā hōṇī*** (***dī***) : w. food, etc. (*see* satiate, satisfaction) ***rajāṇā***, ***sēr-k.*** (U.), be s. -ed, ***rajjṇā***, ***sēr-h.*** (U.) :
Saturday, ***haftā***. m. : ***abbaḷ haftā***. m. : Hindu words, ***saniccar***, ***saniccarwār***, ***chanicchar***, ***chaniccharwaār***, ***chiṇchiṇ***, ***chiṇchiṇwār***, all m.
sauce, ***sā̃s***, f. : ***grēbbi***, f. (gravy), chutney, ***caṭṇi***, f.
saucer, ***pirc***, f.
savage, ***waihshi***, ***jāngli***
save, ***bacāṇā*** : of Christ, ***bacāṇā***, ***najāt dēṇī*** (***nū̃***) : be s. -ed, ***bacṇā***, ***najāt milṇī*** (***nū̃***).
Saviour, ***bacāṇwāḷā*** (also human), ***Najāt Dēṇwāḷā***.
saw, n., small, ***ārī***, f. : large, for two men, ***kalwattar***, m., ***ārā***, m. : large, in frame, two men, ***parnāhi***, f. : v., ***cirnā*** (***ārī nāḷ***, etc.).
sawdust, ***būrā***, m.
say, ***ākhṇā***, ***ākhṇā wēkhṇā***, ***kaihṇā*** : caus., ***akhwāṇā***, ***bulāṇā***, G. 109.
saying, n., ***akhāṇ***, m.
scab, ***khrīṇḍ*** (***bajjhṇā***) : *see* scar :
scabbard, ***miān***, m.
scald, ***sāṛnā***, int. ***saṛnā***.
scales, small, ***trakkṛī***, f. : large, ***kaṇḍā***, in. : weighing machine at station, etc., ***kaṇḍā***. m. : gldsmith's, ***kaṇḍī***, f., one side of basket s., ***chābbā***, m.
scam, ***ṭhaggi*** f.
scandal, use slander and spread, *see* spread, slander.
scar, ***zakhm dā nashān*** or ***dāg***, m. (both also of fresh mark) : *see* scab.
scarce, *see* rare.
scarcely, ***masā̃***, ***masā̃ kiwē̃***, ***masē̃ kiwē̃*** : *see* difficulty.
scarcity, *see* famine, rare.
scarecrow, ***daraoṇā***, m.
scarlet, ***shōkh lāl***, ***lāl sūhā***, ***gul anārī***.
scatter, v. tr., ***khalārnā***, ***khaṇḍāṇā***; int. ***khillarnā***, ***khiṇḍṇā***.
scattered, ***vikkarēā hōyā*** few, *see* few.
scene, ***nazārā*** *see* sight, view : s. of crime, ***maukyā***, m.

scenery, ***nazāra*** *see* scene.
scent, ***khashbō*** *see* perfume, small.
scholar, learner, ***paṛhnwāḷā***, ***tālib ilm*** (U.) : ***skūl dā munḍā*** : learned, *see* learned.
scholarship (money), ***wazīfā***, m. : learning, ***ilm***, m. : *see* learned know.
school, ***skūl***, m., ***madarsā***, m. : special Hindu, ***pāṭhsālā***, m. (for girls. ***puttrī pāṭhshālā***).
schoolboy, *see* scholar.
schoolfellow, ***jamāt-ī***, fem. ***-aṇ***.
school-master, -mistress, *see* teacher.
science, gen., ***ilm***, m : physical s., ***sains***, f.
scissors, ***kaincī***, f.
scold, *see* reprimand.
scorch, v. int., ***saṛnā***, ***jhalūhṇā*** : tr., ***sāṛnā***.
score, twenty, ***wīh***, G. 21, 22, 93.
scorn, ***hikārat dī nazr nāḷ wekhṇā*** : *see* despise.
scorpion, ***ṭhūhā̃***, m.
scoundrel, *see* blackguard.
scrape, ***khurcṇā***, ***khōtarnā*** (esp. clean by scraping).
scraper, for horse, ***kharkṇā***, m.
scratch, for itch, ***khurkṇā*** : get a s., ***jharīṭ paṇī*** (***nū̃***) : *see* scrape.
scream, ***cīkṇā***, ***cīk mārnī***, ***caṅghāṛnā***, ***caṅghāṛ mārnī*** : *see* howl.
screen, *see* chikk, curtain : anything to s. fr. sight, wind, etc., ***ohlā***, m. : v. tr., *see* save, preserve, guard : hush up, ***pardā pāṇā***, ***pōcā phērnā*** (both ***gall utte***) : *see* quiet.
screw, ***pēc***, m. (***lāṇā***. ***kassṇā***).
screw-driver, ***pēckass***, m.
scrub, ***kūcṇā*** : metal vessel, ***mānjṇā*** : table, chair, etc., ***dhōṇā***, ***ragaṛke dhōṇā***.
scuffle, ***āpe icc hatthī paiṇā*** or ***khaihṇā*** : *see* rush.
scullion, ***masālcī***.
scum, ***jhagg***, f.
scythe, ***dātrī*** *see* sickle.
sea, ***samundar***, n). : *see* shore.
seal, ***mohr***, f. (***lāṇī***, int. ***laggṇī***).
sealing-wax, ***lākh***, f. (***lāṇī***, int. ***laggṇī***).
search, ***labbhṇā***, ***ḍhūṇḍhṇā***, ***talāsh karnī*** (***dī***) : turn over things, ***phōlṇā*** : police s. of house, person, for stolen goods, ***talāshī***, f. (***laiṇī***, ***dī***).
season, ***bahār***, f., ***mausam***, m.
seat, n., in railway carriage, ***banc***, f., ***thā***, m. f. : *see* chair, stool, bench.
seat, v. tr., ***bahāṇā***, ***bahāḷṇā*** : *see* teach, sit.
second, ***dujjā***, ***dūsrā***.
second, motion, ***tāīd karnī*** (***dī***).
second-hand, ***purāṇā***.
second-sight, n., ***gaibdānī*** f. : possessings., ***gaibdān***.
secret, ***bhēt***, m., ***bhēt wālī gall*** f. : *see* hide : adj., ***gujjhā*** : s. agent or one in the s., ***bhēt-ī***, fem. ***-aṇ***.
secretly, ***cōrī***, ***cōrī chappī***, ***bhēt nāḷ***.
sect, ***firkā***, m. : *see* party.
section, *see* part : of orange, lime, lemon, pomelo, etc., ***phāṛī***, f. ***hissā***, m.

secure, firm, ***pakkā, ṭhīk tagṛā, huṇ khlōwegā*** : *see* safe, servant.
security, ***hafāzat*** *see* bail, safety, trust.
sedition, ***balwā*** *see* mutiny.
seduce, ***baihkāṇā*** (pron. ***bakhāṇā***), ***wagāṛnā, warglāṇā*** : *see* incite.
see, ***wēkhṇā*** (pa. p. ***ḍiṭṭhā, wékheā***), ***wékhnā-cākhnā.*** we shall *see*, ***wékhī jāégī*** : be seen, *see* visible : able tó *see*, not blind, ***sujākhā.***
seeing that, *see* since.
seed, ***bī̃***, m. : (v. tr. s. cotton, ***wēlnā.***
seek, ***labhṇā, talāshnā*** *see* search.
seem, ***jāpṇā, malūm, hōnā, zāhr hōnā*** : *see* visible, evident.
seize, ***phaṛnā, phagaṛnā, khōhṇā*** (int. ***khussṇā***), ***nappṇā, napaṛnā, mallṇā, zore laiṇā*** : *see* snatch, confiscate.
seldom, ***ghaṭṭ ghaṭṭ waddh*** : *see* sometimes.
select, ***cuṇṇā, pasand-k.***
self, myself, himself, etc., ***āpi, āpū̃, āpe, āpõ*** : genit. ***apṇā*** (when distributive, ***apṇā apṇā, āpo dhāpṇā, āpo apṇā***) : acc. ***apṇe āp nū̃*** : G. 27, 28, 87, 88.
self, n., (relig. sense, evil self), no word, use, ***apṇī marzī, apṇe khyāl, gunāh***, m.
selfish, ***k͟hudgarz. matlabī, garzī.***
selfishness, ***k͟hudgarzī.***
sell, v. tr., ***wēcṇā*** : int. ***wikṇā.***
semolina, ***samlīnā***, m. (K.).
send, ***ghallṇā, ṭōrnā, apṛāṇā, pucāṇā*** : s. for person, ***sadd ghallṇā*** : thing, ***maṅgā ghallṇā, maṅg ghallṇā*** : s. and ask, ***pucch ghallṇā*** : send message, ***āk͟h ghallṇā, sanēhā ghallṇā.***
senior, ***waḍḍā.***
sensation, *see* feeling, astonish. surprise.
sense., ***hōsh***, f., ***akl.***, m. f., ***sudh.*** f., ***budh***, f., ***magz***, m., ***ṭhēṭh***, f. : *see* understanding : come to senses, ***hōsh auṇi*** (***nū̃***), M. 117. 7 : out of senses, *see* mad, fool meaning, *see* meaning.
senseless, ***behõsh*** (***unconscious***) : *see* mad, fool
sensual, ***luccā, shaihwati.***
sentence, in book, ***jumlé***, m., ***fikrā***, m. : of judge, ***hukm***. m.
sentry, ***santrī, paihrewāḷā.***
separate, adj., ***wakhrā, adrā, aḍḍ, wakkho - wakkh, aḍḍo-aḍḍ, waḷo waḷī, nawēkḷā, alaihdā, alagg*** : *see* apart.
v., ***nakheṛnā*** (int. ***nikkharnā***), also any adj. for s. w. ***karnā*** : int. ***wiccharṇā*** (w. sadness), or any adj. for s. w. ***hōṇā.***
separation, ***alaihdgī***, f., ***judāī***, f. : ***wachōṛā***, m. (w. sadness).
September, ***satambar***, m., ***assū̃***, m. (about Sept. 13 to Oct. 12).
series, ***silsilā***, m.
serious, solemn, ***sanjīdā*** : important, ***bhārā.***
sermon, ***wāhz***, f. m. : ***wāhd***, f. m. : ***k͟hutbā***. m. (M) : *see* preach.
servant, ***naukar*** (fem. do), ***taihliā*** : Govt. s., ***mulāzam*** : s. of God, ***Rabb dā bandā, sēwak,***

(H.) : person rendering services for fixed amount of grain, ***sēp-ī***, fem. ***-aṇ*** (master also called ***sēpī***) : night and day s. of farmer, ***āthṛī*** : farm s., ***kāmmā*** (fem. ***kāmmī***) : secure s., ***baṇāṇā***. A.

serv-e, -ice, ***naukrī***, f., ***ṭaihl***, f., ***mulāzmat***, f., ***khidmat***, f., ***sēwā*** : s. of ***sēpī***, ***sēp***, f. : all year : day labour, ***mazdūri karnī***, ***dihāṛīā̃ karnīā̃*** : religious service, ***bandgī***, f., ***duā bandagi girjā***, m. (church) .

set, ***lāṇā***, int, ***laggṇā*** : *see* place, put : s. limb, ***jōṛnā***, int, ***juṛnā*** : s. jewel, ***jaṛnā*** : of sun, moon, stars, ***ast h.***, ***ḍubbṇā*** : s. table, *see* table : of cement, etc., ***ḍāhḍā h.***, ***pakkā h.***

settle, *see* srrange, decide : dispute, ***faisla karnā***, *see* umpire : s. matter, ***nabēṛnā***, int. ***nibbaṛnā*** : ***bhugtāṇā***, int. ***bhugtṇā*** : of earth in water, ***baihṇā***, *see* clear : of building, earth (sink), ***baihṇā*** : dwell, ***wassṇā*** : debts, *see* pay : not quite settled, *see* uncertain.

settlement, ***faislā***, m. : land-s, ***bandobast***, m. (***k.***) : *see* assess- - ment, tax..

settler, ***raihṇwālā***, ***wassaṇwālā***, m.

seven, ***satt*** : -th, ***satuā̃*** : G. 19.

seventeen, ***satārā̃*** : -th, ***satāhr-wū̃*** : shoe s. fingers long, ***satāhrī juttī*** : G. 19-24, 123.

seventy, ***sattar***. ***s-hattar*** : -one, ***ak-hattar*** : -two, ***bahattar*** : - three, ***tihattar***, ***tarhattar*** : -four, ***cuhattar***, ***curhattar*** : -five, ***panjhattar*** : -six, ***chěhattar*** : - seven, ***satattar***, ***sathattar***. -eight, ***aṭhattar***, ***aṭhhattar*** : -nine, ***unāsī***, ordinals add ***-wā̃*** : 79 adds high tone h, ***unāhsīwā̃*** : G.19-24, 123.

several, ***kaī***, ***kujjh*** : *see* few.

severe, ***ḍāhḍā***, ***sakht***, ***zōr dā***.

severity, ***ḍāhḍpuṇā***, m., ***zōrāwarī***, f., ***sakhtī***, f. : *see* oppress.

sew, ***syūṇā***, pa. p. ***sītā***.

sewing, ***salāī***, f. : -machine, ***mashīn***, f., ***syūṇwāḷī mashīn***.

sex, ***jiṇs***, f. : use man, woman ; for animals, *see* male, female.

shade, ***chā̃***, f. : in the s., ***chā̃we*** : *see* shadow.

shadow, ***parchāwā̃***. m. : overshadow, of tree, ***sāyā pāṇā*** (int. ***paiṇā***, ***utte***).

shady, ***chā̃wāḷā***.

shaft, of carriage, ***bamb***, m.

shake, v. tr., ***halāṇā***, int. ***hallṇā*** : *see* wobble, tremble : s. hands, ***hatth maḷāṇā*** or ***suṭṭnā*** (***nāḷ***), ***panjā suṭṭṇā*** (***nāḷ***).

shallow, water, ***pāṇī thōṛā e*** or ***langhaṇwāḷā e*** : of person, ***kaccā***, ***sōcdā nehī***.

sham, ***pakhanḍ*** *see* pretence, imitation : adj., ***naklī***.

shame, ***sharm***, f. : ***namoshī***, f. (humiliation) : both w. ***auṇī***, ***nū̃***, M. 117. 3 : feel ashamed, ***bhaiṛā paiṇā***, M. 125. 7 : *see* shy : for s. ! ***tōbbā tōbbā***, ***hoe hoe***, and words for bravo used ironically.

shameless, ***besharm***, ***behayā*** (strong words, of woman mean immoral).
shameful, ***sharm dī gall***, f.
shampoo, ***muṭṭhiā̃ bharniā̃*** (***nū̃***) : w. feet, ***latāṛnā***.
shape, ***shakal*** *see* form.
share, ***hissā***, m. : *see* part, divide, partner, common.
sharp, not blunt, also of sight, intelligence, ***tēz***.
sharpen, knife, axe, etc., ***canḍṇā***, ***tēz-k*** : *see* grindstone.
sharpness, ***tēzī***, f.
shave, ***munnṇa*** : get shaved, ***munāṇā*** (w. word for beard, head, etc.) : -ed patch on head, ***tāḷū*** (***kaḍḍhṇā***, caus. ***kaḍhāṇā***).
shavings of wood, ***sak***, m., ***sakṛā***, m., ***būrā***, m.
shawl, *see* sheet : ***loī***, f., ***cutahī***, f., ***khēs***, m., ***dushāllā***. m. : wrap s. round head, ***bukkaḷ mārnī***.
she, ***eh***, ***oh***.
sheath, ***myān*** *f. see* scabbard.
shed, ***dhārā***, m. : railway s., ***chiḍḍ***, m.
sheep, ***bhēḍ***, f., ***bhēḍī***, f. : fattailed, ***dumbā***, m. : *see* ram : adj., ***bākrā*** (or goat's).
sheepfold, ***wāṛā***, m.
sheeshum tree, ***ṭāhlī***, f.
sheet of paper, ***tā***, m. : of cloth, ***cādar***, f. (***palangh dī***, ***manjī*** (***aī***, of bed) : pull s. overone, ***cādar utte laiṇī*** : *see* cloth.
shelf, niche, ***ālā***, m. : on wall, ***paṛchattī***, f. : in wall-press, ***drāz***, f.
shell (sea, river) ***sippī***, f. : cowrie ***kauḍḍī***, f. : explosive, ***gōḷā***, m. *see* husk, peel.
shelter, ***ōhlā***, m. (esp. against something coming from side) : ***ḍakkā***, m. (gen.) : ***bacā***, m. (gen.) : ***sāyā***, m. (someone's protection) : *see* guard, save, preserve.
shepherd, ***ājrī***, ***chēṛū***, ***ayāḷī***
shield, ***ḍhāl***, f.
shin, ***sukṛanj***, f.
shine, ***lishkṇā***, ***camakṇā***.
ship, ***jahāz***, in.
shipwreck, ***jahāz ṭakkar khāke ṭuṭṭ geā***.
shirker, ***kamm cōr***, *see* lazy.
shirt, ***kamīz***, f., ***jhiggā***, m., ***kuṛtā***, m.
shiver, *see* tremble, chatter.
shock, sorrow, etc., ***saṭṭ*** (***laggṇī***, ***nū̃***), ***sadmā***, m. (U. ***h.***, ***nū̃***), *see* grief, collide.
shoe, ***juttī***, f. : English, ***būt***, m. : pair of s., ***juttī***, ***jōṛā***, m., ***būṭ*** : G. 73, 74 : Hindu wooden s., ***paūā***, m., ***khṛā̃***, f. : repair s., ***ganḍhṇā*** : put on, ***pāṇā*** : take off, ***lāhṇā*** : horse-s., ***khurī***, f., ***nāḷ***, m. : cattle-s., ***khurī***, f. : old worn-out s., ***chittar***, m. : size, of s., thirteen, fourteen to eighteen finger-breadths, ***tehrī***, ***cauhdī***, ***pandhrī sohḷī satāhrī***, ***aṭhāhrī***, G. 123; small 14, ***narm cauhdī*** : large 16, ***pakkī sohḷī***.
shoeless, *see* bare.
shoot, *see* fire (2), and add following : ***calāṇā*** (ink. ***calṇā***) and ***mārnā*** used of both gun,

cannon, etc., and missile (bullet, arrow, etc.), also ***chaḍḍṇā*** of gun, cannon, etc. : but ***calāṇā*** and ***chaḍḍṇā*** mean merely "fire," "fire off," whereas ***mārnā*** implies hitting (w. ***nū̃*** of thing, person hit) : go shooting, ***shikār khēḍṇā*** or ***kornā*** : *see* stone.

shoot, of tree, ***gullā***, m.

shop, ***haṭṭī***, f., ***dukān***, f. : keep s., ***haṭṭī*** or ***dukān karnī*** : start s., ***haṭṭī pānī*** or ***kholhṇī***.

shopkeeper, ***haṭṭīwāḷā***, ***baṇīā***, ***dukāndār***.

shore, ***kanḍhā***, m., ***dandā***, m. (lit. edge).

short, things in gen., *see* small : person, ***madhrā***, ***mandhrā***, ***nikkā*** : *see* dwarf : letter, speech, *see* brief : in short, ***muddā***, ***gall kāhdī*** : in s. time, soon, ***thōṛe cir nū̃***, ***zarā ku nū̃***.

short-lived, ***thōṛe cir dā***, ***chōṭī umar icc moeā***, ***thōṛā cir rehā*** : *see* transient.

shot, grains of, ***charrā***, m. : *see* shoot (1).

shoulder, n., ***monḍhā***, m. : v., ***monḍheā̃ te*** or ***kandhāṛe*** or ***dhangāṛe cukkṇā*** : *see* back, also back in A. : s. one's way, ***dhakke nāḷ lanġhṇā*** (also means by force) : *see* shove.

shout, ***awāz mārnī***, ***kūk mārnī*** : *see* call, scream : speak loudly, ***uccī*** or ***zōr-nāḷ*** or ***dabbke kūṇā***, ***uccī ditlī bōlṇā*** loudly or angrily, ***kaṛakke kūṇā***.

shove, ***dhakkā dēṇā*** (***nū̃***), ***dhikkṇā*** : s. off (esp. in water), ***ṭhelhṇā***, int. ***ṭhillhṇā***.

shovel, ***bēlcā***, m. : ***kaṛch***, m. (v. large iron spoon).

show, v., ***dassṇā***, ***wakẖāṇā***.

show, n., ***wakhāḷī***, f., ***dakẖāwā***, m : for s., ***wakẖāṇ wāste***, ***apṇī izzat wadhāṇ wāste*** : display, grandeur, ***chūkā shākī***, f. (***k.***) : ***tash*** or ***tash ṭush kaḍḍhṇī*** : ***daddh kaḍḍhṇī*** (affect style) M. 120. 48 : *see* splendour, sit.

shriek, *see* scream, shout.

shrill, ***tēz***.

shrine, (M.) ***k̲h̲āngāh***, f. (tomb) : (H.) ***sthān***, m., ***mandar***, m. (temple).

shrink, v. int., cloth, etc., ***sangaṛnā*** : through pain, ***sī karnī*** : s. back, ***pishā̃ haṭṇā***.

shrivel, *see* wither, wrinkle.

shroud, n., for burial, ***khapphan***, m.

shrub, ***jhāṛī***, f. : small, ***bucc***, m.

shun, ***parhēz karn-ī***, ***-ā*** (***tõ***, esp. of food, actions) : ***bacṇā*** (***koḷõ***) : ***dūr raihṇā*** (***tõ***) : *see* avoid, abstain.

shunt, train, ***shanṭ karnā***.

shut, ***band-k.*** : s. door, window, ***mārnā*** (int. ***wajjṇā***) : fasten hook of door, etc., ***kunḍī mārnī*** (***dī***) : ***hukk mārnī***, (***dī***) : ***kunḍa mārnā*** (***dā***) : close door, etc., *see* close : s. u, ***band-k.***

shy, be, ***sangṇā***. ***jhakṇā***, ***jhijhakṇā*** : adj. ***sangā wāḷā*** : *see* ashamed, shame, synyness.

shyness, ***sangā***, f. : ***jhākkā***, m. (both w. ***auṇā nū̃***) *see* shy.

sick, ***bamār*** *see* ill, sorry, vomit : be s. of, ***jī*** or ***rūh*** or ***dil caṛhnā*** (***tõ***) : *see* tire, (tired of).
sickle, ***dātrī***, f.
side, direction, ***pāsā***, m., ***lāhmb***, f., ***bāī***, f., ***bāhī***, f., ***guṭṭh***, f. (corner) : get to one s., ***lāhmbe*** or ***ikkī pāse hōjā*** : in what direction, *see* direction : on all sides, ***sabbhnī̃ pāsī̃***, ***cawhī̃ pāsī̃*** : everywhere, ***sabbh dare***, ***har kite*** : round, near, ***āḷe duāḷe*** : *see* round : on this s., ***urār*** : on that s., ***pār*** : s. of body, ***wakkhī***, f. : *see* party, bed, door.
sideboard, ***sālbōt***, m. (K.).
side-dish, ***ḍoṅghā***, m.
siege, ***muhāsrā***, m. (***k.***), ***ghērā***, m. (***pāṇā***).
sieve, ***chāṇṇī***, f.
sift, ***chāṇṇā*** : separate husk fr. grain, ***chaṭṭṇā***.
sigh, ***hāhukā mārnā***.
sight, eyesight, ***nazr***, f. : view, ***nazārā***, m. : spectacle, ***tamāshā*** (*see* entertainment) : of holy place or person, *see* visit.
sign, ***nishān***, m. (***k.***, mark) : ***ishārā***, m. (***k.***, sign) : *see* effect, proof, result.
signal, railway, ***saṅgaḷ***, m. : go down, ***hōṇā ḍaun h.*** : ***hatth***, m. (***ḍiggṇā*** :) *see* sign.
signature, ***daskhatt***, m.
signet, ***mohr***, f. (***lāṇī***, ***laggṇī***) : engrave, *see* engrave.
signify, ***ohde maihṇe kī ne***. ***ohdā matlab kī e*** : *see* meaning : it does not s., *see* matter.
silence, ***cup-cāp***, f., ***khamōshī***. f. (U.).
silent, ***cupcapītā***, ***cup***, ***cupkītā***.
silently, ***cup capītā***, ***cup cāp***, ***maikṛī***, ***hauḷī hauḷī*** : *see* secretly.
silk, ***paṭṭ***, f., ***rēsham***, m., ***ṭassar***, m. : adj., these words w. ***dā***, also ***rēshmī***, ***ṭassarī***.
silly, ***jhallā*** *see* fool.
silver, ***cāndī***, f., ***ruppā***, m.
silversmith, ***sunyārā***.
similar, ***wāṅgar***, ***wāṅgū̃***, ***wargā***, ***hār***, G. 35 : ***jehā***, G. 91, 92 : ***ajehā***, ***ehojehā*** : like what ? ***kehā***, ***kehojehā*** : relative, ***jehā***.
simmer, ***matthe tā pakkṇā***.
simple, ***sādā*** (not ornamented) : of person, ***bhoḷā***, ***siddhā***, ***sādā***, sometimes ***bātshāh***.
simultaneously, ***ikse weḷe***, ***nāḷo nāḷ***, ***kaṭṭhā***.
sin, ***gunāh***, m. (k.) : ***pāp***, m. (***k.*** H.) : *see* evil, wickedness.
since (1), time, ***jadõ dā***, ***jis weḷe tõ*** : ***jadõ dī oh āī e***, ***maī ohnū̃ nehī̃ ḍiṭṭhā***, I have not seen her since she came : time since, pa. p. with ***nū̃*** : ***ohnū̃ khote tõ ḍiggeā̃ dō dojāṛe hoe ne***, it is two days since he fell from the donkey ; G. 79, last line : *see* ago.
(2) reasoning, *see* because, also ***jis hāl wicc***, ***jadõ***.
sincere, ***saccā***, ***saccā***, ***dilī***.
sincerely, ***dil nāḷ***, ***dilõ wajhõ hōke***.
sinew, ***nāṛ***, f. (also vein, artery).
sinful, *see* sinner.
sing, ***gauṇā***.

singer, ***gavaiyā*** *see* musician.
singe, v. tr., ***sāṛnā***, int. ***saṛnā***.
single, one fold, ***akāhrā***, ***ighrā***, *see* fold, bachelor.
singly, ***ikk ikk karke***.
singular (grammar), ***waihd***, f. : *see* strange, wonderful.
sink, in water, ***ḍubbnā*** (also of sun, etc. : tr. ***ḍōbṇā***) : in something soft, mud, etc., ***khubbhṇā***, tr. ***khōbhṇā*** : *see* drown.
sinless, ***bēgunah*** : faultless, ***beaib***, ***bēkasūr*** : innocent, ***masūm***, ***mashūm***.
sinner, ***gunāhī***, ***pāpī*** (H.).
siris tree, *see* acacia.
sister, ***bhaiṇ***, ***hamshīrā*** (U.) : s.-in-law : wife's s., ***sāḷā*** : wife's brother's wife, ***sāḷehā-r***, ***-j*** : brother's wife, ***bhābbī***, ***bharjāī***: husband's sister, ***naṇān***, ***nanāṇ***: husband's elder brother's wife, ***jaṭhāṇī*** : younger do., ***darāṇī***.
sit, ***baihṇā***, pa. p. ***baiṭhā***, G. 64 : sitting. ***baiṭhā hoeā***, G. 108 : *see* squat : s. on eggs, ***baihṇā*** : sit up, *see* rise : at someone's feet as scholar, ***baihṇā***, M. 117. 13, 19 : *see* teach : sit upon, reprimand severely, (jocular), ***khabar laiṇī*** (***dī***), ***makkū ṭhappṇā*** (***dā***), ***lamb kaḍḍhṇī*** (***dī***). ***sukranjā bhannṇīā*** (break shins, ***dīā̃***), ***babbar bhannṇe*** (break ribs, ***de***), ***ākkaṛ bhannṇī*** (take down pride, ***dī***). N.B.—In some places, ***lamb kaḍḍhṇī*** means "affect style" : *see* reprimand, reproach.
site, ***jaghā***, f.
sittingroom, ***baiṭhak***, f. : *see* drawingroom.
situated, simply say ***kitthe we***, etc.
situation, service, ***naukrī***. f. ; ***asāmī***, f. (vacancy) : place, ***jaghā***, f. (also for service).
six, ***chē*** : -th, ***chēwā̃*** : G. 19–24.
sixteen, ***sōḷā̃*** : -th, ***sohḷwā̃***: sixteem finger shoe, ***shoḷī juttī*** : G. 19-24, 123.
sixty, ***saṭṭh*** : -one, ***akāhṭh*** : -two, ***bāhṭh*** : -three, ***trehth*** : -four, ***cauhth*** : -five, ***paīhṭh*** : -six, ***cheāhṭh*** : seven, ***satāhṭh*** : -eight, ***aṭhāhṭh*** : -nine. ***unhattar*** : ordinals add ***-wā̃***, ***saṭṭhwā̃***, etc., G. 19-24, 123.
size, of person, ***kadd***, m. (U.) : of boot, shoe, *see* shoe : in gen. no word, use ***ēḍḍā***, ***ōḍḍā***, so large ; ***kēḍḍā***, how large; ***jēḍḍā***, as large : *see* big.
skein, ***gunjī***, f.
skeleton, ***pinjrā***, m., ***pinjar***, m.
skewer, ***sīkh***, f (also iron bar).
skill, skilful, skilled, *see* clever-, -ness.
skim, milk, ***malāī lāhṇī***.
skin, n., ***camm***, m. : ***camṛā***, m. : hide, ***khall***, f. : water-s., mashk, f. : do. for crossing river, ***sarnāhī***, f. : of fruit, vegetable, *see* peel.
skin, v. tr., ***camm lāhṇā***, ***khall lāhṇī***, ***khullṇā*** (used by scavengers) : *see* pare.
skirmish, ***laṛāī bhiṛāī***, f.
skirt, ***ghagghrī***, f., ***laihngā*** m.,

kōrā, m. (2nd and 3rd ornamented) : worn by men and women, ***taihmat***, m., ***luṅni***, f., ***lācā***, m., ***dhōtti***, f. (H.).
skull, ***khōprī***, f.
sky, ***asmān***, m.
slack, ***ḍhillā***. loose : *see* lazy, careless.
slake, thirst, ***treh maṭṭhī karnī*** or ***bujhāṇī***.
slander, use ***jhūṭhā***, false. w. "accusation" : ***bakhīlī k.*** (***dī***), ***tohmat*** (***lāṇī***, ***utte***, U.), ***nakhiddhṇā***, ***mukāḷā k.*** (***dā***), ***kulāhṇā***.
slant, m., ***urēb***, m., *see* slope, sloping.
slanting, ***kuāsā*** ; ***ḍingā***, crooked, *see* slope.
slap, ***capēr***, f., ***caṇḍ***, f., ***dhapphā***, m. (***mārnā***, ***khāṇā***).
slate, ***slēṭ***, f. : wooden, ***takhtī***, f.
slaughter, *see* kill.
slave, ***gulām*** : slavery, ***gulāmī*** f.
sledge-hammer, *see* hammer.
sleep, n., ***nīndar***, f. (sleepiness), *see* sleepy.
sleep, v., ***saũṇā***, pa. p. ***suttā***, G. 64 : fast asleep, ***ghūk suttā hoeā*** : sleeping, ***suttā hoeā***, G. 108 : to have just fallen asleep, ***akkh laggṇī*** (***dī***) : to be getting up fr. s., ***suttā peā uṭṭhṇā***. M. 125. 8 : go to s., of limb, ***saũṇā***.
sleeper, wooden, ***gellī***, f., *see* log.
sleeplessness, ***unīndrā h.*** (***nũ***) : ***jagrāttā kaṭṭnā*** : *see* vigil.
sleepy, feel, ***nīndar auṇī*** (***nũ***), M. 117.5 : ***uṅghlāṇā***, ***uglhāṇā***, nod drowsily : ***jāgo mīṭī***, half asleep on one's bed.
sleeve, ***bā̃h***, f.
slice, of bread, ***tōs***, m. (whether toasted or not) : of fruit, ***phāṛī***, f. (whether cut as in melon, or section of orange, etc.).
sling, n., ***gulēl***, f. (like bow) : ***kubhāṇī***, f. (real sling) : *see* pellet.
slip, ***tilhkṇā*** : down, ***riṛhnā***.
slipper, ***gurgābī***, f : ***slīpar***, m.
slippery, ***tilhkaṇwālā***, ***oāhkṇā***.
slit, n., ***trēṛ***, f., (***paiṇī***, ***nū***) : v. tr., ***cīrnā***, ***pāṛnā*** (also tear) : *see* cut.
slope, ***nuāṇ***, m., ***salāmī***, f., ***ḍhaḷwāṇ***, m., ***urēb***, m. : *see* slanting.
sloping, ***ḍhāḷwā̃***, and words for slope w. ***-wālā***.
slow, ***dhillā***, ***maṭṭhā*** : *see* lazy : s. fire, ***maṭṭhe tā*** (***pakāṇā***, *see* simmer).
slowly, ***hauḷī hauḷī***, ***saihje*** : go s. ***jũ dī ṭōr turnā*** : *see* steadily.
slowness, ***ḍhill***, f., ***ḍhill maṭṭh***, f.
slur, ***dhabbā***, m., ***dāg***, m. (both ***lāṇā***, int. ***laggṇā***).
small, ***nikkā***, ***chōṭā*** : of person, *see* short, dwarf.
smallpox, ***mātā̃***, f. (***nikḷṇī***).
smart, adj., ***sajā sajāeā***, in appearance; and words for show : ***cust*** in action.
smart, ache, *see* pain, hurt.
smartly, ***custi nāḷ***.
smash, v. tr., ***ṭōṭe ṭōṭe k.***, ***phīṭe phīṭe k.***, ***cūr cūr k.*** (all ***nū***) : int., same words w. ***h.*** : *see* collide, knock.

smattering, speak language badly, ***ṭis mis karnā*** : *see* poor.
smear, w. oil, butter, etc., ***cōpaṛnā*** : *see* plaster.
smell, v. tr., ***sunghṇā*** : int. (bad s.) ***bō chaḍḍṇi*** or ***karni, bō auni*** (***tō̃***).
smell, n., sweet, *see* perfume : bad, ***mushk***, f. : ***bō***, f. (by itself means bad s.).
smile, ***muskrāṇā*** : jocular words, ***guṭakṇā, guṛhkṇā.***
smoke, n., ***dhū̃***, m. : *see* soot.
smoke, v. int., ***dhū̃ niklnā*** : s. pipe, hukka, tobacco, etc., ***piṇā***: of hukka also ***chikknā.*** have turn at hukka, ***sūṭ***, m., ***sūṭā***, m., ***wārī***, f. (all w. ***lāṇā***), ***wārī lainī.***
smooth, to touch, ***kūḷā*** : road, ground, ***padhrā*** : gen. ***sāf, suāhrā.***
smother, ***sāh band karke mārnā, saṅgh ghuṭṭke mārnā*** : *see* choke, strangle, stifle.
snaffle, ***kazāī***, f.
snake, ***sapp***, fem. ***sappṇī*** : -skin, cast off, ***sappkunj***, f.
snake-charmer, ***sapyādhā.***
snap, fingers, ***cuṭkī mārnī.***
snare, ***phandhā***, m. : net, ***jāḷ***, m. A.
snatch, kite, cat, hand, ***jhuṭāh mārnā, jharāṭ*** or ***jharuṭṭ mārni*** : *see* seize.
sneer, ***tāhne mārne*** (***nū̃***) : ***mehṇā dēṇā*** or ***mārnā*** (***nū̃***).
sneeze, ***nicch mārnī*** : severe w. cough, ***dhraññā, drā̃snā.***
snore, ***ghurāṛe mārne.***
snout, ***būthī***, f. : pig's, ***thunnī***, f.
snow, ***warf***, f., ***barf***, f. : fall, ***paiṇī.***
snuff, ***naswār***, f.
so, *see* thus : so and so, ***falāṇā***, *see* such and such : so so, ***ajehā kajehā*** ; in indifferent health, circumstances, ***heṭhā̃ utā̃.***
soak, v. tr., ***bheō̃ṇā***, int. ***bhijjṇā*** : *see* wet.
soap, ***sabūṇ***, m. : ***sāban***, m. (U.).
soap-nut, ***rēṭhā***, m., ***rēṭhrā***, m.
sob, ***haṭghōre laiṇe*** or ***bharne, bilkṇā.***
sober, ***hōsh wicc*** : ***sanjīdā*** (solemn).
sociable, ***miḷṇwāḷā, maḷāprā.***
society (also a society), ***susaitī***, f. : M. ***anjuman***, f. : H. ***sabhā***, m., ***samāj***, m.
sock, ***julāb***, f., ***jurāb***, f., ***jarēb*** f., ***mauzā***, m. : ***massī***, f.
socket, ***ghūā̃***, m. : *see* pivot.
soda, ***sōḍā***, m. : s.-water, ***sōḍā***, m. ***khārā pāṇī***, m. : bottle of, ***khārī bōtal***, f., ***sōḍe dī bōtal.***
sofa, ***waḍḍī kursī***, f. : ***kauc***, m.
soft, ***kūḷā***, tender of flesh, meat, skin, trees, shoots, leaves, bones (of children, young animals), smooth of skin, cloth : ***narm***, soft of heart, cloth, skin, leather, also of meat if result of cooking : ***pōllā***, of earth, soil.
softly, not loudly, *see* gently.
soil, ***zamīn***, f., ***jīwī.*** f., ***bhoē.*** f., ***miṭṭī***, f. : good, damp s., ***chambh***, f., ***rohī*** f. : also good, ***mairā***, m., ***pakkī jīwī*** : not good, ***rētā***, m. : barren, ***rakkaṛ***, m., ***banjar***, m., ***kallar***, m.

good, adj., of soil, saras, ***caṅgī***, ***missī***, ***bhōrī*** : bad, ***māṛī***, ***niras***, ***karlāṭhs***.
soil, soiled, *see* dirty.
solder, ***kalī kornī*** (***nū̃***) : *see* patch.
soldier, ***sipāhī***, ***jaujī ādmī*** : English, ***gōrā*** : *see* officer.
sole, of foot, ***taḷī***, f. : of boot,, shoe ***taḷā***, m.
solemn, *see* serious, sober.
solid, ***piḍḍā***, ***ṭhōs*** (not hollow, U.).
soliloquise, ***sōcṇā***, *see* think, meditation.
solitude, *see* alone, lonely.
solve, sum, problem, ***hall-k.***, ***kaḍḍhṇā*** : riddle, ***bujjhṇā*** (guess).
some, ***kujjh***, ***bāze***, ***koī***, ***koī koī*** (G. 87), ***ikknā̃*** (only oblique), G. 28 : some ...others, ***koī ...*** ***koī***, G. 87 : *see* few.
somehow, ***kiwē̃***, ***kise tarhā̃***, ***masā̃*** : *see* difficulty, scarcely.
someone, ***koī*** : s. or other, ***koī nā koī***.
something, ***kujjh*** : s. or other, ***kujjh nā kujjh***.
sometimes, ***kade***, ***kade kade***, ***kadī kadāī*** (implies seldom).
somewhat, rather, -ish. ***jehā***, G. 27, 92 : or add ***-ērā***, as ***waḍērā***, biggish, G. 18 : colour, yellowish blackish, etc., ***piḷī*** or ***kāḷī bhai mārdā e***.
somewhere, ***kite***, ***kitale***, ***kidhare*** : s. else, ***hōr kidhare***, ***hōr dare***.
son, ***puttar***, ***bētā***, leg. ***wald*** : Europeans', ***bāwā*** : s.-in-law, ***juāī***, ***juātrā***, ***majmān*** : ***ikko puttar mar geā***, only one son died : ***ikkse puttar dī saūh***, oath by only son.
song, ***gavn***, m., ***gīt***, m.
soon, ***jabde***, ***jhabdē***, ***jhaw jhaw***, ***thōṛe cir nū̃***, ***zarā ku nū̃***, ***huṇe***, ***jaldī***.
soot, ***kāḷakh***, f. : ***dhū̃***, m. (smoke).
soothe, *see* comfort, condole, add ***dalāsā dēṇā*** (***nū̃***), ***pī***? ***maṭṭhī karnī*** (***dī***).
soothsayer, ***najūmī***, *see* astrologer, magician.
soporific, ***suāṇwāḷī duāī***, f.
sorcerer, *see* magician, astrologer, soothsayer.
sore, n. (wound), ***phaṭṭ***, m., ***zakhm***, m : (blow), ***saṭṭ***, f., on back of horse, mule, etc. ***lāggā*** (***laggṇā***, M. 121. 14) : *see* boil (1).
sore, adj., *see* chafe, painful.
sorrow, *see* grief.
sorrowful, *see* sad.
sorry, see sad, grieve, regret : s. for oneself, ***nimmā*** (***jāpṇā***).
sort, n., ***jiṇs***, f., ***kism***, f.
sort, v. tr., ***chāṇṭṇā***.
so so, *see* so.
soul, ***rūh***, m : often ***dil***, m., heart ; ***jān***, f., life.
sound, n., ***ǎwāz***, f., ***wāz***, f. : *see* noise.
sound, adj., horse, etc. ***bilkul tagrā***.
sound, v. int. ***ǎwāz dēṇī***, ***shāor karnā*** : v. tr., a person, ***patā***

lāṇā (***koḷõ*** of person, ***dā*** of thing) : coin, pot (to test it), *see* ring : a letter, *see* pronounce.

soup, ***shuruā***, m. :- plate, ***supleṭ***, f. (K.).

sour, ***khaṭṭā*** : milk become s., ***phiṭṇā***, ***saurnā*** (G. 113), ***kharāb hō jāṇā***, ***wigaṛnā***.

source, spring, ***cishmā***, m., ***cashmā***, m. : origin, ***jaṛh***, f., ***asl***, f., ***muṇḍh***, m.

sourness, ***khaṭeāī***, f.

south, ***dakkhaṇ***, ***dakkhaṇ pāsā***, m. : -wards, ***dakkhaṇ wall*** or ***pāse*** : south-west, ***dakkhaṇ te laihnde dī guṭṭh*** : south-east, ***dakkhaṇ te caṛhde dī guṭṭh***.

sovereignty, ***rāj***, m., ***bādshāhī***, f., ***saltanat***, f., ***hukūmat***, f.

sow, n., *see* pig.

sow, v. tr., ***bījṇā*** : sowing, n., ***biāī***, f., ***bijāī***, f.

space, ***khappā***, m., ***witth***; f., ***thā̃***, m. f. (place) : ***wāṭ***, f., ***paiṇḍā***, m. (distance).

spacious, ***mōkḷā*** : ***waḍḍā*** (big).

spade, ***bēlcā***, m : inverted, ***kahī***, f.

span, ***giṭṭh***, f.

spare, adj., ***fāltū***, ***waddh***.

spare, v. tr., do without, ***ohde bājhõ guzārā karnā*** : *see* forgive.

sparingly, ***sarfe nāḷ***, ***thōṛā***.

spark, ***ciṅgāṛā***, m. (from fire) : ***ciṇag***. f., from. flint, iron, etc., also small ***ir***. newly kindled fire.

sparkle, ***lishkṇā***, ***camakṇā***.

sparse, ***wirlā***, ***tā̃wā̃ tā̃wā̃***, ***thoṛā***.

spatter, ***chiṭṭā̃ pāṇiā̃*** int. ***paiṇiā̃*** : ***chaṭṭe mārne*** : *see* splash, sprinkle.

spavin, ***haḍḍ mūtrā***, m.

speak, ***kūṇā*** (pa. p. ***koyā***), ***kūṇā saihṇā***, ***bōlṇā***, ***bōlṇa cālṇā***, ***gall karnī***, ***kuskṇā*** : also note ***maĩ ohde nāḷ ā̃***, I am speaking to him : *see* speech : s. against, *see* accuse, slander.

spear, ***burchā***, m., ***barchī***, f., ***nēzā***, m.

special, ***ucēcā***, ***khāss***.

specially, ***ucēcā*** (of set purpose), ***khāskar*** (U.).

species, ***jiṇs***, f., ***kism***, f.

spectacle, ***nazārā***, ***tamāshā*** *see* sight, entertainment.

spectacles, ***aiṇak***, f. ; wear, put on, ***lāṇī*** : take off ***lāhṇī***.

spectator, ***wekhaṇwāṇā*** : *see* audience.

speech, *see* language, and add speak lang., ***bōlṇī*** ; know, ***jāṇṇī***, ***auṇī*** (***nū̃***), M. 117. 2 : speak badly, *see* smattering : make a s., ***spīc dēṇī*** : *see* conversation.

speed, ***kinnā tēz***, ***kinnī jaldī*** : *see* swift.

spell, *see* charm : s. a word, ***jōṛ karnā*** (***dā***), ***hijā karnā*** (***dā***).

spelling, ***jōṛ***, m., ***hijā***. m., ***spěl***, m.

spend, money, ***kharc-k.***, ***lāṇā***, ***paṭṭṇā*** : be spent, ***laggṇā***, ***kharc-h.*** : s. time, ***weḷā laṅghāṇā*** (pass time), ***wakat lāṇā***, ***dihāṛe lāṇe*** (int. ***laṅghṇā***, ***laggṇā***) : *see* squander.

spices, ***masālā***, m.

spider, ***bambohyā***, m.
spike, *see* nail.
spill, v. int., ***ḍulhṇā***, ***ruṛhnā*** (in tr. mean pour, *see* pour) : tr. ***ḍulhaṇ*** or ***ruṛhan dēṇā***.
spin, ***kattṇā*** (object thread or spinning wheel) : *see* spinning-bee, spinning-wheel, turn, top.
sinach, ***sāg***, m., ***pālak***. f.
spindle, *see* spinning-wheel.
spine, ***kaṅgrōṛ***, f.
spinning-bee, ***triñaṇ***. m., ***bhohrā***, m.
spinning-wheel, ***carkhā***, m : needle, ***trakḷā***, m.
spirit, ***rūh***, m : Holy Spirit, ***Pāk Rūh***, m. : in phrases like "s. of pride" or "faithfulness." omit "spirit" : intoxicating, ***sharāb***, m., ***nashā***. m.
spirited, poor-s., ***dil chōṭā***, G. 122 : M. 128. 9.
spiritual, ***ruhānī***. ***ātmak***, ***adhiātmak***.
spit, ***thukkṇā*** : *see* saliva, vomit.
spite, *see* envy, hate.
splash, n., ***chaḷak***, m. : noise of, ***ghṛam***, m. : v. int., ***chaḷakṇā***, ***chiṭṭā̃ pāṇiā̃*** (drops): tr. ***chaḷkāṇā***, ***chaṭṭe mārne***, ***chittā̃ pāṇiā̃*** : *see* spatter, sprinkle.
spleen, ***tiḷī***, f., ***lif***, f.
splendour, ***bhaṛak***, f., ***rauṇak***, f. (many people) : *see* show glory.
splice, ***bannhṇā*** : village style, ***gāṇḍhā laṇā*** (***nū̃***, int. ***laggṇā***).
splinter, wood, ***chiltar***, f. : brick, stone, ***ciṭṭh***, f
split, ***pāṛnā*** (int. ***pāṭṇā***), ***cīrnā*** : *see* tear, cut, chop.
spoil, ***wagāṛnā***, int. ***wigaṛṇā*** ; ***kharāb-k.***, int. ***h.*** : be spoiled, of matter, affair, ***guggaḷ jāṇā*** : *see* destroy, rob, steal.
spoilt, child, ***lāḍḷā***, ***lāḍā***, ***lūḍā***.
spoke, in wheel, ***ār***, m.
sponge, ***spane***, m.
spontaneously, ***āpū̃***, ***āpe***, ***āpi apõ***.
spoon, ***cimcā***, m.. ***cammac***, m. ***ḍoī***, f. (wooden), ***kaṛchī***, f., ***kaṛch***, m. (v. large).
sport, ***khēḍ***, f. (game) : shooting, fishing, etc., ***shikār kheḍṇā***.
sportsman, ***shikārī*** : player, ***khaḍārī***.
spot, *see* stain : drop, ***chiṭṭ***, f. (***paiṇī***) : *see* spatter, splash.
spotted, ***dāgwāḷā***, ***ḍabbā***, ***ḍab khṛabbā***.
spout, of teapot, etc., ***ṭūṭī***. f. : on roof for rainwater, ***pārchā***, m., ***parnāḷā***, m.
sprained, be, foot, ***moh ghattnā***, ***moheā jāṇā***, ***moh nikḷnī*** (***dī***) : other parts, ***waḷ paiṇā*** (***nū̃***) : *see* strain.
spread, carpet, cloth, ***wachāṇā***, int. ***wichṇā*** : separate out, ***khalārnā***, int. ***khillarnā*** : s. abroad, ***phalāṇā***, int. ***phailṇā*** : s. rumour, ***dhumāṇā***, int. ***dhummṇā***.
spring, season, ***cētar wasākh***, m.. ***basant***, f.
spring, steel, etc., ***kamānī***, f.
spring, water, ***sōtā***, m., ***sumb***, m., ***cishmā***, m., ***cashmā***, m.
spring, *see* jump.
sprinkle, ***chiṇakṇā***, ***traūkṇā*** ; *see* splash, spatter.

sprout, ***phuṭṭṇā, puṅgarnā*** grow, ***uggṇā.***

spur, ***kāṇṭā,*** m. (***mārnā***).

spurious, ***jhūṭhā,*** false ; ***jāhlī,*** forged.

spurn, *see* scorn, despise.

spy, ***jāsūs*** ; ***mukhbar*** (informer) : *see* espionage.

squander, ***uḍāṇā, phūk chaḍḍṇā, ujāṛnā, luṭāṇā*** (often of extravagant alms) : *see* waste, destroy.

square, ***cauras, murabbā*** : of land, ***murabbā,*** m.

squash, ***citthṇā, napittnā*** ; ***cūrk.,*** into small pieces : *see* squeeze, burst, crush.

squat, on heels, ***pairā̃ bhār baihṇā*** : cross-legged, ***caukṛī mārke*** : w. legs stretched out, ***nisḷiā̃ karke*** : on knees and feet, ***gōṭh mārke, kutte baihṇī baihṇā, ūṭh baihṇī baihṇā, goḍe mūdhe mārke baihṇā.***

squeak, ***cī cī karnī,*** rats, mice, etc. : *see* creak.

squeeze, ***ghuṭṭṇā, nacoṛnā*** : wring, ***nacōṛnā, napīṛnā*** ; press, ***dabāṇā*** : so as to burst, ***phennā,*** int. ***phissṇā,*** *see* burst : s. sugarcane, oil, etc., ***pīṛnā*** ; of fruit, ***nacoṛnā, napīṛnā*** : *see* squash, press, crush.

squib, ***paṭākā*** (***calāṇā,*** int. ***calṇā***).

squint (eyed), ***bhaiṅgā*** : v., ***bhaṅgāṇā.***

squirrel, ***gālhaṛ,*** m. ***gālhaṛ cūhā,*** m.

stab, ***talwār,*** f., ***khanjar,*** m., ***churī,*** f. : all w. ***mārnā*** and ***nū̃***

stable, ***tawēlā,*** m., ***stabal,*** m., ***astabal,*** m.

stack of hay, ***kupp.*** m.,

staff, *see* stick.

stage, ***harn,*** fem., ***harnī*** : ***bārā̃siṅgā,*** m.

stage, ***paṛā,*** m., ***manzal,*** f.

stagger, ***ḍōlke ṭurnā, ḍigdeā̃ ṭurnā.***

stagnant, ***khlōlā hoeā, gandā*** (dirty).

stain, both moral and lit., ***dāg,*** m., ***dhabbā*** (moral), m. : both w. ***lānā,*** int., ***laggṇā*** : *see* delete.

stair, ***pauṛia,*** f. pl. : one step, ***pauṛī,*** f.

stake, for impaling, ***sūḷī,*** f., ***sīkh,*** f. : *see* nail.

stale, ***behā*** from yesterday ; ***tarbehā*** from day before : ***behā,*** also gen.

stalk of wheat, barley, ***nāḷī,*** f. millet, maize, sugarcane, ***ṭāṇṇā,*** m.

stallion, ***sāhn,*** m.

stammer, ***thathlāṇā.***

stammerer, ***thatthā.***

stamp, seal, etc., ***mohr,*** f. (***lāṇī,*** int. ***laggṇī***) : postage, ***ṭīkaṭ.*** m. f. (***lāṇā,*** int. ***laggṇā***).

stand, ***khlōṇā,*** ps. p. ***khlōtā. khaḷā*** : standing, ***khlōtā, khaḷā,*** G. 108 : caus. ***khalhārnā*** : *see* rise.

stand, I won't stand that ; paraphrase : ***eh mĕnū̃*** , ***manzūr nehī̃*** ; ***maī tĕnū̃ ēs tarhā̃ nehī̃ karn dēṇ lagā*** ; ***maī ēs tarhā̃ nehī̃ hōn dēn*** ; ***lagā*** ; ***ēs tarhō̃ mērī tērī nehī̃ nibhaṇ lagī.***

stand, n., for tumtums, carriages, etc., ***aḍḍā***, m.
standard, *see* flag.
star, ***tārā***, m. : *see* rise, set, comet : for names *see* A.
starch, ***kalf***, f., ***māyā***, m.
stare, ***tāṛī lāṇī*** ; angrily, ***gharākī wēkhṇī***, ***ghūrnā***.
start, be startled, ***traihṇā*** (pa. p. ***traṭṭhā***), ***trāh nikḷṇā*** (***dā***) : *see* startle.
start, set out, ***tur paiṇā***, ***ruānā h.***, ***llāh bēlī h.*** (God be your, his friend, farewell). : ***alī panj h.***
startle, v. tr., ***trāhṇā***, *see* start
starvation, ***baṛī bhukkh***, f.
starve, ***baṛā bhukkhāh.***, ***bhukkh nāḷ marnā***, ***bhukkhā marnā***.
state, ***hālat***, f., ***hāl***, m., ***hāl hakīkat***, f. : Native State, ***riāsat***, f. : ***rāje dā rāj***.
stately, building, ***waḍḍā te sohṇā***.
statement, ***beān***, m., ***ākhṇā***, m
statesman, ***bādshāh dā salāhkār***
station (railway), ***ṭeshn***, m., ***sṭēshn***, m.
stay, ***ṭhaihrnā***, ***raihṇā***, ***ṭiknā*** : *see* wait : place where one can stay, friend's house, etc., ***ṭhāhr***, f. A.
steadily, go slowly but s. ***raḷakdā jāṇā***.
steal, ***cōrī karnī***, gen. ; ***curāṇā*** (must have object) : *see* stealthily, receiver.
stealthily, ***cōrī***, ***cōrī chappī*** (or ***chappe***), ***cup capitā***. *see* quiet-, -ly, silent-, -ly.
steam, real or vapour from kettle or hot food, ***hawāṛ***, f. : from ground, ***bhaṛās***, f.
steamer, ***jahāz***, m.
steel, ***aspāt***, m., ***fulād***, m.
steep, ***siddhī caṛhāī***, f. ; ***siddhā utā̃ jāndā e*** ; ***sak͟ht caṛhāī***, f.
stench, *see* small.
step, ***kadam***, m. : stepping. stone, ***painṭrā***, m. : *see* stair, ladder.
step, ins. -son, brother, etc., ***matrēā***, fem. ***matrēī*** : step brother or sister on father's side, ***pyō̃ mātar*** ; on mother's, ***mā̃ mātar*** : wife's child by former husband, ***pishlagg***.
stew, n., ***ishṭū***, m. (K.) : v., ***rinnhṇā***, (pa. p. ***riddhā***, int. ***rijjhṇā***).
stick, n., ***sōṭī***, f. : cane, ***baint***, m. : stout, s., ***sōṭā***, m. (short), ***ḍaṅgōrī***, f. (for old people) ; ***ḍang***, f. (long), ***ḍanḍā***, m. (short) : *see* switch.
stick, v., gen, ***laggṇā***, tr. ***lāṇā*** : s. in mud, etc., ***khubbhṇā***, tr. ***khōbbṇā***.
sticky, *see* viscous.
stiff, dough, ***ākrā*** : proud, ***ākṛwāḷā***, ***ākṛeā hoeā***.
stifle, v. int., ***boṛā waṭṭ laggṇā*** (***nū̃***) : *see* sultriness : tr., *see* smother.
still, yet, ***aje***, ***phēr wī***, ***tā̃ wī***.
still, ***halldā nehī̃***, *see* quiet, calm (1).
sting, ***ḍaṅg mārnā***, (***nū̃***), int. ***laggṇā*** (***nū̃***) ; ***laṛnā*** (***nū̃***).
stingy, *see* miser-, -liness.
stink, *see* smell.

stipulation, ***shart***, f., ***karār***, m. (promise).
stir, *see* excite, disturbance : fire, ***bhakh̲āṇā***.
stirrup, ***rakāb***, f.
stitch, ***trōppā***, m. (***lāṇā***, int. ***laggṇa***) : *see* patch.
stocking, same as sock, or add ***lammā***, long.
stomach, ***ḍhiḍḍh***, m. ***pēṭ***, m.
stone, ***waṭṭā***, m., ***patthar***, m. : *see* pebble, limestone : in baldder, ***patthrī***, f. : in fruit, ***giṭak***, f., ***hikkaṛ***, f. : pip of orange, apple, etc., ***bī̃***, m. : in ring, ***thēwā***, m.: throw s., ***saṭṭṇā***, ***mārnā*** (hitting someone or -thing).
stone, v. tr., fruit, ***giṭkaā̃ kaḍḍhṇiā̃*** : person, etc. : *see* stone (1).
stony, ***waṭṭcā̃wāḷā***.
stool, ***tūl***, m., ***caukī***, f. : village, ***pīṛhī***, f., ***pīṛhā***, m. : of reeds, ***mūṛhā***, m. : *see* chair, seat.
stoop, ***uṛnā***, ***nyūṇā***, ***jhukṇā***, ***nī̃wā h.***, ***sir jhukāṇā*** : *see* bend, lean (2), crooked.
stop, v. tr., *see* hinder, forbid, leave off, and add ***mōṛnā***, int. ***muṛnā*** ; ***ṭhākṇā*** : int. ***rukkṇā***.
stopper, in bottle, plug, ***ḍaṭṭ***, m. : *see* lid, cork.
store, ***zak̲hīrā***, m., ***k̲hazānā***, m. (treasure) : stores, ***saudā***, m. ; European, ***shtōr***, m. (K.).
store-room, -house, ***gudām***, m.
storey, of house, ***chatt***, m. (ceiling), ***manzal***, f. : two-, three- four-storied, ***du-***, ***tar-***, ***cu-chatta*** or ***-manzlā***.
storm, wind, ***hanērī***, f., ***jhānjhā***, m. : gust, ***jhakkhar***, m. : heavy rain, ***phāṇḍā***, m., heavy squall of rain, ***sharlāṭā***, m.
story, narrative, ***kahāṇī***, f. (***pāṇī***, ***suṇāṇī***) : ***bĕān*** (***karnā***).
stove, ***aṅgīṭhī***, f.
straight, ***siddhā***, ***suāhrā***.
strain, (sift), ***chāṇṇā*** : strain through cloth, ***puṇṇā*** : cloth for straining. ***pōṇā***, m.
strain, arm at socket, through throwing, etc., ***bā̃h*** w. ***chaṇak jāṇī***, ***cuṭak jāṇī***, ***chaṇ jāṇī***, ***chaṇkī jāṇī***, ***chanak ghatlṇī***.
straits, in, ***awāzār***, ***taṅg***, ***aukkhā***, ***k̲hajjal***; (going here and there), ***k̲hajjal k̲huār*** : *see* knock, difficulty.
strange, ***õprā*** ; ***bagānā*** and ***parāyā*** (not one's own) : ***ajīb***, ***ajaib***, ***anōkhā*** ; *see* stranger wonderful.
stranger, ***ōprā***, ***obbhar***, ***parāyā***, ***pardēsī***.
strangle, ***saṅgh*** or ***gaḷ ghuṭṭṇā*** : *see* hang, smother, choke.
strap, ***waddīrī***, f., ***tasmā***, m.
stratagem, ***dā*** (***lāṇā***. int. ***laggṇā***, ***khāṇā***) : *see* trick, deceit.
straw, *see* chaff.
straw-coloured, ***kakkā***.
stray, v. int. ***khunjhṇā*** (***rāhō***, etc.). ***ghussṇā*** (***rāhō***, etc.), ***thaṛukṇā*** : *see* astray, wander.
stream, ***nadī***, f., ***naḷī***, f. : *see* river.
street, ***bazār***, m., ***gaḷā***, m. : lanc, ***gaḷī***, f.

strength, ***zōr***, m., ***tākat***, f. : *see* power, strong.
stretch, *see* spread, pull : s. oneself, ***ākaṛnā***, ***akar auṇe*** (***nū̃***).
strict, ***kaide***, ***dā paband***. ***sakht***, ***ḍāhḍā***, ***karṛā***.
strike, *see* beast, blow, mark, prod : add ***saṭṭ lāṇi*** : of missile, ***laggṇā*** (***nū̃***) : M. 244. 26 : of stick, etc., ***wajjṇā*** (***nū̃***), ***laggṇā*** (***nū̃***) : s. tent ***puṭṭṇā***: s. off name, *see* delete ; do. on payment of debt, ***nāwā̃ walṇā*** or ***lāhnā*** (int. ***laihṇā***), ***āgat pāṇā*** or ***karnā*** (int. ***paiṇā***).
strike, refuse to work, ***kamm chaḍḍṇā***.
string, ***rassī***, f., ***ḍōrī***, f., ***sūtrī***, f. : on bed, ***wāṇ***, m. : on ***ṭiṇḍ*** at well, ***warhī***, f. : bundle or ball of, ***pinnā***, m., ***gunjī***, f.: as sold, ***charā***, m.
string, together papers, ***natthik***.
strip, clothes, bark, etc., ***lāhnā***.
stripe, ***dhārī***, f. : mere line, ***līk***, f.
strive, *see* effort.
stroll, ***sail***, m., ***sair***, m., ***sail sapaṭṭā***, m. (all ***k.***).
strong, ***tagṛā***, ***tākatwāḷā*** : of things, ***mazbūt***, ***dāhḍā*** : of tea, ***sanhṇī***, ***gūhṛī*** : *see* strength, power.
struggle, *see* scuffle, effort.
stud, collar, shirt, ***shṭaḍ***, m.: *see* button.
student, *see* scholar, disciple.
studious, ***mehntī***.
study, v., ***paṛhnā***, ***sṭaḍī karnī*** : n. (room), ***daftar***, m.
stuff in, ***tunnṇā***
stumble, ***ṭhuḍḍā laggṇā*** (***nū̃***) or ***kkāṇā***.
stumblingblock, *see* offence.
stump of tree, ***muṇḍh***, m. : *jagged* bit of wood, ***khuṅghī***, f., ***muḍḍhī***, f., ***muṇḍhī***, f.
stun, ***behōsh-k.***, int. ***h.***
stupid, ***beakl***, ***allhaṛ*** (inexperiened), ***ḍhaggā*** : *see* fool.
stupidity, *see* foolishness.
subject, n., persons, ***raiyal***, f., ***parjā***, f. (both always sing.) : of book, letter, ***mazmūn***, m.
submerge, ***ḍōbṇā*** : *see* sink.
submission, ***hār*** *see* obedience.
subordinate, ***mataiht***.
subscri-be, -ption, give, ***candā dēṇā*** : raise, ***ugrāhṇā*** (int. ***uggharnā***).
subside, building, ***baihṇā*** : *see* collapse, lessen.
subsist-, -ence, ***guzārā***, m. (***k.***, ***h.***).
substitute, ***iwzī*** : *see* exchange, change, relief.
subterfuge, *see* trick, deceit, stratagem.
subtract, ***tafrīk karnī***, ***minhāk***. (educ.), ***ghaṭāṇā***.
succeed, ***kamm ṭōrnā***, ***matlab kaḍḍhṇā*** ; ***kāmyāb h.*** (U.).
succeed, ***ohde thā̃ auṇā***, ***ohde magar auṇā***.
such ***ajehā***, ***ehojehā*** : s. and s., ***falāṇā***.
suck, ***cuṅghṇā***, ***cūpṇā*** (fruit) : *see* eat, suckle.

suckle, ***duddh piāṇā*** or ***cuṅghāṇā.***
suddenly, ***acāṇcak, cāṇcakke, accaṇcēt, awāghatt.***
suffer-, -ing, ***dukh, dukh pāṇā*** *see* endure, pain, grief.
sufficient, ***kāfī*** *see* enough.
suffocate, ***sāh ghuṭṭṇā*** *see* choke, hang, smother.
sugar, ***miṭṭhā,*** gen. : ground fine, ***būrā khaṇḍ,*** f. : not so fine, ***dāṇedār khaṇḍ*** (or both simply, ***khaṇḍ,*** f. ; European variety, ***cīnī,*** f.) : tablets, ***mishrī,*** f. : unrefined, ***guṛ,*** m. : finer than ***guṛ, shakkar,*** f. : without s., of tea, etc., ***phikkā.***
sugar-cane, ***kamād,*** m. : each cane, ***gannā*** m. : different kinds, ***pōnnā,*** m. (very thick), ***pēṭkū,*** m. ***treṛū,*** m., ***dhauḷū*** m., ***ciṇkhā*** m. (v. thin, also called ***kāṭhā,*** m.) : s. juice, ***rauh,*** f. : eat s., ***cūpṇā.***
suggestion, ***salāh*** *see* hint, say.
suicide, ***phāh laiṇā,*** hang oneself ; ***gaḍḍī agge baihke marnā,*** sit before train : gen. ***khudkushī,*** f. (U.).
suit, in law, ***mukadmā,*** m. : *see* case, lose.
suit, clothes, ***jōṛā,*** m., ***sūṭ,*** m.
suit-, -able, v., ***phabbṇā, munāsib h., caṅgā laggṇā*** also ***de gōcrā. de jogā, de laik,*** G. 38 ; ***jogā*** w. infl. infin. *see* proper, right, advisable.
sulk, ***russṇā, mūh waṭṭṇā*** : *see* displeased.
sulpur, ***gandhak.*** f.
sultriness, (outside) ***gummā, gōmmā gum, ghummā, ghōmmā, cumāsā*** (all m., ***laggṇā, nū̃***) : (in room or outside), ***watt*** (***laggṇā, nū̃***) : physical feeling, ***hussaṛ.*** m. (***h. nū̃***), and v. ***hussaṛnā.***
sum, in arithmetic, ***suāl,*** m. : of money, ***rakam.*** f. : total, ***jōṛ,*** m., ***jamhā,*** f., ***mizān,*** f. (U.).
summary, ***nacōṛ,*** m., ***khulāsā*** m., ***samrī,*** f.
summer, ***garmīā̃,*** f. pl. : often ***hāṛh,*** m. (lit. the month June 13-July 12), ***unhāḷ,*** m.
summer-school, ***paṛhāī,*** f.
summit, *see* pinnacle, peak.
summon, *see* call.
summons, leg., ***sammaṇ,*** m.
sun, ***sūraj,*** m., ***dyū̃h,*** m., ***diṇ*** or ***din,*** m. : s. come out fr. cloud, ***dhupp laggṇī*** : have five or six days of sunshine, ***panj che dhuppā̃, laggṇīā̃,*** G. 125 : M. 129. 27 : warm oneself in sun, *see* bask : put it in the sun, ***dhupp icc rakkhṇā, sukṇe pāṇā*** : *see* sunshine.
sunday, ***aitwār,*** m.
sunshine, ***dhupp,*** f : *see* sun.
superfluous, ***wāfar, wādhū, fāltū, fazūl*** (useless).
superintend, ***kamm wekhṇā*** (***dā***), ***nigrānī karnī*** (***dī,*** U.), ***nigābānī karnī*** (***dī,*** U.).
superintendent, ***kamm wekkhaṇwāḷā, mainajar*** : head workman, ***mēṭ.***
superior, ***behtar*** *see* good, better, one's s. officer, ***afsar.***

superstition, ***waihm.*** m.
superstitious ***waihmī.***
supervise, *see* superintend.
supine, lying or fallen on one's back, ***utāṇā, kaṇḍ parne*** or ***bhār.***
supper, ***safar,*** m. (K).
supplant, ***dhokhe nāḷ. thā̃ mallṇā.***
supple, ***lifaṇwālā, kūḷā.***
supply, ***aprāṇā pucāṇā*** : *see* produce, obtain, secure.
support, *see* prop, pillar, lean : gen. ***sambhāḷnā, madad deṇī*** (***nū̃***) : hold up, ***cukkī rakkhṇā*** : provide for, ***pāḷṇā, parwarish karnī*** (***dī***) : *see* endure.
suppose, ***farz karnā*** : *see* think, guess, calculate, what, if.
suppress, *see* hide, stop, hinder.
suppurate, ***pakkṇā, pāk paiṇī.***
sure, *see* certain.
surety, *see* bail, certain.
surgeon, *see* doctor, operation.
surpass, ***wadhṇā, de nāḷõ caṅgā h.***
surprise, *see* astonish-, ment.
surrender, ***hār mannṇī*** : ***hathyār saṭṭṇe.***
surreptitiously, *see* stealthily.
surround, ***waḷṇā, ghērnā, gherā pāṇā*** (***de duāḷe***).
surveillance, ***nazr,*** f. : keep under s.. ***nazr icc rakkhṇā*** : *see* detenu.
survey, measure land, ***kacchnā pamaish karnī*** (***dī***) : *see* look, measure.
suspect, *see* suspicion.
suspend, ***muattal-k.*** (U.).
suspicion, ***shakk karnā*** (***dā***), ***zan karnā*** (***dī***) ***bābat***), ***badgumāṇī karnī*** (***dī bābat***).
swagger, ***ākaṛke calṇā.***
swaddling-clothes, ***pōlṛe,*** m. pl.
swallow, ***nigaḷnā, laṅghāṇā*** : *see* anger.
swamp, *see* marsh.
swarm, of bees, ***ghaṇ,*** m. : of flies, ***ḍār,*** m. : *see* flock.
swear, ***saunh khāṇī*** *see* oath.
sweat, *see* perspiration.
sweep, ***jhāṛū phērnā*** or ***dēṇā*** : s. up leaves, papers, etc., ***hūnjṇā.***
sweeper, ***mehtar, jhāṛū dēṇwālā,*** addressed often as ***jamādār*** : caste, ***Cūhṛā, Kāḷakẖ dās*** : one who has become Muhammadan, ***musall-ī,*** fem. ***-aṇ*** ; Sikkh, ***mazbhī Sikkh,*** fem. ***-ṇi,*** or simply ***mazbh-ī,*** fem. ***-aṇ.***
sweet, ***miṭṭhā,*** both of people and things : s. drink, ***sharbat,*** m.
sweets, gen., ***miṭhāī,*** f. : many kinds.
swell, flesh, etc., ***sujjṇā*** : something hollow, as stomach, ***āpharnā.***
swelling, ***sōj,*** f. : ***aphrā,*** m. : *see* swell : fr. bite of insect, ***dhrapphaṛ,*** m. : *see* lump.
swift, ***trikkhā, tēz*** : in a hurry, ***kāhḷā*** : go swiftly, ***khurī karke jāṇā, khiṭṭ dēṇī*** or ***mārnī.***
swim, ***tarnā*** : water deep enough to s. in, ***tārū pāṇī,*** m.
swimmer, ***tārū.***
swimming, the art, ***tārī,*** f. (***auṇī, nū̃***)

swing, n., ***pingh***, f.
swing, on a swing, ***pingh caṛhāṇi***, ***pingh de hūṇte laiṇe*** (tr. ***dēṇe***) : gen., ***ṭangke halāṇā*** (int. ***hallṇā***) : *see* hang.
switch, little stick, ***chamak***, f. ***chūjak***, f., ***shūshak***, f. : *see* stick.
swoon, *see* faint.
swoop, *see* pounce.
sword, ***talwār***, f. (***mārni***, int. ***laggṇi***, ***nū̃***).
sympathiser, ***dardī***.
sympathise w., ***ohdā dard karṇā***, ***ohnū̃ ohdā dukkh hōṇā*** (this may mean envy) : G. 125 : M. 130. 34–6 : ***hamdardī karnī*** (***nāl***) : or ***ohnū̃ ohdā dard hōṇā*** or ***auṇā***.
sympathy, *see* sympathise.
sympathetic, ***dardī*** ; ***hamdard*** (U.).
symptom, ***nishāni***, f.
syringe, ***pickāri***, f.
syrup, ***shīrā*** m. : golden, ***ṭrikal***, m.
system, ***kaidā*** m. : ***tarīkā***, m.

T

table, ***mēz***, m., ***mēc.*** m. : lay. set t., ***mēz lāṇā*** (int. ***laggṇā***) : take away things. ***mēz cukkṇā***.
tablecloth, ***mēz dī cādar***, f.
tablet, ***ta<u>kh</u>ti***, f.
taciturn, ***gall nehī̃ kardā***, ***cuppū***, ***mū̃h waṭṭdā raihndā e***.
tack, n., ***brinji***, f. : *see* nail.
tack, sew, ***kaccī suāī karnī***, ***kaccā karnā*** (***nū̃***).
tail, ***pūshal.*** f. : of bird, fish, ***būṇḍā***, m. : tailless, ***luṇḍā***.
tailor, ***darz-i***, fem. ***-an***.
tainted, be, ***bō chaḍḍnī***, ***trakk caleā***, ***wigar caleā***, ***muss caleā*** ; of milk, ***wigar caleā***, ***phiṭ caleā*** : *see* bad, sour. A.
take, ***loiṇā***. G. 64 : t. away, ***khaṛnā***. ***lai jāṇā*** : *see* seize, conquer ; t. out stain, *see* delete : t. off clothes, hat, shoes, ***lāhṇā***, sometimes, ***wadhāṇā***, G. 113.
talc, ***abrak***, m. (mica).
tale, *see* story : t.-bearer, ***cugal<u>kh</u>ōr*** (U.), ***ba<u>kh</u>ili*** or ***cuglī karnwāḷā*** : *see* accuse, slander.
talent, money, ***tōṛā***, m. (100o rupees).
talent, *see* ability, able, clever.
talisman, ***tilism***, m. (U.).
talk, *see* conversation.
talkative, ***galāhdaṛ***, ***gappī*** (esp. of what is untrue), ***bakwāsi***, ***baṛiā̃ gallā̃ karnwāḷā*** : *see* chatter.
tall, ***lammā***, ***uccā***.
tallow, *see* fat.
talon, *see* claw.
tamarind, ***imbḷi***, f.
tambourine, ***ḍaph.*** f., smaller, ***ḍaphṛā***, m., ***ḍaphḷi***, f., ***<u>kh</u>anjarī***, f. : *see* drum.
tame (quiet), ***asīl***, ***garīb*** : kept, not wild, ***rā<u>kh</u>wā̃***.
tank, ***talā***, m.
tap, ***naḷkā***, m. ***ṭūṭi***, f. : *see* spout.
tape, ***fītā***, m. : for beds, ***nuār***, f. (adj. ***nuāri***) : for fastening drawers, ***nāḷā***, m. : *see* measuring -t.

tapioca, ***ṭāpiū***, m. (K.).
tar, ***lukk***, f.
target, ***takhtā***, m.
tariff, ***nirkh***, m. : ***bhā***, m. : t.-list, ***nirkhnāmā***, m.
tassel, as in fez cap, ***phummaṇ***, m. : as in the cloth called ***khēs***, ***bumbaḷ***, m.
taste, ***suād***, m., ***mazā***, m. (U.) : t. for, inclination towards, often used in connection with stealing, ***jhass***, m., ***caskā***, m. (both ***paiṇā***, and ***dā***) : *see* desire.
taste, v. tr. ***cakkhṇā***.
tasteless, *see* inspid, add ***alūṇā***, ***belūṇā***.
tasty, ***suādlā***, ***mazedār***, ***karārā*** (well-spiced).
tattoo, ***ukkhaṇṇā***, ***guddṇā***, both w. thing tattooed as obj.
taunt, ***tāhne mārne*** (***nū̃***), ***mehṇā dēṇā*** or ***mārnā*** (***nū̃***, ***kise gall dā***), ***nōk lāṇi*** (***nū̃***, int. ***wajjṇi***, ***laggṇi***) : *see* ridicule.
taut, *see* tight.
tax, ***masūl***, ***maihsūl***, m. : octroi, ***cuṅgī***, f., ***cuṅgī***, ***dā masūl*** : (octroi post, ***cuṅgī***, f. : octroi official, ***masūlīā***, ***cuṅgīwāḷā***) : land-t., ***muāmlā***, m. : (collect t., ***laiṇā***, ***ugrāhṇā***) : on sales, ***āṛhtaḷ***, f., ***dharth***, m. : *see* collect, assess, settlement.
tea, ***cāh***, f. : *see* teapot.
teach, ***paṛhāṇā***, ***sikhāṇā***, ***talīm dēṇī*** (***nū̃***), ***sikkhyā dēṇī*** (***nū̃*** H.) : sit at feet of teacher to learn, ***baihṇā*** (caus, ***bahāḷnā***).
teacher, ***ustād***, ***māsṭar***, ***munishī*** : of Persian, Arabic, ***maulwī*** : of Sanskrit, ***paṇḍat*** : relig. t., M. ***murshad***, ***maulwī*** : H. ***gurū***, ***paṇḍat*** : female t. in school, ***ustādṇī***.
teaching, *see* teach and add ***paṛhāī***, f.
teapot, ***cāhpōcī***, f. : vessels of similar shape, ***astāwā***, m., ***satāwā***, m., ***lōṭṭā***, m.
tear, v. tr., ***pāṛnā***, int. ***pāṭṇā***.
tear, n., ***atthar***, f., ***hanjū̃***, f. pl.
tease, ***chēṛnā***, ***satāṇā***, ***dikk-k.*** : t. by disappointing, ***jhakhāṇā*** : *see* annoy.
teat, animal, ***thaṇ***, m. : *see* nipple.
teaze, ***tumbṇā*** : *see* card (1).
telegram, ***tār***, f.
telegraph, ***tār ghallṇī*** or ***dēṇī*** : -wire, ***tār***, f. : -post, ***waḷā***, m.
telescope, ***dūrbīn***, f.
tell, ***ākhṇā***, ***dassṇā***.
temper, tempered good-, ***caṅge subhā wāḷā***, ***saihndaṛ*** (patient) : bad-, use easily angry, annoyed.
temperament, ***tabīat***, f.
temperate (person), ***parhēzgār***.
temperature, ***garmī***, f. (heat) : of body, do., and ***bukhār***, m. (fever).
temple, ***mandar***, m., ***shiwālā***, m.
temporary, ***thōreā̃ dinā̃ wāste***, ***ārzī*** (of employment, U.) : t. piece of work ***calā̃wā̃ kamm***, m.
tempt, v. difficult idea, ***azmāṇā***, ***warglāṇā***, ***bakāṇ dī kōshish karnī***, ***khiccṇā*** (draw) : *see* incite, test, seduce.
temptation (idea) difficult), ***azmaish***, f., ***partāwā***, m., ***khics***, f. (drawing).

ten, ***das*** : -th, ***daswā̃*** : G. 19–24.
tenaciously, ***cambaṛke, khaihṛā nā chaḍḍke.***
tenant, ***sāmī,*** f., ***asāmī,*** f.
tender, soft, ***kūḷā,*** *see* soft : loving, ***mhabtī.***
tendon, *see* sinew.
tendril, ***wall,*** f., ***wēl,*** f.
tenet, ***akīdā,*** m., ***asūl,*** m. : point of doctrine, ***maslā,*** m.
tent, ***tambū,*** m., ***ḍērā,*** m., servants' t., ***chōldāri,*** f. : nomads' small, ***pakkhī,*** f., ***tapri,*** f. : *see* nomad : wall of t., ***kanāt,*** f. : put up t., ***lāṇā*** : strike, ***puṭṭṇā.***
tentatively, ***wēkkhan wāste, azmāṇ wāste.***
tepid, ***kōssā, khūh-nuāyā.***
terrible, ***ḍarnwāḷā, jis tõ ḍar āwe, ḍarauṇā.***
terrify-, -ing, *see* fear, terrible.
terror, ***khauf,*** m., ***ḍar,*** m.
tertian fever, ***treiā,*** m. (***caṛhnā.*** come on : ***laihṇā,*** go off).
test, ***azmāṇā, parkhṇā, wēkhṇā, azmaish karnī*** (***dī***) : examine, ***imtihān lainā*** (***dā***) : test exam., ***ṭēsṭ.*** m., (***ṭest*** or ***azmaishi imtihān,*** m. (educ.).
testament, *see* will : New T., ***Nawā̃ Aihdnāmā,*** m., ***Injīl.*** f., ***Anjīl,*** f. : Old T., ***Paurāṇā Aihdnāmā,*** m. : *see* Pentateuch, Psalms.
testi-fy, ***guwhāī - deṇā*** -mony, *see* witness, evidence.
testimonial, ***sāṭifkaṭ,*** m., ***sanad,*** f.
than, ***nāḷõ, thõ, tõ, thī̃,*** G. 18 : *see* rather, comparison, time.
thank, ***shukr karnā*** (***dā***) : t. you : ***tuhāḍḍī mehrbānī e*** : t. God, ***shukr e, Khudā dā shukr e*** : the strange phrase ***Rabb dā bhalā howe*** is often heard.
thankful, ***shukrguzār*** : *see* obligation.
that, conj., ***paī,*** ke : sometimes ***akhe, makhe,*** G. 121. 40 : M. 127–42.
that, pron., ***oh, parlā, pailā*** : that is, ***yānī.***
thatch, ***chappar,*** m.
the, ***eh, oh.*** or omit.
theft, ***cōrī,*** f. : *see* robbery.
their, ***ohnā̃ dā, ehnā̃ nū̃, ne, ṇe,*** G. 82–6.
them, ***ohnā̃ nū̃, ehnā̃ nū̃, ne, ṇe,*** G. 82–6.
then, reasoning, ***whalā, tā̃, te, phēr, khā̃*** (only with imperat.), ***tadde*** : time, ***odõ, odū̃, ōsweḷe, ōtweḷe, tadõ, tadū̃.***
thence, ***ōtthõ,*** *see* there.
theolog-y, -ical, *see* A.
theory, ***maslā,*** m., ***dalīl,*** f.
there, ***ōtthe, oddhar, parhā̃*** ; ***ōttal*** (gen. motion to) : there it is, le voilá, ***oh wekhā̃.***
therefore, ***ēs wāste, ōs wāste, tā̃ ī, tadde, tā̃ karke, tā̃hīē.***
they, ***eh, oh.***
thick, ***liquid, gūṛhā, gāṛhā, sanhnā*** : dirty water, ***gandhleā hoeā,*** *see* dirty : dense, trees, crowd, ***sanhnā*** : close friendship, ***gūṛhī*** or ***pakkī dōstī*** : not thin, ***mōṭā.***
thickness (not thinness), ***muṭeāī,*** f. ***muṭāpā,*** m.

thief, ***cōr*** : *see* robber, receiver.
thigh, ***paṭṭ***, m.
thimble, ***aṅgūṭhi***, f.
thin, not fat or thick, ***patlā*** ; ***lissā*** (persons, animals only) : not coarse, ***mhīn*** : fine and small, ***barīk*** : ill-looking, ***māṛā***, ***lissā***.
thing, ***cīz***, f., ***cīz wast***, f., ***shai***, f.
think, ***sōcṇā***, ***gaur karnā*** (consider), ***dhiān karnā*** (meditate) : I believed or thought, ***maĩ ākheā***, ***maĩ samjheā***.
third, ***tījā***, ***tīji*** *see* three : t. day fever, *see* tertian.
thirst, ***treh***, f., G. 108 : (intense) ***bhaṛkī***, f. : ***andar saṛdā e***.
thirsty, ***trihāyā***.
thirteen, ***tērā̃*** : -th, ***tehrwā̃***, G. 19—24, 123 : thirteen-finger shoe, *see* shoe.
thirty, ***trīh*** : one, ***akattī***, ***akattrī*** : -two ***battī***, ***battrī*** : -three, ***tēttī***, ***tētrī*** : -four, ***cauttī***, ***cautrī*** : -five, ***paĩtī***, ***paĩtrī*** : -six, ***chattī***, ***chattrī*** : -seven, ***saĩtī***, ***saĩtrī*** : -eight, ***aṭhattī***, ***aṭhattrī*** : -nine, ***unṭālī***, ***unṭāḷī***.
ordinals add ***-wā̃*** with tonic ***h***, (***trīh*** already has it) : as ***akatlīhwā̃***, ***untāhḷīwā̃***, G. 19–24, 123.
this, ***eh***, ***urlā***.
thither, *see* there.
thong, ***wadhrī***, f.
thorn, ***kaṇḍā***, m. : t.-branch, ***dhiṅgar***, m., ***dhiṅgri***, f., ***moṛhā***, m., ***moṛhī***, f. : tiny thorny plant injurious to rubber tyres, ***bhakkhṛā***.
thorny, ***kaṇḍeā̃wāḷā***.
thoroughly, ***bilkull***, ***pūrī tarhā̃***, ***pūre taur nāḷ*** : *see* absolutely, altogether.
thou, ***tū̃*** : people like thee or you, ***tumhātar***, G. 28.
though, ***bhāwẽ***, ***bhāwẽ jikar***.
thought, gen., ***sōc***, f., ***sōc wacār***, f. : ***k͟hyāl***, m., idea, opinion : ***gaur***, m., consideration : ***dhiān***, m., meditation : ***dalīl***, f., reasoning : *see* anxiety.
thoughtful, ***sōcā̃ icc***, ***dalīlā̃ icc***.
thoughtless, ***lāparwāh***, ***sōcdā nehī̃*** : ***bēparwāh***, beyond need of caring, as God, rich man.
thousand, ***hazār*** : -th. ***hazārwā̃*** : hundred t., ***lakkh*** : -th, ***lakkhwā̃*** : G. 20–4, 93.
thread, ***dhāgā***, m., ***tand***, f. : sacred Hindu t., ***janeo***, m. : three-fold t., ***paṛkatteā dhāgā*** : *see* string.
threat-, -en, ***dhaũs dēṇī*** (***nū̃***), or ***cāṛhnī*** (***utte***) or ***wak͟hāṇī*** (***nū̃***), ***dhamkī dēṇī*** (***nū̃***), ***dābba dēṇā*** (***nū̃***), ***dabkāṇā***, ***ghurkī dēṇī*** (***nū̃***), ***ḍarāṇā*** : *see* reprimand, frown.
three, ***trai***, ***tinn*** : third, ***trījjā***. ***tīsrā*** : G. 19–24 : t.-fold (actual layers), ***treohrā*** ; three times as big or much, ***triṇā***, ***trai hisse waddh*** : *see* time, thread : thrice, ***trai wārī*** or ***werī***.
thresh, v. tr., ***gāhṇā***, int. ***gaihṇā***.
threshingfloor, ***piṛ***, m. A.
threshold, room at, ***ḍeoḍhī***, f. : of door, ***brū̃***, f., ***dalhīz***, f.
throat, outside, ***gaḷ***, m., ***gāṭṭā***, m. : inside, ***saṅgh***, m. : *see* neck and add ***saṅghī***, f.

throne, ***ta<u>kh</u>t***, m. : of ruling princes, ***gaddī***, f.
throttle, ***galā ghoṭnā*** *see* strangle.
through, ***wiccdū̃***, ***wiccõ dī*** : t. Jesus Christ, ***Yesū Masīh dī rāhī*** or ***de wasileõ*** : t. door, window, *see* way : *see* because of, means.
throw, ***saṭṭnā***, ***suṭṭnā***, ***mārnā*** : t. away, ***suṭṭ*** or ***saṭṭ charnā*** or ***chaḍḍṇā***) : t. away liquid, ***roṛh charṇā***, ***ḍolh charṇā*** : t. at, strike w., ***mārnā*** (acc. of missile, ***nū̃*** of person.)
thrust, stuff in, *see* stuff in : t. out, ***dhikhṇā***, ***kaḍḍhṇā***.
thumb, ***aṅgūṭh***, m., ***aṅgūṭhā***, m. : affix t.-mark, ***aṅgūṭhā lāṇā*** (int. ***laggṇā***).
thunder, v. int., ***baddaḷ gajjṇā*** (sometimes ***kaṛakṇā***).
Thursday, ***jumerāt***, f., ***wīr*** or ***wīrwār***, m. (H.).
thus, in this way, ***eñ***, ***iñ***, ***aiñ***, ***eõ***, ***eñ karke***, ***aikkaṇ*** : in that way, ***owẽ***, ***aukkaṇ***, ***uñ*** : (***owẽ*** also just then, immediately).
thy, *see* you.
(1) tick, n., in dogs, etc., ***ciccaṛ***, m.
(2) tick of clock, etc., ***ṭik ṭik***, f. (***k.***).
ticket, ***ṭikaṭ***, m. f. : return t., ***wāpsī ṭikaṭ***, ***auṇ jaṇ dā ṭikat*** : (travel) without t., ***baraṅg***, ***beṭikṭā***.
tickle, v. tr., ***kutkutāṛī kaḍḍhṇī*** (***dī***), int. ***nikḷṇī*** (***dī***), often in plur.
tidy, ***sāf suthrā*** (clean), ***ṭhīk sāhmke rakkhṇā***, ***koī shai kuthāẽ nā howe***, ***thā̃ pathā̃ī rakkhṇā*** : *see* untidy.
tie, v. tr., ***bannhṇā***, pa. p., ***baddhā***, int. ***bajjhnā*** : *see* knot : tie arms or hands behind back, ***mushkā̃ bannhṇiā̃*** (***diā̃***).
tie, n., muffler, ***guḷūban***, m. : *see* neck-tie.
tiffin, ***ṭipan***, m.
tiger, ***shēr***, fem. ***shērnī***.
tight, ***kasseā hoeā***, ***ghuṭṭeā hoeā*** : *see* narrow.
tighten, ***kassṇā***, ***ghuṭṭnā***.
tightly, ***kasske***, ***ghuṭṭke***.
tile, ***khaprail***, f. (U.).
till, v. tr., *see* plough, cultivate.
till, up till, ***tīkar***, ***tāṇī***, ***toṛī***, ***tāṛī***, ***tā̃ī***, ***tākar***, ***sidhā***.
till, conj., ***jicar tīkar*** (or ***tā̃ī***, etc.), ***jicar nū̃***, ***jicar . . . . nā***.
tilt back, of carriage, ***ullarnā*** : *see* weight.
time, gen., ***wakat***, m., ***weḷā***, m. : the present, past or future age, ***zamānā***. m., ***samā***, m. : fixed period, ***miād***, f. : length of t., ***cir***, m. : short t., ***jhaṭ***, m., ***ghaṛī***, f. (*see* short, long) : in t., at the right t., ***weḷe sir***, ***wakat sir*** ; at the wrong t., late, ***kuweḷe*** (*see* late) : this t., ***aitkī***, ***aitkā̃***, ***es wārī***, ***es werī***, ***es phēre*** : *see* meanwhile. o'clock : for A.M., P.M., *see* A.M. time in four, five times, etc., ***wārī***, ***werī*** : the first, second t., ***paihlī***, ***dujjī wārī*** or ***werī***, ***paihlā phērā***, etc.
five, six times as big, ***panj guṇā***, etc., or reversing it, ***ohdā panjwā̃ hissā*** (a fifth part of it) :

fr. two to five, special words, ***dūṇā***, ***trīṇā***, ***cauṇā***, ***panjauṇā***.
time-server, *matlabī*, *gaṛzī*.
timid, *see* coward.
tin, material or a tin, ***ṭīn***, m. : for soldering, ***kalī***, f. (***k.***) : canister, ***kanastar***, m., ***pīpā***, m. : bath-tin, ***bhabkā***, m.
tinkle, *chaṇakṇā*, *wajjṇā*, *chaṇ chaṇ karnī*.
tip, *nōk.* f.
tiptoe, on, ***pabbā̃ bhār*** (***pabb***, m., is ball of foot).
tire, v. int., ***thaknā***, ***thakāṇā***) : tired, ***thakeā hoeā*** : *see* faint : get tired of ***akkṇā*** (***tõ*** tr. ***akāṇā***), *see* sick of.
title, of book, etc., ***nā̃***, m. : heading, ***surkhī***, f. : of person, ***lakab***, m. : honorary t. given by Government, ***khatāb***, m.
to, dat., ***nū̃*** : of place, ***nū̃***, often loc. case, G. 9, 10, 77 : of purpose, infin w. ***wāste***, ***laī***, ***nū̃***, up to, *see* up.
toast, n., ***tōs***, m. (slice whether toasted or not) ; v., ***tōs sēkṇā rōṭī sēkṇī*** : foment or heat limb at fire, ***sēk karnā*** (***hatth nū̃***, ***latt nū̃***, hand, leg) : *see* warm.
tobacco, *tamākū* (***pīṇā***, ***chikkṇā***).
to-day, *ajj* : a week fr. t., *see* week : emphatic, ***ajjo***, ***ajjo ī***, ***ajje ī***.
toe, *uṅgaḷ*, f. : big t., ***aṅgūṭh***, m., ***aṅgūṭhā***, m. : little t., ***cicci***, f. : fleshy part of t., ***pōttā***, m. : ball of toe, *see* tiptoe.
together, *katthe*, *ralke*, *nāḷo nāḷ*.
toilsome, *taklīfwāḷā*, *see* difficult.
toll, *masūl*, m. : *see* tax.
tomato, *ṭamāṭar*, m.
tomb, *kabar*, *samādh* *see* grave, shrine.
to-morrow, *bhaḷke*, *kall* : *see* yesterday (last clause) : day after t., ***parsõ*** : day after that, ***cauth*** : fifth day, ***panjauth*** : sixth day, ***cheauth*** : (***satauth***, ***aṭhauth***, seventh, eighth day, are perhaps jocular) ; also ***panjwā̃ din***, etc. : t. week, *see* week.
tonga, *ṭāṅgā*, m.
tongs, *uccā*, m., ***cimṭā***, m. : *see* pincers.
tongue, *jībh*, f., ***zabān***, f. : *see* language : t. of bell, *see* bell.
to-night, *ajj rātī̃*, *ajj rāt nū̃*, also last night.
too, as in too much, etc., gen. omit, show by context, ***bauhtā tattā***, too hot, etc.
too, also ***wī***, ***bī***, *see* moreover.
tool, *hathyār*, m. : pl., ***racch kāṇ***, m. : barber's t., ***racch***, m.
tooth, *dand*, m. : double t., back t., ***haṇhū̃***, f. : show teeth (dog in anger, or derisively of person laughing), ***dand kaḍḍhṇe*** : tooth in saw, ***dandā***, m. : *see* dentist in A.
toothbrush, *dāttan*, f.
toothed, *dandeā̃wāḷā*.
top, of box, lid, ***dhakkaṇ***, m. : of chest of drawers, bookcase, etc., ***chatt***, m. : of page, ***ṣirā***, m., *see* bottom, foot.
top, plaything, ***lāṭū***, m. : spin t., ***lāṭū saṭṭṇā***, ***wagāṇā*** or ***bhuā̃ṇā*** ; int. ***wagṇā***, ***bhaū̃ṇā***.

topsy turvy, ***hēṭh utte*** (one on top of other) ; ***ugṛā dugṛā, agaṛ dugṛā, wigḷeā shigḷeā*** : *see* untidy, upside down.

torch, ***mashāl,*** f. : t.-bearer in marriage, ***mashālci.***

torment, *see* tease, annoy, torture.

tortoise, ***kaccukummā,*** m., ***khacōprā,*** m.

torture, ***puls ohde nāḷ burī kītī,*** (not used of woman) ; ***mārnā*** ; ***sakhtī karnī (nāḷ)*** : *see* tie.

total, ***jamhā,*** f., ***mizān,*** f. (U.), ***jōṛ,*** m.

totter, *see* stagger.

touch, ***hatth lāṇā, chohṇā*** : feel, ***ṭohṇā*** : t. heart, ***dil utte asar karnā.***

touching, *see* pathetic, sad, and add ***afsoswāḷā, dil te asar karnwāḷā.***

touchstone, ***ghaswaṭṭī,*** f.

tough, no word ; say ***camm wãngar*** or ***lif jāndā e par uñ ḍāhḍā e, pāṭdā nehī̃.***

tour, on duty, ***daurā,*** m. (***k.***) : pleasure, ***sail*** or ***sair,*** m. (***k.***) : very brief, ***phērā,*** m. (***mārnā***).

tow, *see* hemp.

towards, ***de wall, de wallõ*** (only w. look, *see,* otherwise ***wall***) ; ***dī sedh, de pāse.***

towel, ***tauliā,*** m. ; ***nhauṇwāḷā tauliā, gusl dā tauliā*** : t.-horse (or rail) ***tauliā̃ dī ghōṛī.***

tower, ***burj,*** m. : small, ***burjī*** f.

town, ***shaihr,*** m., ***naggar,*** m. (large village).

toy, ***khaḍauṇā,*** m.

trace, ***patā,*** m. (for verbs, *see* discover), ***nishān (labbhṇā, dā)*** ; ***sūh (kaḍḍhṇī, dī)*** : *see* track, path.

track, of wheels, ***gail,*** f. : of feet, hoofs, etc., ***khurā,*** m. : v. tr., ***khurā kaḍḍhṇā,*** *see* path, trace.

tracker, ***khōjjī*** (chiefly for cattle, horses, etc.).

trade, ***tajārat,*** f., ***byopār,*** m., ***wanj byopār,*** m., ***sudāgrī,*** f. (all w. ***k.***) : *see* profession, merchandise.

trader, *see* merchant.

tradition, gen., ***rawait,*** f. : ***hadīs,*** f. (M.) : ***waddeā̃ dī gall.***

traffic, ***auṇā jāṇā,*** m. : ***rauṇak raihndī e.***

train, v. tr., *see* teach : t. animals for ploughing, also metaph, boy for work, ***hāḷī kaḍḍhṇā,*** int. ***nikḷṇā*** : for burden bearing, ***lādū kaḍḍhṇā,*** int. ***nikḷṇā.***

train, n., ***gaḍḍī,*** f. : mail, t., ***dāk gaḍḍī*** ; Bombay mail, ***bambaī mēl,*** f. ; Calcutta mail, ***kalkattā mēl,*** f. : passenger t., ***suārī gaḍḍī, psanjar,*** f. : local t., ***lōkal,*** f., ***nōkal,*** f. : goods t., ***māl gaḍḍī*** : the Lahore, Wazirabad, t. has come, gone, ***Lahaur (Wazīrābād) āeā e, ṭur geā e.***

trait, ***sift,*** f.

traitor, ***gaddār, dagābāz*** no good word, *see* treacherous, treason.

trample, upon, ***mindhṇā, mindhāṛnā, latāṛnā, utte ṭurnā, utte pair rakkhṇā,*** *see* crush.

transaction, ***kamm, m., laihṇ dēṇ, laiṇ dēṇ,*** m.

transfer, ***badlī karnī, hōṇī.***
transfigured, be, ***sūrat badal jāṇī*** (***dī***).
transform, ***sūrat, shakl badalnī*** (***dī***).
transient, ***fānī, caũh dihāṛeā̃ dā,*** *see* shortlived.
translate, ***tarjmā karnā*** (***dā,*** int. ***h.***).
translation, ***tarjmā,*** m. : literal t., ***lafzī tarjmā.***
translator, ***tarjmā karnwāḷā, mutrajjam*** (for ***mutarjim***)
transmigration, ***awāgaũ,*** m., ***āwāgauṇ,*** m., ***curāsī,*** m. (all H.).
transport, ***bārbardārī,*** f. : man engaged in mule t., ***khaccarpātrī***: sentence to transportation, ***kāḷe pāṇī dā hukm dēṇā*** (***nū̃***), ***kāḷe pāṇī ghallṇā.***
trap, ***kuṛikkī,*** f., ***pinjrā,*** m.
trash, ***raddī cīz,*** f. : *see* useless, worthless, nonsense.
travel, ***safar karnā*** ; for pleasure, ***sail*** or ***sair karnā*** : t. distance, ***paiṇḍā mārnā*** or ***k.*** (esp. walking) ; go a stage, ***paṛā jāṇā*** (but ***paṛā karnā,*** halt).
traveller, ***rāhī, musāfar.***
traverse, ***pār karnā*** *see* travel.
tray, ***trēḷ,*** f. (K.) : t.-cloth, ***trēḷ dī cādar.***
treacher-ous, -y, no good word, ***namak-harām-***(n., ***-ī,*** f.), ***dil icc bāgī, beimān-***(n., ***-ī,*** f.) : *see* treason.
treacle, ***cāshnī,*** f. ***ṭrīkal,*** m. (also golden syrup).
tread, *see* trample.
treason, use ***bagāwat,*** f., ***bādshāh*** or ***sarkār dā badkhāh*** : *see* treacherous.
treasure, ***khazānā,*** m.
teasury, ***khazānā,*** m.
treasurer, ***khazāncī,*** m.
treat, well, badly, kindly, ***kise de nāḷ cangā, burā, mehrbānī dā salūk k.*** : t. disease, sick person, ***alāj karnā*** (***dā***) ; be treated (sick person), ***duāī karnī*** (by, ***dī***), ***alāj karāṇā*** (by, ***koḷõ***).
treatment, *see* treat.
treaty, ***aihd,*** m., ***āpe icc likhke karār karnā.***
treble, *see* three.
tree, ***rukkh,*** m., ***būṭā,*** m., ***darakht,*** m. : bark, ***chill,*** f., ***chillar,*** f., ***rang.*** m. : piece of bark, ***sakk,*** m., ***sakṛā,*** m. : family tree, ***shajrā,*** m.
tremble, ***kambṇā, kambṇī laggṇī*** (***nū̃***) : ***kambṇī chiṛnī*** (***nū̃***), begin trembling.
trial, leg., ***mukadmā,*** m. : each appearance, ***pēshī,*** f. : send up for t., ***calān k.*** (***dā***) : *see* test, try, examine.
triangular, ***targuṭṭhā, tarnukrā.***
tribe, ***kaum,*** f.
tributary of river, ***shākh,*** f., ***sūā,*** m. : *see* canal.
trick, n., v. ***pakhaṇḍ,*** m. (***khēḍṇā, nāḷ***), ***chaḷ,*** m. (***khēḍṇā, nāḷ***) ; ***dā,*** m. (***lāṇā, nū̃,*** int., ***khāṇā, laggṇā***) ; ***dā farēb karnā, nū̃***) ; ***khuṭṭar,*** m. (***k., nāḷ***) ; ***waḷ*** pec, m. (***k., nāḷ***) ; ***luṭṭ,*** m., or ***luṭṭ, khruṭṭ*** (***k., nāḷ***) ; ***dhōkhā*** m (***d., nū̃***), (int., ***khāṇā***) ; ***hīlā,*** m. (***k., nāḷ***), ***ḍhang,*** m. (***k., nāḷ***).

trickle, ***cōṇā*** : n., ***coā***, m. (***paiṇā***) : *see* drip, ooze.
tricky, ***pakhaṇḍī***, ***khuṭṭarī***, ***ḍhaṅgī***.
trident, ***tarsūl***, m.
trifle, n., ***nikkī cīz***, f., ***nikkī gall***, f. : v. small amount, ***ruāḷ jehā*** : he's only trifling w. you, ***hujtā̃*** or ***jugtā̃ huṭṭar kardā e*** : *see* waste.
trigger (also cock), ***ghōṛā***, m.
trim, hair, ***katrnā*** : trees, plants, ***chāṅgṇā***, ***katṛnā***.
Trinity, ***Taslīs***, f.
trip, ***ṭhuḍḍā khānā*** make stumble : v. tr., ***ṭhuḍḍā lāṇā*** (***nū̃***, also kick), int. ***laggṇā*** (***nū̃***).
triple, ***tyōhra***, ***-ī*** *see* three.
trivial, *see* trifling.
trolly, on railway, ***ṭhēllā***, ***ṭhelhā***, m., ***trāllī***, f.
trooper, ***suār***.
trot, ***duṛkī calṇā*** or ***ṭurnā*** : tr ***lāṇā***, ***ṭōrnā***, ***calāṇā***.
trouble, ***taklīf***, f., ***janjāḷ***, m., ***kaziā***, m., take t., ***taklīf k.***, ***sir khapāṇā*** (mental): experience t. in getting something done, ***khajjal h.***, ***khajjal khuār h.***, ***bhambaḷ bhūse khāṇe*** : give t., ***taklīf d.*** : *see* inconvenience, difficulty, straits, annoy.
trough, ***khurlī***, f. same as manger.
trousers, Indian for men, ***tambī***, f., ***salwār***, f. (baggy), ***sutthaṇ***, f. (baggy), ***ghuṭannā***, m., ***pajāmā***, m. : for women. ***sutthaṇ*** : English, ***patlūn***, f.
trowel, ***rambā***, m., ***khurpā***, m.
true, ***saccā*** : f. to his word, ***gall dā pakkā***, *see* promise, word : t. friend, ***pakkā*** or ***saccā*** or ***dilī*** or ***jānī dōst*** : t. Sahib, ***pakkā Sāhb*** : *see* real, truthful.
truly, ***saccī muccī***.
trumpet, ***turam***, m., ***turī***, f., ***bigal***, f., all ***wajāṇā***, int., ***wajjṇā***.
trunk, of tree, ***pōrī***, f. : of men, animals, ***dhaṛ***, m.
trunk, of elephant. ***suṇḍ***, f.
trunk, *see* box.
trust, n., ***wasāh***, m., ***bharosā***, m., ***āsrā***, m. : in t., ***amānat wicc*** : v., t. to sthg., ***ohdā māṇ k.*** : *see* faith, believe, confide, reliance, untrustworthy.
trustworthy, ***ehtbārwāḷā***, ***pakkā***, *see* worthy.
truth, veracity, ***sacāī***, f., ***saceāī***, f. : reality, ***hakīkat***, f. : *see* real, reality.
truthful, ***saccā***, *see* true.
try, ***koshish karnī***, ***kōsht karnī*** : t. hard, *see* effort, difficulty : t. one's best, ***apṇe wallō̃ ghaṭṭ nā karnī***.
tube, ***naṛī***, f. (of reed) : ***phūkṇī***, f. (blowpipe) ; ***nalkā***, m. : bicycle t., ***tūp***, f., ***tyūb***, f.
tuft, of Hindu's hair, ***bōddī***, f. : *see* crest.
Tuesday, ***maṅgḷ***, m., ***maṅgaḷwār***, m.
tumbler, acrobat, ***naṭṭ-***, fem. ***-ṇī*** : ***bāzīgar-***, fem. ***-nī***.
tumbler, glass, ***gilās***, m. : *see* drinking-vessel.
tumour, ***gilṭī***, f. : ***rasauḷī***, f. : *see* boil (1)

tumult, ***rauḷā-rappā***, m. *see* disturbance, riot.
tune, air, ***rāg***, m. : pitch, ***sur***, f. : in t., ***ṭhīk sur nāḷ***, ***sur raḷāke*** : out of t., ***besur***, ***besurā***, ***sur nehī̃ raḷdī***, ***sur ṭhīk nehī̃*** : being out of t., ***besurī***, f. : tune, v. tr., ***sur raḷāṇī***, ***sur ṭhīk karnī*** ; *see* play, instrument. Note also ***mērī ohde nāḷ sur nehī̃***, we are not friendly.
tunnel, ***ṭanḍaḷ***, m., ***suraṅgh***, f. : for water, ***saifal***, m.
turban, ***pagg***, f., ***pagṛī***, f., ***sāfā***, m. : red or black, ***cīrā***, m. : blue and white, ***lunnī***, f. : put on t., ***bannhṇā*** : take off, ***lāhṇā***, ***wadhāṇā***, G. 113.
turbulent, ***fasādī*** : *see* rebel, rebellion, riot.
turmeric, ***hardaḷ***, f., ***wasār***, f.
turn, n., ***wārī*** f. : my t., ***mērī wārī*** : take one's t., in game, ***wār laiṇī*** : by turns, ***wārī wārī***, ***wāro waṭṭī*** : t. in canal, road, ***mōṛ***, m., ***goshā***, m. : t. or twist in road, ***waḷā***, m., ***warāṅgḷā***, m. (all four ***paiṇā***, tr. ***pāṇā***).
turn, v., ***bhaū̃ṇā***, G 64 (tr. ***bhuā̃ṇā***) ; ***phirnā*** (tr. ***phirāṇā***, ***phērnā***) : tr. also ***ghumāṇā*** t. in lathe, *see* lathe : t. cattle, horses, by heading them off, ***waḷṇā***, ***waḷke leauṇā*** : t. wheel, esp. well, ***gēṛnā*** (int. ***giṛnā***, caus. ***gaṛāṇā***) ; *see* spin : t. out., *see* expel and add ***hikkṇā***, *see* excommunicate : t. out, prove, ***nikḷnā*** (t. out theif, ***cōr nikḷnā***) e: t. back, ***muṛnā*** (tr. ***mōṛnā***), *see* return : t. over papers, etc., ***phōlṇā*** : t. round (head), *see* dizzy : t. upside down, *see* upside down.
turnip, ***gōṅgḷū***, m.
turnscrew, ***pēckass***, m.
turnscrew, ***pēckass***, m.
turquoise, ***fīrōzā***, m.
turtle, ***kaccūkumhā***, m., ***khacoprā***, m.
twelve, ***bārā̃*** : twelfth, ***bārhwā̃***, G. 19–24, 123.
twenty, ***wīh*** : twentieth, ***wīhwā̃***, G. 19–24, 93, 123.
twice, *see* two.
twig, *see* branch.
twilight (morning), ***mū̃h anhērā***, m., ***muhānjḷā***, m. : (evening) ***hanēre paie***.
twins, ***jauṛe***, m. pl. : he is one of t., ***jauṛeā̃ dā e***, ***jauṛeā̃ wiccō̃ e***, ***jauṛeā̃ dā bhrā*** or ***puttar*** (t. brother or son). A.
twine, v., *see* twist, cling : n., *see* string.
twinkle, ***camakṇā***.
twist, ***marōṛnā***, ***waṭṭnā*** (t. round and round, esp. of rope, etc.).
two, ***dō***, *see* second : t. and a half, ***ḍhāī*** : adj. fr. ***ḍhāī*** is ***ḍhāyā*** : G. 19–24 : t.-fold, actual layers, ***dohrā***, *see* fold : double, *see* double : twice, ***dō werī***, ***dō wārī*** ; twice as big as, ***dūṇā***, ***dō hisse waddh***, *see* time.
typewriter, ***likkhaṇwāḷī mashīn***, f.
tyranny, ***atyācār***, ***zulam***, m. *see* oppress.
tyrant, *see* cruel.

tyre, (bicycle, etc.), ***ṭair***, m.

U

udder, ***hawānnā***, m. : *see* teat.
ugly, ***kojhā***, ***bhaiṛī sūrat wāḷā*** : *see* awkward.
ulcer, *see* boil (1), eye-ulcer.
ultimate, *see* last (1).
ultimately, *see* finally.
umbrage, *see* offence.
umbrella, ***chatṛī***, f. : u.-cover, ***uchāṛ***, m. : put up u., ***lāṇī*** : take down, ***band-k***.
umpire, ***tarfain***, m. : in game, ***ampair***, m. : *see* mediator.
unadulterated, *see* adulterat-e, -ed, pure.
unanimous, use ***sāreā̃ dī salāh*** or ***rā*** : ***itfāk nāḷ***, ***mutfik hōke*** (U.).
unanimity, ***itfāk***, m. (U.).
unaspiring, ***choṭe dil wāḷā***.
unaware, ***bekhabar***, ***patā nehī̃*** : *see* ignorant.
unbeliever, ***kāfar*** (M.).
unblemished, ***beaib***, ***bedāg*** : *see* defect, fault.
uncertain, ***shakk e*** (***wicc***), ***pakkī khabar nehī̃***.
uncertainty, ***kacc pakk***, m.
uncharitable, ***badzan***.
uncivilised, ***waihshī***, ***jāṅglī***, ***ḍhaggā jehā***.
uncle, father's elder brother, ***bābbā***, ***tāea*** (H.) : father's younger do., ***cāccā*** : mother's brother, ***māmmā*** : father's sister's husband, ***phupphaṛ*** : mother's sister's do., ***māssaṛ*** : husband's or wife's uncle, *see* father.
unclean, ***gandā*** *see* dirty : ceremonially, ***palīt***, ***napāk***, ***mlēcch*** (H.) : morally, ***napāk***, ***palīt*** : *see* pure, holy, clean.
uncleanness, ***palītī***, f., ***napākī***, f.
uncommon, *see* strange.
unconquerable, ***jehṛā nā hāre***.
uncooked, ***kaccā*** : half-cooked, ***ḍaḍḍrā*** : *see* ripe.
uncover, any word for lid or covering with ***lāhṇā*** or ***uttõ lāhṇā*** : ***naṅgā-k***.
uncultivated, ***pei hoi zamīn***, ***raṛā***, m.
under, ***hethā̃*** underneath, *see* below.
undergo, ***bhugatnā***, ***bhognā*** *see* suffer.
underground room, cellar, ***bhohrā***, m.
understand, ***samjhṇā***, ***samajh auṇī*** (***nū̃***), M. 117. 4 : be understood, of thing, ***sujjhṇā*** (***menū̃***, etc.) ; ***palle paiṇā***, ***piṛ palle paiṇā***, M. 129. 10 : G. 112 (last two only in negative and interrogative sentences).
understanding, n., ***samajh***, f., ***thauh***, m. : *see* sense, wis-e,-dom, intelligen-ce, -t, clever.
undertake, ***zimmā cukkṇā*** (***dā***), ***bīṛā cukkṇā*** (***dā***), ***zimmewar h.*** (***dā***).
undo, sewing, ***udhērnā*** (int. ***udhaṛnā***) : gen. ***kholhṇā*** : bed, machinery, ***ukhērnā*** (int. ***ukkhaṛnā***) : *see* destroy.

undress, ***kapṛe lāhṇe, wadhāṇe*** G. 113 : caus, ***lauhāṇe.***

undutiful, of children, ***kuputtar***: servants, *see* lazy, unfaithful.

uneas-iness, -y, ***becain, -ī,*** f. *see* restlessness.

uneducated, ***anpaṛh.***

uneven, *see* rough, level, smooth.

unexampled, ***es tarhā̃ dā hōr koī nehī̃, eñ kadī nehī̃ hoeā*** : *see* unique.

unfaithful, gen. ***bēwafā*** : of subordinate, ***namak-harām.***

unfavourable, opinion, report, ***de khalāf, de barkhlāf, caṅgā*** or ***acchā nehī̃.***

unfit, ***laik nehī̃, dī laik dā nehī̃, nafiṭṭ*** : *see* able.

unfortunate, gen., ***wacārā*** (v. mild word) : unlucky, ***badkismat, mandeā̃ bhāgā̃ wāḷā.***

unfortunately, ***afsōs e pai, badkismatī nāḷ*** : the opposite is ***abihāre***, luckily.

unfounded, ***ohdī bunyād*** or ***as līat koī nehī̃.***

unfruitful, trees, etc., ***apphal*** : morally, ***apphal*** : *see* barren.

unfurnished, ***samān koī nehī̃, bussā*** : *see* empty.

ungrateful, ***nashukrā, kirtghan.***

ungrudgingly, ***khushī nāl, khulhe dil nāl.***

unhappy, *see* sad.

unholy, *see* holy, unclean.

uniform, ***wardī***, f.

uninhabited, of house, ***khālī*** : *see* unoccupied : of place, desolate, ***suñā, bēabād.***

uninteresting, ***suād koī nehī̃, besuādā*** : ***dilcasp nehī̃*** (U.).

uninvited, ***bin saddeā̃, saddeā̃ binā.***

unique, ***bēnazīr*** (U.), ***lasānī*** (U.) : *see* unexampled, matchless, peerless.

unjust, ***bēinsāf, bēniā̃.***

unjustly, ***nahakk, bēinsāfī nāḷ.***

unkind, ***beraihm*** ; ***betars.***

unknowable ***bandeā̃ dī samajh wicc nehī̃ aundā.***

unlawful, gen., ***najaiz*** : ***harām***, forbidden by religion, gen. food (M.) : illegal, ***kanūn de khalāf.***

unlimited, ***behadd*** : *see* endless, innumerable.

unload, ***bhār lāhṇā.***

unlock, ***khōhlnā*** (***jandrā***) m. *see* lock.

unluck-y,-ily, *see* unfortunate-,-ly.

unmarried, ***kuārā***, fem. ***kuārī*** : ***chaṛā, chaṛā chāṇḍ, chaṛā muṛā*** (last three also "alone"), *see* alone.

unmentionable, ***dassaṇ, de laik*** (or ***dī laik dā***) ***nehī̃, jihde ākkhaṇ tõ sharm aundī e,*** (***gall***) ***karnwāḷī nehī̃.***

unmerciful-, -ly, ***beraihmī nāḷ, betarsī nāḷ*** : *see* unkind.

unmindful, *see* careless.

unnecessary, ***loṛīdā nehī̃, ohdī lōṛ nehī̃, zarūrī nehī̃*** : (spare) ***fāltū, wadhīk, wādhkū.***

unoccupied, house, ***wehlā, khālī***: out of work, ***wehla, wāndā benaukar*** (out of service).

unpleasant, of matter, word, etc., ***mandī gall*** (or ***kauṛī, maṭṭhī, burī***)

unpopular, ***oste koī khush nehī̃, sāre ohdī shikait karde ne.***
unravel, ***khōhlnā*** (***rāz***) *see* solve, undo.
unreliable, *see* untrustworthy.
unripe, ***kaccā*** : half-ripe, *see* ripe.
unruly, ***sarkash*** (U.) : *see* disobedient.
unsafe, *see* danger-, -ous.
unseasonable, ***manāsab nehī̃*** *see* untimely.
unstable, *see* shake, vacillate, wobble.
unsteady, *see* unstable.
untidy, *see* topsy turvy, and add ***samān ẽwẽ peā hoeā e, cizā̃ ẽwẽ peiā̃ hoiā̃ ne, betartībī nāḷ.***
until, *see* till.
untimely, adv., ***kuweḷe, bewakt*** : n., ***kuweḷā,*** m., ***kuwēḷ,*** f.
untrustworthy, ***beatbārā, wasāh de laik nehī̃.***
unused, leather, blank paper, water-pot, cloth (or unwashed), ***korā*** : *see* new.
unventilated, ***wā dā koi rāh nehī̃, bārī nehī̃,*** *see* ventilate.
unwilling-, -ly, *see* force, reluctant, sick of, oath.
up, ***utte, utā*** : up to, ***tikar, tāṇi, toṛī, tākar, sīdhā, tāī*** : *see* upon.
upbraid, *see* reprimand, reproach.
uphold, *see* maintain, support.
upon, ***utte, de utte, te*** : upon arriving, *see* while.
uppermost, ***utlā.***
upright, ***siddhā, -e, -ī, imāndār*** *see* perpendicular, stand, good honest.
uproot, ***ukhēṛnā*** (int. ***ukkhaṛnā***), ***jaṛhõ puṭṭnā.***
upset, ***ḍēgṇā, garāṇā*** (U.).
upside down, ***mū̃hdā, puṭṭhā*** : on one's face, *see* face : turn u., ***mū̃hdā mārnā*** or ***k., puṭṭhāk.*** ; of bricks, bread, ***thullṇā*** : *see* topsy turvy.
upwards, ***utte wal*** *see* up.
urge (warm against forgetting), ***pakkī karnī*** (***nū̃***), ***jhī karnī*** (***nū̃***) : (emphasise) ***gall utte zōr dēṇā :*** (annoy) ***tang-k*** : (keep on) ***khaihṛā nā chaḍḍnā, picche paiṇā*** : *see* excite, incite, emphasise.
urgent, ***zarūrī*** : of command, ***takīdī.***
us, ***sānū̃*** : *see* we.
usage, *see* custom, treat.
use, v. tr., ***wartṇā, istemāl-b.*** (U.) : u. unnecessarily, of big words, etc., ***wāhṇā,*** G. 121, M. 127. 34 : have no u. for, ***mai jarebā̃ kī karniā̃ ne,*** what use have I for socks ? G. 118 : be used of road, ***wagṇā*** : become used to, state of being used to, *see* accustom.
useful, ***baṛe kamm dā e, baṛā kamm dendā e*** : ***waddhriā̃ baṛe*** or ***baṛiā̃ kamm aundiā̃ ne,*** thongs are v. useful.
useless, ***kise kamm dā nehī, raddī*** : *see* worthless.
uselessly, ***dhigāṇē, ẽwẽ.***
usual, ***ām, sadhāran*** *see* custom, common, ordinary.
usually, ***aksar, ām, bauht karke.***
usurp, ***hakk mārnā*** or ***dabāṇā*** or ***laiṇā*** or ***dabbṇā*** : *see* seize.

utmost, ***jitthõ torī hō sake, apṇe wallõ ghaṭṭ nā karnī.***
utterly, ***bilkul,*** adj. *see* absolutely, altogether, thoroughly.

V

vacancy, *see* post.
vacant, *see* empty, unoccupied, uninhabited.
vacation, *see* leave.
vaccinate, ***ṭikā lāṇā,*** int. ***laggṇā***; caus. ***luāṇā, ukhṇāṇā.*** *see* inocculate, tattoo A.
vacillate, ***galle galle phirnā, dalīlā̃ badaldeā̃ raihṇā, ḍōldeā̃ raihṇā, ḍāwā̃ḍōl, lāī lagg*** (easily persuaded) : ***etthe kujh te otthe kujh,*** *see* back out, wobble, changeable, pliable.
vagabond, ***awārā*** (fem. the same), *see* nomad.
vain, ***nazākti, nakhreā̃ wālā, baṛī mizāj wālā, baṛe damāg wālā*** : *see* conceit, delica-cy, -te, air, proud : in v., ***muft dā*** (or ***mukhat dā***), ***ẽwẽ, dhigāṇe, befaidā.***
valet, ***baihrā.***
valid, ***ṭhīk, jāiz, kamm dā, aje caldā e,*** still current, etc.
valley, ***wādī,*** f. : pass, ***darā,*** m.
valuable, *see* costly, good, excellent.
value, n., *see* cost : v., ***mull ṭharhāṇā*** (fix price), ***kadrpāṇā*** (***dā***) ; esteem, hold dear.
valueless, ***bekār, nakammā*** *see* useless, worthless.
vanish, ***gaib, -hōnā*** *see* disappear.
vanquish, *see* conquer, defeat, win : in argument, ***lājuāb-k, bōlaṇ jogā nā chaḍḍṇā.***
vapour, ***bhāp*** *see* steam.
variable, *see* vacillate, changeable.
variation, ***wādhā ghāṭā,*** m. : *see* change.
varicose vein, ***nārā̃*** *see* vein.
variety, ***kism,*** f., ***jiṇs,*** f. ; *see* various, change, variegated.
variegated (colours), ***raṅg baraṅgī.***
various, ***kism kism dā, bauht kism dā, wakkho wakkh*** : *see* variety, change, variegated.
varnish, n. and v., ***rogan karnā*** (***nū̃***).
veer, *see* vacillate, changeable.
vegetable, ***salūṇā,*** m., ***sabzī,*** f., ***bhājī,*** f., ***sāg pattar,*** m. (***tarkārī*** means meat) : v.-bed, *see* flower-bed : v-curry, ***chichkī,*** f. (K.).
vehemently, ***zōr nāḷ, zore*** : *see* force.
vehicle, ***gaḍḍī, sawārī*** *see* carriage, cart, train.
veil, ***cādar,*** f. : H. woman's, covering body, ***addhaṛwanjhā,*** m., ***sāṛhī,*** f. : M. woman's, all over, ***bhurkā, burkā,*** m. : v. oneself, ***ghunḍ kaḍḍhṇā*** : draw v. over, *see* screen.
vein, ***nāṛ,*** f. (also sinew, artery) : varicose v., ***phullī hoī nāṛ.***
velvet, ***makhmal,*** f.
venerate, ***mannṇā*** : *see* honour.
vengeance, ***badlā*** *see* revenge.
venomous, ***zaihrī.***
ventilate, ***būhe bārīā̃ lāhṇiā̃, wā nū̃ andar auṇ dēṇā*** : s. sultry.

venture, ***himmat karnī, dalērī karnī, haũslā karnā*** (all ***dā, dī***).
venturesome, ***dalēr, bekhauf.***
veracity, ***sac*** *see* truth.
verandah, ***barāṇḍā***, m. : on the v., ***barāṇḍe icc.***
verb, ***fehl***, m.
verbal-, -ly, ***zabānī*** : hear v. from him, ***ohlī zabānī suṇṇā*** : G. 37.
verbatim, ***lafz lafaz.***
verdant, *see* green, verdure.
verdigris, ***ullī***, f. (***laggṇī, nū̃***).
verdure, ***hariauḷ***, f., ***harā***, m., ***sabzi***, f.
verge, ***sirā, kanāra***, *see* edge : on the v. of doing, *see* about, almost, nearly.
verify-y, -ication, ***tasdīk karnī*** (caus. ***karāṇī, dī***).
vermicelli, ***warmseli***, f. : native, ***sẽwiā̃, waṭṭniā̃***, make).
verse, ***nazam, pad*** of Bible or other sacred book ***āit***, f. : *see* poem : of poetry, ***wars***, m. (educ.).
very, ***baṛā*** (G. 34, never ***waḍḍā***), ***ḍāhḍā, bauht, bāhḷā, cokhā, bauhtā, tagṛā, pujjke, parle darje dā, sagõ*** : also ***wāhwā*** (used of good things alone) ; *see* emphasis.
vessel, domestic, ***bhāṇḍā***, m., ***bartaṇ***, m. : *see* ship, boat.
vest (under-), ***banyāṇ***, f., ***baṇaiṇ***, f. : *see* waistcoat.
vestige, ***atā-patā*** *see* trace.
veterinary, surgeon (native), ***salōtrī.***
vex, *see* annoy, tease, angry, displeased.
viâ, ***de rāh***, *hoke.*
viaduct, ***puḷ***, m.
vice, ***burī ādat***, f. : *see* sin, evil, bad.
vice, blacksmith's, ***jamūr***, m.
Viceroy, ***mulkhī lāṭ*** (also Lt.-Gov.), ***waḍḍā lāṭ.*** Lt. -Gov. is often ***choṭā lāṭ.***
vicinity, *see* neighbourhood, near.
vicious, *see* bad blackguard : of horse, ***cak mārnwāḷā*** (biter), ***dulatte mānwāḷā*** (kicker).
victory, ***jitt***, f., ***fatāh***, f.
view, scene, ***nazārā***, m. : *see* opinion.
vigil, ***jagrātā*** (***kaṭṭṇā, raihṇā***) : *see* wake, sleeplessness.
vigilance, ***hushyārī***, f., ***khabardārī***, f : *see* care.
vigour, ***tākat.*** f., ***zōr.*** m. : *see* power, strong.
vigorous, ***jōrdār, sakht*** *see* vigour.
vile, ***makrūh***, *see* bad, unclean, dirty.
village, ***piṇḍ***, m., ***grā̃***, m. : large, ***naggar***, m.
villager, ***piṇḍ dā, pēṇḍū*** (slightly contemptuous).
vindicate, ***saccā sābot-k.***
vine, ***dākh***, f., ***angūr dī wēl or dā būṭā,***
vinegar, ***sirkā***, m.
vineyard, ***dākh dā bāg.***
violence, *see* oppression and add ***dhakkeshāhī***, f. : by v. (physical or mental), ***dhakke nāḷ, zore*** : *see* confess force.
violent, *see* violence, severe.
violet, flower, ***binafshā***, m., ***binashkā***, m. : colour, ***kāshnī.***

virgin, ***kuārī.***
virtue, ***cangiāī, guṇ*** *see* goodness.
virtuous, ***nēk, pāk, bhalā lōk*** : *see* good.
viscosity, ***lēs,*** f.
viscous, ***lēslā.***
visible, to be, ***dissṇā, nazrī̃ paiṇā, labbhṇā, wakhāḷī dēṇī*** : come into sight, ***huṇ dissaṇ*** (or other verb) ***lagā*** or ***lagg peā*** : cease to be v., *see* disappear and add ***akkhiā̃ thī ohle hō jāṇā, nazrd ghuss jāṇā, chāī̃ māī̃ hō jāṇā.***
visit, ***miḷṇ jāṇā*** (***naū̃***), ***mulākāt nū̃ jāṇā*** (***dī***) : go away from home, ***wāhṇḍā jāṇā*** : v. holy place or person, ***ohde didār*** or ***ohdī ziārat*** (M.) or ***ohde darshaṇ*** (H.) ***nū̃ jāṇā*** : v. of inspection, often simply ***phērā mārnā*** : *see* inspect.
visitor, ***muḷākāti*** : on a visit, ***wāhṇḍā*** : *see* guest.
vital, ***nāzak thā̃*** (v. place) : *see* important
viva voce, ***zabānī, mū̃h zabānī, takrīrī*** (U.).
vivid, of colour, *see* bright, colour.
vocabulary, ***firist,*** f., *see* dictionary.
voice, ***awāz*** or ***wāz,*** f. m. : *see* call, hoarse.
void, make, become, *see* abolish, cancel, repeal : fizzle out, ***guggaḷ jāṇā, fisk hō jāṇā.***
volcano, ***ātshi pahāṛ,*** m., ***aggwāḷā pahāṛ,*** m.
volley, ***wāṛ,*** f. (firing).
volume, ***jild,*** f.
voluntarily, ***apṇī marzī*** or ***khushī nāḷ, āpū̃, āpō̃, āpī, āpē, khushī razāī*** : *see* gladly.
volunteer, v., use words for voluntarily w. ***jāṇā,*** go, etc. : n., ***wālanṭīr.***
vormit, ***uḷṭī auṇī*** (***nū̃***), ***uttō̃ suṭṭnā, kai karnī*** ; ***jī utā̃ auṇā,*** feel inclined to v. (***dā***), G. 117, M. 117.7 : v. up, ***ugaḷṇā, ugḷācṇā*** : vomiting and ***diarrhoea, haizā,*** m. (***h., nū̃***).
vote, n. and v., ***rā dēṇī, wōṭ dēṇā.***
vow, n., ***mant,*** f., ***nazr,*** f. : make v., these words w. ***mannṇī*** : fulfil v., same w. ***pūrī karnī, cārhnī.***
voyage, ***samundar dā safar,*** m.
vulgar, of person, ***waihshī jehā, jaṭkā, kamīnā*** : of word or thing, ***ḍagg, jaṭkā, moṭā.***

W

waft, ***udāke laijāṇā.***
wager, ***shart*** *see* bet.
wages, ***tankhāh,*** f. : of day labourer, ***mazdūrī.*** f. : each day's, ***dihāṛī.*** f.
wagon, ***gaḍḍā, gaḍḍī*** *see* carriage, cart.
wail, *see* weep, mourn.
waist, ***lakk,*** m.
waistcoat, ***phatūhī,*** f., ***salūkā,*** m., ***kurtī,*** f., ***wāskaṭ,*** f.
wait, ***udīkṇā thaihrnā, baihṇā*** (sit), ***khlōṇā*** (stand) : w. for, ***udīknā, udīk rakkhṇī*** (***dī***), ***rāh wekhṇā*** (***dā,*** look out for) :

caus., ***uḍīk karwāṇī***, or use ***uḍīkṇā peā*** : lie in w., ***dhrumbhḷā hōke baihṇā*** : w. at table. ***khidmatgāri karni*** : *see* attend, serve : w. a bit, ***khlō jā*** : *see* waiting.

waiter, ***khidmatgār***, m.

waiting for, n., ***uḍīk***, f. : *see* wait.

wake, waken, v. int., ***jāgnā*** : w. up, ***nīndar uggharnī*** (***dī***), ***jāg auṇī*** (***nū̃***), ***jāg uṭṭhṇā*** : v. tr, ***jagāṇā, uṭhāṇā*** : to stay awake, ***unindrā raihṇā*** (***nū̃***) : observe vigil, *see* vigil : to have just got up fr. sleep, ***suttā peā uṭṭhṇā*** : half-awake, ***jāgo miṭī, jāgo miṭā, jāgo nūṭā***.

walk, v., ***ṭurnā*** : *see* go : go for w., ***wā bhakhṇī, sair*** or ***sail karnā, sail sapaṭṭe jāṇā*** : walking, on foot, ***ṭurdā, paidal*** : to w. a horse, ***kadmī lāṇā*** or ***ṭōrnā*** (***nū̃***).

walk, n., style or rate of walking, ***ṭōr***, f. : garden-w., ***rāk***, m., ***paṭri***, f.

walking-stick, ***sōṭī***, f. : *see* stick.

wall, ***kandh***, f. : ***duāl***, f. : roofless, crumbling w., ***kholā***, m. : w. of tent, *see* tent.

walnut, ***khrōṭ***, m., ***akhrōṭ***, m. : w. very thin shell, ***kāgzī khrōṭ***.

wander, ***bhaundeā̃ raihṇā, awārā phirnā*** (idle and useless, fem. ***awārā***) : *see* astray, stray : be knocked about, *see* knock.

wanderer, wandering, *see* nomad and add ***pharautū***.

wane, ***ghaṭṇā*** : *see* lessen.

want, *see* desire, long for lack : be wanting, ***nā hōnā*** : for w. of, ***khuṇō***, sometimes ***bājhō***, *see* without.

war, ***laṛāī***, f. (also battle) : ***lām***, m., expedition, (occ. f., ***laggṇā***) : ***jaṅg***, m (U.) H. holy war, ***judh***, m. ; M., ***jihād***, m. : civil w., use ***āpe icc***, among themselves : go to the w., ***lām icc jāṇā***.

wardrobe, ***kapṛeā̃ wāḷī almārī***, f.

warehouse, ***gudām***. m., ***māl gudām***, m. : *see* storeroom.

warm, *see* hot, tepid : w. oneself at fire, ***agg sēkṇī*** ; in sun, ***siyyā, dhupp sēkṇī***.

warn, ***khabrdar-k.*** : *see* tell, inform, caution.

warp, v. int., of frame, bed, etc., ***kāṇō̃ pai jāṇī*** (***nū̃***), ***ḍiṅgā h.*** : tr. ***ḍiṅgā k.*** : *see* twist, crooked, bend.

warp, n., *see* loom.

warrant, for arrest ***waranṭ***, m. pl. (***kaḍḍhṇe, nikḷṇe***) : authority, *see* authority : guarantee, *see* bail, responsible.

wart, kind of, ***mohkā***, m.

wary, ***hushyār, samajhdār*** : *see* caution.

wash, clothes, separate parts of body, things in gen., ***dhōṇā*** (int. ***dhuppṇā, dhuccṇā***) : *see* bathe : ceremonial, *see* ablution : *see* scrub, clean.

washerman, ***chimbā, dhōbbā, dhōbbī*** : fem. ***chimbī, dhōbbaṇ***.

washing, single w., set of clothes for one w., ***jugān***, f.

wasp, ***dhamūṛī***, f. : long, thin, ***ghuraiṇ***, f. : *see* hornet.

waste, adj., gen., as w. paper, ***raddī***; *see* useless, worthless : w. land, ***ujār***, m., ***rarā*** (not used), ***kallar***, ***banjar*** (both barren), *see* soil, barren, desert.

waste, v., *see* squander. destroy, devastate, lose.

watch, timepiece, ***gharī***, f.

watch, v., *see* look, guard, wait, wake.

watchful, *see* wary.

watchmaker, ***gharīsāz***.

watchman, *see* sentry, guardian : village w, ***barwālā*** (caste), ***rabtī*** (lit. reporter), ***caukīdār***.

water, n., ***pāṇī***, m. : in eyes, blister, etc., ***pāṇī*** (***paiṇā***) : in food, ***pāṇī***, ***tarī***, f., ***shōrā***, m. (soup), ***lās***, m. (soup) : *see* shove off.

water, v. tr., land, ***piāṇā*** (int. ***picṇā***), ***chiññā*** : w. basket by hand, ***jhaṭṭā jhaṭṭṇā*** or ***chiññā*** (the basket is ***jhaṭṭā***, m.) : *see* sprinkle ; cattle, larger animals, ***pāṇī ḍāhṇā*** (***nū̃***) ; human beings, smaller animals, ***pāṇī piāṇā*** or ***dēṇā*** (***nū̃***) : also ***pāṇī dassṇā*** (animals) ; place for giving people water free as charity, ***chabīl***, f. (***lāṇī***, int. ***laggṇī***) : land watered by rain (not irrigated), ***barānī*** ; by well, ***cāhī*** ; by canal, ***naihrī***.

water-carrier, M. ***māshk-ī***, fem. ***-aṇ*** ; caste, ***mācch-ī***, fem. ***-aṇ*** : H. ***jhiūr-***, fem. ***-ī***.

water-channel, -course, in fields, from canal, ***khāl***, m. (***khāḷṇā***) : v. small w., ***āḍ***, f. (***kaḍḍṇā***) : drain, *see* drain.

water-fowl, *see* dabchik, duck. etc., under heading "bird."

watering-can, ***phuhārā***, m.

water-man, *see* water-carrier. sailor.

water-melon, *see* melon.

water-mill, ***ghrāṭ***, m. : *see* mill.

waterpot, *see* pot.

waterproof (material), ***barsātī***, f. : coat, ***barsātī***, ***brāṇḍī***, f.

water-tax, ***ābyānā***, m.

watery, gen. and food, ***jihde wicc pāṇī baṛā e*** : food, ***patlā*** : *see* damp, moisture, wet.

wave, n., ***ṭhallh***, f., ***ṭhāṭh***, f. : v. small, ***laihr***, f.

wave, v. tr., ***halāṇā***. waver, *see* hesitate.

wax, n., ***mōm***, m. : sealing w., ***lakh***, f. : in ears, ***kannā̃ dī maiḷ***, f.

wax-cloth, ***mōmjāmā***, m.

way, actual and metaph., ***rāh***, m. : *see* path, road : manner, *see* manner, method : half way, ***adhwāte*** : show the w., *see* guide : off the w., lose w., *see* astray, stray : by w. of the door, window, ***būhe rāh***, ***bārī rāh*** ; byw. of the house, well, ***ghar***, ***khūh de uttō dī***.

wayfarer, ***rāhī***.

waylay, *see* wait, lie in.

we, ***asī̃*** : people like us ***hamātaṛ***, G. 28.

weak, gen. ***māṛā***; ***kamzōr*** : of people, animals, ***māṛā. lissā*** : w. in character, ***kaccā***, ***gallā̃ dā***

kaccā, *see* vacillate : w. tea, ***patlī*** : heart become w or faint, ***dil ḍubṇā*** or ***chapṇā*** or ***ghaṭṇā***.

weaken, words for weak w. ***karnā***.

weal, on body, ***laūs*** or ***lās*** (***paiṇī***).

wealth, ***daulat***, f., ***māl*** m., ***hasīat***, f., ***dhaṇ***, m.

wealthy, *see* rich.

wean, child, ***duddh chuḍāṇā*** (***dā***) : from habit, fault, ***chuḍāṇā***.

weapon, ***hathyār***. m.

wear : put on, ***pāṇā***, ***lāṇā*** : he wears a waistcoat (is in the habit of putting on), ***phatūhī pāndā hondā e*** : is wearing trousers, has put on, ***tambī pāī hoī e*** ; or ***pāke lagā jāndā e***, etc. : put on. bed-clothes, shawl, etc., ***utte laiṇā*** : v. int., wear (well or badly), ***haṇḍhṇā*** : tr. ***haṇḍhāṇā***, wear out or for certain time (only of things that one wears) : *see* wear out.

wear away, *see* rub.

wear out, int., ***haṇḍh jāṇā***, tr., ***haṇḍhāṇā, haṇḍhā chaḍḍṇā*** : (n., ***haṇḍhepā***. m.), of non-wearable things, ***purāṇā hōjāṇā***: wear out a person w. words, ***sir khapāṇā*** (***dā***), ***kann khāne*** (***de***) ; int. ***sir khappṇā*** (***dā***) : *see* tire, weary.

wearisome, ***thakāṇwāḷā***, ***akāṇwāḷā***, *see* weary, tire, sick of.

weary, ***thakkā hoeā*** : *see* tire, sick of.

weather, no word, *see* climate, reason, spring, summer, autumn, winter, rain : fine w., ***kharā***, after rain, ***wānd laggnī***, ***nimbaḷ h.***, ***kharā ho jāṇā***, ***farakkā laggṇā***.

weave, ***uṇṇā***, ***khaḍḍī uṇṇī*** : *see* loom.

weaver, ***julāh-***, fem. ***-ī***.

web, cobweb, ***jāḷā***, m.

wed. wedding, *see* marriage, marry.

wedge, ***phānnā***, in., ***cappar***, f.

Wednesday, ***buddh***, m., ***buddhwār***, m.

weed, v. tr., ***gōḍḍī karnī gōḍṇā*** : n., ***būṭī***, f., ***jāṅgḷī būṭī***.

Names of common weeds :-

(i) occasionally eaten : ***bughāṭ***, m., ***jaũsāg***, m., ***maiṇā***, m., ***maiṇī***, f., ***mrikkaṇ***, f., ***papoḷī***, f., ***saũcaḷ*** f.

(ii) not eaten : ***āthū bāthū***, m., ***billī būṭī*** f., ***dodhak***. f., ***kaṭiṭṭaṇ***, f. (dock-leaf), ***lelhī*** f., ***madhrāṇī***, f., ***narī dodhak***, f.

week, ***haftā***, m., ***aṭṭh din***, m. pl., ***aṭhwārā***, m (rare) : next w., ***agle hafte*** : last w, ***pishle hafte*** : this day next or last w, ***ajj dā dihāṛā***, ***ajōkā dihāṛā*** : tomorrow w., ***bhaḷak de dījāre***. A.

weekly, adv. ***aṭṭhwẽ de aṭṭwẽ dihāṛe*** or ***din***, ***aṭṭhī̃ dinī̃***, ***aṭṭhī̃ dī aṭṭhī̃*** : adj., use adv., also ***haftewār*** (U.).

weep, ***rōṇā***, ***atthrū wagāṇiā̃***, ***karlāṇā*** (gen. aloud) : slightly, ***atthrā̃ wagṇiā̃*** (***diā̃***) : sadness, almost crying, ***gacc*** (***auṇā***, ***nū̃***) :

w. for person or thing, ***rōṇā*** (***nū̃***).
weigh, ***tōlṇā*** (int. ***tulṇā***) : estimate weight by lifting. ***hāṛnā***, ***jācṇā*** : w. anchor, ***cukkṇā*** : metaph., *see* consider, think.
weighing-machine, at railway station, ***kaṇḍā*** : *see* scales.
weight, ***bhār***, m., ***wazn***, m. : weight too much forward, ***dābū***, m. : too much back, ***ulār***, m. : weight for scales, ***waṭṭā***, m. ; two-ser w., ***duserī***, f. ***waṭṭī***, f. : weights and measures, *see* A.
welcome, v., ***wēkhke khush h.***, ***mhabbat*** or ***khushi nāḷ milṇā*** (***nū̃***) : welcome ! ***jī āeā̃ nū̃***, *see* means, gladly, willingly.
welfare, ***khair***, f. ***khariat***, f., ***sukkh sāṇḍ***, m. (ask after, ***pucchṇ-ā***, ***-ī***) : *see* health, healthy, well (2).
well, n., for irrigation, ***khūh***. m. : for drawing water, no Persian wheel, ***khūhī*** f. : deserted w, ***ḍall***, f. : w. steps down, ***baolī***, f. : the chief parts of a w. are vertical cogged wheel, ***ḍhōl***, m. : horizontal do., ***carhakḷī***, f., ***cuhakḷī***, f : wheel w. pots, ***buiṛ***, m. : pole through last two, ***laṭṭh***, f. : earthen wall, ***cannā***, m. : pole across above, ***kāñaṇ***, f. : rope for pots, ***māhl***, f. : pot, ***ṭiṇḍ***, f. : ox-walk, ***paḍāṇā***, ***purāṇā***, m. : hand-pulley, ***carakhṛī***, f. : work w. ***wāhṇā*** (int. ***wagṇā***) : turn by hand, ***gērnā*** (int. ***girnā***).
well, adv., ***caṅgi*** or ***acchī*** or ***wall tarhā̃ nāḷ*** : adj. in good health, ***wall***, ***caṅgā bhalā***, ***rāzi***, ***caṅgā*** : *see* welfare, health, healthy : all's well, ***khair e khair mehr e*** : all being well, e.g. where are you going, all being (I hope) well ? ***kitthe khair nāḷ*** or ***khairī mehrī*** (H. sukkh ***nāḷ***) ***caleā ē̃*** ? well done ! *see* bravo : v. well, all right, ***halā***, ***caṅgā***, ***acchā***.
well, particle of reasoning, ***khair***, ***whalā***.
well-bred, *see* courteous, polite.
well-dressed, use ***acche kapṛe***, m. pl. : *see* fop.
well-known, ***mashāhūr*** : *see* common, famous.
well-meaning, ***nēkniyyat***.
well-wisher, ***khairkhāh***.
west, ***laihndā***, ***laihndā pāsā*** : westwards. ***laihnde***, ***laihnde wall*** or ***pāse***.
wet, adf., ***wattreā hoeā***, *see* damp, moisture : v. tr., ***bheōṇā*** (int. ***bhijjṇā***).
wet nurse, no ward, use ***duddh piāṇwāḷī***, etc. : occ ***dāī***.
wharf, ***ghāt***, m. : ***bandargāh***, f. (harbour).
what, ***kī*** : (obl. ***kāh***, ***kās***) : what if (depreciatory), lest, ***mate***, ***cētā***, ***par je*** : but what, ***kī par*** : what else (often means why not), ***to hōr***.
whatever, ***jō̃ kujjh***.
wheat, ***kaṇak***, f. : different kinds, ***ḍāgar*** f., ***nikkī kaṇak***, f., ***waḍāṇāk***, f., ***kaṇkū***, m. : *see* grain.

wheedle, ***dhokhā dēke manāṇā, gallā̃ icc phasāke manāṇī*** *see* coax.
wheel, ***pĩñ***, m.: ***pahīā***, m., ***cal kā***, m. : Persian w., *see* well w. -barrow, ***reṛhī***. f.
when, ***jad, jadō̃, jsi weḷe, j ghaṛī***: inter. ***kadō̃, kad.***
whence, inter. ***kitthō̃*** : rel. ***jitth***
whenever, ***jad kadī, bhāwē̃ kadī***
where, inter. ***kitthe*** : motion to ***kitthe, kittal, kiddhar*** : ***re jitthe, jittal, jiddhar.***
wherever, ***jitthe kite, bhāw jitthe.***
whet, whetstone, *see* sharpen, grindstone : metaph., ***wadhāṇā.***
whether, conj., ***paī*** : w. . . . or, ***bhāwē̃ . . . bhāwē̃, cāhe . . . cāhe.***
which ? ***kehṛā*** ? which, ***jehṛā.***
while ; repetition of infl. pres. part. : w. walking, ***ṭurdeā̃ ṭurdeā̃.*** G. 80 : w. going, returning, ***jāndī wārī, partdī wārī***, M. 239. 22 ; 268. 17 : while or upon ; upon arrival, ***appaṛdeā̃ sār***, G. 91, ***appaṛdeā̃ ī***, M. 273. 40, 41 (and so w. other verbs) : cf. ***lō laggdeā̃***, while it was getting light ; lo ***hondeā̃***, while it was light : *see* when.
whimper, ***ū̃ ū̃ karnī***, *see* groan.
whine, *see* whimper.
whip, lash, ***trāṭṭ***, m., ***chāṭ***, m. : wooden part, ***parāṇī***, f. : English w., ***cābak***, m. : v. tr., these words w. ***mārnā, nū̃*** : *see* bea flog, strike w. cream, beat eggs, etc., ***phēṇṭṇā.***
whirpool, ***cakkī*** f., ***ghummanghēr***, m.
whirlwind, ***wā warōḷā***, m.
whisper, no real word ***kann icc ākhṇā*** : ***koī kuskeā wī nehī̃***, no one even whispered.
whitsle, ***sīṭī*** (***mārnī***), both the sound and the instrument.
white, ***ciṭṭā, baggā, safēd*** : whitish, *see* somewhat : w. of egg, ***safēdī***, f. : w. hair, *see* hair : w. and black, *see* A.
whitewash, ***safēdī***, f. (***karnī***) : brush for w. -ing, ***kūcī***, f. (***phērnī***).
whither, *see* where.
whitlow, ***phimmhṇī***, f. : *see* boil (1).
who, ***kauṇ***, obl. ***kih-, kis-.***
whoever, ***jehṛā koī, jō koī.***
whole, unbroken, ***sābat, sābat sabūt*** : all, *see* all complete.
wholesale (sell), ***kaṭṭhā*** (***wēcṇā***) ; ***thōk*** (U., ***wēcṇā***) : retail, ***parcūṇ*** (***wēcṇā***).
wholesome, *see* good, advantageous, profit.
wholly, ***bikul***, *see* altogether.
whooping-cough, ***kāḷī khangh***, f. (***h, nū̃***).
why, ***kāhnū̃, kāhde jogā, kāhde laī, kāhde wāste, kyū̃, kis karke, kehṛī galle.***
wick, ***battī***, f. (also lamp)
wicked, ***badmāsh*** *see* bad, blackgurad, sinner, and add ***ucakkā*** (especially robber).
wickedness, *see* bandness, evil, sin, and add ***sharārat***, f.
wide, ***cauṛā, caiṛā, mōktā.***

widow, ***raṇḍī, bewā*** (villagers use former).
widower, ***raṇḍā.***
width, ***cuṛāī,*** f., ***pēṭ,*** m. : of cloth, ***bar,*** m.
wife, ***wauhṭī, suāṇī, ṭabbar,*** m., (***mēre,*** etc. ***gharõ***) ; ***zanānī, bīwī*** (w. educated people first three uncommon) ; sometimes ***wāīf,*** wife : wife, ***saukaṇ.*** Note that ***ṭabbar*** (lit, family) is masc.
wild, ***waihshī, jāṅglī*** : of plants, animals, ***jāṅglī.***
wilderness, *see* desert (1), wood, forest.
wilful-, -ness, *see* obstina-te, -cy.
will, n. (written), ***wasīatnāmā,*** m. : *see* bequesth, inheritance.
willing, ***rāzī, mannaṇwāḷā.***
willingly, ***khushī nāḷ,*** *see* voluntarily : by all means, *see* means.
willingness, ***razā,*** f., ***khushī,*** f. : *see* pleasure.
win, ***jittṇā*** : game, *see* game.
wince, *see* flinch.
wind, ***wā,*** f., ***hawā,*** f. : east w., ***purā,*** m., west, ***pacchõ,*** f. : hot summer w., ***lō,*** f. : blow, cf w., ***wagṇā*** : in the w., open air, ***waule*** : absence of w., *see* sultriness : strong w., *see* storm ; contrary w., ***wā sāhmṇī e*** : favouring w., ***wā picche we.***
wind, watch, clock, v. tr., ***cābī*** or ***kunjī deṇī*** (***nū̃***) : twist, *see* twist.
winding-sheet, ***khapphaṇ,*** m.
window, ***bārī,*** f. : through the w., ***bārī rāh*** : *see* open, shut.
wine, ***sharāb,*** m., ***dārū,*** m. (both any wine or spirit, latter also medicine), ***nashā,*** m. (any intoxicant).
wing, ***par,*** m.
winged, ***parā̃wāḷā.***
wink, ***akkh mārnī.***
winnow, in open fields, ***uḍāṇā*** : with basket in hand, ***chaṭṭṇā*** : winnowing, ***uḍāīā,*** f. pl. : winnowing basket, ***chajj,*** m. : *see* sift.
wipe, ***pūnjhṇā.***
wire, ***tār,*** f. : wire gauze or netting, ***jāḷī,*** f.
wisdom, ***danāī,*** f., ***akl,*** f. m., ***siāṇap,*** f. : *see* sense, intelligen-ce, -t, understanding, philosophy.
wise, ***danā, aklwāḷā, siāṇā*** : *see* wisdom, clever.
wish, ***iccheā, khaish*** *see* desire.
wits, *see* wisdom, sense.
witch, ***cuṛel, ḍain, jādūgarnī.***
with, along with, ***nāl, sane sang,*** *see* together : instrument, ***nāḷ*** ; for parts of body existing in pairs, loc. plur., as ***akkhī, kannī.***
wither, plants, etc., ***kurmāṇā, kumlāṇā.***
within, *see* in.
without, ***bin, binā, de binā, tõ binā, bājhõ de bājhõ, bagair, de bagair, khuṇõ*** : do without, *see* do.
witness, person, ***guāh,*** *see* eyewitness : from hearsay, use ***suṇī suṇāī gall*** : evidence, *see* evidence.
wizard, ***kamālī*** *see* magician.

wobble, ***ḍōlṇā*** (tr. ***ḍulāṇā***) : *see* vacillate, changeable, back out, shake.

wolf, ***bhageāṛ-***, fem. ***-ī***.

woman, ***zanānī***, ***janānī***, ***buḍḍhī*** (married, of any age), ***aurat*** : "womankind," ***khodāmhaiṇ***, m. (slightly jocular) : my good woman, ***whaī***, M. 130. 32 : G. 125 : adj. ***zanānā***, as ***zanānī gaḍḍī***, carriage for women only : ***zanānā kamm***, women's work.

womanish, ***zanānī tabiat dā***.

womb, ***kukkh*** f., ***dharn***, f., ***rehm***, m. (U., all uncommon). ***ḍhiḍḍh***, m., ***pēṭ***, m., both meaning stomach, may be used.

wonder, feeling of, *see* astonish-, -ment : wonderful thing, ***tajjab dī gall***, ***harānī dī gall*** : I w. if he'll come, ***patā nehī̃ khabre āwe ke nā***, ***wēkhīye āwe ke nā***.

wonderful, ***ajaib***, ***acarj***, ***anōkhā*** : *see* strange.

wood, gen., ***lakkaṛ***, f, ***lakṛī***, f.. ***kāṭh***. m. : firewood, ***bāllaṇ***, m. : heap of for sale, ***ṭāl***, m. : piece of split firewood, ***phāṅg***, f. (***k.***). cut across, ***mochā***, m. (***pāṇā***) ; any piece, ***ṭōṭṭā***, m. : *see* log, beam : saw w., ***cīrnā***, *see* chop : lot of trees, *see* forest copse : forest of dhak trees, ***ḍhakkī***, f., *see* dhak : wood and grass land near river, ***bēllā***, m.

wood-boring insect, ***ghuṇ***, m.

wooded, use ***baṛe rukkh ne***.

wooden, ***lakkaṛ dā***, ***kāṭh dā***

woof, *see* loom.

wool, ***unn***. f. : soft hair or fur, ***jatt***, f. : silky w., ***pashmīnā***, m.

woolly, ***unn dā*** : ***pashmīne dā***, of silky wool.

woolly insect, destroys clothes, ***lehā***, m.

word, single word ***lafaz***, m., ***lafs***, m. : phrase, matter, thing, speech, ***gall***, f. : one's w., promise, *see* promise and add ***kalām***, f. m., ***kaul karār***, m. : Word of God, ***Khudā dī Kalām*** : w. by w., *see* verbatim, literal : a few words, written, ***dō cār harf*** of conversation, *see* converse

work, n. ***kamm***, m., ***kamm dhandā***, m. ***kamm kāj***. m. : literary w., use ***kitāb***, f., book ; ***rasālā***, m., pamphlet, etc. : work involved in message, *see* message : w. turn up to be done, ***kamm paiṇā*** (***nū̃***), M. 125. 6 : G. 120 : w. go on, ***calṇā***, ***ṭurnā*** (tr. ***calāṇā***, ***ṭōrnā***) M. 126. 29 : out of w., *see* unoccupied : leave off w., *see* leave : permanent w., *see* permanent in A.

work, v., ***kamm karnā***, ***kamm kāj***, ***kamm dhandā karnā*** : literary, ***likhṇā*** : finish work badly, w. carelessly, ***traṅgaṛnā*** : he has begun working, is at work, ***oh kamm lagg peā e*** : work out at per rupee, maund, etc., ***baihṇā***, M. 117. 12, 14 : G. 117 : work, be working, of machine, etc., ***calṇā***, ***ṭurnā*** ; of well, ***wagṇā***.

workman, skilled, mason, builder, etc., ***rāj*** : unskilled, ***kulī***, ***mazdūr*** : paid by day, ***dihāṛīdār*** : *see* labourer, servant, clever.

workmanship, ***kamm***, m., ***kārīgarī***, f., ***baṇāwaṭ***, f.

workshop, ***kārkhānā***, m.

world, earth and people, ***dunyā***, f., ***jahān***, m. : H. sometimes ***jagat***, m., ***jagg***, m. : the earth, ***dunyā***, f., ***zamīn***, f., H. ***dhartī***, f. : the next w., ***aglā jahān***, ***parlōk***, m. (H.) : ***aglā jagg*** (H.) : *see* heaven.

worldly, ***dunyāwī***, ***dunyā dā***.

worm, ***kīṛā***, m. : blindworm, slow-worm, ***dumũhī***, f. ; *see* ant, snake.

worry, worried *see* annoy, angry, bore, displease, tease, trouble, inconvenience, difficulty, straits.

worship, Christian, ***bandgī karnī***, ***duā bandgī karnī***, ***girjā karnā***, ***duā namāz karnī*** (of officiating person, ***karāṇī***, ***karāṇā***), occ. ***namāz paṛhnī*** : H. and M., *see* pray : ***pūjā karnī*** (***dī***), w. idols.

worshipper, use words for worship w. ending ***-wālā***, or paraphrase : ***pujār-ī***, fem. ***-an***, worshipper of idols.

worth, ***-de laik*** *see* value, cost.

worthless, *see* useless and add (things) ***bakār***, ***bakārā***, ***nikammā***, ***kujjh nehī̃*** : matter, words *see* nonsense : persons, ***raddī***, ***kucajjā*** or ***becajjā*** (doing things badly), ***nighreā hoeā***, ***nāmurād***, ***bēhadaitā*** (rather strong word) : *see* bad, etc.

worthy, man, ***bhalāmāṇas***, fem. ***bhalīmāṇas***, *see* deserve, right.

would that, use ***Khudā kare pai*** ; ***kadī kare*** (***kare ā***, ***kardā***) ***kehī sohṇī gall howe*** (***howe ā***, ***hondī***), what a good thing, if he does it, did it or were to do it : M. 270. 36, 37.

wound, ***phaṭṭ***, m., ***zakhm***, m. : blow, ***saṭṭ***, f : v. tr. use beat, strike, etc., ***ohde lāṇ*** or ***mārn nāḷ phaṭṭeā geā or zakhm hoea*** : be w., ***phaṭṭeā jāṇā***, ***zakhm h.*** (***mī̃***), w. the feelings, ***dil dukhāṇā*** : *see* grieve.

wrap, ***walhētnā*** : *see* fold.

wrath, *see* anger.

wreak, *see* revenge.

wreck, of ship, ***ṭuṭṭṇā***, ***ṭakkar wajjī te ṭuṭṭ geā*** : *see* ruin, destroy, downfall.

wrestle, ***ghulṇā*** : wrestling match, ***ghōḷ***. m.

wrestler, ***ghulāṭīā***, ***palwhāṇ***.

wretch, ***kambakht*** : *see* bad, wicked.

wretched, *see* poor, straits.

wring, out water, etc., ***nacoṛnā*** : twist round, ***maroṛnā*** : *see* squeeze.

wrinkle, in face, ***jhuṛrī*** (***paiṇī***) ; gen. plur. : *see* crease, fold, frown.

wrist, ***guṭṭ***, m. : w. and forearm, ***wīṇī***, f.

writ, ***sammaṇ***, m.

write, ***likhṇā*** : enter in book, ***likhṇā***, ***darj-k.*** : *see* ealigraph-y, -ist, copyist.
writer, *see* author, clerk, copyist : petition-writer, ***arzīnawīs*** : appeal-w., ***apīl nawīs***.
writing, handwriting, ***khatt***, m. : act or price of w., ***lakhāī***, f.
wrong, adj., ***galt*** : *see* bad.
v., ***hakk mārnā*** (***dā***), *see* damage.
n., *see* damage, injure, loss.
wrongfully, ***nahakk***, ***dhigāṇe***, ***befaidā***, ***ẽwẽ***.

Y

yard, length, ***gaz***, m. : *see* wts. and meas. A : a yard measure, ***gaz***, m.
yard, *see* courtyard.
yawn, ***ubāsī laiṇī***, M. 122. 35 ***ubāsī auṇī*** (***nū̃***), M. 117. 5.
year, ***warhā***, m., ***sāl***, m. : of era, ***san*** m. : every y., ***sāl de sāl***, ***warhe de warhe***, ***warhe dinī̃*** (G. 78), ***har sāl*** : in a y., ***warhe dinī̃***, ***warhe nū̃***, ***sāl nū̃***, ***warhe din icc*** : next y., ***aunde sāl*** : last year, ***par***, ***parū̃***, ***par de sāl***, ***parōke sāl*** : y. before last, ***parār***.
yearly, ***sālānnā***, adj., *see* year.
yearn, *see* long (2).
yell, *see* scream, shout.
yellow, ***pīḷā*** : pale y., ***khaṭṭā*** : dark, *see* orange : of egg, *see* yolk : yellowish, *see* somewhat.
yes, answering question, ***āho***, ***ākho***, ***āh***, ***hā̃*** : answering call, ***hā̃*** : G. 93, 94.
yesterday, ***kall*** (never ***bhaḷke***) : day before y., ***parsõ*** : day before that, ***cauth*** : fifth day, ***panjauth*** : sixth, ***cheauth*** : seventh, eighth *see* week, tomorrow : ***satwẽ***, ***aṭṭhwẽ dihāṛe*** or ***din***, etc., are also used.
yet, *see* still (1), besides.
yield, *see* give in, surrender : owing to threat, ***dabb jāṇā*** : n., *see* produce.
yoke, n., ***panjāḷī***, f. : v., ***jōṇā***, ***jōtṇā*** (int. ***juppṇā***, ***juttṇā***), ***haḷ jōṇā*** (for ploughing).
yolk, of egg, ***zardī***, f.
you, ***tū̃***, ***tusī̃*** : acc. ***tenū̃***, ***tuhānū̃*** : your, ***tērā***, ***tuhāḍḍā*** : for acc., and your, also pronom. suff. (sing.), ***ū̃***, ***-ī***, ***-ā***, ***-ī*** : (plur.), ***je*** : G. 82-6.
young, ***thoṛī umr dā***, ***nikkā***, ***chōṭā*** : the y. of anything, ***baccā***, m. : *see* child : y. man, ***gabhrū***, ***juāan*** : y. woman, ***muṭeār***, ***juān aurat***.
youth, state of, ***juānī***, f.

Z

zeal, ***sargarmī***, f., ***jōsh***, m.
zealous, ***sargarm***, ***joshwāḷā***.
zero, figure, ***sifar***, m.
zest, ***shauk***, m. (desire, keenness,) : ***suād***, m., ***mazā***, m. (both taste) : *see* taste.
zinc, ***jist***, m.
zoological gardens, ***ciṛīā ghar***, m.

APPENDIX I

ADDITIONS TO VOCABULARY

absolutely, add ***ukkā mukkā*** : *see* altogether, thoroughly.
adulterate, add ***khōṭ pāṇā*** (***wicc***): *see* mix.
allow, add *see* permit, liberty.
angry, ***lūsṇā*** suggests inward, not outward anger.
anklet, add ***bā̃k*** f., ***lacchā***, m., ***sā̃ṭ***, f., ***saglā***, m.
annual, *see* cancel, abolish, repeal.
apologise, add ***koḷō*** of person a.-ed to, and ***dā*** of thing a. -ed for.
appease, add ***ṭhaṇḍā-k.*** : a.-hunger. ***lāhṇī***, int. ***laihṇī*** : *see* slake.
arm, of chair, ***bā̃h***, f. : of coat, ***bā̃h***, f. : *see* next word.
armlet, ***ṭāḍḍ***, f., ***ṭāḍḍ***, f.

back (1), (lying) on back, ***utāṇā*** : (carry) on shoulders or high up on b., ***kandhāṛe***, ***dhangāṛe*** : lower down, also pick-aback, ***magar picche***.
bracelet, ***add kaṛā***, m. : *see* armlet in A.
bride, add ***wauhṭī***. wife.
butterfly, add ***titrī***, ***tittrī***, f.
buttermilk, milk and water, ***kacī lassī*** : boiled and curdled,, ***pakkī lassī***.
cajole, *see* coax, wheedle.
cantankerous, *see* irritable.
card (1), ***piññā*** is softening before spinning, ***jhambṇā*** softening before seeding : to seed cotton is ***wēlṇā***.
Cargo, ***māl asbāb***, m., ***asbāb***, m.
carniverous, ***māskh̲ōr***, ***mās*** or ***gōsht khānwālā***.
cash, v., add ***trōṛnā***. ***bhannnā***.
cataract in eye, add ***motiābind***, m.
catch, ***phaṛā dēnā***, *see* explanation on pp. 143-4.
chaff, fr. rice, ***parāḷī***, f.
chain, on door, ***kundī***, f.
chink, opening, split, ***trēṛ***, f.
chink, sound, *see* tinkle.
compensation, *see* damage A.
cook (2), ***rōḷī lāṇī*** (int. ***laggṇī***), means to slap the "***chupattee***" on to side of oven.
cud, chew, *see* ruminate A.
cut teeth, ***dandīā̃ kaḍḍṇīā̃*** (int. ***nikḷṇīā̃***), of children; but back teeth, ***hanū̃*** (***kaḍḍhṇīā̃***, ***nikḷṇīā̃***): animals, ***dand*** (***kaḍḍhṇe***, ***nikḷṇe***).

damage, legal, ***harjā***, m., ***harj***, m. : damages, ***harjānnā***, m. : ordinary compensation, ***iwzānnā***, m.

dentist, ***dand baṇāṇwālā***.
dismiss, add. ***-chuṭṭi, dēṇi*** (***nū̃***), discharge, also give leave : ***makūf-k.***, dismiss.
disqualify, add ***nā̃wā lāhṇā*** (***dā***, int., ***laihṇā***).
divine, ***Rabb dā, K͟hudā dā, Parmeshwar dā***, etc., *see* God : also ***ilāī*** (U.).
divinity, godhead, ***k͟hudāī***, f. : *see* theology A.

feed, dogs, cats, etc., ***ṭukkar pāṇā*** (***nū̃***) : cattle, ***patthe pāṇe, ghāh pāṇā, gutāwā pāṇā***, (***al nū̃***) : horses, ***ghāh pāṇā, nihārī dēṇi*** (both ***nū̃***).
fellow, *see* pair.
fever, *see* also quartan, tertian
fire (2), *see* shoot.
forget, add ***menū̃ ohdā thauh nenū̃ rehā***, I forgot it.
free, adj:, ***add marzi dā mālak.***

gallop, v. tr., ***poīā*** or ***sarpaṭṭ ṭōrnā*** : ***cak͟huriā*** or ***caukhuriā saṭṭṇā*** (***nū̃***).

hereabouts, ***etthe jaie*** : thereabouts ***otthe jaie*** : where-abouts (inter.). ***kitthe jaie***, (rel.) ***iitthe jaie*** : (***jaie*** for ***jaihe*** fr. ***jehā***).

immoral, ***badkār*** *see* blackguard.
inborn, add from birth, ***jamāhndrū*** : deaf from birth, ***jamāhndrū ḍōrā.***

lie down, for woman use ***lēṭṇā***, not ***lammā paiṇā*** : lying down, ***leṭī hoī e.***
luckily, ***abihāre.***

permanent (resident, servant, service, work), ***naṭhāhū, nāṭhehū.***
pip, of orange, apple, etc., *see* stone.
place (2), ***ḍaihṇā*** not used for water.
purgative, take effect, ***laggṇā.***

reddish, ***lāl jehā*** *see* somewhat.
reliable, add ***atbār wāḷā.***
renounce, add ***hakk chaḍḍṇā*** (***dā, apṇā***).
ruminate, chew cud, ***ugāḷi karni***: *see* meditate, think.

safe, add ***rāzi bāzi.***
serv-ant, -ice, *see* permanent A.
sharpen, pencil, ***gharṇā.***
snare, add ***phāhi***, f.
stars ; Bear, the Great, ***palhang pihṛā***, m.
Canopus, ***agath***, m.
Orion's Belt, ***trangaṛ***, m.
Pleiades, ***khittiā̃***, f. pl.
Procyon and Sirius, ***lohnde***, m. pl.
Pole Star, ***kutub tārā.*** m.
Venus (evening star), ***shām dā tārā***, . m. : (morning star), ***waihṛ tārā***, m.

tainted, be, of meat, add ***humh jāṇā.***

theology, ***Khudā*** or ***dīn dā ilm***, ***fikā***, m. (U.) : *see* divinity in A, God.

thereabouts, *see* hereabouts A.

threshing-floor, add ***khalāṛā***, m.

whereabouts, *see* hereabouts A.

white and black, piebald, ***ḍabbā***, ***ḍabb khṛabbā*** : small spots, lines, ***tetrā metrā***.

work, *see* permanent A.

APPENDIX II
List of Common Birds

Great confusion exists in the nomenclature, and Panjabis are certain of none but the best-known.

babbler (seven sisters) ***sehṛ***, f.
bee-eater, ***harī ciṛi***, f.
bulbul, ***bulbul***, f.
cock, ***kukkaṛ***, m.
crane, ***kūnj***, f.
crow, ***kā̃***, m.
crow, jungle, Indian corby, ***pahāṛī kā̃***.
cuckoo, pied crested, ***bambīyā***, m.
dabchick, ***ḍubkū***, m. ; ***jalkukkaṛ***, m.
dove, ring-, ***ghuggī***, f.
dove, little brown and red turtle, ***ṭoṭrū***, m.
duck, ***bata<u>kh</u>***, f., masc. ***bat<u>kh</u>ā***.
duck, wild, ***mugrāī***, ***murgābī***, f.
duck, Brahminy, ***nikkā maggh*** or ***maṅgh***, m.
eagle, ***bāz***, ***ukāb***, m. : often ill, f.
falcon (lugger), ***lagaṛ*** (often used for tawny eagle)
flamingo, ***lamḷhing***, f.
goose, ***bata<u>kh</u>***, f. : rare, ***hans***, m. : wild g., ***maggh***, ***maṅgh***.
goshawk, ***bāz***, f.
grebe, *see* dabchick.
grouse, ***bhaṭiṭṭar***.
hen, ***kukkṛī***, f.
heron, pond, ***baglā***, m.
heron, grey, ***waḍḍā baglā***, ***naṛī***, f.
hoopoe, ***cakkī rāh***, m.
ibis, black, ***bōjā***, m.
jay, *see* roller
kestrel, ***cūhe mār***, m.
king-crow, ***lāt***, f. : ***kāḷ kṛicci***, f. : ***kāḷ kḷicci***, f.
king-fisher, ***macchī mār***, m.
kite, ***ill***, f.
koel, ***koēl***, f. : ***kōl***, f.
lapwing, ***tatauḷī***, f.
lark, ***canḍōl***, m.
merlin, ***turmtī***, f. : ***turmcī***, f.
minivet, ***lāl***, m. : ***sur<u>kh</u>***, m.
myna, common, ***lāllī***, f. : ***lālṛī***, f.
myna, bank, ***shārk***, f.
nightjar, ***cabākhī***, f.
owl, ***ullū***.
owlet, ***bilbataurī***, f. : ***cabākhī***, f.
paddy bird, *see* pond heron.
parrot (nose-ringed paroquet), ***tōttā***, m.
parrot (large Indian paroquet), ***rā tōttā***, m.
partridge, ***tittar***, m. : ***bhaṭiṭṭar***, m.
peacock, ***mōr***, fem. ***mornī***.
pigeon, ***kabūt-ar***, m., fem. ***-rī***.
pigeon, hybrid (tame), ***<u>kh</u>umrī***, f., ***kumrī***, f.
pipit, same as lark.
quail, ***baṭérā***, m.
raven, ***ḍhoḍḍar kā̃***, m., ***ḍhoḍḍrī***, f.
redstart, same as robin.
robin, and any bird like it, ***piddī***.

roller, ***lalāran***, f. : ***gaṛaṛ pōpō***, m., ***garaṛ***, m.
sandpiper, ***kakaūā***, m.
shikra, ***shikrā***, m.
shrike, bay-backed and rufous-backed, ***syōṇ ciṛī***, f. ***sōṇ ciṛī***.
shrike, grey, ***laṭōr***, f.
sparrow, ***ciṛī ghar dī ciṛī***, f. : masc., ***ciṛā***.
starling, common Indian, ***tilyar***, m.
starling, rose-coloured, ***gulābī tilyar***.
stork, ***lamḍhiṅg***, f.
swallow, ***abābīl*** f.
swift, ***abābīl***, ***i***.
tern, ***jhiūrī***, f. : wrongly ***ṭaṭauḷī***, f.
tree-pie, often ***bambīyā***, m.
turkey, ***pērū***, m.
vulture, any large v., ***girjh***, f.
vulture, Egyptian (larger white scavenger), ***ganjā***, m. : sometimes ***baggī ill***, f. : or smiply ***nikkī girjh***, f.
wagtail, ***mamōlā***. m.
warbler, particularly ashy wren w., ***camūṇā***, m. : ***ṭimmā***, m.
woodpecker, golden backed, or any large w. ***ṭōkkā***, m : ***tarkhiṇ***, m.
woodpecker, pied, ***nikkā ṭōkkā***, ***nikkā tarkhiṇ***.

APPENDIX III

Weights and Measures

Measures of Length

inch, ***incī***, f.

about 3 inches, ***cappā***, m. (hand-breadth).

about 8 inches, ***giṭṭh***, f. (span).

Cloth

2¼ inches one ***girhā***, f.

16 ***girha's*** one yard.

Distance

12 inches one ***fuṭ***, ***fiṭ***, m. (foot).

3 feet one ***gaz***. m. (yard).

220 yards one ***farlāṅg***. m. (furlong).

8 furlongs one ***mīl***, m. (mile).

1½ miles one ***koh***, m. (***kuhāṭṛā***. m., approximately, or less than, a ***koh***).

Land Measure

5½ feet one ***karū̃***, m.

22 feet one ***jarīb***, f. (chain).

Square Measure (land)

one sq. ***karū̃*** is one ***sarsāhī***, f.

9 sarsahi's one ***marlā***, m.

20 marla's one ***kanāḷ***, f.

4 kanals one ***wighā***, m. (half acre).

8 kanals one ***ghumā̃***, m. (acre) or ***killā***, a killa is 40 karu's long by 36 broad.

25 acres one ***murabbā***, m.

Weight (precious metals or stones)

1/240 oz. (nearly) one ***ratti***, f.

8 ratti's one ***māssā***, m.

12 massas one ***toḷā***, m.

5 tolas one ***chaṭākī***.

16 chataki's or 80 tolas one ***sēr***, m. (2 lbs. 0.914 oz.).

Food and general

about 2 oz. one ***chaṭākī***. f.

16 chatakis one ***sēr*** as above).

2 chatakis ***addh pā***.

4 chatakis one ***pā***, m. (quarter ser) : 8 chatakis ***addh sēr***.

6, 10, 12, 14 chatakis ***ḍeḍh*** or ***ḍuḍh***, ***ḍhāī***, ***trai***, ***sāḍhe trai pā***.

40 ser one ***maṇ*** m. (maund).

Grain, etc.. actually measured by toppas (see below)

20 ser one ***maṇ***, m.

3 man one ***paṇḍ***. f.

4 pands one ***māṇī***, f. (12 ***maṇ*** of grain),

also the following:—

Capacity (chiefly grain, etc.)

4 cuha's one ***paṛōppī***, f. (***cuhā***, m. : accent on second sylable).

2 paroppis one ***ṭōppā***.

2 toppas one ***daṛōppā***, m.

The weight of a toppa of grain varies from village to village.

A 1¼ ser toppa is called ***suāeā ṭōppā*** (from ***sawā sēr***) : a 1½ ser toppa is ***ḍeḍh serā ṭōppā*** : a 1¾ ser toppa is ***sai pāeā ṭōppā*** : a $1^7/_8$ ser toppa is ***sāṛhsutpāeā ṭōppā*** (from ***sāḍhe satt pā***), while a 2 ser toppa is called ***dusērā ṭōppā***.

These weights and measures have since been overtaken by metrication and decimalization. So this part is only of historic interest.

LINGUASIA

Borden Villa, Borden Lane
Sittingbourne, Kent ME10 1BY